New Cinema, New Media

New Cinema, New Media:
Reinventing Turkish Cinema

Edited by

Murat Akser and Deniz Bayrakdar

Assistant Editor Melis Oğuz

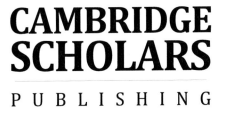

**CAMBRIDGE
SCHOLARS**

P U B L I S H I N G

PN
1993.5
.T8
2014

New Cinema, New Media: Reinventing Turkish Cinema,
Edited by Murat Akser and Deniz Bayrakdar

This book first published 2014

Cambridge Scholars Publishing

12 Back Chapman Street, Newcastle upon Tyne, NE6 2XX, UK

British Library Cataloguing in Publication Data
A catalogue record for this book is available from the British Library

Copyright © 2014 by Murat Akser, Deniz Bayrakdar and contributors
Front cover image: Ismail/The Sun (Ahmet Rifat Sungar) from *Üç Maymun/Three Monkeys*
(Nuri Bilge Ceylan, 2008) © NBC Film and Zeynep Özbatur Atakan-Zeyno Film/Yapımlab.
Back cover image: Eyüp/The Father (Yavuz Bingöl) from *Üç Maymun/Three Monkeys*
(Nuri Bilge Ceylan, 2008) © NBC Film and Zeynep Özbatur Atakan-Zeyno Film/Yapımlab.
Cover design: Adam Brown

ISBN (10): 1-4438-5688-6, ISBN (13): 978-1-4438-5688-1

CONTENTS

Part V: New Reception

Part VI: New Methodology

LIST OF IMAGES AND TABLES

ACKNOWLEDGEMENTS

This volume could not have been realized without the support of our assistants, colleagues and contributors. The eleventh conference of The New Directions in Turkish Film Studies on 'Cinema and the New' at Kadir Has University was the starting point of this volume. Later, we have called for articles and after a blind referee 20 out of 43 articles made into this volume. During this process, we are grateful to my university and especially to our Rector Prof. Mustafa Aydın and provost Prof. Hasan Bülent Kahraman for their invaluable support for this conference and book.

We are grateful for the support to our assistant Zeynep Altundağ in the organisation phase of the 2010 conference. The regular conference gang from the very beginning in 1999, Melis Behlil, Tül Akbal, Savaş Arslan, Kaya Özkaracalar, Dilek Kaya, Ahmet Gürata and Zahit Atam helped with the refereeing of the articles.

We also would like to several keynote speakers for the conference whose contribution can also be found in our book. Murray Pomerance and Seth Feldman kindly accepted our call and deliver superb lectures.

The call for papers and editing process coincided with the establishment of our new Film and Television MA program at Kadir Has University. The newly arriving graduate students and assistants also inspired us with their enthusiasm during the editing of this volume. We are thankful to Mine Paşamehmetoğlu, Elif Kahraman, Selen Gökçem, Tan Tolga Demirci and Özüm Ünal, who provided much needed work during the crucial stages of the preparation of this volume.

We would like to mention the continuous efforts and support of a long line graduate assistants Sarphan Uzunoğlu, Fatma Tekin and Hazal Malkoç, who helped in formatting the volume. I thank them all for *being always out there to solve our problems*. Along with them our friends in the arts world Pelin Tan, Başak Şenova, Jalal Toufic, Feride Çetin, Görkem İldaş, Zeynep Kesler, Vildan Öztürk, Sedef Olgaç and Selin Söl helped a great deal during the preparation of the volume. Sevinç Baloğlu and Zeynep Özbatur Atakan helped with the copyright clearance of images on the cover.

Mark Wyers as the Writing Centre coordinator made huge contributions in copyediting parts of this volume. Along him, our copyeditors Maria

Alba Brunetti and Elizabeth Salvedra for their detailed and incredible hard work on this volume.

Thanks to Carol Koulikourdi and Amanda Millar from Cambridge Scholars Publishing for supporting this enterprise in patience while we in return tried to meet the deadlines.

When we began to compile this volume, Melis Oğuz joined us as assistant editor to complete the work in progress. She did coordination, paperwork, formatting in general, assisted in the editing and the communication with the contributors and our publishers for the Turkish version of this volume. With her help, we could finalize this work.

Near the completion stage of the book vital support came from School of Creative Arts, University of Ulster from the research team lead by Cormac Newark and Frank Lyons from Arts & Humanities Research Institute in the form of two doctoral students, Siobhan O'Halloran and Darach MacDonald, who helped with the final proofreading. Justin Magee of Design program along with his most talented students helped with the design of the cover. Adam Brown, Heather Mallon and Matthew McDowell did superb job in book cover design.

Finally, we would like to dedicate this work to the memory of Halit Refiğ, Metin Erksan; the forerunners of film criticism and new cinema in Turkey in the 1960s and the late Seyfi Teoman whose sudden death in May 2012 reminds us every day of how precious life is and how we must cherish every moment of it.

INTRODUCTION

TEN PROPOSITIONS ON THE POSSIBILITY OF A NEW CINEMA

MURAT AKSER AND DENIZ BAYRAKDAR

How can we define "new" in cinema? Is it creating a new film movement where a new group of filmmakers emerges to call themselves the next independent movement? Is it a new cinema in an age when every day some new technological delivery system (3D, Blu-ray, VOD) changes methods of distribution and exhibition? What about a sudden shift in production economics of a nation's cinema that goes from no film-audience to millions in dollars and audience attendance, a year later? Identifying a new cinematic phenomenon is one thing. How to define and analyse it, what methodologies to use in understanding the dynamics of that *new* core requires novel approaches. Yet how does one define the novelty of a group of films? Should they add a new style to the world of cinema? Should there be a manifesto appealing to an audience? Should it be accompanied by new modes of production? Who decides and defines a new cinema: filmmakers, critics or the audiences? Let us take *neo-realismo* as a new film movement that came out of Italy in the 1950s. Socio-political conditions (in the aftermath of war) created a shortage of camera and film stocks. This necessity of low tech gave rise to use of streets with real people. This in turn fuelled a new film aesthetic. What of French New Wave cinema that came about in the 1960s? It came about because of artistic boredom, as a rebellion of young filmmakers rejecting a stale salon aesthetic of the older generation of directors. French Nouvelle Vague could claim the streets because of the high-tech, the new hand-held camera and sound recording devices that allowed for shooting in the streets. These two countries share two opposing social and political conditions in two different decades, and yet they also share similarities in artistic sentiment. The new in cinema is a new aesthetic vision, fuelled by a new desire to tell human stories differently with the assistance of new media technologies.

Then how would we define what New Turkish Cinema is? We would like to make ten propositions on what post-1994 Turkish cinema is.

New Cinema, New Media: Reinventing Turkish Cinema comprises a wide range of essays by scholars from different corners of the world and is enhanced with contributions from England, the USA, Canada and Turkey. The essays mainly focus on various themes around films, directors and producers of Turkish and world cinema. We have tried to categorise the different parts of the book with the help of a virtual map of our knowledge about the creation and interpretation of new cinemas around the world.

The essays on New Criticism in Part One refer to new technologies, older regimes of cinematic production and New Criticism of the twenty-first century. The first chapter by Murray Pomerance "A World That Never Was: Old Special Effects, New Eyes" explores the changing perceptions of "new special effects technologies" in American cinema through the 1950s and up until now. The author states that styles and methods for representing reality in art have always been subject to the dictates of technical possibility. Effects and realism change over time with audience competence and horizons of expectation. Special effects often demonstrate features of optically perceivable reality the human eye wouldn't pick up in real life which Pomerance calls "surface splendor". Pomerance mentions problems of watching old movies with new sensibilities and watching new movies with old, social class problems. Surface splendor is also invoked by the screen, more frequently and opulently as cinema advances. Spectatorially powerful effects, close-ups, fragments of the scene, of characters' makeup are used to demonstrate to viewers that they are in the hands of expert computer animators who could achieve fine-grain graphic detail that would read as hyper-informative. Pomerance comments that this new exceptional professionalism shuns the labour-intensive cinema of the old Hollywood. Instead, it valorises a computer graphics technique intensive approach. The loss here is that "old" cinema that was plainly offered in the character of the visual experience is now more and more replaced by action. We are losing something else, too, in fact, have now virtually all but completely lost it: the talents of particular individuals who gave their lives to the creation of screen illusions in the "old" days and who are now no longer among us. This is a lament in particular innovative (low-tech) experiments in illusion.

Seth Feldman's contribution is titled "Flaherty, Fatty Arbuckle and the Invisible Bride: *Nanook of the North* and the Origins of Documentary". Feldman rejects the idea that single notable individuals are the sole shapers of their historical eras or that there are lone inventors of any new technology. In the creation of documentary narrative techniques Robert

Flaherty's *Nanook of the North* (1922) is given as an example whereas filmmakers before him had other approaches that are still prevalent today. Feldman comments that *Nanook*'s new cinematic originality is that it sparks a dialogue between the two realities: the actuality we feel like we are seeing and the craft of applying a "creative treatment" that will evoke emotional certainty.

Selim Eyüboğlu, in his piece "The Radical Novelty of Robin Wood's Political Film Criticism," summarises the multifaceted, mind provoking and politically controversial aspects of Robin Wood's film scholarship. The article was first presented in the fashion of in-memoriam style at the opening of the "New Directions in Turkish Film Studies XI Conference" in Istanbul at Kadir Has University in 2009, the year Robin Wood passed away. Eyüboğlu finds the new film criticism of Wood practical and engaging as he analysed shifting discourses of class, genre, and race. For him, Robin Wood's new approach came from the fact of his being a cinephile, a film fan and a critic; in this way, he could form a dialogic and a dialectic approach applying his comparative and communicative method. The birth of a new cinema can come from the use of such new critical approaches. One can easily point to the connection between the creation and interpretation of New Turkish Cinema as the writers of the Turkish film magazine *Altyazı* applied some of Wood's psychoanalytic and class based methods in analysing new cinema's subtext.

In Part Two: Defining New in Cinema, there are four articles dealing with the different aspects of cinematic novelty in relation to the writing of history and defining the new features of cinema. The writing of history and defining the new features of contemporary Turkish cinema. Murat Akser, in "Towards a New Historiography of Turkish Cinema," indicates that the time has come to write the history of Turkish cinema from a fresh perspective. The current histories take a modernist approach that divided film history into progressive eras. A new way of writing Turkish film historiography as the writer suggests, will be to look at social and cultural changes as well as local, global and economic and technological changes in film production in Turkey since 1997. This essay shows that the access to historic resources and evaluation of first hand sources rather than secondary readings of other historians will reveal a new history.

Zahit Atam, in his paper "In the Beginning Was the Father: Why Papa? The 'New' in Nuri Bilge Ceylan's Cinema," presents Nuri Bilge Ceylan as one of the founding directors of new Turkish cinema. As a director Ceylan takes the viewers on a journey through an existential and intellectual past of his own and confronts us with the past of Turkey: Ceylan's cinema draws conclusions of his philosophy of life, of Ceylan's generation giving access to the conflicting relations between Ceylan and his rendering of Turkish society. Atam takes us through this creative journey between Ceylan's existence and his creativity.

Aslı Daldal's contribution is entitled "The Concept of National Cinema and the 'New Turkish Cinema'". Aslı Daldal's purpose in this study is twofold: Firstly, to (re)define the notion of "national" cinema in the age of globalism and discuss its relevance to account for "national" film movements. Secondly, to examine the current situation in new Turkish cinema and try to investigate whether the current developments in filmmaking practices signal the birth of a new film "movement". Can we talk about a new Turkish "national" cinema as we talked about the "new German cinema," the "new Danish cinema" or "the new Iranian cinema"?

Savaş Arslan, in "Realism alla Turca–*Valley of the Wolves*," comments on the mixing of fiction and reality in new Turkish television and cinema. The difference of new realism in Turkish cinema comes from the fact that in Turkish cinema the relation between narrative realism and reality is conceived as quite a distinct form of realism than in Western cinematic realism. The new televisual experience of Turkish dramatic storytelling underlines a different fold of narrative realism in television series by allowing the possibility of real-time interaction with current news and events. Instead of displacing us from the world or blocking reality from the screen, the cinematic and televisual fiction in Turkey offers a contingency in which the mythological expression of fictional fulfilment is realised in both reality and fiction. Arslan comments that the viewer is left in between the West and the non-West, the cinematic and televisual illusionism and the narrativised reality. In this respect, the reality of the narration and/or storytelling ties the filmic and televisual culture in Turkey to its historical/cultural forms that bring together the presence of the storyteller or the bard. It is this very presence of the storyteller–not only in the fictional world, but also in the real world of the storyteller's performance–which denies the displacement of the viewer from the represented world.

Part Three: Canons Refined deals with naming new, alternative, underground or hyphenated cinemas in Turkey. Özgür Çiçek, in "The Old and the New Ways of Kurdish Filmmaking in Turkey: Potentials and Risks" takes the definition of ethnic cinema in Turkey to a new level. The writer questions the position of Kurdish filmmaking within the realm of cinematic production in Turkey. She theorises Kurdish filmmaking in Turkish cinema, referring back to the theoretical framework of a national cinema. The cinema of an ethnic minority group that does not have a recognised nation-state and that does not want to merge within another national cinema realm/territory bears difficulties for the definition of a "new" national cinema. Thus, she finds in Yılmaz Güney's cinema the nature of censorship motivated a new film language that is much more metaphoric, and that uses facial expressions rather than words. The restrictions motivated a narration that deals with social realities on the level of image and sound rather than in words or performance. This new Kurdish national cinema uses the experience of the present time in the new discursive space that would be incomplete if it was not mediated by memory, nostalgia and loss, censorship and isolated use of sound.

Tuncay Yüce's "New Documentary, New Cinema and New Media" approaches the changes in new media technologies and their impact on cinematic art. The new technologies of the visual give rise to innovation in cinematic language. As a genre, documentary cinema takes advantages of these developments within contemporary art-making practices. These technological developments give new ground for ordinary citizens to tell their stories. This increasing availability of production can also mean multiplicity in narratives in a multimedia platform such as *youtube*. Yüce believes that when we trust in the deep-rooted tradition of the documentary because the documentaries that arises is limited by the artistic production. What really matters is the exposure of the subject of the documentary not the way it is made. This is an era providing us to means to create the new cinema, new documentary and the new media.

In Part Four: New Ways of Seeing, alternative approaches to the new cinema in Turkey are reflected on by three writers. Deniz Bayrakdar in "Old Beginnings, New Ends: Why Do New Turkish Films End by the Sea?" comments that the sea stands for "loss" and the "disappearance of desire" and the new and old value system of the region. She also mentions the importance of the "oceanic feeling" in "final" scenes as a key point in new Turkish cinema. Bayrakdar elaborates that Fatih Akın draws the imaginative line of genealogical evolution in time and space and in ending their films by the sea. In the cinema of Turkey of the 2000s, the directors direct our gaze toward the sea. We experience a "pause" in between: a move from the New Turkish Cinema to the Cinema of Turkey or Cinema in Turkey to continue our stories, to remember our past, to forgive and end at the same "ocean".

Eylem Atakav's "Do One's Dreams Become Smaller As One Becomes Bigger? Memory, Trauma and the Child in Turkish Cinema" touches on the considerable efforts by post-1980 filmmakers in Turkey to come to terms with the national trauma of the military coup. The outpouring of cinematic texts since 2000 focusing on the coup's consequences on individuals' lives (through stories of children suffering) calls attention to notions of memory, remembering trauma, torture and more importantly the child in cinema. This article focuses on the ways in which children are represented in recent films as it critically examines the implications of these representations.

Özüm Ünal in her essay "Post-Apocalyptic Science Fiction: A New Genre in Turkish Cinema?" intends to examine the theme of the "post-apocalypse" in *Gelecekten Anılar* (*Memories from the Future*) (Erverdi 2010), a post-apocalyptic science fiction short film project. Furthermore, her contribution speculates on the reasons why Turkish Cinema has not produced films that are related to or centre on the theme of post-apocalyptic Science Fiction genre so far, and also the reasons why post-apocalyptic narratives should be taken into consideration as a religious, historical, and socio-cultural fear formation in relation to the methods of cultural and political theories.

Elif Kahraman, in "Arm-wrestling a Superpower: The Representation of the United States and Americans in Turkish Films," discusses the cinematic representations of American characters in Turkish comedy films with an interdisciplinary approach. Her article claims that, through comedy films, Turkish society expresses its feelings and thoughts about Americans. The study suggests that Turkish comedies that represent American characters are not only aimed at providing amusement to a Turkish audience but also express feelings on changing the power relations of the real world.

Part Five: New Reception brings theoretical ideas around how the audiences perceive the differences in "old" and "new" cinema to the fore. In Chapter Fourteen, "A New Look at Film Reception: Summer Theatres," Hilal Erkan looks at Turkish open-air theatres as the important entertainment and socialising places of the recent past. The replacement of open air theatres by indoor multiplex theatres brings the loss of spontaneity and freedom produced in public places, which enabled social sharing. Erkan acknowledges the necessity of interacting with others in order to create a bond with audiences. This bonding disappears when one retreats to the satisfaction provided by subjectivity, the urban fabric, which includes plazas, malls and movie theatres that are "constructed" as places isolating individuals pursuing leisure-time activity and entertainment instead of socialising them. The open-air movie theatres united people from different age groups and socio-economic levels in an atmosphere of festivity like a *carnival* and opened the doors to enthusiastic experience. Open-air cinemas served not only as places to watch films but also as gathering places where people could engage in various forms of social interaction.

Tülay Çelik in the study "International Film Festivals: A Cinema Struggling to Exist between New Resources and New 'Dependencies'," states that the development of the auteur cinema field in Turkey can be evaluated in the context of international film festivals. As well as examining the opportunities offered to the director-producers in Turkey by the international film festivals in terms of international financing, sales, distribution and viewing, the study highlights the negative effects of the commercial structure of the festival network on the process of film production in Turkey. Çelik focuses on the thesis that the structure of the international film festivals—which may be creatively limiting the directors of the field of art cinema and exposing them to external interventions through the concern to be elected—is pushing the New Turkish Cinema into a new dependency relationship at the level of form and content.

In Chapter Sixteen, "Thinking Out Loud: On the Adaptations of *Hürmüz with Seven Husbands*," Pınar Asan compares four versions of a Turkish film musical to form a ground on which some facts concerning the (time) periods when the films were shot can be revealed. She discusses the parallel reading of the 2009 film with a female protagonist to illustrate the ways in which "women's films" were part of the social agenda, particularly during the 1980s in Turkey and how this discussion is reflected in our day. Asan comments that migration to the cities from various parts of the country and the encounter with a cosmopolitan environment that resulted from such a migration led to diversification of genres, stereotypes and space depictions in plays. Comedy attracted great attention in the city as it was a genre that could continue the critical tradition that transcended social classes.

Part Six: New Methodology is the closing philosophical section on defining a new cinema. Tül Akbal Süalp's article is entitled "Cinema of Thresholds, Without Gravity, under Urgent Times: Distant Voices, Still Lives". She mentions the September 12, 1980 military coup as a historical event that triggered long-time trauma with no mourning period. Together with other conditions such as growing unemployment, Turkish society began to experience insecurity and desperation and individuals became indifferent as if lost in time and space. Süalp comments that a new time-space chronotope is created with this trauma in Turkish cinema. This new alienated, "*outsider*" cinema has the "outsider" quality coming from the directors' standpoint. These directors detached themselves from the recent past, the memories of the political and social trauma and became indifferent and numb. In this new cinema, there is a total disregard of social criticism, a lumpen nothingness, disappearance of the voices of women and hatred for the other. These films glorify rural life, the slowness of the towns and the claustrophobic world and indirectly, the petty bourgeois life style as well, as they desperately seek for an escape from the metropolitan condition. Süalp points towards a new and emerging poetics of showing and telling. It is a two-dimensional dream stalk. Because the real might be so painful to face, and both remembering and forgetting are more problematic than ever, the directors of new cinema prefer to raise the curtains of the old shows and open up the boxes of fairy tales. Fortunately, she comments, there are alternative tracks of filmmaking other than commercial or personal (mostly male) such as women directors' feminist cinema and a rising political cinema.

Gülengül Altıntaş finds finds liminality to be a way of resistance in Erdem's cinema. Reha Erdem is one of the most prominent directors of Turkish Cinema since the 1990s. Gülengül Altıntaş, in her article "Inbetweenness as a Mode of Resistance in Reha Erdem's Cinema" argues that Erdem's films complement each other through a constant dialogue, while investigating the conflicts that arouse from humanity's encounter with culture through the quest for freedom and happiness. Looking at the *time-spaces* of adolescence in Erdem's films, Altıntaş argues that the repeating theme of adolescence becomes a means of representing this conflict at its climax and also, proposes its state of *in-betweenness* as a way of resistance which we should preserve all through our lives.

Hülya Alkan Akyüz, in "Spatial Realism: From Urban to Rural," discusses the cinematographic inclination from a cosmopolitan metropolis (especially Istanbul) to Anatolian towns in Turkish Cinema. The city is not just a visual background in recent epoch Turkish movies, but a dramaturgical element giving direction to the story. Anatolian cities and rural towns that are chosen as the site of the movies appear with their specific culture and real names. This spatial transition can be attributed to the fact that in many cases the directors were born and raised in these towns. The will to tell personal stories, a quest for belonging shaped by the space are the basis of the films discussed in this essay.

Ten Propositions

After looking over these articles, we can draw ten propositions about the existence of a new cinema:

1. New cinema of Turkey is an entirely new mode of cinematic production. Its directors are film school educated or at least university graduates compared to the artisanal directors of old cinema. This new cinema is part of global transformations such as the resurgence of

nationalism and, on the other hand, the impact of globalisation and post-nationalism (see Derman 2001; Arslan 2009).

2. It is a continuation of Yeşilçam and art cinema at the periphery. The duality that existed in Turkish cinema for the last fifty years still continues. There is the popular cinema of sensory pleasure, and there is the existential-contemplative cinema of personal experiences (Akser 2010). The genres, star system and audience appeal exist with the help of the television industry, its advertising and recycling of Turkish cinema. There is a new audience for new genres such as religious-horror as well as parodies of Yeşilçam classic genres (Arslan 2011; Özkaracalar 2012; Akser 2013).

3. It is a cinema of film festivals. As Tülay Çelik shows, the new cinema of Turkey has an organic connection to national and international film festivals for development and distribution. Film development funding and guidance of film festivals orient a new cinema towards being a more transnational marketable elite cultural product (Dönmez-Colin 2012).

4. The new cinema is that of memory, loss, forgetting, trauma and migration from rural to urban areas. This loss is seen in the new lumpen apolitical films as Tül Akbal Süalp illustrates of Nuri Bilge Ceylan, Zeki Demirkubuz and others (Suner 2004; Atakav 2011).

5. The new cinema is initiated by technology. New means of presentation, use of computer graphics and editing new delivery systems orient the viewer towards a new reception regime. As Murray Pomerance explains, there is a new level of high-tech special visual effects; the audience of today will look at labour intensive and more organic effects of the old cinema as passé, defunct and outmoded. A new reality is presented to the viewer that looks more real than the previous cinematic representation. The new cinema is always more real than the old cinema. New networks of distribution are also available through governmental film policies (Behlil 2010).

6. Alternative forms and genres of filmmaking are introduced. Transnational networks by expat/émigré directors like Fatih Akın and Ferzan Özpetek are part of this new cinema (Göktürk 1999; Bayrakdar 2009; Hake and Mannel 2012; Arslan 2012).

7. Minor cinemas like Kurdish or women's cinema are called new. The cinema of Yılmaz Güney was a first in the expression of the Kurdish minority. The new films dealing with alternative identities are the independent part of new cinema (Robins and Aksoy 2000; Kaftan 2000; Dönmez-Colin 2010).

8. New cinema is about new urban lifestyles and alienation in big cities (Göktürk, Soysal and Türeli 2010; Köksal 2012).

9. There is a new audience that looks at the real and the fictional narrative from a different perspective (Arslan 2009b). Documentary film production is on the rise touching on traumatic issues. Narrative films more and more use *cinema verité* techniques blurring the boundaries between fact and fiction (Spence and Kotaman-Avcı 2013).

10. New Turkish cinema is partially created and totally endorsed by a new breed of film criticism. For every new cinema, there is new film criticism. As Selim Eyüboğlu elaborates, the existence of film critics who redefine the films from political viewpoints of class, genre and race makes a difference in the amount of attention given to a new cinema. As Seth Feldman states, the choice of film historians to define what was standard filmmaking practice in a given genre and era depends on their own personal preference.

At last, the New Turkish Cinema revealed the need for hope for a "new cinema" to begin newly after a long silence in Turkish cinema as a counterpoint to the European cinemas' stagnation. Where the East found a fresh perspective was in the ashes of the Revolution in Iran, social movements in Korean and Chinese cinemas. The awards received at film festivals are a motivation not only for the directors but also for the spectator (Arslan 2010). New cinema in Turkey owes much to the presence of the newly found audience, without whose large numbers of attendance the true success of new directors' films would not have been acknowledged by the critics, the funding bodies, the festivals and the rest of the world.

Works Cited

Akser, Murat. 2010. *Green Pine Resurrected: Film Genre, Parody and Intertextuality in Turkish Cinema*. Saarbrucken: Lambert Academic Publishing.

—. 2013. "Blockbusters". In *Directory of World Cinema: Turkey* edited by Eylem Atakav, 124-145. London: Intellect.

Arslan, Savaş. 2009a. "The New Cinema of Turkey". *New Cinemas: Journal of Contemporary Film* 7 (1): 83-97.

—. 2009b. "Venus in Furs, Turks in Purse: Masochism in the New Cinema of Turkey". *Cinema and Politics: Turkish Cinema and the New Europe*: 258-67.

—. 2011. *Cinema in Turkey. A New Critical History*. New York: Oxford University Press.

—. 2012. "Fatih Akın's Homecomings". In *A Companion to German Cinema*, edited by Terri Ginsberg and Andrea Mensch, 249-259. London: John Wiley and Sons.

Atakav, Eylem. 2011. "'There are Ghosts in These Houses!': on New Turkish Cinema: Belonging, Identity and Memory". *Inter-Asia Cultural Studies* 12 (1): 139-144.

Bayrakdar, Deniz, ed. 2009. *Cinema and Politics: Turkish Cinema and the New Europe*. Newcastle-Upon-Tyne: Cambridge Scholars Publishing.

Behlil, Melis. 2010a. "Better Late than Never? The Role of Policy in the Turkish Cinematic Revival". *Film International* 8 (6): 21-29.

—. 2010b. "Close Encounters?: Contemporary Turkish Television And Cinema." *Wide Screen* 2 (2):1-14.

—. 2012. "East is East?" In *A Companion to Eastern European Cinemas*, edited by Anik Imre, 504-517. London: Wiley-Blackwell.

Çakırlar, Cüneyt and Özlem Güçlü. 2012. "Gender, Family and Home (land) in Contemporary Turkish Cinema". In *Resistance in Contemporary Middle Eastern Cultures: Literature, Cinema and Music*, edited by Karima Laachir, Saeed Talajooy, 167-183. New York: Routledge.

Derman, Deniz ed. 2001. *Türk Film Araştırmalarında Yeni Yönelimler I (New Directions in Turkish Film Studies I)*. Istanbul: Bağlam.

Diken, Bülent. 2008. "Climates of Nihilism". *Third Text* 22.6: 719-732.

Dönmez-Colin, Gönül. 2010. "Women in Turkish Cinema: Their Presence and Absence as Images and as Image-Makers". *Third Text* (24) 1: 91-105.

—. 2012. "Film Festivals in Turkey: Promoting National Cinema While Nourishing Film Culture". In *Coming Soon to a Festival Near You*, edited by Jeffrey Ruoff, 101-116. St. Andrews: St. Andrews Film Studies.

—. 2013. *The Routledge Dictionary of Turkish Cinema*. London: Routledge.

Göktürk, Deniz. 1999. *Turkish Delight-German Fright: Migrant Identities in Transnational Cinema*. University of Oxford: Transnational Communities Programme.

Göktürk, Deniz, Levent Soysal and Ipek Türeli, eds. 2010. *Orienting Istanbul: Cultural Capital of Europe?* New York: Routledge.

Hake, Sabine and Barbara Mennel, eds. 2012. *Turkish German Cinema in the New Millennium: Sites, Sounds, and Screens*. New York: Berghahn Books.

Hartley, Paul. 2011. "The 'Return to Home': The Musical Construction of a Common Trope in New Turkish Cinema." *CINEJ Cinema Journal* 1: 76-88.

Kaftan, Eylem. 2000. *Identity in Crisis: Turkish Cinema Post 1980*. York University, MA Thesis.

Köksal, Özlem. 2012. *World Film Locations: Istanbul*. London: Intellect Books.

Özkaracalar, Kaya. 2012. "Horror Films in Turkish Cinema: To Use or Not to Use Local Cultural Motifs, That is Not the Question". In *European Nightmares: Horror Cinema in Europe Since 1945*, edited by Patricia Allmer, Emily Brick, and David Huxley, 249-260. New York: Columbia University Press.

Paça-Cengiz, Esin. 2009. *Film As A Tool To Re-Write History: New Political Cinema In Turkey*. MA Thesis, Kadir Has University.

Robins, Kevin and Asu Aksoy. 2000. "DEEP NATION: The national question and Turkish cinema culture" In *Cinema and Nation*, edited by Mette Hjört and Scott Mackenzie, pp.203-221. London: Routledge.

Spence, Louise and Aslı Kotaman Avcı. 2013. "The Talking Witness Documentary: Remembrance and the Politics of Truth". *Rethinking History*: 1-17.

Suner, Asuman. 2004. "Horror of a Different Kind: Dissonant Voices of the New Turkish Cinema". *Screen* 45 (4): 305-323.

—. 2009. "Silenced Memories: Notes on Remembering in New Turkish Cinema". *New Cinemas: Journal of Contemporary Film* 7 (1): 71-81.

—. 2011. "A Lonely and Beautiful Country: Reflecting Upon the State of Oblivion in Turkey Through Nuri Bilge Ceylan's *Three Monkeys*". *Inter-Asia Cultural Studies* (12) 1: 13-27.

—. 2014. "Between Laughter, Tears and Nationalism: The Rise of a New Popular Cinema in Turkey". In *Understanding Media and Culture in Turkey: Structures, Spaces, Voices*, edited by Christian Christensen and Miyase Christensen, (forthcoming). London: Routledge.

PART I:

NEW CRITICISM

CHAPTER ONE

A WORLD THAT NEVER WAS:
OLD SPECIAL EFFECTS, NEW EYES

MURRAY POMERANCE

To begin, a note about the Orient Express, which made its virgin eastbound journey from Paris to Istanbul (at the time, still Constantinople) on the first of June 1889, eight weeks after the inauguration of the Eiffel Tower. This train, paragon of modernity, operated by the *Compagnie Internationale des Wagons-Lits*, would have stopped in Munich, Vienna, Budapest, and Bucharest, stocked with as many as four sleeping coaches, two baggage cars, and a restaurant coach in which one could have eaten oysters and sipped turtle soup. The Istanbul terminus was the Sirkeci Station, in Eminönü; passengers continuing into Asia would have ferried over to the Haydarpaşa Garı in Kadıköy. For lovers, devotees, and students of trains, as anyone interested in modernity will surely be, the Orient Express is important chiefly because of its extremely luxurious style, a kind of late nineteenth-century special effect, if you will. In terms of style, design, and pleasant physical accommodation, this service epitomises what railway travel had become as the century drew to a close.

My reason for invoking railways here is connected to pleasure and technology, but is a step removed from simple description. In his masterful treatise on railway travel, Wolfgang Schivelbusch draws our attention to the relation between socially organised technologies and frivolous pleasure when, commenting upon carriage riding, the precursor to the development of trains, he notes that the "final fate" of this "traditional mode of travel" was "to become the amateur sport of the privileged classes" (1986, 14). Quite beyond the application of technology to the production of entertainment then, traditions and technologies gone by come in themselves to constitute entertainment when they are outmoded (note in this respect, the so-called "delights" of Michel Hazanavicius's *The Artist* and Martin Scorsese's *Hugo* [both 2011], which allow audiences to revel pleasurably in fundamental cinematic techniques of the past). Once, the train existed to annihilate for travellers the topography of the landscape, by substituting with the level track on which a relatively smooth ride could be experienced, the horse-driven carriage, in earlier days vital as a means of locomotion, now only for play. We may reflect that transformations like this are widespread in capitalist culture.

I want to suggest another technical eclipse that, in the wake of a new cultural experience considered precious by those who share it, left a trail of defunct and relatively primitive operations, quite fascinating in their own right, but now considered hopelessly impractical and out of touch, material fit for only those who like to play and imitate; good for writing history or cultural analysis but not, as the multitudes wish, rushing forward to new and more smoothly-designed excitements with inventions of the moment. Television programmes of the 1950s, for example, at the time considered the crest of the wave by all who addictively watched them, are now available as sentimental downloads for those who wish to look back with superiority on their primitive charms. They represent a kind of televisual archaeology; while at the time of their first airing they were taken just as seriously, considered a rich treasure of dramatic possibility, as *Boardwalk Empire* or *Glee* or *The Boss* are today. In this age of cellular communication, "old-fashioned" dial telephones are sold for decorative purposes. And with the advent of digital cinema, special effects produced from the early days of the twentieth century and for decades afterward through matte and rear projection techniques are valued now as quaint historical toys: optical printers are sold off at auction for esoteric collectors; clips from the films adorn museum exhibitions; the works themselves are screened for esoteric cinephiles on TCM. Already by 1974, the Orient Express was in decline, relegated to the status of a glamorous film set as travellers who wanted to get from Paris to Istanbul took the plane. What I want to consider here is the use of technical effects in cinema to represent what viewers would call "reality," specifically the way in which when they are past their prime, outdated techniques become less serious and less believable for audiences. In the end, technique toys with belief, that quintessential substrate that we cannot quite define or touch but that guides and focuses our lives.

Nerves

Styles and methods for representing reality in art have always been subject to the dictates of technical possibility. We can think of the nineteenth-century posing stand that held photographic subjects' heads still so their expressive faces would not be blurred, and how the realism of representation achieved thereby facilitated the work of such cataloguers as Berthillon or photographers like Edward S. Curtis who photographed North American Indians (see Scherer); or the way painting could be advanced once the colour blue "became aristocratic and fashionable" in the eleventh and twelfth centuries (Pastoureau 2001, 49 ff). Beyond technology, fashion and public judgement have also played their roles, as we can see by the denigration and ridicule that the French critical establishment offered in response to the first shows of *Impressionisme*, one sniping observer writing of Monet in 1874 that he "has frenzied hands that work marvels. But to tell the truth, I never could find the correct optical point from which to look at his *Boulevard des Capucines*. I think I would have had to cross the street and look at the picture through the windows of the house opposite" (Jules-Antoine Castagnary, *Le Siècle*, 29 April) and another thinking it possible in 1886 that Seurat was "a cold-blooded mystifier" (Octave Maus, *L'Art Moderne*, 27 June). Of cinema, Maxim Gorky's often-quoted July 4, 1896 newspaper account of some of the earliest Lumière projections, for example "Des Ouvriers sortant de l'usine" (1895), reveals a certain self-protective equivocation of sentiment, since even while aghast at some of the effects of the experience he couldn't help seeing film evoking a rather negative, ghostly twin world to his own comparatively lively one, "a kingdom of shadows…without sound, without colour…Everything…dipped in monotonous grey…no sound of footsteps or of speech". Cinema of the golden age (between about 1930 and 1960) was frequently misunderstood or undervalued in its evocation of reality. The locust storm in Sidney Franklin's *The Good Earth* (1937), a special effect if ever there was one, the *New York Times* believingly found "terrifying," but the utterly splendid and often technically complex *Vertigo* (1958) the same newspaper found notable for nothing more than its "dramatic color". And watching *The Wizard of Oz* (1939), a film that has enchanted hundreds of millions of viewers again and again, one critic ignorantly saw only "betraying jolts and split-screen overlappings" (Frank S. Nugent, *New York Times*, 18 August 1939, 16). Viewers unceasingly carry their own cultural expectations and biographically cultivated hopes, and construct their viewing experience through an unfolding negotiation between what is offered on the screen and what they wish for, think proper, and remember. This negotiation becomes complicated when history enters the formula by way of a temporal lag between a work and the audience's experience of it, as when, for example, people look back upon cinematic effects produced before they were born but with unavowed anticipations based in their present-day experience.

I will never forget the contemptuous laughter my undergraduate class produced, year in and year out during the late 1970s and early 1980s, and in the very best of spirits, when I showed them François Truffaut's *Fahrenheit 451*, produced in London in late 1965 by Lewis M. Allen, who had earlier produced the entirely credible *Lord of the Flies* for Peter Brook. At one point in *Fahrenheit 451*, the hero, a futuristic fireman named Montag (Oskar Werner), in flight from repressive state authorities, arrives at the edge of a river, which is the beginning of the underground road to freedom. Hearing a high-pitched drone, he quickly hides under a tarpaulin in a rowboat. The sound persists, and turns out to be produced by a team of four airborne police agents, skimming along the river with hover jets tucked under their arms and scanning beneath them for any sign of the fugitive. It's a chilling narrative moment. The sequence contains two shots, one with a very long lens for establishment showing the stretch of the river, then one with a medium-long lens that focuses on the policemen approaching, twisting this way and that as they search for Montag, but miss him. This second shot ends with a close-up featuring the jet equipment, since the agents have by now approached the camera; in this moment, actually, the matte process being used is *less* obvious than it was before. But every time this sequence came up in class, and especially this particular close-up, my students broke up laughing. Not just laughing: laughing with a kind of relief. They had endured more than an hour and fifteen minutes of the film in rapt engagement, including very elaborately designed modernist representations of a monorail, a futurist fire station and fire wagon, a wall-sized television, and even an obtrusive though extremely dramatic optical wipe, all this without even a snicker of disengagement, but now their deriding sense of superiority could be held in no longer. "Who do you think you're kidding?" they seemed to say, "Don't you know this kind of cheesy effect is beneath our dignity?" Mattes like this were all over the place in the late 1960s and early 1970s. At the end of *Willy Wonka and the Chocolate Factory*, a film made five years after *Fahrenheit*, there is a similarly "cheesy" group of matte and rear-projection shots of the Chocolate King's glass Wonkavator flying over a European town. This sequence, neither particularly sophisticated nor particularly cheap, didn't move audiences to laughter because it claimed to constitute a happy ending, not a tense climax. Nabokov's observation, "Some people, and I am one of them, hate happy ends. We feel cheated. Harm is the norm. Doom should not jam. The avalanche stopping in its tracks a few feet above the cowering village behaves not only unnaturally but unethically" (25-6), did not apply to most viewers of Hollywood fantasy and science-fiction films of the 1960s and 70s, for whom any contrived special effect could be tolerated if it would lead directly to a smooth resolution of tension and conflict, and thus soothe the audience.

Obtrusive effects such as the matte shot from *Fahrenheit 451* irritate the viewer who is trying to remain convinced that cinema offers not a construction, but a veritable window on the world. (Such viewers depend upon cinema as a window or means of transportation, not a form of art.) The clarity of the effects technique *as such* tends to suggest manipulation, disingenuousness, insincerity, and a kind of low charlatanry, and provides a behind-the-scenes glimpse that (rather demanding) viewers would prefer not to have, since it seems to ruin the illusion by pointing to it. Audiences watching a reprise of this Truffaut sequence in Steven Spielberg's *Minority Report* (2002) never flinched, although the same type of matte technique was in use, albeit in a more contemporary version.

Figures 1 and 2 Matte of air-bound police from *Fahrenheit 451* (François Truffaut, 1966) and from *Minority Report* (Steven Spielberg, 2002). Both digital frame enlargements. Note how the darker background in the Spielberg shot obscures the technical effect.

Serious narrative disengagement is produced for the viewer who notices that he has not been hoodwinked. Such critics populate current audiences looking back suspiciously, for example, on the attack sequences in Alfred Hitchcock's *The Birds* (1963), sequences that were seen by audiences at the time—I sat among them—in thoroughgoing suspension of disbelief even though we knew what we were seeing could not be happening in fact. The point was: it rather looked as though it was happening—unless, of course, we allowed ourselves to withdraw and began to see it as artistry (but *who wanted to withdraw!*). Perhaps audiences today actually do wish to withdraw when they encounter such a film, only because it is from, as Montag says in *451*, "before".[1] In 1963 at any rate, an age before the flood of popular cinematic criticism (on television and the internet) that makes an expert out of every viewer, viewers simply believed what they saw, committed to the entertainment, the indeterminacy of a direct optical experience that could not discern "special effects" as such since it had not been educated by a postmodern media to do so. The postmodern age of distrust and cynicism that was born with the assassination of John F. Kennedy was still just short of eight months away when *The Birds* came out. Watching it, audiences relished an optical experience that attached itself to characters and their fates and wondered, not why, how, or that the birds were fake, but why the birds might have wanted to take over the world. Viewers today very often see only a failure in object realisation, a reason for critical distancing and for disaffiliation with the screen. This coolness notwithstanding, one must affirm that affiliation is the transforming, the redeeming stance.[2]

In the early 1940s, audiences went along with—even profoundly enjoyed—some rather simplistic effects in Charles Reisner's Marx Brothers comedy *The Big Store* (1941), effects that already by 1963 could have seemed unacceptably bald and elementary. One would be the optical printing and matte work in the Bedroom Department scene, as a tent automatically unfurls from the back of a camper van, then collapses back again. A more emphatically false moment shows Harpo and Groucho

---

1. *Fahrenheit 451*, indeed, is an exegesis on the theme I am addressing here, advancements in sensory technology and their political and social effects.
2. I here respectfully bypass the significant critical estimation of apocalypse thrillers offered by Christopher Sharrett (see, for just one example, "American Sundown: *No Country for Old Men*, *There Will Be Blood*, and the Question of the Twilight Western," in Pomerance and Sakeris'2010 *Popping Culture* 6th edition, 261-68); since regardless of whether one adopts his powerfully critical critique of apocalyptic cinema or not, nevertheless the vision of the apocalypse as "real" is a matter that must be negotiated between filmmakers and audiences.

singing to a cobra in a basket, and the cobra, clearly nothing but a puppet, appearing to dance with them (and making a face at Groucho). Perhaps the simplicity of these effects lends a childlike innocence to the project. We can write off the audiences who enjoyed them, less than six months before Pearl Harbour, as childlike and innocent, too.

The issue of historicising the audience's response to visual effects is continually with us. We see it raised by George Lucas's much publicised digital revisions of his original three *Star Wars* films, so as to "improve" on the effects sequences, that is, so as to render his work less vulnerable to audience criticism and disengagement on the basis of what could be seen as "inadequate" realism (this although no one thought the realism of the first *Star Wars* films inadequate when they first came out).[3] Even more bluntly interesting is the aspect of cinematic effects most widely discussed by viewers around the world, namely their easy obsolescence: the apparently obvious importance of producers continually raising the bar as to quality and detail. For example, the perfectly enchanting, and groundbreaking *TRON* (1982), with animation, visual, rotoscope, and matte effects by Harrison Ellenshaw and a team of six or seven dozen artists; or the somewhat ridiculous *Clash of the Titans* (1981), with stop-action animation by Ray Harryhausen, are both completely insufficient to our current demands for a more objective realism, and must be remade as *Clash of the Titans* (2010)—with hundreds of specialists handling digital compositing, match-move photography, rotoscoping, creature modelling, shader writing, asset modelling, texture art, digital matte creation, fluid simulation, and so on—and the similarly pumped *TRON Legacy* (2010), both films in appallingly seductive if perhaps not so very convincing 3-D.

The formula of repeating obsolescence applies not only to special effects hardware (such as the Fusion 3-D system, used for James Cameron's *Avatar*, that involves a pair of SONY high-definition cameras yoked together in a harness); or techniques (such as motion capture that, advancing rotoscoping into the twenty-first century, was used in *Avatar* to model Na'vi body movement on the movement of human actors covered with electronic sensors; or in *TRON Legacy* to make a performance out of Jeff Bridges' isolated gestures); but also to a kind of moral/economic imperative. One must continually purchase, adapt, and utilise newer and bigger computer programs to achieve animation effects; employ more and more technicians, even armies, flooding the vast battlefield of the narrative

---

3. I sat with an audience deep underneath Times Square when, in the very first of the films to see the screen, Han Solo and Chewbacca switched into hyperdrive for the very first time. It will suffice to say that more than twelve hundred people, most of them streetwise and young, roared with astonishment and pleasure.

project like the digitally-cloned armies in *Lord of the Rings* (see Thompson) to do the enormous (basically uncredited) grunt work of retouching, surfacing, modelling, shaping, and colouring (just as, in 1937, Walt Disney employed armies of uncredited female artists to paint in animation cells between his key frames for *Snow White* [see Zohn]). Once one has invested in the big-chip computers and the high-end software, they must be used or the costs cannot be amortised. The destruction of Santa Monica and Brentwood in Roland Emmerich's *2012* (2009), is a good example of this kind of usage:

Figure 3 The destruction of Santa Monica and Pacific Palisades from *2012* (Roland Emmerich, 2009). CGI matte shot. Digital frame enlargement.

Apparently in actuality and almost infinitely detailed in rendition, the entire western side of Los Angeles from at least the 405 onward breaks off and crumbles into the sea; this is the area where so many movie stars and celebrities of the golden age lived, including Claude Rains, Paul Henreid, and, in a new home where she was discovered dead with a smile on her face one morning in August 1962, Marilyn Monroe. Computer animation allows artists to zero in on any part of a frame, amplify it, and increase its pixellation: more, one can add to the representation of the world, painting in reflections in mirrors, dewdrops on flower petals, tears on the face of an actor who has forgotten what it is to cry.[4]

---

4. Computer animation, however, does not necessarily improve on older techniques. The Astrodome moon landing sequence in Kubrick's *2001: A Space*

Special effects often demonstrate features of optically perceivable reality the human eye wouldn't pick up in real life. Based on photo-realist painting of the late 1960s and beyond, we now see a hyperrealism replacing what used to be called pictorial realism. This is partly owed to the nervous camera (born in 1976 with the Steadicam), a device that must always have the freedom to move, to move anywhere; but hyperrealism has been aggravated with fast editing in the style that David Bordwell has called "intensified continuity," one that cuts rapidly from shot to shot— with shots lasting only about a quarter of a second—as though the action suffers from a kind of attention deficit disorder. The films of Quentin Tarantino and Paul Greengrass show good examples of this A.D.D. camera—as we might call it—which zooms and swoops into scenic details no human observer would care about or need to catch. Detail is presented because it can be, not because the viewer would want to search for it or give it meaning. The camera that is everywhere sees everything, a perfect tool of surveillance.

By comparison with a view from this always shifting, always magnifying, always dramatising camera-eye, this hypervigilant, hyperventilating, surveillance camera, films from the 1930s, 1940s, and 1950s seem tediously slow moving and static and their pictures of the world painfully limited. In them, after all, the camera position has been selected to encompass an artist's personal choice of the relevant action of a shot, not a distanced, objective, always modified and improved scientific display of facts. The new nervous camera takes position only to launch itself. Immediately it races through a shot to gain and dispense information as the shot develops, indeed, jumping so as to show a scene as a Cubist would, from many points of view that the audience is meant to sum up. The shot, made this way, becomes a field. Where once the filming artist had selected from the field of situational possibility the key elements necessary for composing a rich and telling shot, the nervous camera operates differently, scooping up and then displaying as much information as possible, no matter its origin or quality. With this informative field the viewer is daunted to compose his own shot, if he chooses. Alternately, he can passively scan the space, reserving the potency to make decisions while never making a decision in fact, thus always feeling empowered. This is

---

Odyssey (1968) was shot not with animations but with rear projections; and the spacecraft travel was accomplished with painted plastic models including "thousands of tiny parts selected from hundreds of plastic model kits, ranging from boxcars and battleships to aircraft and Gemini spacecraft. Cameras could get very close to models with no loss of detail or believability" (Douglas Trumbull quoted in Agel 1970, 89).

related to that grand invention of modernity, the technique of the suspended judgement.

A good example of the nervous camera is given by the airliner crash sequence of Bryan Singer's *Superman Returns* (2006), where we are outside and inside the vehicle, behind it and ahead of it, looking up and looking down at it, penetrating into its every interior niche while examining passengers for their facial expressions, bodily postures, twitches, spasms, and contortions. We see the oxygen masks drop down hopelessly, the pilots in their face masks stunned into paralysis, Superman zipping ahead of the plane and grasping it as it plummets down, down, down. Then quickly, a baseball game at Yankee stadium, the players, the crowd, everybody looking up as smoking death approaches from the sky. And a calming side view as Superman holds the thing off the ground, gently slides it down to rest on the pitcher's mound. No single one of these points of view can be taken seriously for long. The kids in the baseball crowd gawking up at the sky, for instance: if we rest on them, and let their expressions develop, we lose the chance in this fixed temporal universe to watch Superman perform his heroics. But if we stayed with Superman and the plane, we wouldn't be able to have the kick of seeing the kids in the crowd. The nervous camera sees it all because it refuses to choose. It devours everything, with no taste, or with unlimited taste. As a topological ride for the audience this is nothing but thrilling, but it depends upon our occupying a trajectory that is uncommitted, deeply uninterested, and therefore, flirtatious. Nervous photography is the mode in a society where social connections are too dangerous for comfort.

"Surface Splendor"

What is generally framed here are the corollary problems of watching old movies with new sensibilities and watching new movies with old, social class problems, when seen in light of Siegfried Kracauer's observation about the movie theatre as a palace of distraction: "Elegant *surface splendor* is the hallmark of these mass theaters" (1995, 323). Kracauer is speaking, of course, about the exhibition space itself; but the "surface splendor" is also invoked by the screen, indeed more and more frequently and opulently as cinema advances. The screen is the jewel box of a new aristocratic celebration. But the question is: which kind of surface is being valorised and rhapsodised as we watch film, a bounded surface framed and made special, or a surface that extends without apparent limit across the conceivable world? Are we fixated upon something that can exist only here, or is the theatre screen a mere section of an elaborate universe conceived through and referenced by the narrative? In the first case, the screen appears to offer the entirety of a visual subject. In the second, it yields to us but an arbitrary fragment of some manifestation far too immense to specify and contain. Indeed, watching the story in "limitless" cinema we can never have any idea of how big the seen world is, how big the event, how substantial its impact, how precisely the pieces are related, since what is outside the screen, undefined and indefinable, always tints and flavours what we see in ways we cannot fix. Think of the world of the matrix in *The Matrix* (1999) or the sunless *cauchemar* of *Dark City* (1998): they recede without restraint, and yawn all around. The "world" of George Stevens' *Giant* (1956), by stark contrast, was the fabulous spread of "Reata," a mere collection of dusty acres in the state of Texas, with a mere mansion cozied at its heart.

A good way to grasp the problem of cinema's "surface splendor" is by thinking about rear projection, especially in the case of driving sequences in classical and recent films. The continuing motorway sequences in Fred Schepisi's *Last Orders* (2001) are shot almost exclusively without special effects, since a very sensitive film stock (that would work to produce a good exposure range in available light) was available along with a lightweight Steadicam that could be positioned inside the car. None of these technologies were possible in the age of classical cinema. Camera operator Alexander Sahla could get astonishingly realistic views of the car interior, a detailed space enclosing Ray Winstone, Tom Courtenay, Bob Hoskins, and David Hemmings driving to their friend Michael Caine's funeral; and a very crisply rendered vision of the motorway outside. Virtually no rear-projection effects are needed, except when a truck pulls up from behind and realistically passes our vehicle as the editor shifts from a rear view to a three-quarter angle. Being able to use a camera in so intimate a way—and in very confined space—is a relatively new development. The road here seems real in the sense of extending beyond the pictorial frame into a geographic space that is contiguous with extra-narrational reality, a reality that is spreading outward as we drive away from it and stretching back into an extensive "past". In earlier films, narrative space was felt to be "real" exactly because it seemed magically cut off, distinct, and complete in itself. In Michael Curtiz's *Mildred Pierce* (1945), for example, there is a rear projection composite of Joan Crawford and Jack Carson driving along the Pacific Coast Highway outside Los Angeles. In this shot the road and its topography seem contained entirely within the bounds of the picture, and indeed, the fact that the road surface is nothing but a picture within the picture assists in this effect. The earlier film seems to give us an opportunity to see a world pictured; the more recent film seems to show a picture in a world.

Figure 4 Ray Winstone (l.), Bob Hoskins, and David Hemmings in *Last Orders* (Fred Schepisi, 2001). Motorway shot without rear projection. Digital frame enlargement.

Figure 5 Joan Crawford and Jack Carson in *Mildred Pierce* (Michael Curtiz, 1945). Motorway shot with rear projection. Digital frame enlargement.

The difference here, no matter to what degree it flows from the filmmaking artists' authorial intent, is made possible by technical developments, not only inspirations. For instance, cameras like the hand-held Aaton or Éclair 16 mm. used by French New Wave filmmakers such as Godard put pressure on manufacturers to develop newer, smaller, lighter, and more efficient cameras that could be stabilised inside a moving automobile, equipped with faster lenses, and loaded with faster, more sensitive films: once this kind of equipment is available, you can shoot while travelling on a highway in broad daylight, and once shooting is possible, filmmakers can start having the idea of making certain kinds of shots and the desire to bring such an idea into practice.

Figure 6 Driving scene from *Lady for a Day* (Frank Capra, 1933). Note central hotspot through car's back window. Digital frame enlargement.

When the shot from *Mildred Pierce*—that at the time of the film's release was stunning and exciting (and that echoed hundreds upon hundreds of similar rear projections from films of the 1930s, 1940s, 1950s, and 1960s)—is judged according to what we can see in *Last Orders*, it seems shockingly flat and contrived, and to the extent that we pull away in disenchantment from its directness, we are also relieved of our commitment to the characters and their condition. Technically even worse is an apparently less accomplished—but also much earlier—driving scene from *Lady for a Day* (1933), a film made when the transition to new cellulose rear-projection screens was just in progress and giveaway "hot spots" still often showed in backgrounds; even the rear projections we can see by the early 1930s, "flawed" as they may seem now, were improvements over the images on ground glass screens shot previously (see Salt 1992, 209). In *A Letter to Three Wives* (1949), the technology of rear projection is more advanced. In some scenes we see a small rear-projection screen used (for a shot outside a kitchen window of a train rushing by, repeated four times in the film), and in some a much, much larger one (for exteriors of a shoreline as a ferry boat meanders down a river, and a scenic panorama behind Ann Sothern and Jeanne Crain). But Arthur C. Miller lit the studio foregrounds too strongly and with too much uniformity, so that the composite nature of the shots is clearly distinguishable. Nevertheless, when the film came out the cinematography was highly praised. Some hypercritical viewers even find reason to complain about Sean Connery and "Tippi" Hedren driving on a superhighway in *Marnie* (1964), where we have Technicolor rear projection plates and much more refinement of the process in Hitchcock's hands.

Such sequences as these seem hollow and artificial by twenty-first-century standards because they do not appear to extend beyond the theatre as we now believe—cultivated as we are by contemporary technical marvels—that they should. We could say that cinema was once intensively framed, and now the frame has been taken off with the effect that the image can migrate into the world that also houses the viewer. The viewer and the image share a space; while with *Mildred Pierce* and other golden age films, the viewer worked to engage with cinematic space, which was not intrinsically his own.

As time goes by and new technologies take the place of old, early special effects seem thin, cheap, bogus, and especially *visible*. More elusive for many viewers is an associated thought: that our most popular special effects today—from *The Dark Knight*, through *Cloverfield*, *The Imaginarium of Dr. Parnassus*, *Mission Impossible: Ghost Protocol* (2011), and *The Twilight Saga* (2008-2012), to *Hugo*—might be surpassed themselves in the near future, with the result that they, too, would look "cheesy," unbelievable, and hopelessly pinioned in history. Thus, every ostensibly stunning, overwhelming, and incomprehensible effect exists simultaneously on the verge of boredom: built-in obsolescence has guided the economy of modernity. Consumers must buy the same product over and over again, in order for manufacturers to realise sufficient profit without having to produce an infinitely expanding catalogue of products. Just as the 3-D wizardry of *Superman Returns* (with the Man of Steel projected toward the audience as he flew into the stratosphere) caused the 3-D wizardry of *The Charge at Feather River* (1953, with a charging band of Indians shooting their arrows into the audience) to stand out as crude and ridiculous; so the 3-D wizardry of *Avatar* upstaged *Superman Returns*; *Hugo* upstaged *Avatar*; and something we don't know yet is going to make *Hugo* seem primitive and uninteresting when evaluated according to its lights. We may even find a way to replicate our actual experience of seeing in three dimensions which, of course, none of these so-called "3-D" films manages to do, settling instead for what I would call "intensified depth of field". Audiences act as though 3-D excites them—they've acted this way since the earliest days of "3-D"—and because they act that way, it does. But no effect leaves us so very satisfied that we are unwilling to try out experiencing a new one.

Effects Close-Ups

"Intensified depth of field" is epitomised by a number of shots in Tim Burton's *Alice in Wonderland* (2010). In one, young Alice is at a garden party being proposed to by a snobbish member of the aristocracy. She turns to look at the assembled multitude of aristocrats, lined up away from the camera as far as the eye can see. Each row stands distinctly apart from the rows in front and behind. The effect is of a children's pop-up book illustration, with the extraordinary sea of white, pale blue, off-white, and pale pink dresses and gray tuxedos spread away from us like tiers of French pastry. This effect is reprised toward the conclusion of the film as the White Queen stands in front of her retinue—a collection of charming and crazy beings, including the Mad Hatter, the Cheshire Cat, and so on, all these more colourful than the people at the garden party and ranged in a snow-white palace between crumbling columns in a stunning tableau that has, again, a distinctly over-pronounced and artificial depth of field. It's interesting that in these intensified depth-of-field shots—the major selling point of the new 3-D—the project of directing the eye from the front to the back of a shot is actually challenged by the distinctness, the objective presence, of the layers in the array one by one. Each plane of focus is fascinating in itself—has to be, in order that the effect of "depth" should be created—and this slows down the eye's passage from one plane to another, since patient discrimination of planes becomes a principal part of the optical task. It bears repeating that in this film Burton makes shots like these because technology has rendered them makeable, not because it is important or meaningful for the continuity of his dramatic action that we should discriminate all these persons and see them clearly. This is a perfect example of art doing what technique permits, and of the artist's "need" being oriented to his ability: the artist seems to be a show-off.

Frequently one comes across what might be called an "effects close-up". The close-up in cinema goes back at least to Griffith's *The Gay Shoe Clerk* (1903), when the filmmaker shot and cut in a close shot of the shoe, ankle, and lower leg of a customer in a shoe shop as the over-romantic salesman fixated upon them in helping her try on the article. The close-up worked to give the audience a telling detail. Later, in *The Lonedale*

Operator (1911), after a brave young woman has saved the company payroll from being heisted by two scruffy robbers in a local railway telegraph station, she holds up (for the camera to see) the wrench, borrowed from her father, which she has made to simulate a pistol. As she holds up the wrench, Griffith gives us a close-up so that we can "get the joke" clearly and pointedly (see further Gunning 2004). In these two close-ups, and in most of the close-up shots that would follow for at least a decade, an informative or crucial point of dramatic action was selected out, specially lit, and featured by the camera as a way of "modifying" or "elaborating" the ongoing narrative. The close-up came out of the story itself; yet it spoke of the author's mode of storytelling. It had a narrative "voice".

Figure 7 Typical 3-D demonstration from *Alice in Wonderland* (Tim Burton, 2010). Digital frame enlargement.

In the 1920s and onward, a crucial development occurred with the advent and presence of film stars onscreen. Now, for economic reasons, it was necessary to draw to the audience's attention in a special way the (beautiful) face of the star who had become one of the reasons for going to the movies. As stars gained power by achieving marquee appeal, they were featured onscreen in shots that made their faces not only recognisable but also especially admirable. By the 1930s, of course, the "star close-up" was a regular feature of Hollywood cinema, a conventional special effect, and cinematographers specialised in being able to construct such shots with professional aplomb, courtesy, and consideration, not to say talent. George Barnes and William Daniels were two such "geniuses" of the camera. As to the narrative close-up, it continued with force as well. We can see a very powerful example in Alfred Hitchcock's *Saboteur* (1942), when in the conclusion the villain is dangling from the hand of the hero who is perched in the torch of the Statue of Liberty. The hero has hold of the villain's jacket cuff. Hitchcock gives us a macro-close-up of the stitching slowly unravelling from the point where the arm of the jacket is attached at the shoulder. When the stitches are gone, of course—and we are watching them go!—the arm itself will slip off in the hero's hand and the hapless villain will plummet to his death. This particular close-up is not only narrative, but mortal.

Figure 8 This effects close-up from *Avatar* (James Cameron, 2009) shows more highlights in the eyes than are necessary to match the situational lighting: they can be added easily, and look pretty. Digital frame enlargement.

By the 1990s, however, something else was going on. The close-up of the star continued, as, in complex action sequences, did that of the relevant narrative detail; but added to these were narratively insubstantial but spectatorially powerful "effects close-ups" —fragments of the scene, of characters' makeup, and so on. The point of these was to demonstrate to viewers that they were in the hands of expert computer animators who could achieve fine-grain graphic detail that would read as hyperinformative. Thus, it was not the author speaking but his technical assistant, in effect the augmented camera itself. "Look what I can see and show you!" Anything would work as long as it was difficult to achieve: a long shot of ships floating out to sea in *Benjamin Button* with snowflakes dallying in the air in front of our eyes, or in *Avatar* a similar effect with tiny, colourful flying insects. In 1903, the narrative close-up itself was a marvel. In 1933, the star close-up became a marvel, and the narrative close-up retreated and became normal. In 2003 and onward, the effects close-up is a marvel, and even the star close-up is taken for granted, unless an effects tweak is managed that reveals perspiration drops slowly trickling down those magnificent cheeks.

One particularly subtle effect of valorising our present-day experience of special effects—taking our own habits and expectations seriously—is that, jaded about the past, we systematically fail to study two features of older effects techniques in general. First, that they were accomplished with exceptional professionalism, given production challenges and standards at the time (so that in being blind to them we neglect the extent and quality of technique available in the Hollywood studios through the golden age and the 1950s). Secondly, that an enchanting residue is left behind by special effects that never were meant to seem like documentary realism, but that aimed instead to carry audiences to a territory or zone somewhere beyond both pragmatic everyday factuality and artfully creative fantasy, a zone in which the reality of the image was not specified by the technology but was instead left up to the viewer's imagination to crystallise.

Painted Life

In the earliest days of the 1950s, a major change in the technology of cinematic realisation took place at MGM. The studio was under severe financial pressures, given the effects of the Paramount Decision of 1948, the tremors of the McCarthy hearings and the anti-Communist witch hunt, and the slowly building cataclysm of domestic entertainment and television that was threatening movie attendance. When in 1951 Louis B. Mayer was ousted as Chief Executive of MGM studios and replaced by Dore Schary, it seemed as though the handwriting on the wall would dictate frantic budget consciousness and cost-saving as a way of addressing the studio's particular vulnerability in the economic climate of the time: all the studios were suffering, but MGM had made fewer adjustments than most and had long been committed to lavish productions undertaken with what now seemed a devil-may-care attitude to the profit line.

As Schary looked for pennies to save on Arthur Freed's scheduled production of *Brigadoon* (1954), to be directed by Vincente Minnelli and choreographed by Gene Kelly, he was able to see immediately that Minnelli's elaborate productions of *An American in Paris* (shot in 1950) and *The Band Wagon* (shot in 1952) had benefited from the care that can be given to soundstage work. When Freed and Kelly suggested that what they wanted for *Brigadoon* was to shoot it outdoors in the Scottish Highlands, Schary nixed the plan flat out and stipulated that the entire picture would be shot indoors, on Stage 27 at Culver City, the largest soundstage in Hollywood. Kelly's visions of the clans dancing through real hills quickly evaporated. The village and surroundings of Brigadoon would have to be built, not found.

The essential problems were two, beyond actually building the thatched huts and structures of the village of Brigadoon itself. First, the sound stage had to be transformed into a Scottish countryside, with rolling hills, implanted trees, wooden fences, a working stream, and a stone bridge crossing it. Since virtually the entire action of the film would be set in this territory, the challenge required an enormous and expansive set, one that could be photographed in small sections or by a camera that travelled across almost all of it. Further, the set had to be populated by living animals, some of whom had to wear false eye patches so that they would appear to be normal while not seeing Kelly and distracting him with sudden moves as he danced. Cinematographer Joseph Ruttenberg would use a huge range of camera angles, many of which involved movement of the huge crane that was Minnelli's favourite perch and his point of view of choice both for rehearsals and for shooting. And the set had to be lit for both daytime and nocturnal sequences. On top of all this, the construction would have to support sophisticated choreography, so the ground had to be "real" at the same time as it was "unreal".

The second challenge was technically as difficult and philosophically even more profound. A background had to be created of such magnitude that viewers would believe they were looking at the Highlands no matter what direction the camera faced. The head of the painting department George Gibson worked with his team to produce an immense drop, running some 450 feet long and 50 feet high and hung on a cyclical rack. Undertaking this background required specially cut canvas, special techniques for stitching the pieces together, special sizing to seal it, special paints, and special lighting, not to mention a special building, the MGM paint frame, in which the huge backdrop could be sketched and painted.[5]

The effect on viewers was that of an indeterminate and thus entrancing space, much the same kind of environment that had been created with Gibson's backing for the "Our Love Is Here To Stay" number in *An American in Paris* (1951), where Kelly and Leslie Caron did a *pas de deux* on a *quai* of the Seine all designed inside a soundstage with a backdrop

---

5. An extended discussion of this film and its effects is given in my *The Eyes Have It: Cinema and the Reality Effect* (2013).

showing the Pont Neuf in mist behind them; and for the highly charged "Dancing in the Dark" number of *The Band Wagon*, where Central Park seems at once very much present and very much replaced with a fantasy. Since the film *Brigadoon* both is and is not a view of real human relations in space and time, it invokes a potent ambiguity in our experience, one that rather than leaving the visual world coldly defined and at a distance approximates to our thought and memory the problem of understanding, grasping, and relating to reality.

Figure 9 Section of 456-foot-long backing for *Brigadoon* by George Gibson and staff (Vincente Minnelli, 1954). Digital frame enlargement.

In more contemporary cases, however, ambiguity of placement is reduced or abandoned. The hand-painted effect achieved by Gibson is often replaced by location shooting, which gives a blunt portrayal of the real that is often at odds with the fabular identities of the stars posing against it; or pixellation, which produces a pictorial grain invisible to the naked eye. Thus, the computerised background—such as we see, for example, in *The Chronicles of Narnia: The Lion, the Witch and the Wardrobe* (2005) or *Prince of Persia: The Sands of Time* (2010)—appears photographically real; the sense of indeterminacy is lost. With *Alice in Wonderland*, another transformation is invoked: what in Lewis Carroll's book was inexplicably eccentric or strange and thus philosophically entrancing is now pinned to unambiguous diegetic locational "facts" undergirding the visual structure. A winding, unending phantasmagoria is transformed into an architecture, and the gardens of Wonderland, no longer a vast extension of our wandering minds (Alice, remember, is dreaming on a summer's afternoon), are reduced to an elaborate design. The film is thus a design triumph, but it repositions and resituates fantasy in a relatively unbounded context, since the design, or at least its impulse, goes on without apparent limit in every direction inward and outward.

One continues nowadays to believe what one sees, but *how do we see*? In "old" special effects, intensive labours are undergone to make for relatively seamless screen compositions, but it is always clear that these are created through standard cinematic optical practices: thus, constructive pieces (pieces of film or pieces of a vision) are seamed together to produce the apparent seamlessness, and part of our way of seeing is an acceptance of the very principle of illusion that underlies our vision. Illusion, indeed, is a phenomenon that alternately shows itself and hides, that is apparent—as it were, in the brushstrokes—while also being invisible—in the camera's treatment of the brushstrokes. And for its own sake, illusion is deemed to be desirable. In watching *Brigadoon* we experience a thrill at a certain staginess, as though all of this is only a dream vision of Scotland made up by talented magicians in a magical moment, which, of course, is precisely what it is: the work of labouring magicians, working on contract. With *Avatar*, *Alice in Wonderland*, *Lord of the Rings*, or the now huge number of computer-animated films that have been redefining screen reality and re-educating viewers as to what to expect when they go to the movies, the feeling is conveyed that we are looking through a microscope not at a contained construction but at an infinitely elaborated world, a world that recedes into layers of recursive detail the further we probe into it. The screen of the digitally animated tends to be fractal, recursive, continuous. The hand of the artist seems to recede, and the visual object seems to obtrude directly into our sight. Computer generated graphics do not absolutely require this optical strategy, as we see very well with *Hugo*, which retains through all its elaborate animations and set designs a sense of indeterminacy and vivid presence before the eye, as we find in *Brigadoon*.

I think part of what makes for the difference between "old" optics and "new" optics is that in the 1940s and 1950s, and largely because of the star system, principal attention was always paid to the humans performing in a scene. The star system has continued, of course, but tends to distance itself from the optical structure of blockbuster cinema, so that blockbusters are frequently about scenes, actions, events, and finally, the quality of depiction, and not about characters with whom we care to identify or of whom we care to have a detailed portrait. The Johnny Depp performance in *Alice* might seem to be a crossover, except that Depp the actor is entirely submerged in an optical surface comprising make-up, costume, and finally, computer animation. If in *Edward Scissorhands* we met an actor employing a costume to create a performance, in *Alice* we meet a design employing an actor to move it through n-dimensional diegetic space.

Loss

There are two great losses we may have endured in our voyage to accommodate our sensibilities to *Inglourious Basterds*, *Avatar*, *Alice in Wonderland*, *Watchmen*, *Clash of the Titans*, *Star Trek*, *Lord of the Rings*, *Prince of Persia*, and the like. First, the distinct and riddling pleasure of ambiguity, something that was not only philosophically part of "old" cinema but was plainly offered in the character of the visual experience we had then, may now be more and more replaced by action. In discussing the active life, Hannah Arendt notes (Arendt 1958)

> among the outstanding characteristics of the modern age from its beginning to our own time we find the typical attitudes of *homo faber*: his instrumentalization of the world, his confidence in tools and in the productivity of the maker of artificial objects…his conviction that every issue can be solved and every human motivation reduced to the principle of utility; his sovereignty, which regards everything given as material and thinks of the whole of nature as of "an immense fabric from which we can cut out whatever we want to resew it however we like". (305)

Our current questions, moment by moment as we flit through films, regard the diegesis: "Where exactly am I at this moment, inside this space that I have accepted and now take for granted? Who is it that I am watching? What is happening?" These are questions relevant to positioning, mapping, navigation, constant circulation. When we looked at special effects techniques of the golden age, we asked instead, "What *kind* of place is this?" I think it possible that our current concerns are more about our own abilities to deconstruct what we see, and thus more about ourselves, than about the image itself, and that we are losing the ability to be confounded, bewildered, entranced, and thus touched by cinema even as we are gaining the experience to be informed and to move. We are losing the sense of touch. Or, to be fair, we are losing a certain touch that made possible a sensation of an ambiguous reality intermediate between everyday focal clarity and dreamlike fantasy, a certain ability to discern a world while being half-awake, or, as Leslie Fiedler liked to say, paraphrasing Caliban and Walt Whitman together, "in dreams awake". Instead we gain a tactile sense for the objective reality that we encounter in a state of hypervigilance. We could say that computer-animated screen realities are a particular side benefit of the surveillance state, and that our way of apprehending them is a requirement of the surveilling attitude.

We are losing something else, too, in fact, have now virtually all but completely lost it: the talents of specific individuals who gave their lives to the creation of screen illusions in the "old" days and who are now no longer among us. Russell Collings, E. Roy Davidson, W. Percy Day, Linwood Dunn, Farciot Edouart, A. Arnold Gillespie, Devereaux Jennings, Nathan Juran, George Turner, Albert Whitlock, to name only a few, whose life labour it was to make the designs, optical photography, split-screen shots, rear projections, and travelling mattes through which we saw another world: these artists, unsung and unheralded while they lived and worked, are now all but forgotten.

In his book *I Have Landed*, the palaeontologist, biologist, and philosopher Stephen Jay Gould (2002) recounts a strange little tale, the point of which, for him, is to show how "respected styles of former explanation became risible and 'mystical' in the light of new views about causality and the nature of the material world". Think of this in terms of cinematic special effects old and new and our perception of reality:

> There was a popular pre-scientific remedy, a soothing salve, for healing wounds from swords and other weapons. This salve had to be rubbed on the wound—it was made of herbs and potions that apparently really worked. But the ancient recipe also required that the salve be applied to the sword that had caused the wound!

Healing, says Gould, required that both the victim and the weapon should be put right, rebalanced. His point about this story is simply that by modern-day standards it is ridiculous, and that when we hear it we tend to laugh at the simplicity, even the ignorance, of our ancestors who would have believed it.

This hollow laughter is what fascinates him. He notes how some thinkers cannot "bear to surrender the comforting and traditional view that human consciousness must represent a predictable (if not a divinely intended) summit of biological existence". Many of us have exactly this thought about the development of realism in cinema, that what we see today represents a kind of glorious summit that we have attained. Just as we are clever and progressive for *not* thinking one needs to rub medicine on the sword, we are clever and progressive for appreciating Tim Burton's *Alice* or James Cameron's *Avatar* rather than Michael Curtiz's *Mildred*

Pierce or Alfred Hitchcock's *The Birds*. How primitive, how stupid, how transparent, how cheesy are the effects of days gone by, we say when we see them with our new eyes. And how brilliant must we be, possessing those eyes, experiencing this newness, and looking back on the primitive past from a regal height.

It is when we find an escape from this kind of arrogance, of course, that we can come to understand what cinema was for our parents and grandparents and their parents before, and understand what it is for us now; that cinema can truly become an object of our love.

Works Cited

Agel, Jerome. 1970. *The Making of Kubrick's 2001*. New York: Agel Publishing Co./New American Library.

Arendt, Hannah. 1958. *The Human Condition*. Chicago: University of Chicago Press.

Gould, Stephen Jay. 2002. *I Have Landed*. New York: W.W: Norton.

Gunning, Tom. 2004. "Systematizing the Electric Message: Narrative Form, Gender, and Modernity in *The Lonedale Operator*." In *American Cinema's Transitional Era: Audiences, Institutions, Practices*, edited by Charlie Keil and Shelley Stamp, 15-50. Berkeley: University of California Press.

Kracauer, Siegfried. 1995. *The Mass Ornament: Weimar Essays*. Translated by Thomas Y. Levin. Cambridge, Mass.: Harvard University Press.

Mathijs, Ernest and Murray Pomerance, eds. 2006. *From Hobbits to Hollywood: Essays on Peter Jackson's Lord of the Rings*. Amsterdam: Editions Rodopi.

Nabokov, Vladimir. 1989. *Pnin.* New York: Vintage International.

Pastoureau, Michel. 2001. *Blue: The History of a Color*. Translated by Markus I. Cruse. Princeton: Princeton University Press.

Pomerance, Murray. 2013. *The Eyes Have It: Cinema and the Reality Effect*. New Brunswick, NJ: Rutgers University Press.

Pomerance, Murray and John Sakeris, eds. 2010. *Popping Culture* 6th edition. Boston: Pearson Education.

Salt, Barry. 1992. *Film Style and Technology: History and Analysis*. 2nd Expanded Edition. London: Starword.

Scherer, Joanna Cohan. 1975. "You Can't Believe Your Eyes: Inaccuracies in Photographs of North American Indians." *Studies in the Anthropology of Visual Communication* 2 (2): 67-79.

Schivelbusch, Wolfgang. 1986. *The Railway Journey: The Industrialization of Time and Space in the 19th Century*. Berkeley: University of California Press.

Thompson, Kirsten Moana. 2006. "Scale, Spectacle and Movement: Massive Software and Digital Special Effects in *The Lord of the Rings*." In *From Hobbits to Hollywood: Essays on Peter Jackson's Lord of the Rings*, edited by Ernest Mathijs and Murray Pomerance, 283-99. Amsterdam: Editions Rodopi.

Zohn, Patricia. 2010. "Coloring the Kingdom." *Vanity Fair* (March). Available online at:
http://www.vanityfair.com/culture/features/2010/03/disney-animation-girls-201003

CHAPTER TWO

FLAHERTY, FATTY ARBUCKLE
AND THE INVISIBLE BRIDE:
NANOOK OF THE NORTH
AND THE ORIGINS OF DOCUMENTARY

SETH FELDMAN

Contemporary thought cautions us to tread carefully around the idea of origins. That there are great "firsts" shaping all that comes after them is as discredited an idea as is the thought that single notable individuals are the sole shapers of their historical eras or that there are lone inventors of any new technology. One thing doesn't follow another; many things follow many. Although historians may present history as narratives with beginnings, middles and ends, there is no reason to believe that events unfold that conveniently. And if there is anything at all interesting about the belief in a specific origin it is what it tells us about the believers.

So what then does it mean for the definition—and definers—of documentary that Robert Flaherty's *Nanook of the North* (1922) has for so long and so widely been regarded as the prototype of documentary film? Despite the massive re-examination of early cinema that has led us to think of it as something like the medium's DNA, classic narratives of documentary history still go to some lengths to draw a line between *Nanook* and various attempts at non-fiction filmmaking before its release. Obligatory credit is given to the early actualities, the evolution of newsreels, propaganda films. We learn that there were documentaries before *Nanook* that had an impact of their own: Herbert Ponting's footage of Scott at the South Pole, screened in various assemblages from 1911 attracted a large audience. *Battle of the Somme* (Geoffrey Malins and John McDowell, 1916) sold more than two million tickets after its release in August, 1916—when the battle was still in progress. Malins even helped define the image of the documentary filmmaker in his 1920 memoir, *How*

I Filmed the War: A Record of the Extraordinary Experiences of the Man Who Filmed the Great Somme Battles.[1]

Work on early cinema tells us that ethnographic filmmaking was more than just a "part" of film's origins; rather, it was the pursuit of the exotic that spread the new medium to much of the non-western world. Ethnographic cinema was also regarded as a scientific tool long before *Nanook*. In the first decade of the twentieth century, the American Museum of Natural History—which happily displayed dioramas of native life, collected the bones of aboriginal peoples and, on occasion, housed live-in exhibits of those people themselves—became known for sponsoring and screening ethnographic films. The circulation of these works was wide enough so that film critics, as early as 1911, began to note the lack of authenticity in the depiction of native peoples in fiction films (Geller 2003, 104). And there were those lost films that certainly sound like near precedents if not incitements for the production of *Nanook*. One of the more intriguing titles is *The Romance of the Far Fur Country* (1920), a film commissioned by the Hudson's Bay Company that, according to Peter Geller, included "a self-contained 'Eskimo Story'" (ibid.).

Interesting as these precedents may be, they seem less than convincing to modern writers. In fact, the surviving film with the most direct influence on *Nanook*, Edward S. Curtis' *In the Land of the Head Hunters* (1914), has been used by Brian Winston to make the distinction between Flaherty's film and all that came before. Curtis screened his work for Flaherty. They also watched together the first footage Flaherty brought back from the Arctic on his earlier expeditions. They may well have shared ideas about producing a more sophisticated form of ethnographic cinema. Curtis, as Winston happily points out, used the term "documentary" more than a decade before Grierson and in a manner closer to our sense of the word. Yet having said that, Winston (2000) too acknowledges *Nanook* as documentary originating work:

> Flaherty's contribution then is not that he was trained (he wasn't); nor that he was uniquely intimate with his subjects (he wasn't); nor that he alone understood the need for drama (Curtis did too). What Flaherty understood, though, was the need for the drama to arise from the life being observed,

---

1. Malins' image of a British mine exploding under the German trenches at the outset of the battle is perhaps the most frequently used motion picture image of the First World War.

not imposed from without...This insight was to prove crucial to the development of the documentary.[2]

It is with these sorts of statements that *Nanook* becomes not only the prototype documentary but also a guarantor that there is a progressive documentary history marked by a succession of breakthroughs. That these incremental insights are critiqued only reinforces the sense of a movement toward our understanding and acceptance of the veracity of contemporary forms. *Cinéma vérité*, as Errol Morris asserts, may well have set documentary practice back twenty years. But it also advanced critical scepticism by at least that many decades. Drama documentary generated a kind of reverse critique of filmed veracity, i.e. that it is, in the end, justified as being no more staged than other forms of what purports to be non-fiction. Reality television, we are told, is this generation's assertion of its right to renegotiate the terms of what constitutes "reality".

As hardened veterans of these many takes on documentary truth, twenty-first century audiences approach new films on a common sense basis. Conventions are just that in and of themselves, unreliable (no system of representation other than mathematics (maybe) is self-verifying). We view all manner of hybrids, yet we know what to believe when we see it. Postmodern scepticism and even the joys of deconstruction become irrelevant when our cause is just. Or to again quote Winston (2000, 253): documentary has "a relation to actuality which acknowledges the normal circumstances of image production but is at the same time consonant with our everyday experience of the world". It is, in other words, a cure for deconstruction.

In this regard, *Nanook* poses a special sort of problem. Whether or not we agree with the stature attributed to the film or are otherwise captivated by it, we know too much about its making and its maker to take it at face value. In *Nanook*, we have a film that from the time of its release has been both the icon of non-fiction filmmaking and a magnet for critiques of documentary veracity. Flaherty's name has become synonymous with the founding of the documentary spirit—just as Grierson's is synonymous with the founding of its ideology. One aspect of Nanook's originality is that it sparks a dialogue between the two realities: the actuality we feel like we are seeing and the craft of applying a "creative treatment" that will evoke just such emotional certainty. Historically, of course, *Nanook* is the product of that battle between instinct and the Word, the Dionysian and Apollonian, the Id and the Superego. To focus this paper, though, let us concentrate on two aspects of the film. One is the historical context of

---

2. *Variety* (June 16, 1922).

Nanook's release and reception—the film of 1922. The other is the complexity of the relationship between the film's subject and its director— as revealed to us since its release.

1922: Fatty Arbuckle's Nanook

In examining *Nanook*'s claim on origin, we should begin by citing the obvious: *Nanook* is widely regarded as the ur-documentary because it competed successfully with feature films in commercial theatres and did so on a global basis. The comparison is frequently made with the way that Griffith's *Birth of a Nation* had been a breakthrough seven years earlier, establishing once and for all the feature film as the industry's gold standard. *Nanook* it is argued, originated the documentary feature by making the form viable—or at least as viable as it is—to film producers and distributors. It was, to be sure, a humble breakthrough. *Nanook* was held over for a total of one week after its week long premiere at the Capitol Theatre in New York.[3] The film was more successful on the road in North America and more successful still in Europe, particularly in London where it ran for three months. *Nanook* spawned an "Eskimo" fad that persisted through the mid-1920s leaving in its wake any number of songs, ice cream bars and collectables.

With all this though, the film was a modest imitation of Griffith's success; Flaherty estimated that, by 1926, it had returned approximately five times its original $55,000 cost. In contrast, *Birth of a Nation's* $90,000 investment was recouped one thousand times over in years-long runs in some cities, leasing to 28 foreign distributors and in its three re-releases. The fad it inspired was in the short term an intensification of American racial struggle and, in the long term, an enduring international recognition of cinema's social and historical importance.

Even if Flaherty's innovation was in any way comparable to Griffith's, it begs the question of why it succeeded to the extent it did. What made *Nanook* so appealing and made it so appealing so quickly? Certainly, part of *Nanook*'s appeal was simply the modernist shock of the new. On June 12, 1922, the morning after the film premiered, readers of the *New York*

---

3. Flaherty recalled *Nanook* as having opened on a double bill with Harry Langdon's *Grandma's Boy*. His brother David later wrote that it in fact ran on its own. Richard Barsam in his 1988 biography of Flaherty, points out that *Grandma's Boy* opens three months after *Nanook*, but concludes that Nanook did in fact premiere on a double bill with Robert C. Bruce's documentary short, *My Country*. To further confuse matters, the Internet Movie Database lists Bruce's film as having been released on May 21, some two weeks earlier.

Times' anonymous film critic found it described in apocalyptic, all but Vertovian terms:

> Beside this film, the usual photo-play, the so-called "dramatic" work of the screen, becomes as thin and blank as the celluloid on which it is printed. And the photoplay cannot avoid the comparison that exposes its lack of substance. It is just as literal as the "travel" picture. Its settings, whether the backgrounds of nature or the constructions of a studio merely duplicate the settings of ordinary human experience—or try to. And its people try to persuade spectators that they are just ordinary people, ordinary that is, for the environment in which they happen to be placed. So the whole purpose of the photoplay, as a rule, is to reproduce life literally. And this is the purpose of the travel film. But the average photoplay does not reproduce life. Through the obvious artificialities of its treatment, through the unconcealed mechanics of its operation, through its reflection of a distorted or incomplete conception of life, rather than life itself, it usually fails to be true to any aspect of human existence. It is not realistic in any sense. It remains fiction, something fabricated. It never achieves the illusion of reality. (Anon. 1922, 18)

A few weeks later, Frances Taylor Patterson, instructor of photoplay composition at Columbia University and author of the 1920 screenwriting text, *Cinema Craftsmanship*, took that argument somewhat further. In the August 7, 1922 issue of *The New Republic*, Patterson, anticipating Robert Sherwood's much quoted analysis that would appear the following year (not to mention Winston's tipping point argument), recognised Flaherty's innovations as providing a dramatic unity to non-fiction footage. She then goes further, labelling *Nanook* as "the beginning of the naturalistic school of cinematography:"

> The director has used his mechanical device to gain the highest quotient of dramatic efficiency. The camera is subordinated to, and in fact almost eliminated from, the final effect. It is an invisible magician. There is no internal evidence that a camera was used. (Patterson 1922 in Pratt 1973, 343)

The beauty of the film, Patterson goes on to argue, is that this disappearance of the camera gives us a taste of pure cinema.

> One other thing about *Nanook of the North*. It is composed and expressed in terms of the motion picture. We are excessively weary of adaptations from the other arts, the art of the stage and the art of the printed word. Here at last begins our native screen language, as original in concept as *The Cabinet of Dr. Caligari*, yet as natural as that is fantastic. It reproduces

actual beauty as *Caligari* reproduces expressionistic beauty. (Patterson
1973, 344)

Again, we are hearing an argument made in terms reminiscent of those
Vertov would have been making at more or less the same moment.
Nanook, in these and similar responses, is taken not simply as a well-made
or intriguing film but as a repudiation of the newly established hold of the
feature film industry and more, of the last vestiges of film's subservience
to other art forms. Another way of looking at this is to see Flaherty's film
as having bracketed and hence defined fiction film—in the same way that
the talkies, a few years later, would necessitate the idea of silent cinema.

That Flaherty had contained Hollywood, had drawn a generic border
around it, was nothing if not timely in the late spring of 1922. For it was
during the winter of 1921-22, in Robert Sklar's much quoted analysis, that
American film had become recognised as the industry we frequently love
to hate.

In its rise to international success the industry had shifted from individual
to corporate enterprise…with new constraining ties to banks and brokers.
Hierarchies of salary, billing and job classification had replaced the old
open camaraderie. The pressure of aspirants and fans had caused studios
and stars to build walls of privacy against the outside world. In the space of
three or four years the movie trade had recapitulated the evolution of
industry from small to large scale organization, and many people had been
distressed by its sudden new impersonality and bureaucracy. (Sklar 1976,
83)

There was another, more specific, set of events generating public
distress with Hollywood during the winter of 1921-22. On September 3,
1921 a woman named Virginia Rappe suffered a fatal internal injury at a
party given by Roscoe "Fatty" Arbuckle. Arbuckle had parlayed his
cherubic face, spherical form and genius for directing silent comedy into a
stardom second only to Chaplin. He was, at the time, being paid one
million dollars per year by Paramount to develop the new genre of feature
length comedies and was doing so with considerable success. Rappe's
death three days after the party and Arbuckle's indictment for rape and
murder was quickly taken up by the Hearst newspapers as evidence of
decadence in Hollywood—anarchistic creative personalities unleashed
with too much money and too many appetites.

This moral panic was kicked up a notch on February 22, 1922 with the
murder of director William Desmond Taylor. Several Hollywood
celebrities were rumoured to be suspects. The first generation moguls

responded. To make sure that it was their employees rather than themselves who would be pursued by a scandalised public and its provocateurs, studio heads formed the Motion Picture Producers and Distributors of America. Will Hays, American Postmaster (and President Warren G. Harding's campaign strategist) was made its head on March 6, 1922. On April 12, Arbuckle, having suffered two mistrials, was acquitted. The newly appointed Hays used the occasion to ban Arbuckle and his films from American screens. No one was ever indicted for the Taylor murder.

When *Nanook* premiered on June 11, Flaherty and his Inuit family had the best possible alibi to clear them of involvement in Hollywood's various crimes. They were somewhere else, commercially, professionally, geographically, stylistically. The film—funded by a French fur company, starring non-actors and distributed by another French enterprise, Pathé— could not be traced to the California industry. Flaherty was no professional Hollywood director but rather the epitome of the civilised explorer, a Fellow of the Royal Geographic Society as even *Variety* (June 16, 1922) reminded its readers. It was his business to be somewhere else. And Nanook, his leading man, could be seen as the incarnation of early Hollywood's heroes: the plucky, hardworking, innocents whose devotion to simple but eternal values overcame all natural obstacles. As Eric Combest (2001, 125) describes the creation of Nanook:

> Flaherty's main insight, I think, was a Dickensian one: it was not necessary to delegate the primitives to the background and to film a white man's encounter with the wilderness, nor was it necessary to make of primitive people mere curios that sated white audience' desires for the exotic and prurient through the depiction of radical cultural difference. Like Dickens with the poor, Flaherty made the Eskimo commensurate with the audience, revealing their difference but in a way that was knowable and useful as well as entertaining. Moreover, Nanook would be both a "man against nature" hero and a citizen drawing on the support of his community, two roles Americans feared were disappearing from the realm of possibility in the corporate capitalist culture of the 20th century.

Flaherty's innovation then was not so much one of plot as of character, and an historically fortuitous character at that. Nanook was a man of his times, a kind of pre-lapserian Fatty Arbuckle. He was the smallest town boy—naiveté incarnate except, of course, for the fact that he had two wives.

The Optics of Polygamy

There are indeed two women who emerge from Nanook's kayak and live with him in his igloo. One is identified in the film's inter-titles as "Nyla, the smiling one" and the other simply as "Cunayoo," (variously spelled in the literature as "Cunayou" and "Cunayow") who seems somewhat older than Nyla and smiles far less. Cunayoo's position in the household is never identified in the film. She might well be taken for one of Nanook or Nyla's siblings or as the mother of one or the other of them. In the more recent literature, though, it is the polygamy theory that has gained ascendency. Shari Huhndorf notes rather matter of factly that she is "probably Nanook's second wife" (2000, 135). We are more apt to accept this interpretation as *Antanajurat, the Fast Runner* (Zacharias Kunuk, 2001) has reminded contemporary viewers that traditional Inuit society indeed tolerated polygamy. And in the much larger context, the sexual practices of the Inuit, particularly the sharing of wives, have been part of the Orientalist mystique accorded to them from a much earlier time. Indignant missionaries railed against the Inuit's traditional approach to gender relations well into the 1930s.[4] By the time *Nanook* was released, the Inuit's sharing of wives with visiting explorers was well known.

Nanook's polygamy, along with passing glimpses of the women's breasts, could simply be dismissed as this sort of *National Geographic* voyeuristic, scopophilic Orientalism—which is pretty much the way Huhndorf dismisses it. Even at (or at least close to) the time, the use of ethnographic documentary as a Freudian "smuggler" of forbidden passions was an open secret. Paul Rotha, for instance, fumes at the expectations the film industry had of Flaherty when it hired him to make another *Nanook* in Polynesia:

> In point of fact…Flaherty was dispatched to the South Seas in the belief that he would bring back a symphony of female nudity, such being the main asset of the native to the film producer. Instead, Flaherty returned with a sensitively composed idyll of the Samoans, a theme that showed how the native, in order to prove his manhood, created a ceremonial ritual of pain—the Tattoo. (Rotha 1935, 82)

One can argue for some time about the erotic vs. the sado-masochistic in Flaherty's reconstructions of "native" life in *Nanook* (1922), *Moana* (1926) or for that matter, *Man of Aran* (1934). What is certain though, is

---

4. See, for instance, Hugh Brody's *The People's Land: Inuit, Whites and the Eastern Arctic* (1975).

that these evocations are intentional. *Nanook*, in particular, was carefully cast—its nuclear family entirely artificial. Neither Nyla nor Cunayoo were the wives of the hunter Flaherty cast as Nanook, actually a man named Allakariallak (whose more common nickname was "Attata," homage to his patriarchal stature). On her part, Nyla was a woman named Alice Nevalinga, generally called "Maggie" by the white men around Port Harrison. Cunayoo, whose real name was Kanajuq, had originally been photographed by Flaherty during the winter of 1913-14. In 1915, he sold the photograph to the *Toronto Star* and it was frequently reprinted. As Robert Christopher puts it (2005, 169; photograph caption), Cunayoo/Kanajuq had become an "Inuit poster girl" well before *Nanook* was filmed.[5]

Flaherty's typecasting of the entirely artificial polygamous family makes us wonder why he would deliberately jeopardise the acceptance of *Nanook* in the midst of the moral panic being endured by the film industry while he edited the work. The even more interesting question is why nobody watching—or at least publically discussing the film—commented on the duality of Nanook's significant others. One answer—and one that could explain at some level *Nanook*'s instant success—is that the film vanquished Hollywood's evil aura while simultaneously offering the unstated pleasures of transgression engendered by its sexual excesses. That Nanook so heroically struggles for his family only facilitates a western audience's accepting that family in whatever form it might take. Extraordinary men are entitled to their own rules and to their extraordinary rewards, a rule of nature here made clear by stripping away the veneer of civilisation.

This would be a rule of nature that Flaherty himself obeyed —or so the more modern commentators on Flaherty might argue. As Huhndorf asserts (2000, 139), "both women were by all accounts Flaherty's common-law wives with whom he bore children". While Hunhdorf doesn't footnote "all accounts," her reference is linked to the short discussion of Claude Massot's 1991 film *Kabloonak* (released in English in 1995 as *Nanook Revisited*), by Fatimah Tobing Rony in *The Third Eye; Race, Cinema and*

---

5.   That the Inuit around the Port Harrison trading post were long accustomed to contact with Europeans and had adapted many European technologies was noted almost from the time of Nanook's release. Suffice it to say that the first Hudson Bay trading posts were established in the seventeenth century not far from Port Harrison. Accordingly, the Inuit we see in the film were descendants of a people who had been dealing with Europeans for a quarter of a millennium by the time Flaherty arrived.

Ethnographic Spectacle (1996, 122-24).[6] In Massot's film, the assertion regarding the two women is made by a modern day resident of Port Harrison (a town now known as Inukjuak). The film also presents a woman whom we are told is the widow of one of Flaherty's Inuit children and a man who is identified as his grandson. More recently, Melanie McGrath has chronicled the life of an Inuit man named Josephie, whom she identifies as the son of Flaherty and Alice Nevalinga. She also notes that Flaherty's northern and southern descendants are now in contact with one another (McGrath 2006).

Flaherty has been, perhaps always was, known for his contributions to the Northern Canadian gene pool. In the lore of frontier exploration, men absent from "civilisation" for months or years at a time were all but expected to take "country wives". Like the explorers and traders before him, Flaherty abandoned these wives and offspring—never returning to the Canadian north after filming *Nanook*. What I would argue here though is that this bit of celebrity gossip has some resonance in the film itself. For what we are seeing onscreen is not merely Nanook's polygamy but also Flaherty's. It is one of the more poignant instances of Flaherty's identification with the character he created as Nanook.

Flaherty, as we have seen in the reviews of the film, is taken as being as innocent of Hollywood's artifice (and crimes) as Nanook is of western civilisation as a whole. This innocence was the essence of his persona. Frances Flaherty (to whom Flaherty was engaged during his first northern expeditions and married at the time he shot *Nanook*) kept the flame of that innocence both during Flaherty's lifetime and after his death in 1954. She insisted that her husband's work was the product of "non-preconception" of his subjects, wandering into their lives in much the same way that the concocted innocent Inuit in *Nanook* stumbled into the white man's trading post. Arthur Calder-Marshall's biography of Flaherty underlined the identity between Flaherty and his documentary subjects in its title, *The Innocent Eye* (1963). And in a note attached to Calder-Marshall's introduction, John Grierson suggests that even *The Innocent Eye* is a corrective for the way in which Flaherty was perceived by his peers:

> As Arthur Calder-Marshall suggests, we have all been somewhat fanciful in our personal accounts of Flaherty. This came partly from the conversational respite he gave us when he blew into town. It was not the least of his gifts that he engaged us richly in that Canadian tradition of storytelling which insists that Paul Bunyan, Holy Old Mackinaw and all

6. Hunhdorf's implied reference to this source has been confirmed via correspondence.

Enchanted Wanderers are not the less real for being improbable. (Grierson in Calder-Marshall 1963, 12)

Nanook then is very much Flaherty's tall tale—with a somewhat blurred line between the protagonist and the teller. For to take up where Winston leaves off, it is not so much that Flaherty created a documentary narrative from the material he shot. He did not. There is no narrative in the "story telling" sense in Nanook, no character arcs, climaxes and denouements. The film indeed presents the "slight narrative" that Kracauer attributes to all of Flaherty's work (Kracauer 1997, 247). The point, though, is in the "slightness". This is a voyage of discovery with a general direction rather than a scenario or map. The explorer meets Nanook and his family at the Port Harrison trading post, follows them through the arctic, dutifully records their hunting, tool making and igloo building but at last can go no further and leaves them mid-blizzard to their fate and our imagination. Our journey, which began at the trading post where Nanook is the helpless child, has come to its end at a place where trading post "civilisation" has been blown away by greater powers. Nanook the child is the only one who can do battle with those powers. The filmmaker departs. Fade out on the polygamous igloo in the blowing snow.

For the European, this fantasised igloo, like the igloo and the tents that Flaherty shared with his Inuit guides on their long expeditions was also the site of regression. In his diaries, Flaherty often refers to the Inuit— including Nanook[7]—as childlike. He depicts himself as the rational westerner, father figure to a childlike crew. He doles out rations and bemoans the Inuit for their illogic. He even gives them nicknames for his own convenience and amusement. Yet those same diaries also reveal that it is Flaherty himself who is infantilised. During the many long winter expeditions, he depends on the Inuit entirely to find the way, drive the dog teams, build the igloos and generally bring him back alive. When the food runs low, it is they who nurture him. Flaherty's paternal dividing up of the remaining tea and splitting the last biscuits is reduced to a child playing with toy food when his Inuit companions save him from starvation by bringing home a newly killed seal. At one point, he reports in his diaries, his Inuit companions declare that they will survive by giving up western food and eating like men.

Perhaps it is too much of a leap but let's say it anyway: the manchild whom we imagine in the polygamous igloo at the end of *Nanook* is not all that different from the repulsive, thus highly alluring, fantasy of the cherubic Fatty Arbuckle making his way among the party girls on the

---

7. The name Flaherty uses for Allakariallak in his diaries.

evening of his downfall. The point of *Nanook*'s narrative is not that the
persona Flaherty has given to Allakariallak has gone from child to man.
Rather it is that the child and the man are one. Innocence and "non-
preconception," yields the intimate life that includes both the older, more
maternal woman and the younger woman who has replaced her in the role
of "Inuit poster girl". And while we are out on a limb, we might also say
that this is the root of salvage ethnography's great oxymoron of the "noble
savage". Within the profound depths of that oxymoron as personified in
the subject/filmmaker relationship in *Nanook*, with all its allure, its
invisibility and the nagging questions it raises, lies the nature of the film's
claim to origin. Like so many origins, *Nanook of the North* was not a
"first," but a "primal" — which is what it remains.

Works Cited

Anon. 1922. "The Screen". *New York Times* (June 12).
Brody, Hugh. 1975. *The People's Land: Inuit, Whites and the Eastern
    Arctic*. Harmondsworth, England: Penguin Books.
Calder-Marshall, Arthur. 1963. *The Innocent Eye; A Life of Robert J.
    Flaherty*. Baltimore, Penguin Books.
Combest, Eric. 2001. *Primitive Encounters: Ethnographic Imagination
    and American Identity, 1910-1930*. Unpublished dissertation. University
    of North Carolina (Chapel Hill), Department of History.
Christopher, Robert J. 2005. *Robert and Frances Flaherty; A Documentary
    Life, 1883-1922*. Montreal: McGill-Queen's University Press.
Geller, Peter. 2003. "Into the Glorious Dawn". In *Screening Culture:
    Constructing Image and Identity*, edited by Heather Norris Nicholson,.
    Oxford: Lexington Books.
Huhndorf, Shari M. 2000. "Nanook and His Contemporaries: Imagining
    Inuit in American Culture, 1897-1922". *Critical Inquiry* 27 (1)
    (Autumn).
Kracauer, Siegfried. 1997. *Theory of Film: The Redemption of Physical
    Reality*. 2nd Edition. Princeton: Princeton University Press.
Malins, Geoffrey H. 1920. *How I Filmed the War: A Record of the
    Extraordinary Experiences of the Man Who Filmed the Great Somme
    Battles, etc.* London: Herbert Jenkins Ltd. Available online at Project
    Gutenberg:
    http://www.gutenberg.org/files/30285/30285-h/30285-h.htm
McGrath, Melanie. 2006. *The Long Exile: A Tale of Inuit Betrayal and
    Survival in the High Arctic*. London: Fourth Estate.

Patterson, Frances Taylor. 1973 [1922]. "Nanook of the North". Reprinted in *Spellbound in Darkness; A History of the Silent Film*, edited by George C. Pratt, . Greenwich, Conn.: New York Graphic Society. Originally printed in *The New Republic* 26 (401), August 9.

Sklar, Robert. 1993. *Movie-Made America: A Cultural History of American Movies*. New York: Vintage Books.

Rony, Fatimah Tobing. 1996. *The Third Eye; Race, Cinema and Ethnographic Spectacle*. Charlotte, North Carolina: Duke University Press.

Rotha, Paul. 1935. *Documentary Film*. New York: Hastings House Publishers.

Variety. 1922. June 16.

Winston, Brian. 2000. *Lies, Damn Lies and Documentaries*. London: British Film Institute.

CHAPTER THREE

THE RADICAL NOVELTY OF ROBIN WOOD'S
POLITICAL FILM CRITICISM

SELIM EYÜBOĞLU

Robin Wood was a scholar driven by his passion of watching, interpreting and writing about movies. Even though he never considered himself an academic, his insights go beyond criticism, opening up many conceptual gateways that have made significant contributions to film studies.

During the 1980s, Robin Wood was one of most influential film scholars, critics and cinephiles, whose work crossed and redefined those boundaries. In this respect, he is more like the André Bazin of the English-speaking world. I would describe his style with three adjectives: profound, thought-provoking and witty. His approach continuously encourages his readers to think about issues in cinematic narration in a way that would be considered outside the box. To illustrate this, let me dive into his seminal work *Hitchcock's Films Revisited* (1989;2002) that single-handedly established the multi-faceted discourse that was his signature. The following passage that I quote in its entirety compares the portrayal of the protagonists from Hitchcock's *Vertigo* (1958) and *Marnie* (1964). It not only delineates the characters' parallels and points of contrast, but also maps the motivations that propel the Hitchcockian narrative:

...had Hitchcock elected to tell *Marnie* from the point of view of Mark Rutland, we would have something strikingly resembling (if significantly different from) *Vertigo*. Look at the film from this point of view and the triangle Mark-Marnie-Lil closely resembles in essentials the triangle Scottie-Madeleine-Midge. Marnie first intrigues and fascinates Mark because of her inscrutability and mysteriousness, by her abnormality. Scottie falls in love with Madeleine because she is remote, dreamlike and inaccessible; and in one of the crucial sequences of *Marnie*, Marnie rounds on Mark with "Talk about dream worlds! You've got a pathological fix on a woman who is not only a criminal but who screams if you come near

her." Like Scottie, Mark rejects a known reality for this "dream world"…
(Wood 1989, 186)

Wood's comparative approach that re-imagines the reversed roles of
the characters is striking as it is comparable to the Freudian definition of
fantasy as an organising force both within the psychic economy of
Hitchcockian narratives and within the formation of the characters of
Marnie and *Vertigo*, who are motivated by fantasy scenarios. In this
respect, projecting a fantasy is not the result of seduction, but the staging
of a mise-en-scène that creates a desire. Wood's thoughts seem to run
parallel with many contemporary Freudian theoreticians, arguing that
Mark and Scottie are not seduced by Marnie and Madeleine/Judy,
respectively, but for the desire of the circumstances and contingencies of
seduction; or, as Laplanche and Pontalis write, *fantasy is a mise-en-scène
of desire* (1988, 214-319; see also Donald 1989 for an elaborate discussion
on this subject). Wood also notes that the reversal of fantasy and mise-en-
scène also occurs on account of Mark's headstrong manner in dealing with
Marnie's traumatic male-hating fantasies, which are then destroyed:

> If Mark is Scottie, then he is Scottie without the vertigo: a Scottie became
> more mature, responsible, and aware. Perhaps the most striking thing about
> *Marnie* is this development in the Hitchcock hero, for of all Hitchcock's
> male protagonists, Mark is the one most in charge of situations, most
> completely master of himself and his environment, most decisive, active
> and purposive. In a sense, he is the reverse of Scottie: where Scottie
> struggled to re-create the dream of Madeleine—the illusory Idea—Mark
> struggles to destroy the unreal shell of Marnie—the provocative exterior—
> in order to release the real women imprisoned within it. (Wood 1989, 186)

As the "revisited" part of his title suggests, Wood's book was re-
worked with an additional second part that includes significant changes in
his view of Hitchcock's movies. It should be noted that these changes also
correspond to some life-altering choices Robin Wood underwent,
including his coming out as a gay man/critic and all the implications of
this change to his personal life. However, a significant shift towards
radical politics reflected in the second part of the book I would argue is
already embedded in the first part as he meticulously analyses the power
relations and sexual politics amongst Hitchcockian characters. To be more
precise, Wood cross-examines the characters via imagined point-of-view
shifts in order to inquire into the fantasies the characters project or by
destroying the female character's persona by means of interference.

In a similar sense, Wood stresses the "time bomb" effect of the
relationships in Hitchcock movies. In the 1956 version of *The Man Who*

Knew Too Much, for example, Jo's prominence in the narrative overshadows her husband's. Unlike the possessive mother figures of some other Hitchcock movies, Jo sacrifices her singing career in order to maintain her marriage. Interrelating the emancipated women of the post-WWII era and the monstrous mothers of Hitchcock movies, Wood argues that it is indeed these types of women who rebel against the manners of a male-dominated world. For Wood, Jo of *The Man Who Knew too Much* differs from those of the caricatured mothers: her marriage seems to have gone sour. Along with the implications of her male name, she is also assertive, competent and independent. Having given up her career to raise her son, she is a good mother only because she is much more than a mother: during the singing of *Que sera sera* at the embassy reception, the strength of her voice reaches her kidnapped son as a coded form of communication. Ironically enough, Wood suggests the couple seems to need the excitement of the spy plot as a distraction from their stale marriage.

Apart from his interest in Hitchcock, Wood is also a Howard Hawks admirer. By way of "rescuing" the perception of Hawks' movies from the strong influence of structural authorship, he stresses his anti-auteurist reading with the title *Hawks deWollenized*, criticising Peter Wollen's pattern-based reading of Hawks' work that focuses on repetitive narrative conventions. That said, Wood's approach is also based on certain repetitive features. Those features, however, are quite broad, crossing over a few centuries in the tradition of other types of narratives. The following text quoted in its entirety by David Bordwell in his memorial blog, not only compares the artistic traditions of Shakespeare and Hawks, but also compares some other forms of storytelling that defy temporal development in the manner of rituals and myths.

> Hawks, like Shakespeare, is an artist earning his living in a popular, commercialized medium, producing work for the most diverse audiences in a wide variety of genres. Those who complain that he "compromises" by including "comic relief" and songs in *Rio Bravo* call to mind the eighteenth-century critics who saw Shakespeare's clowns as mere vulgar irrelevancies stuck in to please the "ignorant" masses...Hawks, like Shakespeare, uses his clowns and his songs for fundamentally serious purposes, integrating them in the thematic structure. His acceptance of the underlying conventions gives *Rio Bravo*, like Shakespeare's plays, the timeless, universal quality of myth or fable. (Bordwell and Thompson 2009)

Bordwell and Thompson note that Wood refuses to evaluate films in terms of a "high" versus "low" art dichotomy. Wood seems to avoid evaluative spectatorship and academic filtration prior to fully absorbing a movie. As one of his students quoting him said, "you have to watch movies six days a week and then on Sunday you have to think about them throughout the day." Generally, there is a fine line between being a fan of the movie, and strolling through the diegetic world of that film and explaining the complexities of its narration. Wood combines the two.

Some time ago, I was looking for an academic explanation of the term "subtext" for a paper. I could not find a satisfactory definition. Many of the definitions were vague, making the concept almost indistinguishable from myth or connotation. What I needed were some solid examples that I could use to base my understanding and work on a definition of my own. And then re-reading the first edition of *Hollywood from Vietnam to Reagan*, I re-discovered Wood's account along with examples of subtext that still held their initial panache after many decades. Illustrating these concepts through *The Night of the Living Dead* (1968) and *The Texas Chainsaw Massacre* (1974), he probed the reasons why many filmgoers chose to see these "insignificant" movies that were ignored by major film critics at the time. He aptly described the death of patriotism and the dissolution of the nuclear family as a result of the Vietnam War as the striking subtext that was perceived by the general public. Needless to say, his pursuit in observing implicit subtexts extends to the work of Hitchcock, *Raging Bull* and many other movies.

In line with Marxist theory, he was interested in the way in which the dominant ideology manipulates our way of thinking and perceiving. Yet, as much as he brings to the fore the multiple aspects of critical theory, he sparked a humanistic controversy within the circles of film theory, criticising *Screen and co.* for pigeonholing movies and criticism into specific disciplines instead of bringing them into broader contexts. He prefers communicative and reader-friendly writing instead of adhering to esoteric scientific language. His writing is self-critical: he confronts his previous naiveté and political shortcomings. Thus, he constantly renews himself. In the preface of the new edition of his *Hollywood from Vietnam to Reagan...and Beyond* he expresses his commitment to raising awareness to the subversive features of the movies made in the '70s, whose edge was lost during the 1980s. As he vibrantly stresses in this passage:

> Today we need political struggle, protest and feminism more than ever before, but the enemy now seems dauntingly pervasive and omnipotent. My aim…is to do everything in my extremely limited power to reactivate revolutionary ideas and ideals of the 60s and 70s and to develop them further, within the context of a word that, at its increasing peril, appears to regard them as redundant. If I have achieved no more of value than a few

allegedly illuminating interpretations of films, then my life, professionally
at least, has been wasted. (Wood 2003a, xviii)

As he revisits his books with major updates as in *Hitchcock's Films
Revisited* and *Hollywood From Vietnam to Reagan...and Beyond*, he shares
the progression and transformation of his thoughts with his reader as he
writes in a dialogical sense. In this respect, he shares his thinking process
with his reader in a manner similar to Pauline Kael's credo: *The reader is
in on my thought process.*

So much has been said about Robin Wood's radical transformation,
both personally and intellectually, which positions him as a gay, feminist,
and left-wing critic with certain ideological responsibilities. Most of his
critics praise his political stance. However, some of them value the
original part of his Hitchcock book, admiring the analysis and finding the
socio-political views of the *Revisited* part superfluous. Dismissing those
views, he replies:

This seemingly common reaction bewilders me: Everything I have written
from *Hollywood from Vietnam to Reagan* onwards seem to me characterized
and structured by my political position, so that it should be impossible to
separate the aesthetics from the politics (in which I include, of course,
sexual politics), the analysis from the radical attitude that animates and
pervades them: if you accept one, you accept the other. (Wood 2003a, xvi)

Nonetheless, Wood's political standpoint caused further controversy as
his pro-feminist question, *"Can Hitchcock be saved for feminism?"* has
been dismissed by Tania Modleski, the writer of *The Women Who Knew
Too Much* (2005), who questions the way in which women are represented
in Hitchcock movies, arguing that Hitchcock's treatment of women is
contradictory and ambivalent. However, taking this dismissal very
seriously, Wood defended his male position as a male critic upholding
feminism as well as his right to be a scholar who grapples with gendered
representations. Finding Modleski's exclusive approach reductive and
separatist, he asks with bitter sarcasm: "Should one have to be black to
fight racism? Or, similarly, should one have to be a cat to defend animal
rights?"

Wood starts the preface of his *Hollywood from Vietnam to Reagan
...and Beyond* with the statement: *I am a critic*, setting his work apart from
that of theorists and scholars. Despite this statement, however, his essays
work through many of the theories that fundamentally influence film
studies. In Wood's reading of *The Texas Chainsaw Massacre*, for example,
he observes the living room of the "bad" family decorated with

lampshades and ornaments made of human bones, arguing that killers are just as bourgeois as we are, thus unsettling the binary opposition between us and them, making their otherness problematic. Though Wood never communicates through academic language, a wide range of contemporary theories are embedded in his work, inspiring readers who may find it difficult to tackle complex academic writing. In other words, it is this quality of writing that contributes to both his academic and critical work. In this respect, it is Robin Wood's personality who will be missed, rather than his work, which will remain indisputably stimulating.

A Postscript by Murat Akser

Born in the UK in 1931 and dying in Toronto, Canada in late 2009, Robin Wood was a scholar, critic and friend. I approached Prof. Selim Eyüboğlu about writing a short piece on Robin as he was considered one of the most important films scholars in Turkey, close to Hitchcock studies and familiar in training and practice with both American and British canons of film scholarship. In return, Prof. Eyüboğlu asked me to add a postscript to his tribute to Wood.

I first met Robin Wood in 1999 when he was giving seminars in the Graduate Programme of Film at York University. His approach to film criticism was fascinating. Soon we enjoyed hours of discussions on a variety of topics ranging from horror cinema to *American Pie* and David Fincher. One day, he told us his life story. He was a Cambridge (F.R. Leavis) trained literary critic. He had already helped establish Queens University's Film Studies programme between 1969 and 1973. He later arrived at York in 1977, becoming an influential force in the department in the years to come. In time, he established with fellow students and colleagues, a radical, film criticism collective that published a journal which still exists today: *CineACTION!* His students and friends—Richard Lippe, Scott Forsyth and Janine Marchessault still publish *CineACTION!* With Robin's passing, the unavailability of some of Wood's previous books became a frequently discussed subject between his friends. We were relieved to hear the news from Barry Keith Grant that he is working on getting various books by Robin Wood reprinted by Wayne State University Press. So far, *Howard Hawks* (2006), *Personal Views* (2006) and *Ingmar Bergman* (2013) have already been published. *Arthur Penn* (1968), *The Apu Trilogy* (1971), *Antonioni* (1971) and *Claude Chabrol* (1970) are in the pipeline. Robin's take on auteur cinema, Hitchcock, horror film (1979), Hollywood teen film cycles (1998) and his views as a gay film critic (1985) has had a tremendous impact on film studies. Robin Wood's dialogic and dialectic approach to film criticism will be studied by generations to come and his mark is firmly affixed on film studies, his memory still fresh among his friends and students.

Works Cited

Bordwell, David and Kristin Thompson. 2009. "Observations on Film Art: Robin Wood". Available online at:
http://www.davidbordwell.net/blog/2009/12/19/robin-wood/
Donald, James, ed. 1989. *Fantasy and Cinema*. London: British Film Institute.
Laplanche, J. and J. B. Pontalis. 1988. *The Language of Psychoanalysis*. London: Karnac Books.
Modlesk, Tania. 2005. The Women Who Knew Too Much: Hitchcock and Feminist Theory. London: Routledge, 2005.
Wood, Robin. 1968. *Arthur Penn*. New York: Praeger.
Wood, Robin, and Michael Walker. 1970. *Claude Chabrol*. New York: Praeger.
Wood, Robin, and Ian Cameron. 1971. *Antonioni*. New York: Praeger.
Wood, Robin. 1971. *The Apu Triology*. New York: Praeger.
Wood, Robin, and Richard Lippe, eds. 1979. *The American Nightmare: Essays on the Horror Film*. Toronto: Festival of Festivals.
Wood, Robin. 1985. "Responsibilities of a Gay Film Critic." In *Movies and Methods Volume II*, edited by Bill Nichols, 649-660. Berkeley: University of California Press.
—. 1999. *Sexual Politics and Narrative Film: Hollywood and Beyond*. New York: Columbia University Press.
—. 1999. *The Wings of the Dove*. London: British Film Institute.
—. 1989/2002. *Hitchcock's Films Revisited*. New York: Columbia University Press.
—. 2003a. *Hollywood From Vietnam to Reagan...and Beyond*, New York: Columbia University Press.
—. 2003b. *Rio Bravo*. London: British Film Institute.
—. 2006a. *Howard Hawks*. Detroit: Wayne State University Press.
—. 2006b. *Personal Views: Explorations in Film*. Detroit: Wayne State University Press.
—. 2011. *Trammel up the Consequence*. Toronto: Lightstruck.
—. 2013. *Ingmar Bergman*. Detroit: Wayne State University Press.

PART II:

DEFINING NEW IN CINEMA

CHAPTER FOUR

TOWARDS A NEW HISTORIOGRAPHY
OF TURKISH CINEMA

MURAT AKSER

Introduction: Questions and Approaches

For every generation of film historians, there are new discourses and methods of film historiography regarding Turkish cinema. The methods, periodisation, and discursive practices of Turkish film historiography have evolved since the publication of Nijat Özön's *Türk Sinema Tarihi* (*History of Turkish Cinema*) that first came out in 1962. Since then the periodisation indexed to political events, attention to auteur-style directors, and the differentiation of film genres can all be traced back to Özön. In time, new writers of film history emerged who preferred to use archival material to go back to the roots of film screenings in Turkey. Burçak Evren (1984a, 1984b, 1984c, 1998), Alican Sekmeç, Ali Özuyar (2008), Özde Çeliktemel-Thomen (2013) along with Agah Özgüç (2012) belong to this school of writing. Lastly, English-language histories of Turkish cinema came out in the 2000s. Aslı Daldal (2003), Dilek Kaya (2007), Gönül Dönmez-Colin (2008), Asuman Suner (2010), Savaş Arslan (2010), Canan Balan (2010), Murat Akser (2010) and Eylem Atakav (2013) all examined the new methodological possibilities in the writing of Turkish film history. This article will discuss the strengths and weaknesses of these approaches and explore new ways of historical writing on cinema. The changing discourse of Turkish historiography can trace a route from structuralist/modernist to post-structuralist approaches (even post-colonial, with Nezih Erdoğan, 1998). The careful division of history marked by turning points/eras, emphasis on the nation-state, and the exclusion of minority cinemas (Özön, Scognamillo) are trademarks of the modernist period in Turkish film historiography. Acceptance of the existence of "new" cinemas, other modes of production and minority (Kurdish, gay, diasporic) works represents the post-structuralist mode of film historiography.

In this article, the main aim is to suggest and search for new methods for writing the history of Turkish cinema. Film studies and history both belong to the field of humanities and as such their methods are more analytical than quantitative. On the other hand, in social science research, the search for an answer begins with research design, that is to say, searching for a methodology for research, a research outline and a research question. The writing of the history of Turkish cinema requires a joint effort: A bringing together of the humanities with the methodologies of social science research. Currently, Turkish cinema studies and history writing are carried out according to the research interests of the people who are studying Turkish cinema. Especially in recent studies, there has been a tendency to present the existing literature repeatedly without going back to their roots (Özden 2009). Every writer of Turkish film history accepts Rakım Çalapala's (1946) or Nurullah Tilgen's (1957) version of events before the 1960s in Turkish film history, although both writers produced texts that can be classified as secondary sources in history writing (i.e., memoirs). In this way, new books and theses are produced based on subjective points of view that summarise these secondary texts (Hakan 2010).

Other attempts to write about Turkish film history have also, to a certain extent, relied on secondary readings and sometimes almost exclusively on memories. Zahir Güvemli wrote a now long-forgotten book on Turkish and world cinema in 1960. The next attempt to chronicle Turkish cinema was made by Giovanni Scognamillo, who first published his work on Turkish film directors in 1973. Scognamillo then went on to extend his work to cover the entire history of Turkish cinema. In 1988, his two-volume history of Turkish cinema was released by Metis Publishing. He later revised his work in 1998, condensing it into a single volume published by Kabalcı. The text is still used today as the primary reference for researchers of Turkish film history after being revised and updated twice, in 2003 and 2010. Other scholars such as Mustafa Gökmen (1989) and Oğuz Makal (1991) wrote their own versions of Turkish film history from the sources available to them.

Özön and his predecessor Scognamillo (1987a, 1987b) are modernist historians who view history as a progression toward better times. They tell a grand narrative of losses, victories, firsts, clearly-defined eras and great warriors. The division of film history into eras by Özön in 1962 can be used to illustrate this point. Özön divides his timeline into eight sections:

-The emergence of motion pictures (1896-1914)
-First feature-length films (1914-1922)

-The era of theatre actors (1922-1924)
-The Muhsin Ertuğrul era (1928-1939)
-The transition period (1939-1950)
-The filmmakers' era (1950-1960)
-Documentary filmmaking
-The film industry

Nijat Özön's periodisation is that of a progression of history into clear-cut eras with certain directors leading the way. His subheadings, such as "The Wasted Years" or "The Eighth Wonder of the World: Turkish Censorship," can be read as representing ideals of a modernist-nationalist Turkish intellectual's comments on the progression of history, which oftentimes runs against his own wishes. History is constructed through theory, and a historian is part of the era and the conditions in which he lives; it is thus only natural that he expresses his point of view in the creation of his writing.

Scognamillo's periodisation of Turkish film history is similar to Özön's except that he adds a post-1960s era to his analysis:

-Social Realism/National Cinema (1960-1970)
-Political Cinema/Yılmaz Güney (1970-1981)
-Art Cinema (1982-1994)
-New Cinema (1994-now)

Scognamillo continues the idea of a progression of film history based on heroes (construed as directors). In this conceptualisation, Metin Erksan, Halit Refiğ, Yılmaz Güney, Ömer Kavur and Nuri Bilge Ceylan represented the decades of filmmaking as a totality. There are also certain journalistic segments in the book. Film genres and the lives of actors and actresses are included throughout the study, partially in an attempt to popularise the book for the general reading public, and the work is bolstered by hundreds of photos from each period.

More recently, Agah Özgüç published a series of journal articles, which divide Turkish cinema into thematic topics. Notably, all of the data was personally collected by the author and then turned into encyclopaedic works: *Dictionary of Turkish Film Producers* (1996), *Dictionary of Turkish Film Directors* (2003), and *Dictionary of Turkish Films* (2012). Özgüç's ability to collect and classify is uncanny, and his studies are painstakingly composed of dates and the names of screenwriters, editors and producers of films. This data was first compiled in CD format in 1998 (in Microsoft's *Cinemania* style) and designed by the company, 3. Boyut, as a CD-Rom (*100 Türk Filmi / CD-ROM*), and began to be used as a primary source by university libraries in the early 2000s. In a similar vein, film director Metin Erksan's stance on Turkish film history comes from the point of view of political developments. Erksan looks at developments in Turkish film history as reactions made in response to state policy. Whenever new regimes come to power, they create their own laws governing cinema through censorship or bans. The time frame that Erksan creates is as follows:

-1895-1923 (establishment of the Turkey as a Republic in 1923)
-1923-1932 (censorship law enacted in 1932)
-1932-1939 (new censorship law in 1939)
-1939-1945 (multi-party politics begin in 1945)
-1945-1950 (first free elections in 1950)
-1950-1960 (May 27 military coup in 1960)
-1960-1971 (March 12 military intervention in 1971)
-1971-1980 (September 12 military coup in 1980)
-1980-1986 (new cinema law in 1986)
-1986-1994 (current period)

(Önder and Baydemir 2005, 115-16)

Such a classification is useful in that it brings to the fore different aspects of historical moments as well as alternative ways of looking at the development of Turkish cinema and new methodologies. As stated above, the problem with modernist Turkish film history is that Özön's method has become the norm but the validity of his methodology has not been questioned by those historians who followed his example. Today, Turkish film history could be written from a variety of perspectives, including cultural, economic, industrial and technological, and could also take into account the ways film is exhibited, formal approaches, the stars themselves, and the archaeology of film. Seçil Büker (2010) mentions a variety of approaches in her essay on film history. She refers to several film historians (Elsaesser 1986; 2004) that treat film history as a process in the making rather than something fixed in the past (Büker 2010, 22). The history of film technology can be explored as Edward Branigan (1976) does in his analysis of the advent of colour in cinema. Douglas Gomery (1976) takes up an industrial model, Robert Sklar (1993) utilises cultural history and Jack Ellis (1979), Allen and Gomery (1985), David Bordwell (2008), Barry Salt (2009), Gomery and Pafort-Overduin (2011) study the history of film style. There are also historians who have written large-scale historical accounts of the field such as Pam Cook (1999), Robert Sklar

(2001), Gianetti and Eyman (2001), David Cook (2004), David Bordwell and Kristin Thompson (2009). Bordwell and Thompson (2009) classify ways of looking into film history, which can be biographical, industrial, economic, aesthetic, technological and social/cultural/political. Studies in archaeological micro-history attempt to recover lost history as in Sobchack's (2000) description of how Peter Brosnan dug into the sand of Guadalupe to discover the lost film set of Cecil B. DeMille's *The Ten Commandments* (1923) or Robert Allen's digital humanities project called "Going to the Show" that documents film-going experience in North Carolina from the introduction of motion pictures in 1896 to the end of the silent film era in 1930. Similar attempts to recover lost history are being made by Bilkent University (turkishcine.ma) and İstanbul Şehir University (www.tsa.org.tr) in 2014.

Some Fundamental Questions

So what should a historian of Turkish cinema do? Let us first start by asking these questions:

1. *What are the criteria used to date Turkish films? Which Turkish films were produced in which years? Which is the original version of each film?* Do we see censored or uncensored version of these films? There have been attempts to preserve films by film archives such as TÜRVAK of Türker İnanoğlu, Horizon International and the Ministry of Culture that give answers to these questions related to authenticating films.
2. *Where are these films? How can we access them?* Many of these films are located in special archives such as the Mimar Sinan University's Film and TV Institute, but they are not easily accessible.
3. *Who has the director credit?* Özgüç points out that with television sales of films, the producers often tamper with credits replacing the names of directors with their own names. So, watching the TV version of a film may mislead us in what we really know about the identity/credits of the movie.
4. *Is there a verifiable film database where we can access information about films and their crews?* Currently, there are websites on Turkish cinema with detailed content such as sinematurk.com. These websites have been created in the image of the Internet Movie Database (IMDb), but their reliability is still questionable. The creation of a national film registry could easily solve the problem of verification.
5. *How can copyright problems be solved?* For film scholars and

researchers, the fair use of films in DVD and data format should be allowed by regulation and by law.

6. *How can we access other primary sources?* Other sources must be made accessible through archives, museums, research centres and libraries. Film set still photographs, company balance sheets, import-export records, posters and screenplays should be made available to researchers. One such service has recently been provided by Necip Sarıcı of Lale Film who has been collecting film-related material since 1949. He has created access to 150 feature film negatives, 250 prints, 5,000 books and 65,000 film stills (Tokuşoğlu 2012).

7. *What about existing films that have not been covered by previous film histories?* This difficulty should not hinder the attempts of researchers. There are private archivists out there, people who would trust the researcher with good intent. But in some cases good intentions may lead to the loss of precious films. In 2008 it was discovered that the original film negative of *Selvi Boylum, Al Yazmalım* (dir. Atıf Yılmaz, 1977) was lost. The broadcaster who owned the rights to the film took the original film negative from the MSU archives and never returned it. After a government-friendly newspaper made an issue of this loss, the Ministry of Culture ordered a search of the broadcaster's archives located the lost film negative (Güven 2008). The film has now been restored and there is a new print available to the general public. But how could we recover a film not previously covered in film histories? There is a number of ways in which this might be achieved, for example, in examining the records of production companies as all payments made to film crew are recorded:

a. Records of the production company: All payments made to film crew are recorded. Since records are kept of all payment (in which archives?) this can give an idea of what a film's production process may have been like

b. Records of the director: The person who works closest to the production team has access to important archival materials.

c. Memories of actors and crew members: Oral history projects can unravel these mysteries, just like a puzzle.

d. Small bits and pieces left at film labs: Even a sequence left from a film can be preserved and classified for further use.

Determination of Primary Sources

Primary sources are considered to be the main source of film history studies. In Turkish cinema history writing, the primary sources could be listed as the:

-Screening copy of a film
-Director's cut of the negative copy
-Shooting script of the film
-Memories of the director and employees (cast and crew)
-Publications, laws and regulations about cinema
-Censor office records
-Official municipal tax records
-Ticket receipt records of movie theatres
-Film critiques in newspapers and magazines
-Economic data, balance sheets, import and export records
-Distribution company records

More could be added to this list, but my focus here was on primary sources.

Historiographical Methodology

The first thing to do is create a complete list of the Turkish films produced until today. To that end, a national registry of films could be created by the Ministry of Culture. Currently, it is impossible to ascertain the production date of a Turkish film. Different encyclopaedias and histories of Turkish cinema show that films like Metin Erksan's *Sevmek Zamanı* (Time to Love) and *Kuyu* (The Well) and Halit Refiğ's *Bir Türk'e Gönül Verdim* (I Lost My Heart to a Turk) were produced in different years ranging from 1966 to 1969. So how do we ascribe the correct date in film histories? Is it the screening date, the date of completion or the date a film got a green light from the censorship board?

How American and British film institutions deal with these questions can shed light on Turkish historians' problems. The American Film Institute (AFI), the British Film Institute (BFI), and Academy of Motion Picture Arts and Sciences (AMPAS) register films released each year and prepare catalogues (*The AFI Catalog of Feature Films*). UCLA has a large archive that allows access to these documents as well as to the AMPAS library. The Library of Congress also contributes to the preservation of prints of films deemed to be national treasures. TÜRSAK and Ministry of Culture of Turkey work to store and restore films located at the Taksim Atatürk Cultural Centre (AKM) as a national film archive project in Ankara which we hope will give similar access to film historians in Turkey.

Let us now look at what could or should be done to avert some of the difficulties encountered by Turkish film historians.

1. *Pre-history should be studied.* Turkish Cinema exists in two main periods: between the years 1895-1928 and the post-1928 era. The main criterion here is the transition to the Latin alphabet. Those who want to investigate pre-1928 resources need to learn how to read the Ottoman (Arabic) script.

2. *Historical geography matters.* The history of Turkish cinema studies is divided into the two geographical categories of pre- and post-1923; referring to these timeframes means before and after the establishment of the Republic of Turkey. This is both a geographical and ideological problem. When the Republic of Turkey was founded it was limited to the borders referred to as the *Misak-ı Milli* (a document outlining borders drawn by the founding fathers) rejecting the heritage of the Ottoman Empire. However, films produced between 1895 and 1923 are arguably interpreted as belonging to the first quarter of the Turkish history of cinema. As this requires in-depth research that takes into account multicultural, multinational and multilingual cinemas, other languages must be learnt as well. For example, films by the Manaki Brothers belong to belong to Turkish as well as Macedonian film history.

3. *The first film thesis is wrong.* Narrowing the beginning of Turkish cinema to *The Destruction of St. Stephanos Monument/Ayastefanos Abidesinin Yıkılışı* (1914) limits the beginning of Turkish cinema to a nationalist, Turkish, Muslim identity and rejects previous attempts at filmmaking and exhibition by Ottoman minority groups such as the Greeks and the Armenians. The existence of the 1914 film itself is debated by scholars today (see Kaya Mutlu 2007).

4. *Archives and digitisation are needed.* Without the documentation of all the books and magazines on Turkish cinema, it is impossible to write a complete history of Turkish cinema. Recently, efforts by Nezih Erdoğan led to the creation of an online database of Turkish cinema documents (http://arsivsinemaseyir.com). Other websites that list the publications on film such as (kameraarkasi.org) list a bibliography of the past and updated current list of publications on film.
(http://www.kameraarkasi.org/sinema/kitaplar.html).

5. *Lost films can be recovered.* It is often argued that all the original copies of Turkish films made before 1950 were accidentally destroyed by fires at state-run archives or in municipal storage facilities. There are even reports that due to the shortage of materials during World War II,

most film prints were melted down and turned into shoe heels in the 1940s. It is said that later, in the 1970s, film producers also ordered film labs to destroy film prints in order to extract silver (see Hızlan 2012). Even though some films are lost, there are individuals who have kept old films in storage, and these may one day be discovered by researchers. Collectors could be approached by guaranteeing the preservation of films. State-private enterprise collaborations could be asked to restore and re-release classics of Turkish cinema and open their archives for film historians. There are two sources for the movies shown on television today, namely, film producers who store their own negatives and the MSU Cinema TV Central Archive established by Sami Şekeroğlu in 1975. With the assistance of the World Cinema Fund led by Martin Scorsese and Fatih Akın, several Turkish film classics have been restored (such as Metin Erksan's *Dry Summer*). The process is long and expensive, but has encouraged private corporations— Yapı Kredi Bank restored Muhsin Ertuğrul's *Halıcı Kız*—and the Ministry of Culture to do more about film restoration.

6. *Avoid rejection of heritage.* Previous histories of Turkish cinema have to be carefully studied to avoid further factual errors.

7. *Institutionalisation.* Long-term academic research design must be developed through collaboration with universities and other institutions based on a long-term digital humanities programme.

8. *Films should be made accessible.* All Turkish films should be collected in a research centre, negatives should be restored and presented to the public on a need-by-need basis, and DVDs of restored films should be produced. BFI Southbank could serve as an example for the creation of such an institution.

9. *Film and crew databases must be created.* There should be a website about Turkish cinema with inclusive content written in multiple languages. The Internet Movie Database (IMDb) could serve as an example.

10. *Copyright problems must be resolved.* The fair-use clause must be legally defined for researchers who need to study scenes from films.

11. *Other sources must be made accessible.* Film set photographs, company balance sheets, import-export records, posters and screenplays should be preserved and easily accessible to researchers.

After making sure that authentic copies of films are ready to use, we can then think about which method of history writing listed below to adopt should be used, which are all useful in different ways.

What Kind of History?

The current categories of the history of Turkish cinema can be divided into the different approaches below:

a) *Popular journalistic history*: The study of Turkish film stars and their impact on audiences. Mesut Kara and Agah Özgüç have been the most productive in this regard.

b) *A history of film criticism*: Atilla Dorsay leads the way in collecting film criticism thematically on Turkish cinema.

c) *History of firsts*: Individual memories and observations. Cemil Filmer (1984) and other veterans of Turkish cinema have published personal memoirs (Akad, Refiğ, Ün). The most recent is by Fikret Hakan (2010).

d) *History of film periods*: This type of history is written by isolating a turning point in political-social-legal change. Esin Berktaş (2010) has written one such study of the 1940s. SİYAD, the Turkish film critics association, started writing a book series on film decades released every year at the Antalya Golden Orange Film Festival. There are currently volumes only on the 1960s and the 1970s.

e) *History of reception*: Currently, there are books on old film theatres (Gökmen 1989, 1991; Beyru 1996; Makal 1999; Akçura 2004) and a detailed study of the cultural history of exhibition by Serpil Kırel (2005).

f) *Thematic histories*: Film history written on themes such as women or genres. Agah Özgüç has written about genres (2005), and Giovanni Scognamillo and Metin Demirhan have written about erotic films (2002) and fantasy films (2005).

g) *Economic history*: Very recent studies by economists are bridging the gap between qualitative and quantitative research (Tunç 2012). New websites such as boxofficeturkiye.com promise to retroactively enter all box office data soon.

The above kinds of history writing can be classified into two approaches. The first of these is subjective, an arbitrary approach resulting from filmmakers' or film critics' interest in cinema and their opportunity to write and get their pieces published. The second is a doctrinal approach about Turkish history writing. Echoing the Republic of Turkey's official version of history, historical societies (TTK-Türk Tarih Kurumu/Turkish Historical Association) and school textbooks are didactical, praising political successes while omitting social history. An elitist history of firsts is created (first director, first colour film, first censored film, and so on). In this version of history, cinema is created by an intellectual elite whose members' artistic achievements are not understood by the public, and who are punished by the state for their political and artistic stance. It is impossible to make such grand definitive statements in history writing. Each generation of historians develops theories according to their need to comment on history. A combination of qualitative and quantitative history could be seen as a cure for the prevalence of didactic history writing. While gathering correct and authentic film credits, and economic data, oral histories and social history could also be written. Social historical methods that could be used in the history writing of Turkish cinema are as follows:

1. *Oral history*: As mentioned above, interviews should be sought with people who worked in Turkish cinema and in comparing them a synthesis could be made. İbrahim Türk's interviews with Halit Refiğ (2001) and Bülent Oran (2004) offer a promising future for this approach. Mithat Alam Film Centre's Oral History Project has produced thirteen DVDs of interviews from the classic period of Turkish cinema, and this project continues today. The MSU Film and TV Centre has an abundance of video interviews recorded by Turkish film directors since 1975. These recordings are closed to the public and should be transcribed for future researchers.
2. *Industrial history*: Subcategories of history writing should be focused on observations of the relationship between producers and consumers. Audience research using past data could also be carried out.
3. *Periodisation from other angles*: This should be done not only according to great political events, but also technological, economic, social and artistic criteria. Researchers such as Douglas Gomery, David Bordwell, Kristin Thompson, Richard Allen, Robert Sklar and Janet Steiger who worked on the golden era of American cinema each studied a specific period of the age in a detailed way. 1952-1977, Turkish cinema's golden age, could be studied in this way as well. But it should not be forgotten in the history writing of Turkish cinema that the use of the Turkish language will be determinative. Related concepts are directly linked to the language of the researcher as well as to history and cinema history studies. A film history based on concepts borrowed from French and American-based methods could be misleading.
4. *Local history writing*: Local, regional cinema cultures must be studied. It is possible to coordinate local citizens and high-school students to

study the history of cinema in their neighbourhoods.

5. *Institutional history*: A history of Turkish film unions, associations, film festivals and film movements could be written.

6. *History of technology*: A history could be written based on areas of expertise pertaining to Turkish cinema in regard to the history of technology, as well as the history of how cinematographers, editors, sound and light technicians, and projectionists started unique practices and using various technologies in Turkish cinema. For example, when was the jump cut introduced in Turkish cinema? What was the impact of Gani Turanlı (Director of Photography) and Mevlüt Koçak (editor) on Turkish cinema? How did Western cinema technologies penetrate Turkey? Have there been any contributions to film technology by Turkish filmmakers? Did Turkish technicians make different hybrid cameras, cinemascope lenses and dollies?

7. *Economic history*: Records of import and export numbers are important in recovering the total economic output of Turkish cinema. Screening statistics of foreign films in Turkey might be accessed by researching the archives of export companies in Europe, Hollywood and other countries' cinemas (Gürata 2004).

8. *Turkish cinema overseas*: How about films produced by Turks abroad? Or Turkish films exported to other countries? A history of expatriate Turkish directors (Vedat Örfi Bengü in Egypt), actors (Muzaffer Tema, Kuzey Vargın, Salih Güney, Derya Arbaş, Tuba Ünsal in Hollywood) and their films could also be written.

9. *Biographies*: Definitive detailed historical biographies of actors and directors are also waiting to be written.

10. *Aesthetic/Stylistic history*: How did certain styles develop in Turkish cinema? Why are there so many wide shots in 1950s films? Why do zoom-ins suddenly appear in the 1970s? Why are colours so different in the 1960s? All of these questions are valid and should be examined in research taking an aesthetic approach.

Works Cited

Akçura, Gökhan. 2004. *Aile Boyu Sinema* (A Family Cinema). Istanbul: İthaki Yayınları.

Akser, Murat. 2003. "Türk Sinema Tarihi Yazılımı: Bir Yöntem Önerisi" (Writing Turkish Film History: A New Method). In *Türk Film Araştırmalarında Yeni Yönelimler 3: Karşılaşmalar* (New Directions in Turkish Film Studies 3: Encounters) edited by Deniz Bayrakdar, 41-48. Istanbul: Bağlam.

—. 2010. *Green Pine Resurrected: Film Genre, Parody and Intertextuality in Turkish Cinema*. Saarbrucken: Lambert Academic Publishing.

—. 2011. "Reinvigorating Film Studies: an Immodest Proposal". *CINEJ Cinema Journal* 1 (1):1-3.

Allen, Robert C. 1980. "Historiography and the Teaching of Film History". *Film and History* 10 (3): 25-131.

Allen, Robert C. and Douglas Gomery. 1985. *Film History: Theory and Practice*. New York: McGraw-Hill.

Altman, Charles F. 1977. "Towards a Historiography of American Film". *Cinema Journal* 16 (2): 1-25.

Arslan, Savaş. 2010. *Cinema in Turkey: A New Critical History*. New York: Oxford University Press.

Atakav, Eylem, ed. 2013. *Directory of World Cinema: Turkey*. London: Intellect.

Balan, Canan. 2010. "Changing Pleasures of Spectatorship: Early and Silent Cinema in Istanbul". PhD Thesis, Film Studies, University of St. Andrews.

Bali, N. Rifat. 2007. *The Turkish Cinema in the Early Republican Years*. Istanbul: ISIS Press.

Basutçu, Mehmet, ed. 1996. *Le Cinema Turc*. Paris: Centre Georges Pompidou.

Beck, Philip. 1985. "Historicism and Historism in Recent Film Historiography". *Journal of Film and Video* 37 (1): 5-20.

Berktaş, Esin. 2010. *1940'lı Yılların Türk Sineması* (Turkish Cinema of the 1940s). Istanbul: Agora Kitaplığı.

Beyru, Rauf. 1996. "İzmir'de İlk Sinema Gösterileri" (First Film Screenings in İzmir). *Antrakt* 53: 43.

Bordwell, David. 2008. "Doing Film History". Available online at: http://davidbordwell.net/essays/doing.php

Bordwell, David and Kristin Thompson. 2009. *Film History: An introduction*. New York: McGraw-Hill.

Branigan, Edward. 1976. "The Articulation of Color in a Filmic System" *Wide Angle* 1 (3): 20-31.

Büker, Seçil. 2010. "Nasıl Bir Tarih?" (What Kind of a History?) in Büker, Seçil and Y. Gürhan Topçu, eds. 2010. *Sinema: Tarih-Kuram-Eleştiri* (Cinema: History-Theory-Criticism). Istanbul: Kırmızı Kedi Yayınevi.

Cook, David A. 2004. *A History of Narrative Film*. New York: W.W. Norton.

Çalapala, Rakım. 1946. *Filmlerimiz* (Our Films). Istanbul: Yerli Film Yapanlar Cemiyeti.

Çapan, Sungu. 1991. "Ne Filmi Gören Var Ne De Belge"(No record of this film that Noone has seen). *Antrakt* 2: 23-25.

Çeliktemel-Thomen, Özde. 2010. "Osmanlı İmparatorluğu'nda Sinema ve Propaganda (1908-1922)" (Cinema and Propaganda in Ottoman Empire). *Kurgu Online International Journal of Communication Studies* 2 (June).

—. 2013a. "Prime Ministry Ottoman Archives: Inventory of Written Archival Sources for Ottoman Cinema History". *Tarih* (3): 17-48.

—. 2013b. "1903 Sinematograf İmtiyazı" (1903 Cinematograph Privilege). *Toplumsal Tarih* 229: 26-32.

Daldal, Aslı. 2003. *Art, Politics and Society: Social Realism in Italian and Turkish Cinemas.* Istanbul: The Isis Press.

Dorsay, Atilla. 1984. "Bu Ay Sinemamızın 70. Yılını Kutluyoruz: İyi ki Doğdun Sinema" (We are Celebrating the 70th Anniversary of Our Cinema: Happy Birthday Cinema). *Video Sinema* (5): 30-31.

Dönmez-Colin, Gönül. 2008. *Turkish Cinema: Identity, Distance, Belonging.* London: Reaktion Books.

Elsaesser, Thomas. 1986. "The New Film History". *Sight & Sound* 55 (4): 246-51.

—. 2004. "The New Film History as Media Archaeology". *Cinémas: Journal of Film Studies* 14 (2-3): 75-117.

Erdoğan, Nezih. 1998. "Narratives of Resistance: National Identity and Ambivalence in the Turkish Melodrama between 1965 and 1975". *Screen* 39 (3): 259-71.

Evren, Burçak. 1984a. "Türk Sineması 70 Yaşında" (Turkish Cinema is 70 Years Old). *Video Sinema* 5: 27-30.

—. 1984b. "İlk Türk Filmi Üstündeki Kuşkular" (Doubt on the First Turkish Film), *Gelişim Sinema* 2: 6-8.

—. 1984c. İlk Türk Filmine İlişkin Görüşler ve Belgeler (Opinions and Documents on the First Turkish Film). *Gelişim Sinema* 3: 18-20.

—. 1995. *Türkiye'ye Sinemayı Getiren Adam Sigmund Weinberg* (Sigmund Weinberg: The Man who Brought Cinema to Turkey). Istanbul: AD Yayıncılık.

—. 1998. *Eski İstanbul Sinemaları: Düş Şatoları* (Old Cinemas of Istanbul: Dream Palaces). Istanbul: Milliyet Yayınları.

—. 2006. *İlk Türk Filmleri* (First Turkish Films). Istanbul: Es Yayınları.

Evrenol, Hilmi Malik. 1933. *Türkiye'de Sinema ve Tesirleri* (Cinema and Its Effects in Turkey). Ankara: Kitap Yazanlar Kooperatifi Neşriyatı.

Filmer, Cemil. 1984. *Hatıralar* (Memories). Istanbul: Emek Matbaacılık.

Giannetti, Louis D., and Scott Eyman. 2001. *Flashback*. New Jersey: Prentice-Hall.

Gomery, Douglas, and Clara Pafort-Overduin. 2011. *Movie history: A survey*. New York: Taylor and Francis.

Gomery, Douglas. 1976. "The Coming of the Talkies: Invention, Innovation, and Diffusion". In *The American Film Industry*, edited by Tino Balio, 192-211. Madison: University of Wisconsin Press.

Gökmen, Mustafa. *Türk Sinema Tarihi* (History of Turkish Cinema), İstanbul: Denetim Ajans, 1989.

—. 1991. *Eski İstanbul Sinemaları* (Old Istanbul Theatres). Istanbul: Turing Yayınları.

Gündeş, Simten. 1998. *Sinema Kaynakçası* (Bibliography of Cinema). Istanbul: Der Yayınları.

Gürata, Ahmet and Louise Spence. 2010. "Introduction" *Cinema Journal* 50 (1): 131-35.

Gürata, Ahmet. 2004. "Tears of Love: Egyptian Cinema in Turkey (1938-1950)". *New Perspectives on Turkey* 30: 55-82.

Güvemli, Zahir. 1960. *Sinema Tarihi: Başlangıcından Bugüne Türk ve Dünya Sineması*. (History of Cinema: Turkish and World Cinema from Its Beginnings to Today) Istanbul: Varlık Yayınları.

Güven, Ali Murat. 2009. "Türk sinemasının başyapıtı kayboldu" (Masterpiece of Turkish cinema is lost). *Yeni Şafak*, 23 November.

Hakan, Fikret. 2010. *Türk Sinema Tarihi*. (History of Turkish Cinema) Istanbul: İnkılap.

Hızlan, Doğan. 2012. "Artık Türk filmlerinin de bir sözlüğü var" (Now Turkish Films Also Have a Dictonary). *Hürriyet*, 15 September. http://www.hurriyet.com.tr/yazarlar/21468770.asp

Kaya Mutlu, Dilek. 2007. "The Russian Monument at Ayastefanos (San Stefano): Between Defeat and Revenge, Remembering and Forgetting". *Middle Eastern Studies* 43 (1): 75-86.

Rongen Kaynakçı, Elif. 2006. "Türk Sinema Tarihi ve Kayıp Filmler". (History of Turkish Cinema and Lost Films) In *Türk Film Araştırmalarında Yeni Yönelimler, Sinema ve Tarih 5*, (New Directions in Turkish Film Studies 5: Sinema and History) edited by Deniz Bayrakdar, 73-79. Istanbul: Bağlam.

Rongen Kaynakçı, Elif. 2009. "Sessiz Sinema ve Film Arşivleri" (Silent Film and Film Archives). *Kebikeç* 28: 69-76.

Kırel, Serpil. 2005. *Yeşilçam Öykü Sineması* (Green Pine Narrative Cinema). Istanbul: Babil Yayınları.

Kutlar, Onat. 1974. "Türk Sinemasının 60 Yılı ve İlk Türk Filmini Çeviren Fuat Uzkınay"(60th Anniversary of Turkish Cinema and The Man who shot First Turkish Film). *Milliyet Sanat* 106: 5-6.

Künüçen, H. Hale. 1996. "Sinemanın 100.Yılında Sinemamızın Bir Dönemdeki 'Tek Adam'ı Muhsin Ertuğrul Sineması Üzerine" (On the Maestro of Our Cinema for a Period). *İletişim*, Gazi Üniversitesi İletişim Fakültesi Dergisi 3.

—. 1999. "Manastır'da Başlayan Türk Sineması Serüveni ve Atatürk'ün Sinema Anlayışı" (The Film Adventure that started at Manastır ana Ataturk's Idea of Film). In *Uluslar arası Atatürk ve Manastır Sempozyumu Bildiri Kitabı*. Ankara: Özten Yayınları.

—. 1999. "Osmanlı'da Başlayan Sinema Serüvenimiz" (Our Cinema Adventure that Stared with the Ottomans), *Osmanlı*, vol. XI, Yeni Türkiye Yayınları, Ankara, 1999.

Künüçen, H. Hale and A. Şükrü Künüçen, 2002. "Sinemanın Türkiye'ye Girişi ve İlk Yılları" (Coming of Cinema to Turkey and Its Early Years), *Türkler*, vol. XV, Ankara: Yeni Türkiye Yayınları.

Liman, Ali Sait. 2011. "Türk Sinemasının İlk Yıllarında Çekim Sonrası Üretim ve Teknik Altyapı" (Post-production and Technical Infrasturucture of Turkish Cinema in its early years) *İstanbul Üniversitesi İletişim Fakültesi Hakemli Dergisi* 40: 37-52.

Makal, Oğuz. *Türk Sineması Tarihi* (History of Turkish Cinema). İzmir: Dokuz Eylül Üniversitesi Yayınları, 1991.

—. 1999. *Tarih İçinde İzmir Sinemaları* (İzmir Theaters in History). Izmir: GÜSEV.

Margulies, Roni. 1994. Ayastefanos'taki Rus Abidesinin Yıkılışı (The Demolishing of Russian Monument in St.Stephanos), *Toplumsal Tarih* 1: 25-26.

Okumuş, Fatma. 2011. "Sinema Tarih Yazımına Farklı Bakmak" (Looking at Writing Turkish Film History Differently). *Journal of Yaşar University* 24 6: 4024-4040.

Onaran, Alim Şerif. 1999. *Türk Sineması* (Turkish Cinema). Ankara: Kitle Yayınları.

Önder, Selahattin and Ahmet Baydemir 2005. "Türk Sinemasının Gelişimi (1895-1939)" (Development of Turkish Cinema). *Eskişehir Osmangazi Üniversitesi Sosyal Bilimler Dergisi* 6 (2): 113-35.

Özen, Emrah. 2009. "Geçmişe Bakma: Sinema Tarihi Çalışmaları Üzerine Eleştirel Bir İnceleme"(Looking Past: A Critical Look at Studies in Turkish Film History). *Kebikeç* 27: 131-55.

Özgüç, Agah. 1988. *A Chronological History of the Turkish Cinema*. Ankara: Ministry of Culture.

—. 1994. *80. Yılında Türk Sineması* (Turkish Cinema at 80). Ankara: T.C. Kültür Bakanlığı.

—. 1996. *Türk Film Yapımcıları Sözlüğü* (Dictionary of Turkish Film Producers). Istanbul: Film Yapımcıları Derneği.

—. 2003. *Türk Film Yönetmenleri Sözlüğü* (Dictionary of Turkish Film Directors). Istanbul: Agora Kitaplığı.

—. 2005.*Türlerle Türk Sineması* (Genres of Turkish Cinema). Istanbul: Dünya Yayıncılık.

—. 2012. *Türk Filmleri Sözlüğü* (Dictionary of Turkish Films). Istanbul: Horizon International.

—.2013. *Türk Sinemasının Marjinalleri ve Orjinalleri* (The Marginals and the Originals of Turkish Cinema). Istanbul: Horizon International.

Özön, Nijat. 1962. *Türk Sinema Tarihi* (History of Turkish Cinema), Istanbul: Artist Yayınları.

—. 1968. *Türk Sineması Kronolojisi (1895-1966)* (Chronology of Turkish Cinema). Ankara: Bilgi Yayınevi.

—. 1970. *Fuat Uzkınay*. Istanbul: Sinematek Yayını.

—. 1974. "50 Yılın Türk Sineması" (Turkish Cinema of 50 Years). *Yedinci Sanat* 11: 3-8.

—. 1981. "Sinemamızda Klasikler" (Classics in Our Cinema). *Gösteri* 6: 70.

Öztürk, Serdar. 2006. "Türk Sinemasında İlk Sansür Tartışmaları ve Yeni Belgeler" (Debates on First Censorship in Turkish Cinema and New Documents). *Galatasaray İletişim* 5:47-76.

Özuyar, Ali. 2004. *Babıâli'de Sinema* (Cinema at Sublime Porte). Istanbul: İzdüşüm Yayınları.

—. 2007. *Devlet-i Aliyye'de Sinema* (Cinema at State Level). Ankara: De Ki Basımevi.

—. 2008. *Sinemanın Osmanlıca Serüveni* (The Ottoman Adventure of Cinema). Ankara: De Ki.

—. 2011. *Faşizmin Etkisinde Türkiye'de Sinema (1939-1945)* (Turkish Cinema under the Influence of Facism). Istanbul: Doruk.

—. 2013. *Türk Sinema Tarihinden Fragmanlar 1896–1945* (Fragments from Turkish Cinema History). Istanbul: Phoenix.

Refiğ, Halit. 2007. *Sinemada Ulusal Tavır* (National Attitude in Cinema). Istanbul: İş Bankası Yayınları.

Refiğ, Halit. 2009. *Doğruyu Aradım, Güzeli Sevdim* (I Searched for the Truth, I Looked for the Beauty). Istanbul: Bizim Kitaplar Yayınevi.

Ross, Steven J. 2004. "Jargon and the Crises of Readability: Methodology, Language, and the Future of Film History". *Cinema Journal* 44 (1): 130-33.

Russell, Catherine. 2004. "New Media and Film History: Walter Benjamin and the Awakening of Cinema". *Cinema Journal* 43 (3): 81-85.

Salt, Barry. 2009. *Film Style and Technology*. London: Starword.

Scognamillo, Giovanni and Metin Demirhan. 2002. *Erotik Türk Sineması* (Erotic Turkish Cinema). Istanbul: Kabalcı.
—. 2005. *Fantastik Türk Sineması* (Fantastic Turkish Cinema). Istanbul: Kabalcı.
Scognamillo, Giovanni. 1987a. *Türk Sinema Tarihi 1: 1896-1957* (History of Turkish Cinema V.1). Istanbul: Metis.
—. 1987b. *Türk Sinema Tarihi 2: 1960-1986* (History of Turkish Cinema V.2). Istanbul: Metis.
—. 1991. *Cadde-i Kebir'de Sinema* (Cinema at Pera). Istanbul: Metis Yayınları, 1991.
Scognamillo, Giovanni. 2003. *Türk Sinema Tarihi* (History of Turkish Cinema). Istanbul: Kabalcı.
Sklar, Robert. 1994. *Movie-made America: A Cultural History of American Movies*. New York: Vintage.
—. 2001. *Film: An International History of the Medium*. New Jersey: Prentice Hall.
—. 2004. "Does Film History Need a Crisis?" *Cinema Journal* 44 (1): 134-38.
Sobchack, Vivian. 2000. "What is Film History?, or, the Riddle of the Sphinxes". In *Reinventing Film Studies*., edited by Linda Williams and Christine Gledhill, 300-315. London: Hodder Arnold.
Suner, Asuman. 2010. *New Turkish Cinema: Belonging, Identity and Memory.* London: I. B. Tauris.
Şekeroğlu, Sami. 1985. *Türk Sinema Tarihi* (Documentary Film). Istanbul: MSGSÜ Sinema-TV Merkezi.
Şener, Erman. 1972. "Yarım Asır Önceki Sinemamız ve Artistleri"(Our Cinema Half a Century Ago and Its Actors). *Hayat Tarih Mecmuası* 2 (10): 84-89.
—. 1979. "İlk Filmlerimiz". *Kurgu* 1: 80-97.
Teksoy, Rekin. 2008. *Turkish Cinema*. Istanbul: Oğlak Yayınları.
Tilgen, Nurullah. "Türk Sineması Tarihi, Dünden Bugüne 1914-1953" (History of Turkish Cinema, From Yesterday to Today) *Yıldız* 30 (18 July 1962).
Tilgen, Nurullah. 2009. "Bugüne Kadar Filmciliğimiz" (Our Filmmaking Until Now). *Kebikeç* 28: 113-33.
Tokuşoğlu, Nazenin. 2012. "Eski Türk filmlerine yeni cennet" (A New Heaven for Turkish Films). *Milliyet*, 26 May.
Tuğrul, Semih. 1967. "Türk Sinemasının 50 Yılı: Karakolda Ayna Var" (50th Anniversary of Turkish Cinema). *Yeni Sinema* 4: 4-5.
Tunç, Ertan. 2012. *Türk Sinemasının Ekonomik Yapısı (1896-2005)* (Economic Structure of Turkish Cinema). Istanbul: Doruk Yayınları.

Türk, İbrahim. 2001. *Halit Refiğ: Düşlerden Düşüncelere Söyleşiler* (Halit Refig: Interviews from Dreams to Ideas). İstanbul: Kabalcı Yayınevi.

—. 2010. *Senaryo: Bülent Oran* (Screenplay by: Bulent Oran). İstanbul: Dergah Yayınları.

Ülkütaşır, Türkan. 1969. "Türkiye'de İlk Sinema ve Kısa Tarihçesi" (First Cinema in Turkey and its brief History). *Belgelerle Türk Tarihi Dergisi* 20: 76-78.

Ün, Memduh. *Memduh Ün Filmlerini Anlatıyor* (Memduh Un on Film), İstanbul: Kabalcı Yayınları, 2009.

—. 2012. *Futbolcudan Yönetmen* (Soccer Player to Film Director). İstanbul: Horizon Yayınları.

Vitali, Valentina. 2010. "Film Historiography as Theory of the Film Subject: A Case Study". *Cinema Journal* 50 (1): 141-46.

Yıldırım, Müjgan. 1991. "Türk Sinemasının Perde Arkası" (Background of Turkish Cinema) *Tempo* 16.

CHAPTER FIVE

THE EXISTENTIAL BOUNDARIES OF NURI BILGE CEYLAN: "IN THE BEGINNING WAS THE FATHER, WHY PAPA?"

ZAHIT ATAM

Nuri Bilge Ceylan is a filmmaker from a generation trying to overcome the impositions of the film business on those who wanted to create conditions to produce films by themselves. These filmmakers have made many sacrifices in order to create films without any artistic compromise, seeking to maintain immediacy between their own identity and cinematographic language (Kızıldemir 1997). This generation of independent film directors has been fundamentally and radically against the "Oriental" melodrama of traditional Turkish Cinema (known as Yeşilçam (Green Pine)[1]), which was mostly producing remakes of Hollywood movies by domesticating them. None of this generation of filmmakers (1994-1997) has entered the mainstream cinema sector. They have all chosen to self-educate themselves in cinematic expression; while they have struggled to constitute their own style, they have succeeded. Attending university in the aftermath of the military coup d'état of 1980, they were part of a

---

1. For Nuri Bilge Ceylan's opinion on Yeşilçam and on the cultural atmosphere in Turkey, see Mehmet Erdem's article "Piyasa Acımasız ve Demirden Yasalarla İşliyor!" 1997, "Our cinema was trying to produce films by using Hollywood strategies. A society with no more words to express itself or with no eyes to see itself adopts the perspective of the other, speaks with the words of the other. Films, commercials and newspapers we see place the audience into a system of social addiction by creating a series of desires that do not fit into each other. Everyone, especially those around my age, now has a feeling and concern that they have lost things that mattered to them. The human's need for a transcendent and reassuring source becomes really clear in such an atmosphere."

generation that was practically excluded from politics, and mostly in opposition to the ideals of the new political regime.

Ceylan's family is from the Western Anatolian town of Yenice where agriculture is the main source of livelihood. His relationship with his father, which left a deep mark on his life and films, has greatly influenced his humanitarian positioning toward life and the relationship Ceylan has constructed between his art and society. In this sense, the personal history of Nuri Bilge coincides with the consequences of post-1980 Turkish social history as his life experience was full of disillusionment in terms of ideals and beliefs. Hence, Ceylan developed a radically disparate position from the artist type who is devoted to society and ascribes great political meanings to art; the prime example in Turkish Cinema being Yılmaz Güney. The question that naturally arises from this set of circumstances would be: How does the personal trauma of Nuri Bilge fit into the trauma of his generation?

Ceylan's father was the first university-educated person in Yenice, Çanakkale. Although there was no primary school in his village, he went to town and attended boarding school there, going on to graduate from Ankara University. After WWII, university scholarship exams offered as a result of the rapprochement between Turkey and the US won him a place to study agricultural engineering in the United States. Upon his return from North America, he was appointed a job in Istanbul; as a result of his studies however, he had a desire to conquer the land where he was born and raised, deciding to relocate to his hometown. This is the reason why Nuri Bilge Ceylan's childhood years were spent in Yenice.

Implementing agricultural reform in Yenice, Ceylan's father completely restructured the area with new irrigation canals. Having developed a new modernist worldview that was in conflict with the traditional institutions and values of the town due to his introduction to science, his experience within the city and his time in America, after a while, and despite his legendary status in and around his hometown due to his professional knowledge, he had conflicts with the status quo and the traditional leaders of Yenice. These tensions gradually prepared for the defeat of his idealistic programme; he revolutionised agriculture, but failed in changing the scope of social relationships. Eventually, tradition overcame him, and he was slowly excluded from the town's social life. The radical idealism of Ceylan's father thus gradually gave way to his withdrawal from social life as he was criticised for losing touch with his roots. In his personal life, this withdrawal meant gradual seclusion into a world shaped by books. Here, living with his deep disappointment, he restricted his interactions only to his extended family. Thereafter, he was known as "Mehmet Emin the atheist" by the peasants and the townspeople.

> It was a typical town with its narrow-minded society and strict ethical standards. In this society, my father's world view was very different from those of the people around him. We lived in that town for eight years. And throughout time, we witnessed my father's idealism slowly turning into disappointment. (Kızıldemir 1997)

An idealistic father, an educated and adventurous person who guides the people around him with ease, this is where the first paradox begins: A father who is trying to dedicate himself to his community, a person who is open to innovation because of his education and experience opposed to a socioeconomically underdeveloped milieu, a backward society that resists change. The source of disappointment is the conflict between modern norms with traditional ones; of moral idealism with moral relativism; of a man of action with the carefree attitudes of those around him. The tensions that his father experienced left a fundamental impression on Nuri Bilge, who has approached any sort of ideals with suspicion throughout his life. He felt an emptiness created by his own failure to find his own great object. He moved within this emptiness for many years, because he deeply agreed with his father's idealism yet he saw how the same idealism overwhelmed his father, distressing and even smothering him. His father understood very well that he could not find any solution other than gradually retreating into seclusion. Nuri Bilge has feared both seclusion and suffering, yet this fear has strongly fed his reaction to regression.

The main character in his film *Small Town* (Ceylan, 1997), who finishes university and then obtains a master's degree in America before coming back to his town to work as an agricultural engineer, surprised many people. It is plain to see however that this is a character entirely based on his father:

> [My father]…is a man who moved into town with idealistic goals, but as his hopes perished. He slowly withdrew into the solitude of his own cocoon or shell. In the beginning, I was afraid of ending up like my father, but I guess there is no escape from destiny, and I feel I am slowly drifting into the same fate. In a way, filmmaking gives me the hope of getting rid of the fate that I fear I am obliged to suffer one final act before going into solitude. (Erkal 1999)

The consequence of this for a typical prospective intellectual from an underdeveloped country was admiration of the West. Ceylan thus found his desire, his great object, with the exaltation/elevation of art that is taken as a substitute for life itself. His success in art turned into real therapy for his neurotic personal character. Nuri Bilge Ceylan is a relaxed, and in his own words, a laidback/lazy person, in regard to obligatory social practices, education and other institutional relationships. However, he turns into a very meticulous and extremely hardworking person, in every aspect from screenwriting to camera work, from editing to audio and colour, once he starts filming. The people working with him on his sets are said to be astonished when they see him still working efficiently after long hours, while they feel completely exhausted.

In general, traditional Anatolian values have more of an impact and are more deeply felt as we go back in time and towards the more rural parts of the country. An element enhancing this intensification is that everything takes place under the watchful eye of the public. Everyone knows each other because of the limited population and lack of social mobility. A lot of things that would have been private in big cities are communally known in a small town, and this leads to stricter social control. Tradition and custom become the important criteria for judgement. Life has little dynamism; therefore, any sort of change is conceived as some sort of corruption. Lack of interaction with the outside world adds to the sharpness of value judgements. The educated intellectual, especially, is in constant conflict with the traditional leaders of public opinion. This typical behaviour of the small-town folk towards the intellectual portrayed in Ceylan's films shows similarities with novelistic depiction of town folk versus intellectuals in Turkish literature for a hundred years since the Ottoman period (Diken 2008).

Nuri Bilge grew up in a rural area, moved to the metropolis and studied at Boğaziçi University, a former American university that is deemed to be prestigious in Turkey. As a result of this background, he has had a constant struggle with "the ideology of newness" with which he has been fascinated, and consequently; the remnants of tradition disintegrated and disappeared.

In the Ceylan household, the father figure is seen to be a well-educated, rule-bound, idealist man of action, whose worldview is close to positivism. However, the townspeople are enveloped in a certain way of life, and they look at new things with suspicion. Even though Ceylan's father is a model for them in agricultural issues, he is seen as a subverter of moral values through his interest in worldly things. The father defends the interests of the community while the notables of the town defended their own privileges. The worldview of the father and the values he represents are therefore always used against him in the conflict between the two. For the town notables, life is lived with pragmatism and cunning.

The third element that completes this dynamic is the decisiveness of the power relations. As conditions become more difficult, these three tendencies within the townspeople become much sharper so that the more the settled rural structure resists change, the clearer the father will see the limits of his own power. Hence, his own ideals will turn into disappointment, to the extent that he faces defeat. There are two remedies he can find for the disappointment: he will either leave the town, or go into solitude, gradually becoming more lonely. As he lives in disharmony with the outside world in terms of values and morals, he will strive, to the extent of his own self-confidence, to create a world in which he sets his own limits. Seclusion turns into some sort of denial of life, and he lives in a world made up of books and ideals while his own social identity decreases in value. In the film *Small Town*, the best friends of the "father" character are his books; the valuable treasure of seclusion. They accuse him of failure: "you are not one of us, or why would you be here if you are that great after all?"[2] Seen from the perspective of the youth of the town, both success and being different are things found in the metropolis. They cannot see a way out of the small town, and the repetitiveness of its routine seems overwhelming to them. The metropolis thus turns into a source for their dreams, all the more so as it is beyond their knowledge as, being unknown, they can project their desires upon it. It is some sort of showdown where they will test themselves, and in a sense, a place to show their courage.[3]

Ceylan's father's disappointment that results in his seclusion is reflected in the depth of his son's mind as a fear of seclusion before he even starts life. However, the issue is not limited to this. The reasons for this seclusion are to be found in the father's ideals. The son's fear turns into an avoidance of any ideal; the foundations of a person who doubts every kind of ideal are laid in this relationship. The father's journey, which started with his departure from Yenice, becomes the main source of his alienation from the people of Yenice, even though Yenice embodied his populist ideology: when he is torn between ideology and the public, he is obliged to deny the public since he cannot deny his ideology. From the

---

2. The dialogue between the grandson (acted by Mehmet Emin Toprak) and uncle can be seen. (Plays the role of Nuri Bilge Ceylan's father in real life).

3. In the films *Small Town* and *Clouds of May* the desire for migration from small towns to the metropolis is depicted, with the latter considered as a place of courage where one can prove oneself. However, in *Distant*, the metropolis is seen as an alternative only when there is no more hope in the town; the temporary residence is the house of a relative that passed away, at the same time metropolis is tempting and is a place of freedom.

son's perspective, the act of catering to the exalted ideals comes to stand for undermining the public, the traditions, national ideals, political radicalism as he sees his father's defeat. The son sustains this alienation in the city and also at university. He sustains the anxiety of seeing his own future in his father. The result is his own alienation from the public, traditions, ideals, and he sinks slowly into work that is his way of engaging with the world, but he does so alone. The art that he began creating with curiosity becomes an elevated form; an elevated space for seclusion, which is his shelter. In addition, he can make a living from photography. This pursuit allows him to observe life abstractly and thus, separates him from it. It places him in an awkward situation where he thinks himself. He repositions his actual life with the image of life that is a direct result of his constant desire for the denial of life. What he seeks is the meaning of life, a meaning that can never be grasped; he takes shelter in art for seeking a better intellectually fulfilled life.[4]

Rather than looking toward the public for answers, art turns into a platform of debate regarding the public's image, history, inside feelings of an individual and the idea of beauty formed within everyone. Art provides Ceylan with a realm of existence in which he can set his own boundaries, and he sees art as a substitute for life because he knows that his father's defeat was as profound as his dreams and innocence. Life itself caused disappointment. In avoiding disappointment himself, Ceylan became infatuated with the image of life. He elevated it, by viewing life from an outsider's perspective in his daily life, by distancing himself from what is social, by drawing strict boundaries in his individual existence, by turning into an exile in his own being, and finally by removing his trace from civilian life—these were the most important characteristics of Ceylan's art and life during this period.

When the past is remembered in the present, it has a deceptive beauty, it turns into a place where solidarity is experienced intensely, and unity is felt even more. Today the past has become a period that can only be regarded with a sense of nostalgia; a sense of belonging is felt for the past, while today only the differences in/of the present are emphasised. Following his third film, *Uzak/Distant* (2002), the actor Mehmet Emin Toprak died in an accident. After this tragic death, the cynical filmic conversations Ceylan had had with him about the nature of people living

---

4. Leyla Sevükten, *Antrakt Sinema Gazetesi*, 5 September 1998, interview with NBC, "Only realistic people can produce good films." "What does cinema mean to you? I do not know who said it now but there is a saying; for human, a good life is the life that he/she spends while searching for it. For me, maybe film-making is the tool I use for searching for the good life."

in Yenice from the perspective of a person from there drew to a close. Consequently, Ceylan stopped going to Yenice. During that period after 2004, he was re-organising his memories and trying to look back at his former life there from the perspective of maturity reached through his relationship with Mehmet Emin. He only returned in 2012 after his father's death for his father's funeral. Today, Nuri Bilge can love his past only from a distance, and this love is bittersweet. For him however, the past is a place that involved intense disengagement and the many disappointments he witnessed. In this sense, it is meaningful that he began his journey by first tracing his past in *Koza* and in the two feature-length films that followed. This can be called a return to an adjourned reckoning and can be interpreted as a review of his past, that is to say, his home for filmmaking, and as an effort of making peace with it before launching into life.

> I consciously focused on my difference. It was like this since my childhood, and it created a feeling of guilt. You know, there is the mechanism of ridicule in childhood. You have to be the resilient in order to avoid being the object of derision. Power relationships start in school during childhood. (Kızıldemir 1997)

While Ceylan experienced feelings of guilt that came out of his relationship with and observation of his father, the responsibility for this guilt was not directed at his parents but rather towards the society. The issue of difference turns into the notion of "self-censorship," the always self-controlling identity turns into an observer, who constantly questions himself and humanity.

In Anatolia, people who have some sort of exceptional quality devote themselves to others (like saints); otherwise, they are isolated in strange ways. In Nuri Bilge's case this was extreme. The idealistic figure of the father in Ceylan's family can be described as a hardworking and honest man who has his own rules, who does not want any trouble and constantly expects success. Therefore, the child is secretly crushed by the presence of this virtuous, proficient, and prominent father, and he also feels guilty. In the same context, the father also expects the child to mature more quickly and more radically than a child possibly can. The father figure settles into the child's mind as part of the inner-self that represents the norm of moral principles during this childhood period, which is in direct contrast with the way that morals and rules are usually learned in childhood, i.e., by breaking the rules.

This situation turns into the strongest tool of moral coercion of the child. As such, the child's desire to have an ideal identity starts conflicting with the nature of his age—the time in which he lives and/or the social, emotional and intellectual quality of his age in years—and with his own personality. This dilemma leads the child to do certain things. As a matter of fact, the clearest reflection on this situation is seen in the film *Small Town*; the child turns the turtle upside down because of his curiosity and because of the attraction of breaking a rule. As a result of the feeling of guilt that he experiences, he sees his mother lying upside down in front of the window. He witnesses the fall of his mother with fear, then he wakes up from his nightmare. If we follow the traces of this period in Ceylan's films and photographs, we can see that this is why he chose his father as a subject and why he portrayed him as an eccentric character. The educated and wise father's perception of the world is described in the film *Small Town* (1997); the same father is alone with his old ideals and his own truths even after Nuri Bilge grows up and receives international awards and visits him again. The relationship of Muzaffer and the father in *Clouds of May* (1999) can be analysed both in terms of the relationship between the urbanised son and the father, who holds on to his land (perhaps taking shelter in his land and thereby, also isolating himself as far as possible), and in terms of the world of the father, how the son perceives this world and dissociates himself from it. The father is still replete with his ideals, and the son does not want to address these ideals. We can call this the differentiation of the ideal "great objective," so that, after many years, the son can only watch the father's resolved and contented state in his own world with astonishment (*Clouds of May*).

Nuri Bilge's "childhood desire of being a normal person" is probably the element behind the fact that later in life he feels drawn to the ordinary stories of ordinary people.

> I don't like marginal stories; I also don't like the extraordinary stories that happen to ordinary people. I like the ordinary stories of ordinary people. (Shrikent 1999)

This can be called a syndrome, which involves being fond of tranquillity. The young Nuri Bilge could see how his father's ideals caused him trouble, how his father's struggle for serving people because of his ideals exhausted him, and the different kinds of issues created by having these ideals, which resulted from his father's inability to accept people as they were. Even after he achieved success, Nuri Bilge neither became involved in artistic struggles of a political nature nor joined public actions. He feared retreat into the type of defeated seclusion he had learned as a child as a consequence of the lesson he learned from his father's defeat. His success did not turn him into a politically or socially active person because he was aware that his father's success was the real reason behind his defeat. His experience of collectivity – a group mentality has clearly shown him how personal flaws and weaknesses are transformed from subjective things into demands as if they are objective things. When approaching his past, Ceylan sees the lessons he learned, especially the realisation that people can selfishly undermine his greatest ideals, and he uses this approach as a guiding principle throughout life. Perhaps he is living from the depths of the part of his personality moulded in childhood that considers everything that is uncommon as tension and even as a source of embarrassment. In the same sense, Nuri Bilge regarded his father's idealistic vision, and the disappointment caused by his father's inability to realise it; it is at exactly this point that his tragedy coincides with the tragedy of his generation. For this reason, on the one hand, he loves his father and his family, but on the other hand, he has acquired the characteristics that remind him of a person who keeps himself away from engaging in people's lives, becoming more pessimistic, more receding, and not following his dreams. Moreover, this is a person who fears being exploited, as a result of his escape from the sum of his father's disappointments.

The same situation also applied to the radical socialist movement in Turkey, which is known as the '78 generation. The revolution was a real possibility; being so close to it meant becoming infatuated with the idea of it. Shortly after the military coup of 12 September 1980, when about one million people were tortured, and a great number of people were murdered (Öktem 2011). While radical socialists were upholding the revolution, to which they were passionately connected and which ran parallel to the intensity of their ideals, dying for the beloved (the revolution) was also to be upheld because of the greatness of that love. Devotion was on the verge of turning into mental illness, which involved denying one's own existence and identity. After the coup, a painful era of defeat arrived. The pain of defeat created a traumatic area of inactivity, and undermined the idea of creating a revolution with the concept of populism at its core. The spirit of this period turned into pessimism, and people began steering clear of politics as well as feeling very suspicious about what was viewed as the public and the ideals of society. After the coup, the integration of the political and social environment with personal tragedies made individual tragedy align with the tragedy of a generation. Taking political action and devoting oneself to a cause started to be seen as wasting time or as entertaining some sort of delusion that things in some way could be different. Feeling responsible for the other (for the public) was labelled as foolish and one could also be accused of defending a hopeless cause. The ego had to put aside its relationship with the public in order to make some space for itself; transforming itself into a pragmatic person, it freed itself from social ideals. This generation strived to create a space in which to exist outside of the social order of life, or something along these lines Alcohol and drugs started functioning as a refuge from life and more importantly, detachment from practical life became evident during the production process in art as a gradual shift to cope with everyday harsh reality (Mutman 2006).

Reading the Films of Nuri Bilge Ceylan

The characters in all of Nuri Bilge Ceylan's films are people who fear engagement at certain levels and keep away from being saddled with the burdens of their relationships, who strive to keep others at a distance and cannot find inner motivation to achieve the things they have in their minds. These psychological tendencies transform Nuri Bilge into a person with a neurotic personality.[5]

The aforementioned is the reason why the main characters of Ceylan's films *Small Town* (1997), *Clouds of May* (1999), and *Distant* (2002) are seen to fear engagement, why there is no sense of belonging to place in those films, why there is a chain of relationships in which the lines of privacy are rigorously drawn, and why the clear signs of pride secretly cause relationships to be kept at a distance. The disappointment that his father experienced, along with the belief that his father was right, became integrated with the social tragedy of his generation and the tiring materiality of reality. Nuri Bilge Ceylan removed himself from his generation by living his own personal tragedy. An existential convergence was formed as a result of the tragedy of his generation. That is why he did not try to delve into any "great ideology". The disappointment that he saw in his father hung over Bilge as his own biggest nightmare. Bilge's approach to life is of a person who removes himself from life; his tragic fear of defeat is also a trigger for his pessimism.

---

5. Nuri Bilge Ceylan often defines himself as a neurotic person, for the same reason he objects to the pace of life. As a person of the past he even has the feeling that a lot of things are now lost. As cinema records the time, as it is an art that can sculpture in time just like Tarkovsky says, Nuri Bilge Ceylan sees the cinema as a secret resistance: an art that allows to make a notch on time, on the ones passing by, on being lost and on history, an art that makes Ceylan feel he exists (for more detail see Mehmet Erdem's article "Piyasa Acımasız ve Demirden Yasalarla İşliyor!" (1997).

The main reason behind his interest in photography is that the very nature of photography allows him to work alone. One of the reasons he refrained from moving on to cinema was that he wanted to be able to work alone. When eventually he preferred to move on to cinema as a medium, he preferred to work with small crews; large crews reminded him of the public, from whom he was still running away, while also attempting to understand through observation.

> One of the things that I worried about most when I was moving on to the cinema was the fact that I was going to be obliged to break the habits I had when I was a photographer. Photography is a thing that you can do alone. However, cinema is a field of art that makes the loneliness of a writer or artist enviable since it has such production conditions that involve many complicated human relationships. (Ceylan in Çetin 1998)

> Probably, this aspect of filmmaking will always be the aspect that I hate the most. Filmmaking directly obliges people to become socialised. It surrounds people with a network of synthetic relationships, far more than a typical life would have. And this can harm inwardness and concentration. (see Erdem 1997)

Although he experienced difficulty in finding something to hold on to, it can be said that Nuri Bilge Ceylan found his own transcendent meaning in filmmaking in spite of his neurotic personality, creating for himself an identity in life only through finding this meaning in filmmaking, thus creating the space necessary for him to experience harmony with his existence.

> Actually, the situations of meaninglessness and melancholy can only be transmuted into something that has a transcendent value. Art is one of these values. Things that we can call neurotic emotions, i.e. the differences of people, can only be transmuted into such a transcendent value. I think that art has been good for this side of me, my melancholy. It worked as a therapy. (Ceylan in Kızıldemir 1997)

We can see a tendency in Ceylan's life to reject the success achieved after hard work; success in itself seems meaningless. For example, although he studied engineering, he never worked as an engineer, he has never worked as an engineer, even for a day. The direct result of this process is the pursuit of meaning that "feels meaningful," or in short, a search for meaning that is worth the burden it causes: "for a human being, a good life is the life that he/she spends while searching for it. For me, maybe filmmaking is the tool I use to search for the good life". In his mind that stands against infinite reasoning, he is also suspicious of everything. Apart from all these, a smart sense of reality, and sufficient experience and knowledge about the trouble that reality can get someone into increases his pessimism and neuroticism:

> I am a person who usually thinks negatively, so I am always surprised when my films are successful or are chosen for something or when something else happens. I usually do not expect something because I am a person that is accustomed to considering the worst case; I have such a nature. Therefore, I am usually surprised, and I always ask myself how it could happen. I make films thinking that this time no one will watch it or this time we are all washed up, etc. Generally I feel a sense of failure as my films come close to being complete, perhaps because my consciousness focuses mostly on insufficiencies, weaknesses and on the negative aspects of the film (Ceylan 2012).

The university experience for Ceylan was a turning point in the realisation life could be different to what he had experienced in his youth. Here, everything from educational conditions to living space is much closer to the ideal, and which also adds a certain pedigree to a person in terms of one's social environment and, which teaches a Western language to a high level of proficiency:

> What affected me the most in Istanbul was probably my education at Boğaziçi University. I do not know how exactly it was formed, but I started developing an admiration for the West, and Boğaziçi University pushed it further. You know; Boğaziçi has a thing that steers people towards the West. It is thought that one way, or another, one will finish school and the next stop will be settling in the West. It appeared to me as if the West was where my fate lay. (Ceylan in Kızıldemir 1997)

In particular, Ceylan developed a great affection for nineteenth century Russian literature which it represents the rational mind of the West and the circle of values of the East in the most unified way in world literature. Russian society experienced a kind of alienation because of the conflicts between westernisation/westernism/pan-Slavism and Orthodoxy similar to Turkey. It is no surprise that the authors Ceylan has said to appreciate in particular are Dostoyevsky and Chekhov: authors who created epic narratives about the dilemmas surrounding the philosophy of life in this conflict of values and identities. Both authors are very important as their work describes realms of reality and confessions which are not included in daily conversations, and includes characters that experience a conflict of values in life and make great efforts at rationalising the things they have done. Thus, as a person who experienced the same things elsewhere, Nuri Bilge Ceylan regards works by these authors as his main sources for understanding and describing his own journey (Ceylan 2012).

In this sense, the East-West conflict lies at the centre of Nuri Bilge's cinematographic creation. Furthermore, he looks both at the eastern world and the western world with a certain externality, shown as a structural feeling of detachment in his films. In life, this feeling is shown in his lack of participation in anything that could put a strain on his inner world and his social relationships. Emerging from a world of values and ideals that has been shaken, in Ceylan's own words, his strongest need lies in "the effort to find meaning and interpretation". He has to recreate his values, meaning and moral code. In this sense, it is understandable that his films (*Distant* (2002), *Climates* (2006), *Three Monkeys* (2008), Once Upon a Time in Anatolia (2011) and *Winter Sleep* (2014) focus on the narratives of people who constantly experience value conflicts. It is only natural then, that these films also fit in with certain issues in both eastern and western societies and that, consequently, each social structure will interpret these films from its own perspective.

When he received the Best Director award for the film *Three Monkeys* at the Cannes Film Festival in 2008, he said, "I dedicate this award to my lonely and beautiful country, which I passionately love". This statement can be read to mean that his "country" is made up of two aspects; "lonely," which represents his father as the superego while "beautiful" represents his mother and compatriots. If we go further into this type of analysis, we see that Ceylan himself is the one that lives alone in conscious isolation, but also the one that makes beautiful films, so these questionable words could actually mean "I dedicate this to myself, who lives alone, makes these beautiful films and presents them to his people". After many years, he was able to merge his present with his past life, and also able to present his country with valid success before going into solitude, which he always feared. The feeling of power attained by the success of surviving alone enabled Ceylan to rid himself of the pain he caused himself through his fear of failure. Even though still feeling alone among people, he was reconciled with them, with them, their community and the reality (identity) of. By escaping he made a comeback and was rewarded with great success.

The Continuity/Disengagement Dialectic in the Films of Nuri Bilge Ceylan

A strange characteristic becomes prominent when all the films of Nuri Bilge Ceylan are analysed together: he cannot abstain from attaching his works like an annotation to each other. Nothing is regarded as a single phenomenon nor presented from only one character's perspective. Ceylan constantly establishes connections between events; events do not develop under the control of any character; characters cannot rule over events; each and every event triggers yet others by changing independently from the intentions and purpose of the characters involved. When we analyse the events of the different films, we see an important emphasis on the portrayal that the same event is experienced and perceived differently by the persons it involves and that their reactions constantly trigger new conflicts. This is exactly what places Nuri Bilge in the tradition of European art; none of the characters is seen to follow a single cause or to be fascinated by this purpose. On the contrary, the films are characterised by their effort to capture "the usual and the ordinary" in the flow of life; the *entr'acte* moments highlight the plotline. For the same reason, this attaches reservations to the things he constantly creates.

Nuri Bilge searches for his own truth, one that is based upon the fact that reality is in its essence plural, reflected differently by different people. What comes across is therefore the notion that no one can shape life by his/her will it seems like life slips through our fingers. Humanity is depicted as weak in the face of our individual, or collective goals, intentions and ideals.

> I do not agree on this saying, at least it does not apply to me: 'One should not make films if he/she does not have something to say'. To be honest, I am a confused person. One of the things that pushed me towards art is that art is a field that gives one the freedom of not being sure of anything. For example, let's consider Dostoyevsky. He is also a very good philosopher— why does he prefer attaching his thoughts to novels? He prefers it because he constantly contrasts certain things that clash. I bet he is not sure which one he believes in, as well. Sometimes he believes in one, and sometimes he believes in another. Honestly, I am a person that cannot be sure of anything. I am not sure what is right and what is wrong. We are born into the system with pressure to conform. There are established moral codes around us, and when they collide with our conscience, some of them gradually become unsound. For me, the process of filmmaking is a learning process and not a teaching process (Ceylan 2012).

If we analyse his first film *Cocoon* (1995) we see; a mother and father living apart; they try to come together to no avail. In the meantime, the son is busy trying to break the rules and discover himself when he is alone in nature. In his second film *Small Town* (1997), a step into the son's world is taken; the son is still searching for himself, and so is his sister. Shame, mischief, kindness, the feeling of trust and the effort needed to find one's own truths, the desire to discover the meaning of mysterious disputes around the world of adults come to the fore in this film. After that, the pragmatic relationship the son establishes with the townspeople, and the son's character—a stand-in for the director—lie at the centre of the film. In the same way, the father is central to the film. He too is represented by a director who has a pragmatic approach and whom the son does not want to understand. This son figure in both *Cocoon* (1995) and *Small Town* (1997), in fact, functions as a sort of auto-criticism of Nuri Bilge's positioning in real-life events. The subject of the next film *Clouds of May* (1999) focuses on an exploration of the family, the world of the townspeople, the social as well as inner world of the townspeople, and the intentions of the director. In the film *Distant*, the character is a photographer unable to find the strength to realise his ideals. The director, who promised to help him come to the city in the film *Clouds of May* (1999), has withdrawn his offer. However, the factory is shut down as a consequence of the financial crisis in Turkey and the photographer goes to the city by necessity. However, he establishes a bonded relationship with the director and tries to ignore him as much as he can. With this, the tangled relationship of the urbanite with the townsman becomes fully formed. The efforts the director made to understand him draw to a close within a dog-eat-dog world. The character is driven away to his own world, a lonely, alienated world of personal relationships, which are full of disappointments.

In *Small Town*, Nuri Bilge focuses on the feelings of guilt, shame, confidence that accompany experiments in living outside the rules and on the first steps that are taken into the world of adults. He then focuses on how the urban character that comes to town detaches from his origins, while also showing the townspeople's craving to come to the city. In the final scene of the later film *Distant*, a continuity in this desire is reflected when we see the arrival to the city of a character from a town. In this film, Ceylan focuses his attention on a series of fractures in the individual existence of the character Mahmut. If we study this character's individuality, we see that he is alienated, he cannot maintain relationships that are rooted in love, he is weak when faced with his own ideals, and he cannot take action to realise those ideals. Perhaps not an individuality from other characters in other films who share these traits, but individuality from other characters seen around him.

Following on from this scheme of films, *Climates* (2006) needs more of an introduction because it delves deeper than the others into the tortured realm of individual existence; social responsibilities are set aside. This film focuses on Ceylan's inner world, on his dark side, especially on his relationships with women, on his reckoning with himself and on his efforts to hold on to things in his social life.

The following film *Three Monkeys* (2009) finally presents internal family relationships for the first time. *Three Monkeys* is also the most atypical of all of Nuri Bilge Ceylan's films: it has a structure that stands outside its story process. Here Ceylan makes a film about distancing oneself from the ordinary, the shattering of the ordinary in an extraordinary way, and about the ordinary, which becomes inseparable from reality. In the final scene, he comes to the town, yet this time to a world of people who hold the power. The social fabric, with which his father could not cope and which resulted in his father's seclusion, is reckoned with again, but this time the focus shifts from town-specific patterns of Anatolia to patterns of the East and more generally, to patterns of mankind. In this sense, *Once Upon a Time in Anatolia* (2011) corresponds to the director's effort to form an insight into the inner worlds of people, characterised by confession, people's thoughts About the borders of their personal existence, and seen in people's efforts to escape themselves by their denial of the reality in which they live, their compromising behaviour as well as in their desire to make a new start in life by leaving their environment (by leaving Anatolia). In other words, the film corresponds to the director's effort to create a representation of the world that his father denied himself.

On *Once Upon a Time in Anatolia*

Once Upon a Time in Anatolia is a film that involves a general analysis of Anatolia, it is not only based on an Asia Minor country, it is based on the East in general, and beyond that it is based upon the parable of humanity. Its structure regarding humankind/humanity is distinctive.

Firstly, it is important to mention that Turkey has never been a normative country which is governed by law or in which the people respect the law in general, and most importantly, it has never been a society in which the lawmakers themselves abide by the law. It is a society in which people always try to be the "biggest repining" regardless of their position or of the authority they have; this is a country of dissatisfied people. More importantly, this is what the East is (Wood 2006).

Secondly, the truth is that Turkish society *is not* a normative society; established, written or unwritten rules do not govern it. Society creates its own norm and the notion of normal in this process. Difficulties exist on a destructive scale; legal and lawful instruments of central political power are never enough, and the main determinant is the mechanism of difficulty. However, even that is not enough; we do not know how to stand in balance even within the shifting normal, abnormal norms and events that are the main determinants. Instability is typical and most of the time destructive for human lives. The rules are violated first by the rule makers, who believe that the rules regarding the operation of society should be established for everyone but them.

There are two significant unifying factors in *Once Upon a Time in Anatolia*: the first is this dissatisfaction, or, as seen in the idiom used by the townsfolk, the "we are incorrigible" attitude. Since not one of the characters is content with his/her position, each has designs on a place of higher-ranking. The second factor is more significant: the people in the film are defeated by reality; they do not have the character qualities to rule their own destiny. Since none of them can carry his/her own ideal into reality, each of them is defeated, and the distinguishing characteristic of this situation is "in the events they experience" as they all adopt the behaviour that involves finding a way to make things look legal as a solution. These two factors combined, of dissatisfaction and defeat, lead to constant conflict between the characters because none of them believes in and loves the work that he/she does, everyone wants others to shoulder the responsibility when there is work to be done, as if there is a ritual of avoidance. This situation is typically found in Chekhov, before him in Gogol, in the Ottoman novel or, to give a modern example, in Kieslowski's analyses of Poland or in his documentaries where he explored the bureaucratic misery caused by the state on people (Zizek 2001).

From the beginning to the end of the film, all of the characters but one endure trials and tribulations. There is a moment for everyone where they are all by themselves, they hide, or at least they do not want anyone to see their naked selves, which they see through the mirror. There is a vital confession that everyone strives to hide carefully. The only character not to have a story is the mentally disabled suspect who "cannot garner any stories," and who "wants a Coke" for himself in an odd moment and place in the film.

Therefore, the film situates/locates Anatolia as a place of/for confession. The film does not push the audience to listen to the confessions, but rather to confess in view of the confessions, by way of accepting their own situation. In this sense, the answer to what this film is about is very simple; we can say that *Once Upon a Time in Anatolia* is the scene of and for the confessions of the Anatolian people. It is a place where one is challenged, where personas are removed and people face themselves. This confessional zone scares people; it scares the person who hides the most, whose innermost feelings range from threatening and killing a person to whom the secret was told, (in order to keep the secret after the confession), and this is shown as an everyday event in this country.

The doctor who comes to the town of Keskin in Kırıkkale, becomes acquainted with the town for the first time from 8 p.m. to 8 a.m., at least this is what he thinks in the beginning. Later, however, the doctor realises something else: this is not only the town Keskin; this is Anatolia. Moreover, this is Turkey, this is Eastern society and finally, this is humanity. That night the doctor witnesses a situation in which one is caught between his or her image and his or her persona. It is only towards morning that the doctor stops asking people unanswerable questions. Everything becomes clear; the doctor gives up his ideals, and understands that he is buried alive. However, he cannot register it and cannot create a record of this. It does not matter whether he is against the death sentence or pities the convict or if this image of reality is too much for him, the film carefully shows that each character is defeated one by one and must do things against their ideals.

The story of the film is based on an actual event that transpired a quarter-century ago, experienced by Ercan Kesal, one of the screenwriters, when he went to Keskin for his compulsory social service at the age of twenty-five. In his own words, he aged ten years that night. As in real life, the film ends with the doctor performing an autopsy on a murdered man. It is important to note here that the film is based on an old story which has left deep scars both in the mind and the conscience of Ercan Kesal even after all this time. What was felt in the past is processed and transformed into the design of a film.

As soon as the opening titles fade the viewer is in for a shock. Through the tire shop's window one can see inside, and there is no tension on people's faces, in fact, they are cheerful. They seem like they are the closest of friends. Then the action begins, with the camera following three cars arriving at empty field. The following scenes from the film take place during the same night, and the film comes to an end the next morning.

Spanning twelve hours, from 8 p.m. to 8 a.m., the actual duration of the film is two hours and thirty-seven minutes.

The paradox of the film *Once Upon a Time in Anatolia* starts at this point because this time the shock, which is experienced by the doctor who witnesses real life, is not intended to be presented from just any character's perspective, but rather to be experienced entirely by the audience. The film itself turns into an area of confession to confront the audience: Yes, this is our society and this is who we are. Whereas some attribute the state of society to capitalism, Kemalism, the hard-bargaining usurer, or the bourgeoisie, in my opinion its ideological roots run deeper; the roots lie in the very essence of the Anatolian people. This can be called an essentialist approach, but "leaving things to chance" and "finding a way to make things look legal" are things we see in Turkish society, from right to left and in every stage of our lives. There is a hidden confessional area in the government of Turkey, whose administrators are always ready to make it appear legal through a bureaucratic maze. People learn to be defeated in the presence of their own ideals at primary school. "Rubbing somebody's nose in it" is the defining element of Turkish society; the one resisting is only a candidate for further oppression. When a new Constitution is issued in Turkey, threats are made before the election(s) to extend military regime. For example, after the 1980 *coup d'état*, the village and settlements that had given a no vote in the constitutional referendum of 1982 experienced oppression due to political pressure.

Once Upon a Time in Anatolia creates a field of discourse far beyond the story it tells. We can interpret that Ceylan's films have entered into a new cinematic era, starting with *Three Monkeys*. References that go well beyond the story leave their marks on the whole film. *Once Upon a Time in Anatolia* invites the audience onto a confessional stage running parallel to the mundane quality of the narrative and focuses on the moments in which the ego is analysed. On the one hand, Nuri Bilge presents "the Anatolia that he passionately loves" and, on the other hand, he shows his own bare identity to society that walks through the ruins of the image of Anatolia his father had denied. His father was defeated by society, and this is the image that Ceylan projects on the screen. Nuri Bilge can love this society, to which he cannot dedicate himself, only by placing himself outside of its realm and making it a narrative object.

Winter Sleep (2014) and Beyond

Nuri Bilge Ceylan has directed eight films, the last being very recently completed *Kış Uykusu/Winter Sleep* (2014). Looking at the progression of his filmmaking shows us that *Small Town* and *Clouds of May* are Bilge's introduction to cinema. They represent the first phase in which he overcomes his fears, improves his technique and of course, gains self-confidence. Among these films, *Small Town* can be thought of more as a "situation" cinema than a "character" cinema; observations and moments of feelings are prominent. There are also observations regarding the phases a child undergoes in the growth process and the process of constructing an identity. With *Small Town* Nuri Bilge Ceylan was not yet ready to construct a certain type of story, to gradually create a discourse that would go well beyond the narrative to build a ground of context/witnessing/confession and questioning on which the viewer would face himself/herself. Neither his mind nor his cinematographic language was sufficient for that yet. We can also think about it this way; that Nuri Bilge Ceylan in this film sought to describe the construction of a personality in his own world of thoughts who gradually drifts into solitude, but narrated it in such a way that the audience saw a theatrical representation of simple, innocent and loving relationships within a social atmosphere. Nonetheless, the social fabric he depicts and the relationships he describes are mainly exploited to show the traumatic consequences of a child's search for the meaning of the world.

I think that his film *Small Town* has been largely misunderstood, not because it is multi-layered, but because it is simple and beautiful. I believe viewers can take a fresh look at this film. Being a film, in the public arena, it is open to new interpretation. The truth is, *Small Town* is a beautiful film and, as a result it has become a kind of orphan.

In *Small Town* everything is shown exactly as it is. Yet, in Ceylan's films, there are associations that can be seen to function as a laboratory for observations that are made about humanity; his is a cinema of discovery of a type of world, a reckoning with the people he grew up among, with his own history and past. Analysis of this process cannot be achieved without modelling the inner worlds of children and the inner mechanics of a rural area.

With *Distant*, he leaves the rural setting, but does not manage to leave who he was (where he was born and raised) behind on going to the city. No longer in accord with this former self in terms of values, culture, and the limiting obligations of existence, he yearns to actualise himself, but becomes weakened as a result of his self-questioning. He becomes defeated. The psychological process now shifts from what is cultural and observational to the world of introspection; on the one hand, there is the inner world, on the other hand, there is a deep feeling of alienation, an emptiness in the inner world of the character. The character cannot devote himself to anything. But he is able to step back and create breathing room for himself against the absorbing power of life. The film *Distant* should be seen as an impressive work on the paradoxes of modernism.

Isa, the lead male character of the film Climates shares Mahmut's behavioural traits in *Distant*, but this time the focus shifts from individual behaviour to the relationships of the character with two women. We see that personal relationships build the dramatic structure. The story is largely included in this process. Besides, the main character is created in such a way that the audience does not have any sympathy for him. On the one hand, he tells a story, on the other hand, he destroys the story. However, while the male lead character puts a firm negative stamp on the film, the two women are depicted far more positively. The fourth character, one of İsa's university roommates, is placed into the story with the purpose of creating a world of men in a sense, and also with the purpose of depicting the personal character of İsa. . İsa is a person who has lost most of his values and who does not have a 'great object' in which to contain himself. He can punish others easily since he has lost himself. In fact, when we examine İsa as a character, in addition to his selfishness, he is a person who judges other people from specific perspectives as a result of his own failures; someone who exhibits behaviour that can be destructive when he shows them the image they project, who knows how to feed his narcissistic aspects and who can be destructive when his own personality is attacked or criticised. It may seem funny but is, in fact, very real. Nothing can reform a character such as İsa (and he is not the only one who is described in this way), except the therapy of personal achievement

Nuri Bilge Ceylan's third cinematic period starts with *Three Monkeys*. We can also come to this understanding from the titles of his films; the name of the film, *Three Monkeys*, corresponds to a social/personal behaviour pattern. This title is used in a way that the point of origin of the title is turned inside out in the process of modernism, and it is used in the sense and in a context that criticises the denial of reality. Similarly, the film *Once Upon a Time in Anatolia* goes far beyond the town it describes. It has a structure that bears a general meaning about our society, our history, and eastern societies and, from there, about humanity. His entry into narrative cinema, which he initially feared, then creating films that are not restricted by the stories they tell, that go beyond the characters and relationships they discuss, as well as their being read as parables, are the common characteristics of his last two films.

Three Monkeys explores the origins of and analyses social behaviour in detail. All those who watch the film respect the architectural success of the narrative. Simplifying the social structure in order to narrate the story in the narrowest way, appears as a way of conveying style and meaning, which model the social interactions of four characters over time. In particular, we are given an image of the one woman (Hacer) at the film's centre, that consists of her identity as a woman, of the things she seeks, of the processes that she has been through to hold on to life, of the limited options available to her, of a yearning for a better life nourished by her poverty, and of a person who has no strength to provide herself the things she desires.

Ceylan's last two films are on the verge of being like a novel. It should be clearly stated that the creation of the characters in these films, and their interactions are quite complete such that nothing seems to be missing in the integrity of the structure and are the result of an insight so deep that only a few filmmakers can grant us.

What is *Once Upon a Time in Anatolia*? What does it strive to tell us and how does it tell its story?

Once Upon a Time in Anatolia consists of three layers. Firstly, the film is a story about alienation. From the occurrence of the main event of the film to the investigation of the judicial case and the finding of the corpse, the story does not slow its pace until all the characters feel a specific instance of alienation leading towards the point where they confess. This continues until their personalities and inner worlds start conflicting with their personas, when they start to feel that their reality is unacceptable, as this dialogue between the police commissioner and the doctor shows.

> "My wife never stops saying the same thing...'Why did God pick us?' I say, you are falling into sin. Don't be rebellious. There's certainly a reason for it...we are worn out, doctor. This job is punishing after a certain age. It's hard to stand. But what should I do? The boy's status is obvious...It's hard to stick around at home, doctor. You find you can't take it. So you go off to work again...You should appreciate the value of these days. You're still young. If I were you, I'd leave everything and clear off now, damn it."

> "Where?" asks the doctor.

> "Wherever, it doesn't matter...then my father got on the bus. I was going to wave to him, but he did not turn around. The bus had gone. I stood there aghast. There was nothing to do. Then I went to the salt lake and sat by it. It was white everywhere. It was blinding. Then I started to cry. I was crying because my father did not wave to me...When I think about it now, I guess I felt that I was never going to see him again...I shouldn't rant on to you so early in the morning, doctor."

> "No, please."

"You're a city boy, doctor, you don't know. Life is tough here. Being without a father is even tougher, especially if you're a boy. That's why I feel a bit sorry for the kid."

When we analyse this dialogue we see:

a) That reality and the status quo are defined by not being accepted. It cannot be changed either. An effort to escape comes to the fore in the form of the police commissioner speaking to himself most of the time, of living within the condition of stalemate, and in order not to rebel against circumstances, of trying to escape by ignoring what has happened.

b) A person with a fretful nature is always exhausted, cannot behave in a stable manner and will certainly explode at critical moments. This produces a feeling of guilt. For this reason, unease, restlessness, and tension have left their marks on every aspect of his or her life. Escape is sought from the truth; that the person is on the verge of rebellion. This fact can neither be ignored nor faced, because it exists in the most unguarded part of the mind.

c) A yearning for what is "other" comes about, the desire to leave everything behind and start life afresh is deeply held, but this desire is also feared: there is neither a place to go, nor can anything be left behind.

d) In psychoanalytical terms, one is in a situation in which he cannot distinguish anything from anything else; he is lost both to yourself and to his past, he is as naïve as he is desperate. He is equally incredibly naïve as you are angry. Life is knotted up with the things he yearns for, and his yearning is endless. For love, for being loved, and for the truth that he can accept. He is living through it, but he does not accept he is living through it. He has no strength of heart because he has been punishing himself. However, his persona should not give way to despair because he is in a dog-eat-dog world.

e) He does not know what to do, because his father is not there, and he also does not know anyone who can play the role of a father for him. There is neither a person who shows the way for him nor someone who shows him a trace of the path. There is no ideological/moral/legal and exalted value that belongs to him. Everybody has a story: but the story points to the other in a double sense. At first, his story materialises in his confession. He is traumatised. He has not overcome anything, and he cannot cope with anything, and he is always trying to play the other. The second story is this: everyone has a story about the other. In a way, the story is being told in a double sense for all the characters: first come the personas of the people, and then the presumption of innocence and the confessions which destroy this persona.

f) *Once Upon a Time in Anatolia* can only be analysed, understood, or felt by conscientious perception. *Once Upon a Time in Anatolia* is a film that questions humanity, sin and reality, however, it can only become complete in the audience's mind, who in turn can only understand the film's meaning if they question themselves.

Secondly, *Once Upon a Time in Anatolia* builds a social fabric. The attitude of the director can easily be understood if we remember the words of Marx: "If the human being is shaped by his or her circumstances, then it is necessary to shape those circumstances humanely".

Finally, the film *Once Upon a Time in Anatolia* is an aesthetic challenge. A pioneering director's challenge toward the conditions of cinema and the boundaries set by the film business, against conventional habits of the audience and decorum, placed against the simplest elements in the language of cinema and against the lies of humanity.

Works Cited

Atam, Zahit. 2011. *Yakın Plan Yeni Türkiye Sineması Dört Kurucu Yönetmen: Nuri Bilge Ceylan, Zeki Demirkubuz, Derviş Zaim, Yeşim Ustaoğlu* (Close-Up New Turkish Cinema The Four Founder Directors: Nuri Bilge Ceylan, Zeki Demirkubuz, Derviş Zaim, Yeşim Ustaoğlu). İstanbul: Cadde Publications.

Çetin, Berna. 1998. "Kendi Doğama Uygun Minimal bir Yapım"(A Minimalist Structure suited to my Nature). Interview with Nuri Bilge Ceylan. *Sinema Dergisi*, January.

Ceylan, Nuri Bilge. 2012. *Söyleşiler* (Interviews). Edited by Mehmet Eryılmaz. İstanbul: Norgunk Publications.

Diken, Bülent. 2008. "Climates of nihilism." *Third Text* 22 (6): 719-732.

Erdem, Mehmet. 1997. "Piyasa Acımasız ve Demirden Yasalarla İşliyor! (The Market operates with Unforgiving Iron Rules" *Sinema Gazetesi* 59, 19-25 December.

Erkal, Seyyid N. 1999. "Koza'dan Kasaba'ya bir bilge" (From *Cacoon* to *Small Town* a Bard). Interview with Nuri Bilge Ceylan, *Zaman Gazetesi*, May.

Kızıldemir, Güldal. 1997. "Kasaba'lı anlam avcısı" (A Meaning Hunter from *Small Town*). Interview with Nuri Bilge Ceylan, *Radikal Gazetesi*, 21 December.

Mutman, Mahmut. 2006. "An Ethics of Images: The Distant." *GMJ: Mediterranean Edition* 1 (1): 101-12.

Öktem, Kerem. 2011. *Angry nation: Turkey since 1989*. London: Zed Books.

Sevükten, Leyla. 1998. Interview with Nuri Bilge Ceylan. *Antrakt Sinema Gazetesi*, 5 September.

Shrikent, Indu. 1999. *Cinemaya Magazine* 43.

White, Rob. 2011. "Nuri Bilge Ceylan: An Introduction and Interview." 64-72.

Wood, Robin. 2006. "Climates and other disasters: The films of Nuri Bilge Ceylan". *Artforum International*, 45 (3): 278-283.

Zizek, Slavoj. 2001. *The Fright of Real Tears: Krystof Kieslowski Between Theory and Post-Theory*. London: BFI.

Interview with Ercan Kesal (the scriptwriter of BZA), September 2011, Istanbul.

Radikal news, 16 April 2010, access on 12 March 2012.

CHAPTER SIX

THE CONCEPT OF "NATIONAL CINEMA" AND THE "NEW TURKISH CINEMA"

ASLI DALDAL

Introduction

In the mid-1990s, the once dormant Turkish film industry saw the rise of a new generation of filmmakers who described themselves as "independent" filmmakers. Among these independent directors, the most prominent were Nuri Bilge Ceylan, Yeşim Ustaoğlu, Zeki Demirkubuz, and Derviş Zaim. They brought a new modern sensibility to the Turkish film industry and then introduced the new Turkish cinema as yet unknown to the outside world, before. Following Nuri Bilge Ceylan's recurring success at successive Cannes Film Festivals after 2003, the number of "independent" filmmakers increased dramatically in Turkey, and Ceylan's style (the use of non-professional actors, minimalist mise-en-scène, sparse narratives) started to become the dominant mode of directing among young artists. Among these young filmmakers (with the exception of Semih Kaplanoğlu, who began his directing career at a rather mature age) the most significant were Pelin Esmer, Özcan Alper, Hüseyin Karabey, İlksen Başarır and Seren Yüce. As the number of unconventional directors multiplied, film historians, as well as film directors, began to discuss the possibility of a new film "movement" in Turkish cinema. In 2010, in order to point to these "new" developments in Turkish cinema, the young directors gathered under the name of "The New Cinema Movement" (*Yeni Sinema Hareketi*) and launched a press release which summarised the basic principles of this "new Turkish cinema". Although it was not a "manifesto" in the classical sense and did not go beyond expressing the hope of creating a common ground of solidarity vis-à-vis the giant problems of the industry, it was, nevertheless, an unconventional declaration in favour of an "independent" Turkish cinema as its opening sentence indicated: "We consider cinema fundamentally an aesthetic practice."[1]

The purpose of this study is twofold: First, to (re)define the notion of "national" cinema in the age of globalism and discuss its relevance to account for "national" film movements. Following the studies of Susan Hayward, Stephen Crofts and in particular, John Hill, it could be argued that contrary to the claims of some film scholars such as Andrew Higson, the concept of national cinemas still had some theoretical weight to describe "local" cinema, which struggled against the dominance of the "Hollywood" method of film production and distribution. Following the footsteps of a well-known article by Fredric Jameson written in the 1980s ("Third World Literature in the Age of Multinational Capitalism") and combining it with Hayward's and Hill's approaches, it could be argued that due to the imperialistic nature of the globalised Hollywood style of filmmaking today, "world" cinemas (which are mostly defined under the general rubric of "national cinemas") should assume a "national" as well as "multicultural" character in order to set limits against the dominance of Hollywood.

Secondly, the aim of this article is to analyse the current situation in new Turkish cinema and try to investigate whether the recent developments in filmmaking practices signal the birth of a new film "movement". Can we talk about a new Turkish "national" cinema as we talked about the "new German cinema," the "new Danish cinema" or "the new Iranian cinema"? Do these new filmmakers in Turkey (Ceylan, Kaplanoğlu, Esmer, Zaim, Demirkubuz, Ustaoğlu, Başarır, Karabey, Öz) have an authentic, independent character to create a unique film style? What can be said about their "political" attitudes? These will be some of the questions this study will try to answer in the second part of the essay.

"National Cinema" and Film Movements

Before starting to search for a proper definition of the term "national cinema," I find it necessary to emphasise that, in the Turkish context, this concept has wrongly been associated with Halit Refiğ, who launched a rather poor intellectual debate in the mid-1960s with an Occidentalist bias against all western influences in Turkish cinema. Halit Refiğ was an important writer and filmmaker who made significant contributions to the

---

1. The entire declaration can be reached at www.yenisinemahareketi.org

Turkish Social-Realist Movement in cinema in the early 1960s with his partner, Berlin Golden-Bear Award winner Metin Erksan.[2]

Nevertheless, after the frustrating elections of 1965 which brought the conservatives back to power, Refiğ adopted a very anti-western attitude which repudiated all traces of modernism (including Marxism) in cinema. Although he rightly claimed that a "national cinema" was indispensable for creating an "anti-imperialist culture," he defined the former as an extension of the popular Turkish cinema of *Yeşilçam* (Pinetree—the figurative name of the street in Beyoğlu where the film companies had offices). It was also the name given to commercial Turkish films and did not attempt to separate the commercial productions of Yeşilçam from earlier progressive intellectual works of Marxist filmmakers. Thus, he claimed that Turkish "national cinema" should reflect the popular demands of the Turkish audience as well as reflecting the national character of the people. To free Turkish culture from western influences, Refiğ suggested that this "national character" should focus on Anatolian folk culture (which meant for him the popular melodramas of Yeşilçam) and the Ottoman cultural heritage of the past (Refiğ 2009).

The concept of "national cinema" is widely used in contemporary film studies and cannot be limited to popular genre films or nostalgic nationalist aspirations. Although (as will be emphasised below) its theoretical origin encompasses the question of national identity and the cinematic image, its current definition in intellectual cinema studies involves an anti-Hollywood stance and the criticism of the dominant mode of commercial film productions. The term "world cinema" which is often used interchangeably with "national cinema" refers to this rejection of Hollywood dominance. National cinema has a critical attitude towards national questions, a philosophical background which often stems from a serious political engagement and a "realist" filmmaking spirit along with independent *auteur* aesthetics. Therefore, the "national" cinemas of particular countries often involve aesthetic "film movements" such as the Italian *neo-realismo* or Brazilian *cinema novo*.[3] Thus, the question is not

---

2. For a detailed analysis of Social Realism in Turkish cinema see Aslı Daldal, *Art, Politics and Society: Social Realism in Italian and Turkish Cinemas* (2010).

3. Italian neo-realism of 1945-1952 is an important film movement associated with Roberto Rossellini, Luchino Visconti and Vittorio de Sica. They cast non-professional actors in their low-budget realistic films, often based on very loose scripts. Brazilian "new cinema" of the 1950s (with Glauber Rocha, Nelson Pereira dos Santos, Carlos Diegues) is an offshoot of Italian neo-realism and focuses on a minimalist-social cinema with the motto "a camera in the hand and an idea in the head".

whether to call these cinemas "nationalist" or "ethnic" cinemas but rather to define "local" cinemas with their own independent spirit, which show the characteristics of a new cinematic *école* (school of film). When we analyse the latest developments in Turkish cinema, it would, naturally, be more appropriate to adopt a rather modest term such as a film "movement" instead of *école*. To reformulate the purpose of the present essay, then, it is possible to ask: Do the recent developments in Turkish cinema signal the birth of a new "national cinema movement"? The following paragraphs will first try to frame the scope of "national cinema" from a deeper theoretical viewpoint, and then clarify the enigma of this "new movement".

The notion of "national cinema" is, in fact, a very broad term with a variety of "subcategories". As emphasised above, a national "film movement" is an important component of this complex setting. Although the impact of some of the *écoles* of cinema (such as *neo-realismo*) in the pioneering countries of the seventh art went beyond national boundaries, these *écoles* have, nevertheless, been the "national cinematic image" of their home countries as they reflected the socio-cultural atmosphere often with a politically sensitive language. As for the film movements in developing countries, they frequently assume a more pronounced "national" tone, for they aspire to prove their authentic identity as distinct from other national cinemas and try to challenge the dominance of globalised Hollywood films with low-budget local productions. It may, therefore, be appropriate to adopt Jameson's main argument in his "Third World Literature in the Age of Multinational Capitalism" to our discussion of national cinema. Although later criticised by Aijaz Ahmad (1992, 95)[4] for his "totalising assumptions" in this essay, Jameson very successfully pointed to the fact that third world literatures are "national allegories" as they are born into a culture which passed through the traumas of colonialism and imperialism (1986, 65). Thus, when the "world cinemas" which cannot fail to feel the hegemonic presence of globalised Hollywood productions, create film movements challenging the globalising imperialistic tendencies of Hollywood, they invent a "national" discourse which, first of all, stresses economic and cultural freedom. It would even be possible to argue in a Jamesonian sense that all the cinemas of the world are "third-world" cinemas vis-à-vis Hollywood, as they have all passed through similar stages of colonialism and resistance (many film movements have flourished as a result of protectionist governmental measures against Hollywood). Ahmad's criticism concerning the problems of language and translation are not valid in the case of cinema as a film

---

[4] Aijaz Ahmad, *In Theory: Classes, Nations, Literatures* (London: Verso, 1992).

depends on a universal visual "Esperanto" and uses a "metonymic" (and not a "metaphoric") language, as Pier Paolo Pasolini stressed, which expresses the image by the image itself (Pasolini 1976). Ahmad's other forceful point against Jameson's argument, namely, the problematical nature of identifying the entire East with, say, only the work of Said can, of course, create some theoretical difficulties for the present analysis. However, despite all the arguments put forth by the theorists of *auteurism*, filmmaking is a different vocation from that of the writer, and a "recognised" director associated with a national movement is more likely to be bestowed their fame by film critics.

Some major national film movements in the history of world cinema are Soviet Expressive Realism and German Expressionism of the 1920s, Italian Neo-Realism of the post-war period and the French New Wave of the 1950s. These major schools inspired many national movements and gave the impetus for the birth of Indian, Brazilian, African and Turkish national cinemas. The "national character" of world cinemas is further strengthened by some qualities peculiar to the film art. Cinematic movements are always microcosmic reflections of political order and mirror the socio-political superstructure of a nation, as cinema is a complex art form which can encompass all other arts and which also depends on a politically sensitive chain of production, distribution and consumption. A national film movement is the subconscious image of a political system. And as Godard states, film movements are born out of countries' need to see an image of themselves. When countries were inventing and using motion pictures in Italy, Germany and Russia, national cinemas then emerged. Godard also states:

> Russian cinema arrived at a time they needed an image of themselves. And in the case of Germany, they had lost the war and were completely devastated and needed a new idea of Germany. At the time the new Italian cinema emerged, Italy was completely lost—it was the only country that had fought with the Germans, then against them. They strongly needed to see a new reality, and this was provided by neo-realism. (Godard in Petrie 1992, 98)

"World cinema" then, adopts a serious stance against Hollywood cinema and its commercial and hegemonic ideology. From the perspective of "state policies," it is also evident that the birth and rise of many acclaimed national film movements have been related to anti-Hollywood measures such as the ban on film importation. If we turn our focus to pure film studies and away from critical theory, therefore, from Fredric Jameson to Roy Armes, we will see the emergence of the notion of "third cinema" and the same "national" emphasis to analyse the complex resistance against the West. But this time Armes separates all the cinemas of the "first world" (not just Hollywood but all the cinemas of the developed countries) from the emerging national cinemas of the developing or underdeveloped (André Gunder Frank 1996) "peripheral" societies. Armes argues "third cinema" is in a "love/hate" relationship with the West. The imperialist West created the infrastructure and set the first models to imitate. It also assumed the role of the cultural invader that third-world countries had to rebel against (Armes 1987). Thus, in many post-colonial societies where the problems of nation-building have not yet been totally solved, the art of film is mostly devoted to the issues of national identity; it may also assume, from time to time, a propagandist tone.

When analysing the "new Turkish cinema," film scholar Asuman Suner underlines the necessity of a multifocal framing model (2010). Suner, who tries to build his argument from two different theoretical perspectives, argues that to understand the "new Turkish cinema" we have to consider two parameters: first, the "national" context that the term "Turk" refers to (and Suner, nonetheless, finds the term "national" a little outdated), and second, the temporal framing of the word "new" which stresses the new-wave cinematic movement. The Turkish context is really a peculiar one, as Turkish cinema is neither the product of the crises of post-colonial nation building nor a member of the "first world" cinemas that Armes sharply separates from the "third cinema". It nevertheless clearly underlines the importance of independence ("an independent cinema" has been the motto of the new cinema in Turkey for more than a decade) from global market pressures and often problematises political issues of "belonging". Thus, this cinema can be considered "national". The "new" cinematic wave is yet to be analysed (and this essay also aims at accomplishing this task). Contrary to Suner's apathetical outlook which sees the term "national" as a rather useless theoretical tool in analysing world cinemas (see Suner 2005), this essay contends that the notion of "national" cinema is not limited to the questions of national identity. Bearing in mind Terry Eagleton's famous statement (1990, 23) that "to wish class or nation away….is to play straight into the hands of the oppressor," this study suggests that the question of "national cinema" encompasses political issues of cinematic independence vis-à-vis the hegemonic power of Hollywood, and aesthetic schools that are particular about specific national cultures. The coming paragraphs will turn to the contemporary discussions as to the use and scope of the "national cinemas" to clarify the above statement.

Theories of National Cinema

There is a variety of conceptualisations, today, in the studies of "national" cinemas. To some, national cinema is one of the important cornerstones of national identity building. Reflecting common fears, anxieties and joys, it may help some individuals to imagine their common denominators as citizens of the same country. For others, national cinemas are the antidotes of Hollywood imperial culture. For them, "national cinema," in fact, represents a leftist and critical attitude often aligned with a developed political consciousness. Another group of scholars (that Suner is also a part of) finds the term "national cinema" very essentialist and proposes instead a transnational and multidisciplinary approach. Although this final approach is surely worthy of great merit as globalism and its postmodern cultural artefacts necessitate the redefinition of national boundaries, in a "world cinematic order" very visibly structured to benefit the hegemony of Hollywood, the "political" defenders of "art cinema" are still clustered under their national umbrella (though today with visible transnational echoes) as in the *Dogma* movement, "the response of a small nation to Hollywood-style globalization" (see Hjört 2005). In the remainder of this section, a summary of basic theoretical viewpoints will be presented.

The first publications on "national cinema" were inspired by the pioneering works of sociologists and political scientists. Ernest Gellner's *Nations and Nationalism* and Benedict Anderson's *Imagined Communities* (both 1983) were among them. According to Gellner, the standardised system of education and the standardised language that it uses played a seminal role in the formation of nationalism. Parallel to Gellner's analysis of official language and official culture, Anderson takes mediated communication to be mainly responsible in the formation of a nationalist consciousness. Anderson, whose work has provided the theoretical starting point for early research on national cinema believes "print-language is what invents nationalism, not a particular language *per se*" (1983, 122). On the other hand, Michael Billig's concept of "banal nationalism," which contends that nationalist discourse reproduces itself through banal rituals and practices of everyday life, also had a considerable impact on film studies. Billig argues that national ideology today (which also influenced the representation of the nation in film) is maintained through the news as "home affairs" (as distinguished from foreign reports), the weather forecast reinforced awareness of political geography, the sporting heroes of national virtues, the televised wars of increased emphasis on a sense of community. Thus, we get accustomed to being part of a "nation" through routine transmissions of signs (Billig 1995).

Going back to Anderson's impact on film studies, it is crucial to analyse British film scholars such as Andrew Higson whose early works focused on the imaginary coherence created by national cinema. Higson suggested that national cinemas were the product of tension between "home" and "away" and there were two conceptual means of identifying the imaginary coherence of a national cinema. On the one hand, a national cinema seemed to look inward, reflecting the nation itself, on its sense of common identity and continuity. On the other hand, it seemed to look across its borders, asserting its difference from other national cinemas (Higson 1989, 36-46). But in his works published in the 2000s, Higson highly revised his earlier Andersonian view. While still conserving the notion of "national cinema," (as it is directly linked to the cultural policies of the national state) he questioned his earlier outlook. Especially in his polemics with John Hill, he contends that it is no longer possible to talk about fixed borders and identities and that the notion of "national cinema" cannot accommodate all the cultural diversity created by transnational processes of production and distribution. As with Suner's contempt of the term "nation," Higson also questions the critical and intellectual tradition framing the definition of the term "national cinema". He proposes in this vein a new theoretical perspective that favours audience preferences, that is box-office success parallel to the postmodern partnership between consumption society and global culture (Higson 2000, 46).

Another British film theorist, Stephen Crofts, on the other hand, prefers to preserve the term "national" but widens its scope of definition. Crofts argues that while until the late 1980s artistic film schools in particular countries competing with global Hollywood productions could easily be defined as "national cinemas," today the framing structure should also include the processes of production, distribution, exhibition, audience response, critical studies, textual analyses and state policies. Contrary to Higson, Crofts is also aware that most of the assumptions prevailing in contemporary film studies are Eurocentric. In an evaluation he bases on the famous French critic George Sadoul, Crofts admits that the film scholars know very little about world cinemas. Reminiscent of the polemic between Jameson and Ahmad, Crofts maintains that there are many small national cinemas around the globe that still remain unnoticed, and that they should be analysed more meticulously (Crofts 2000).

Susan Hayward, known for her research on third world cinemas as well as French national cinema, also deals with the polysemantic nature "national" cinema acquired within the postmodern context. She argues that, in defining national cinemas, it is essential to examine what is "included" and "excluded," the nature of the knowledge produced through this complex issue of exclusion/inclusion and the choice of the specific aesthetic codes. Aware of the paradoxes of globalism, she underlines how the "local" becomes more valuable as the "global" acquires more power and how identity co-existing with difference becomes reality. Therefore, a "national cinema" should assume a "multicultural" character and combat assimilation. For example, national films may unmask a nation's alleged discourse of homogeneity and thus demystify the practice of the dominant ideology. On the other hand, working against what she calls Hollywood's *para-nationalism* and modes of new colonialism, the space of national cinemas also creates a culture in which to combat the oppressor. Adapting Franz Fanon's concept of "native poet" to the realm of film studies as "native-poet filmmaker," Hayward contends that the "native-poet filmmaker" should advance from the pre-liberation moment of denouncing his/her oppressor to the moment of liberation, acting as a mediator and joining people to their repressed culture (Hayward 2000, 89). To sum up, "national cinemas" should thus have two major characteristics for Hayward. They should problematise the hegemonic discourse within the nation and combat against the pathological *para-nationalism* of Hollywood through independent and culturally specific products.

Parallel to Susan Hayward's complex definition, another film scholar, John Hill, also has a twofold approach towards "national cinema". In addition to Hayward's sensibility of protecting the local culture through negating the *para-nationalism* of Hollywood, Hill discusses the critical issue of "economic freedom". So for Hill the issue of "national cinema" should be examined firstly from an economic point of view and secondly, from the perspective of cultural politics. From an economic viewpoint, a "national cinema" should financially be "national," thus, independent. To have a "national" film industry is still crucial despite the fact that the numbers of transnational productions have increased dramatically over the last few years. Similar to Hayward's emphasis on the role of the "native-poet filmmaker," Hill also underlines that in order to resist the culture of Hollywood and its global financial web nations should develop specific subsidies for their national film industry. Secondly, from the aspect of cultural politics, that it is the national image that films are expected to reflect, Hill is again as libertarian as Hayward. Like Hayward's stress on "multiculturalism," Hill also contends that, from a cultural point of view, national cinema should be able to register the multiple national, regional and ethnic complexities of social life. It will be, then, neither uniting nor agreed (Hill 1992). This socio-cultural pluralistic approach to the "nation" that Mette Hjört is also underlining when examining the new Danish cinema, breaks with the tradition of "imagined homogeneity" of the nation and gives attention to the voice of formerly marginalised groups. This does not mean "the withering away of the nation" as the "nation" has never been unitary or an agreed-upon definition anyway (and homogeneity was only "imagined"). It is a new and more realistic reflection of the fissures within society, and with the understanding that diversity is not threatening but, in fact, "enriching". When analysing the new Turkish "national" cinema, this essay will follow in the footsteps of Hayward and Hill. The definition of "national cinema" that this study is trying to elaborate on is therefore based upon:

a. An economic conservatism (a strong wish of independence from hegemonic commercial practices);
b. A cultural pluralism regarding the reflection of the nation itself;
c. An attempt to create a culturally-specific language distinct from popular Hollywood *genres*—the culture of the colonialist in Hayward's analysis based on Fanon.

A socio-politically sensitive "independence" is thus one of the key elements in the formation of a modern national cinematic language. Metaphorically speaking, the independence from the "colonialist" (in the rejection of the Hollywood cinematic practices) is the starting point for creating new and authentic film movements. So, a "new" wave is also a "national" wave, as posited by the previous definitions that, in contemporary film studies, "national cinema" means an independent and authentic cinema. "National" also symbolises a multicultural approach to the diversities within the nation. Thus, it should have a socio-political empathy towards the pressing problems of the marginalised groups within the official national discourse. A commonly shared attitude of creating an original film language—although there can be many *auteurs* with their specific aesthetic codes within a national cinema, there should, nevertheless, be some basic points of agreements between the filmmakers if one is to talk about a "film movement"—should also be present among the filmmakers regardless of the box-office success they have. Contrary to Higson's emphasis that the popularity of films with "national" audiences is also a key factor in determining the nature of "national cinema," this study follows Hill's dictum concerning British cinema that "British cinema" (that is, the British National Cinema) and the "cinema in Britain" (all films produced or consumed within Britain) are not the same. The coming section will examine the nature of the new cinematic developments within

Turkey. Are we, thus, talking about a new Turkish national cinema movement or only a new cinema in Turkey?

The New Turkish Cinema

In the 1990s, a new cinematic sensibility in Turkey began to flourish. It is possible to examine this phenomenon through two historical periods. In the mid-1990s, some independent filmmakers that were producing self-financed films with tiny budgets began to produce "personal" films with a very particular cinematic language. Although unique, these films also had universal appeal as their aesthetic and political subtexts reflected a certain global awareness of modern cinema. Unable to achieve box-office success within Turkey, these films survived thanks to international film festivals and a handful of Turkish film fans.

The positive impact of the Istanbul Film Festival organised by the Istanbul Foundation for Culture and Art (a private organisation founded by leading industrialist and film cinephile Şakir Eczacıbaşı) is also worth mentioning here, as this festival introduced film lovers to world cinema and initiated the annual "national best film award" to promote independent directors.

The young filmmakers of note were Nuri Bilge Ceylan, Yeşim Ustaoğlu, Zeki Demirkubuz, Derviş Zaim and Reha Erdem. Apart from them, other filmmakers such as Kazım Öz, Handan İpekçi and Tayfun Pirselimoğlu also made important contributions to the new rising art cinema in Turkey.[5] Films made by these directors were varied in their subject matter, but had a major point in common: all of them aspired to be "independent". This independence came from their autonomy from local market pressures. They were "art" films, disinterested in popularity and commercial success. Some of these films were not well received and were harshly criticised by traditional critics. For example, Nuri Bilge Ceylan's early films such as *Kasaba/Small Town* (1997) and *Mayıs Sıkıntısı/Clouds of May* (1999) were disapproved of because of their unusual minimalistic style and use of nonprofessional actors (mostly from Ceylan's own family).

Parallel to this "independent" attitude, these films also rejected the popular codes of entertainment promoted by Hollywood cinema and its

---

5. The Turkish cinema, of course, had already produced many internationally acclaimed directors. The most famous among them, Yılmaz Guney, was preceded by the Social Realists such as Halit Refiğ, Lütfi Akad and the "Golden Bear" awarded Metin Erksan. In the 1980s Ömer Kavur made very important contributions and became the first *auteur* filmmaker in Turkish cinema in the modern sense.

international extensions. On the other hand, these filmmakers did not care too much about the traditional Turkish film industry's (Yeşilçam) filmmaking practices either. Mostly educated in newly opened film departments of public universities and some from acclaimed English-speaking Turkish universities such as Boğaziçi (Bosphorus) University and METU, these filmmakers had international backgrounds, and they opened up Turkish cinema to the world. But as emphasised above, they had a "selective" perspective. These independent filmmakers had *auteur* features and often reflected very personal *sui generis* aesthetic codes while also demonstrating the impact of the new French, British, and Middle Eastern national cinemas (especially that of Iran).

This spirit of renaissance in Turkish cinema acquired a new dimension in the aftermath of Ceylan's prestigious Cannes award in 2003. Those "art" films which did not have the characteristics of a film "movement" between 1994-2003 except for the "independent" nature they shared, began to show some discernible patterns that could, perhaps, be examined within the general rubric of a "national cinema movement". After 2004, the following factors played an important role in giving Turkish cinema a new direction.

Firstly, Nuri Bilge Ceylan's unexpected success at Cannes with *Distant* (his film won the Grand Jury prize as well as the best leading actor award) greatly inspired young filmmakers and re-energised the older ones: after years of silence, Reha Erdem started shooting films one after another and Semih Kaplanoğlu started his *Yusuf* trilogy. Ceylan's international triumph also showed the new generation that local box-office success was not crucial, and that they could establish themselves and find subsidies through international festivals and funds. Thus, young filmmakers began to develop a minimalistic 'hybrid' style, mixing documentary realism and feature film, with a view to satisfying international festival tastes as well as to develop a counter-mode of filmmaking that was in opposition to popular codes of entertainment. In that respect, Turkish cinema's recent positive reception in international film festivals was similar to the recent international acclaim garnered by Iranian cinema, which came to be epitomised by Kiarostami's films of innocence (Farahmand 2002, 86).[6]

Secondly, a career in film, which had formerly seemed to be a risky adventure, became possible for young aspirants as access to international funds became easier, and low-budget productions could have a voice in international film festivals. Digital technology also facilitated the shooting

---

6. For a critical account on the popularity of Iranian films in international festival markets, see Azadeh Farahmand's paper, "Perspectives on Recent International Acclaim For Iranian Cinema" (2002).

of films and thus, the number of young filmmakers multiplied drastically within a few years. These positive developments also encouraged female filmmakers to enter the profession. The traditionally male-dominated field of cinema has been challenged surprisingly by the first feature films of female directors such as Pelin Esmer, Aslı Özge and İlksen Başarır.

Thirdly, the number of films produced increased dramatically after 2004. Commercial cinema as the heir to Yeşilçam was already on the rise after the great success of Yavuz Turgul's *Eşkiya/The Bandit* (1996). But after 2004, the popular film industry experienced a great boom and films such as *Neredesin Firuze/Where Are You, Firuze?* (2004), *Mustafa Hakkında Her Şey/All About Mustafa* (2004), *GORA* (2004), and *Vizontele Tuuba* (2004) had great box office returns (Akser 2010; 2013). These films were not part of the "independent" national cinema that this study undertakes to examine (although they might comply well with some of Higson's categories), but nevertheless contributed to the expansion of the industry and created a new interest from local audiences for Turkish films. These popular films shared the commercial mentality of the Turkish popular film industry, that of the Yeşilçam. They were much less naïve in their strategies of promotion and distribution. Part of a global network of hegemonic cinema which "national cinema" stood against, these films created an interest in Turkish cinema and pushed politicians to reconsider the much-debated measures on supporting a national film industry.

Going back to the previous theoretical structure based on Jameson, Hayward and Hill, what do these new developments in Turkish cinema in the period of 1994-2003 and from 2003 to the present tell us about the possibility of a new national cinema movement? If we focus on "art" cinema and leave aside the commercial popular films which are necessary for the development of the industry, but do not contribute to the development of an "independent" and "politically progressive" national cinema, the films produced after 1994 (the year Zeki Demirkubuz shot *C Blok*) mostly show characteristics of an independent national cinema in line with John Hill's emphasis on financial conservatism (a keen determination of economic independence from global market pressures). Financially speaking, from 2004 onwards, the multiplication of festival funds and the increased number of co-productions seem to emphasise the transnational characteristics of some contemporary film productions especially for the films of Yeşim Ustaoğlu such as *Journey to the Sun* (1999) and *Waiting for the Clouds* (2003), the fact that these transnational funds are created to promote local cinemas against the dictates of global capital make them compatible with the national criteria of "independence from Hollywood hegemony". The films produced through the co-production market (as The Berlin Film Festival website calls it) also often examine the issue of national belonging and call into question (as Hayward and Hill indicate) the official discourse within the nation. On the other hand, a great many acclaimed independent films were not co-produced and were shot with the limited financial resources of the directors themselves or the help of some small production companies within Turkey, such as Erman Film and Bulut Film. As to the second emphasis of Hill and Hayward, namely, on a critical and multicultural approach to the problem of national belonging, the first phase of the "new Turkish cinema" (1994-2003) also satisfies the criteria, although it had adopted a micro-political outlook and refrained from directly targeting the "centre". The films produced in this first phase (as well as in the second phase) often question the official discourses on national homogeneity and reflect the forgotten lives of many "outsiders" ethnically and culturally speaking. These politically "progressive" films can be categorised as films constructed around the themes of the "road" and the "journey" such as Yeşim Ustaoğlu's *Güneşe Yolculuk/Journey to the Sun* (1999), Demirkubuz' *Masumiyet/ Innocence* (1997), Tayfun Pirselimoğlu's *Hiçbiryerde/Nowhere* (2002), and as films of "rupture" focusing on liminality and isolation such as Derviş Zaim's *Tabutta Röveşata/Summersault in a Coffin* (1996), Reha Erdem's *Kaç Para Kaç/A Run for Money* (1999), Zeki Demirkubuz's *Üçüncü Sayfa/The Third Page* (1999), Nuri Bilge Ceylan's *Uzak/Distant* (2002), Ümit Ünal's *9* (2002), and Handan İpekçi's *Büyük Adam Küçük Aşk/Big Man Little Love* (2001). However, as emphasised previously, the only real common denominator to the heterogeneity of subjects and styles, was the "independent" spirit shared by the young filmmakers and the number of films produced prevented this national cinematic attempt to turn into a national film "movement" for the period between 1994 and 2004. Thus, though we can safely call this new cinema (in Jameson's, Hill's and Hayward's frameworks) a "national cinema," we cannot talk of a new national cinema "movement" such as the Italian neo-realism, the Danish Dogma or the new Iranian cinema.

The crucial question of the existence of a cinematic "movement" can only be viable for the second phase of the new cinema in Turkey (2003 onwards). The increase in the number of films produced and some common preferences towards a visible style (a hybrid mixture of documentary with feature film, choice of nonprofessional actors, location shooting, minimalism, social criticism through the stories of innocence narrated by children, emphasis on an "accented" cinema) are mostly discernible in the films produced after 2003. Film movements (or cinematic *écoles*) fall within the broad category of "national cinema".

However, not all "national cinemas" generate a national film "movement". A cinematic movement (such as the German Expressionism, the Italian neo-realism, or the Brazilian cinema novo) is often the product of a rich intellectual tradition and frequently adopts a particular political perspective. Even the films that are not politically engaged share a Hegelian *geist* with the rest of the movement. In fact, film movements generally coincide with specific socio-political developments within a unique historical segment.[7] When we examine the independent films produced after 2004, apart from all the surface similarities in style and the micro-political criticisms towards official discourses, it is impossible to talk of such a *geist*, an authentic commitment shared by the members of the new wave which gives a *raison d'être* to the new cinematic movement.

Although the young filmmakers (who call themselves "The New Filmmakers") of contemporary Turkish cinema recently issued a common declaration stating the basic principles of their novel approach to the cinema, it was not a manifesto (with a *geist)* in the classic sense and did not go beyond expressing the hope of creating a common attitude of solidarity vis-à-vis the giant problems of the industry. While far from being a national cinematic "movement" for the present (it may take a more vigorous direction in the near future), the new Turkish cinema of the post-2003 period has produced intense national cinematic "activity" worth examining. The following questions and their respective answers may help to clarify the nature of this new cinematic "activity" and explain why it cannot yet be tagged as a national "movement".

What are the common styles and subjects shared by the members of this new national cinematic activity?

In terms of production, we see a huge increase in the number of so-called "independent" filmmakers (those who make use of independent funds, reject big capital, and so on.). When we examine their preferred styles and subjects, we see that:
a) A great majority of films are set in small towns, with mostly unknown or nonprofessional actors (generally children) telling the stories of ordinary people: Ceylan's *Kasaba/Small Town* (1997), Uluçay's *Karpuz Kabuğundan Gemiler Yapmak/Boats Out of Watermelon Rinds* (2004), Erdem's *Beş Vakit/Times and Winds* (2006), Aksu's *Dondurmam*

---

7. For a detailed analysis of film movements and socio-political change, see Aslı Daldal's *Art, Politics and Society: Social Realism in Italian and Turkish Cinemas* (2010).

Gaymak/Ice Cream I Scream (2006), Kaplanoğlu's *Yusuf Trilogy* (2007-2010), Karabey's *Gitmek/My Marlon and Brando* (2008), Alper's *Sonbahar/Autumn* (2008), Teoman's *Tatil Kitabı/Summer Book* (2008), Taşdiken's *Mommo* (My Sister) (2009), Doğan and Eskiköy's *İki Dil Bir Bavul/On the Way to School* (2008), Baş' *Zefir* (2010), Emin Alper's *Tepenin Ardı/Beyond the Hill* (2012).

b) Many films continue the dominant micro-political discourses of the previous generation (1994-2004) and are reflected in the simple story structure of a "road movie," the pain of frustration, the search for identity, and the anguish of being isolated: Özcan Alper's *Sonbahar/Autumn*, Demirkubuz' *Kader/Destiny* (2006), Hopkins' *Pazar Bir Ticaret Masalı/The Market: A Tale of Trade* (2008), Karabey's *My Marlon and Brando*, Zaim's *Nokta/Dot* (2008), Coşkun's *Uzak İhtimal/Wrong Rosary* (2009).

c) The films set in big cities generally adopt a realistic and minimalistic approach and although frequently unable to maintain straightforward political tone (except for the directors of Kurdish origin such as Kazım Öz) assume, in the spirit of Hill and Hayward, a multicultural perspective which focuses on the stories of those marginalised by the official national discourses or lost in the "hygienic" crowds of the national bourgeoisie. Emphasising these micro-narratives of the isolated urban dwellers, those films adopt a "progressive" political attitude in the postmodern sense: Öz's *Bahoz/The Storm* (2008), Temelkuran's *Bornova Bornova* (2009), Esmer's *11e 10 Kala/10 to 11* (2009), Özge's *Köprüdekiler/Men on the Bridge* (2009), Başarır's *Başka Dilde Aşk/Love in Another Language* (2009), Yüce's *Çoğunluk/The Majority* (2010).

Why would it be impossible, at present, to call this national cinematic "activity" a new national film "movement"?

a) *The problems of authenticity and sincerity*: In order to call a group of films the product of a real film movement, these films should possess certain authentic qualities unseen in other national cinemas. This unique "aura" can be present either in the preferred styles or in the intellectual background of the movement. It has already been underlined that acclaimed film movements often have a progressive political attitude (though sometimes with implicit methods of expression) or at the least, emphatic social engagement. A genuine movement has a reason to develop, a mission to perform, in sum, a *geist* of its own. The styles and narratives, therefore, are not chosen haphazardly to "decorate" the product, but are genuine reflections of the interaction of the artist within the social milieu. Personal style, therefore, persists as long as the nature of the interaction remains unaltered. At present, there are very few filmmakers in Turkish cinema whose filmic styles reflect an authentic search for meaning. It is also dubious whether the vogue in choosing nonprofessional actors, children, minimalist narratives and micro-political criticisms are sincere preferences on the part of the new directors. In other words, do these young filmmakers really believe in what they do or are they just trying to satisfy a contemporary demand in international festival markets?[8] Are they only following closely in the footsteps of Nuri Bilge Ceylan, who developed an original style of minimal-pastoral narrative (although somewhat inspired by the new Iranian cinema) and was, thus, able to draw the attention of the Cannes Film Festival? It is not yet very clear whether some of the new Turkish films are blank *pastiches* or original works of young *auteur*s.

b) *The problem of "independence"*. This study has often pointed out that the issue of independence from global networks of Hollywood is the most important in determining the nature of a national cinema. It has also been emphasised that the new Turkish cinema has adopted an independent path since 1994 after the collapse of old Yeşilçam film industry that produced commercial films since the birth of the cinema making in Turkey. The so-called "young filmmakers" of the post-2003 era also followed *grosso modo* that independent spirit of filmmaking. Some of these young directors, though, recently produced films that were ostensibly self-financed, but, in point of fact, not totally detached from the ethical dilemmas of the market. In some recent "independent" films such as Karabey's *My Marlon and Brando* and Başarır's *Love in Another Language*, there were some commercials cleverly concealed inside the film's script. In Karabey's film, for instance, the main protagonist always reads and watches the same media network which belongs to a giant media group in Turkey (Doğan Holding). In addition, the protagonist also

---

8. For example, Aslı Özge, the director of *Köprüdekiler/Men on the Bridge*, who uses a very radical cinéma-verité inspired technique to depict the real life stories of people she crosses every day on the Bosphorus Bridge, in a panel organised by Boğaziçi University Film Centre (MAFM) on March 4, 2010, said that she was not particularly interested in the cinéma-verité technique as such, and could switch to another form if the circumstances required it. As an answer to the question of the moderator Enis Köstepen on the political implication of her film, she simply underlined that she was not surprised by the success of her film in the festivals, as she had picked an unconventional subject that might interest contemporary film viewers.

complains explicitly of a cell-phone network (Turkcell) with whom, at the time of shooting this same media group was in conflict, and which does not function well outside the confines of Turkey, does not function well outside of the confines of Turkey. So the film was not only advertising the network of a media corporation, but simultaneously "anti-advertising" a rival company. As the press release of the "New Filmmakers" underlined in 2010, the continuation of an "ethical" as well as "independent" method of filmmaking—as seen in the work of the previous generation—is vital if we are to commit ourselves to the creation of an authentic national film spirit in Turkey.

Conclusion

This article aimed to redefine an important concept in world cinema studies, namely, the notion of "national cinema" in the age of globalism when everything solid "melts into the air". My argument was based on an "adapted" Jamesonian schema (or structure) that due to the imperialistic nature of first-world filmmaking practices (mostly symbolised by Hollywood) defines all other cinemas as necessarily "national". They first struggle to become independent of global hegemonic power. This study held, in the spirit of John Hill and Susan Hayward, that national cinemas today should still struggle for financial and cultural independence, with a contemporary multicultural and democratic approach to the nation. Contrary to the contention of some well-known scholars such as Higson that the classic usage of "national" cinema is now a *passé* theoretical preoccupation and that audience dynamics should be reflected in the analysis of this "post-national" cinema, this article followed on from Eagleton, who wrote that "to wish class or nation away….is to play straight into the hands of the oppressor". I suggested, therefore, that the concept of national cinemas can still be used to describe "local" cinemas, which fight against the omnipresent dominance of "Hollywood" methods of film production and distribution.

Secondly, this study undertook to examine the current situation in the so-called new Turkish cinema and tried to investigate whether the recent developments in filmmaking practices signal the birth of a new national film "movement". The essay argued that, since 1994, there exists a new Turkish national cinema that can be analysed from two historical periods. Until 2003 (the year Nuri Bilge Ceylan won the Grand Jury Prize at Cannes) a small number of self-financed directors made independent films for a select national audience. After the international success of Ceylan's, *Distant*, a new generation of filmmakers started to produce films for festival markets while more or less retaining the same independent and progressive spirit. Despite the increasing number of these original and self-financed new filmmakers that now adopted a more or less discernible pattern of directing (minimalism, non-professional actors, and so on), it is still impossible to talk of a national film "movement" in Turkey. The new filmmakers, although dynamic and collaborative—as their common declaration in March 2010 under the name "the new cinema movement" (*yeni sinema hareketi*) shows—seem at present to lack an authentic and really independent "aura" which will enable them to compete with other national cinematic movements.

Works Cited

Ahmad Aijaz. 1992. *In Theory: Classes, Nations, Literatures*. London: Verso.

Akser, Murat. 2010. *Green Pine Resurrected: Film genre, parody and intertextuality in Turkish Cinema*. Saarbrucken: Lambert Academic Publishing.

—. 2013. "Blockbusters". In *Directory of World Cinema: Turkey*, edited by Eylem Atakav, 124-145. London: Intellect.

Anderson, Benedict. 1983. *Imagined Communities*. London: Verso.

Armes, Roy. 1987. *The Third World Filmmaking and the West.* Berkeley: University of California Press.

Billig, Michael. 1995. *Banal Nationalism*. London: SAGE.

Crofts, Stephen. 2000. "Concepts of National Cinema." In *World Cinema*, edited by John Hill and Pamela Church Gibson, New York: Oxford University Press. 385-394.

Daldal Aslı. 2010. *Art, Politics and Society: Social Realism in Italian and Turkish Cinemas*. Piscataway, NJ: Gorgias Press.

Eagleton, Terry. 1990. "Nationalism, Irony and Commitment." In *Nationalism, Colonialism and Literature*, edited by Eagleton, Jameson and Said, 23-42. Minneapolis, MN: University of Minnesota Press.

Farahmand, Azadeh. 2002. "Perspectives on Recent International Acclaim For Iranian Cinema." In *The New Iranian Cinema*, edited by Richard Tapper, pp. 86-108. I.B.Tauris.

Frank, Andre Gunder. 1996. Capitalism and Underdevelopment in Latin America. New York: Monthly Review Press.

Gellner, Ernst. 1983. *Nations and Nationalism*. Ithaca: Cornell University Press.

Hayward, Susan. 2000. "Framing National Cinemas." In *Cinema and Nation*, edited by Mette Hjört and Scott Mackenzie, 88-102. London: Routledge.

Higson, Andrew. 1989. "The Concept of National Cinema". *Screen* (30)4, 36-47.

—. 2000. "The Limiting Imagination of National Cinema." In *Cinema and Nation*, edited by Mette Hjört and Scott Mackenzie, 63-74. London: Routledge.

Hill, John. 1992. "The Issue of National Cinema and British Film Production." In *New Questions of British Cinema*, edited by Duncan Petrie, 10-21. London: British Film Institute.

Hjort, Mette. 2005. *Small Nation Global Cinema: The New Danish Cinema*. Minneapolis, MN: University of Minnesota Press.

Jameson, Fredric. 1986. "Third World Literature in the Era of Multinational Capitalism." *Social Text* 15: 65-88.

Pasolini, Pier Paolo. 1976. "The Cinema of Poetry". In *Movies and Methods*, *Vol. 1*, edited by Bill Nichols, 542-557. Berkeley: University of California Press.

Petrie, Duncan J. ed. 1992. *Screening Europe: Image and Identity in Contemporary European Cinema*. London: British Film Institute.

Refiğ, Halit. 2009. *Ulusal Sinema Kavgası (The National Cinema Debate)*. İstanbul: Dergah Yayınları.

Suner, Asuman. 2005. *Hayalet Ev (Ghost House)*. Istanbul: Metis.

—. 2010. *New Turkish Cinema: Belonging, Identity, Memory*. London: I. B. Tauris.

CHAPTER SEVEN

REALISM *ALLA TURCA*:
VALLEY OF THE WOLVES

SAVAŞ ARSLAN

Since 2003, every Thursday evening around 8 p.m. during the television-series season which runs roughly from September to June, the streets are not as crowded as on other days.[1] If one goes to a coffee house, or a tea garden next to the historical Süleymaniye mosque, one can notice crowds of men (maybe a few hundred) silently concentrating on watching television. When one of the main characters in the programme says or does something good, the crowd reacts by applauding and cheering, or when one of the bad guys—often depicted as a threat to Turkish nationalism— shows up, they show their distaste by grumbling or booing. Turkey is used to such scenes of crowds applauding and cheering when its national football team plays an important game or when there is a derby match between one of the three big clubs of Istanbul. However, on Thursday nights this communal male gathering occurs due to an extremely successful television series, *Valley of the Wolves/Kurtlar Vadisi*. The series follows the adventures of a Mafioso agent and his buddies fighting against the "enemies" of Turkey—ranging from the US to the Kurds and/or the liberal-democratic portions of Turkish society. The communal aspect of gathering and sharing the mythology of the series continue after the screening has ended. Not only do fans continue having conversations about what might happen in the next episode, but some define their lives according to the characters in the series, frequently repeating famous lines, naming their children after the characters, and even organising real-life "fake" funerals for dead characters.

Such aspects of fandom are neither novel nor exceptional if one thinks of *Star Wars* or *Harry Potter* fans. What is unique about *Valley of the*

---

1. Since this article was written in early 2009, it only covers the series' episodes and films which were released between 2003 and 2008.

Wolves is not its fandom however, but rather how it combines fact with fiction by directly using and referencing events from actual life, thus creating an incessant crosscurrent between fact and fiction. Moreover, since the television-series market in Turkey is a fast-paced one where the episode to be aired is filmed and edited the preceding week, the series often addresses current events. For example, in a feature film based on the series, *Valley of the Wolves Iraq/Kurtlar Vadisi Irak*, the capturing of Turkish soldiers by the US. forces is dramatized. In the film, the lead character of the series, Polat Alemdar, with the help of his buddies takes revenge against the American soldiers who were responsible for the event. In another instance, the murderer of Armenian-Turkish journalist Hrant Dink Proudly proclaimed to be a fan of the television series, feeling partially justified in his hatred through the series' own glorification of extreme nationalist zeal (*Today's Zaman* February 23, 2009). Then, in this mishmash, the realism of the fictional series and its crosscurrents with reality are at stake.

Situating this television series within the rendering of realism in Turkish popular cinema, this article addresses how the relationship between narrative realism and reality could be conceived as quite a distinct form of realism from that of Western cinematic realism, which has a background in perspectival representation. In doing this, I will first propose a rendering of cinematic realism, which does not depend on a creation of the illusion of reality produced by the visual arts and cinema, but rather acknowledges what Stanley Cavell calls "the myth of film" (Cavell 1979, 39). Secondly, I will discuss the above in relation to the televisual experience, which underlines a different fold of narrative realism in television series by allowing the possibility of real-time interaction with current news and events. Finally, I will try to pinpoint this televisual and cinematic experience in Turkey through an analysis of the series by looking at its narrative, themes and viewership, as well as at the reactions to it and the real events which, in one way or another, the series re-enacted or referenced.

In the Western history of visual arts, the invention of perspective as a visual system to organise and represent the world underlies the development of the camera. The realism and naturalism of literature, painting and cinema have often been related to a representational regime in which the artist or the writer is put into a position of observer separate from the represented world. This sense of perspectival representation has far-reaching interrelations with the sciences and philosophy, as well as with the social and political organisation of this relationship that ranges from empiricism to rationalism and the panopticon. In literature and cinema, the rendering of classical realist text or classical cinema assumes a set of characteristics, which allows for the spatio-temporal continuity and coherency of the represented world. In the Bazinian sense of cinema, the ability of the medium of cinema resides in its realistic presentation of the world and cinema incessantly moves toward complete realism. However, what is yearned for is not the reality as such, but the completeness and perfection of its illusion. It is this sense of illusionism which underlines the Western modes of representation (Bazin 2004).

Modernist self-reflexivity and postmodern forms of self-consciousness and reflexivity as practices and tactics which dissolve the sense of illusion of these media may be considered as alternative routes. For instance, contemporary televisual practices ranging from talk shows to reality TV are often thought to be reflexive forms which distract from illusionistic language. However, such instances of reflexivity do not present a differential relationship between presence and absence, which is not just a coefficient of the relationship between reality and the illusion of it. Instead, the presence-absence dynamic owes itself to a different relationship, one which deals not with illusion and mimesis, but with the presence of the work which ties the artist to the spectator. As Robert Stam (2000) notes, film is also about "an act of contextualized interlocution between socially situated producers and receivers. To say that art is 'constructed' should not be the end of discussion but the beginning". For him, one may deal with the choices in representation of social voices and ideologies. While Stam's point reflects an ideological criticism of visual representation, the previous point is of an experiential alterity in which the culture of a people is at stake.

A distinction between narrative and non-narrative forms of representation is now necessary in order to delve into cinematic and televisual realism and illusionism. Whenever reality is juxtaposed with fiction, one needs to distinguish the non-narrative forms ranging from the actuality films of early cinema to newsreels, documentaries, live television, and television news. In presenting an alternative to narrative cinema and its historicised evolution, as it tells the story of the creation of narrative cinema, especially by introducing Griffithian continuity editing, Tom Gunning speaks of early cinema as a cinema of attractions, which was exhibitionistic, "establishing contact with the audience" without residing in illusion, but relying on showing,: "a cinema that displays its visibility, willing to rupture a self-enclosed fictional world for a chance to solicit the attention of the spectator" (Gunning 2000) . What Gunning underlines here is a certain disinterest in the creation of illusionism, by siding early cinema's exhibitionism against classical Hollywood narrative and the voyeurism attached to it by psychoanalytic film theory. This does not inform us about a non-Western narrative cinema which is completely different from classical narrative cinema and thus presents us with a different understanding not only of visual representation but also its viewership.

While this rendering of Western cinema may be put against its alterity in a non-Western context, it will still inscribe the re-presentation of a visible space. The mechanisation of this process of inscribing by way of the camera brought yet another relationship, this time between automatic recording and reality. However, while photography as a mechanical record of reality allows for this relationship, cinema offers yet another quality. The primary condition of cinema, of the viewer's displacement from the represented world is an underlining trait of the visual arts in the Western context. According to Stanley Cavell, cinema's capacity to represent the world magically resides in its capacity to permit us to view the world unseen (Cavell 1979, 40). Because movies give us a chance to be invisible to the world represented, they also allow us to be displaced. It is this sense of displacement that Cavell underlines in proposing a different understanding of cinema's potential. For him, reality is treated in cinema by being "photographed, projected, screened, exhibited, and viewed". In all of these senses of cinema, reality is treated through displacement because it is there before we even attempt to know it:

> The epistemological mystery is whether, and how you can predict the existence of the one from the knowledge of the other. The photographic mystery is that you can know both the appearance and the reality, but that nevertheless, the one is unpredictable from the other. (Cavell 1979, 185)

According to Cavell's distinction between the filmic and the non-filmic, between reality and its re-presentation, a sense of scepticism comes to the fore:

> Film is a moving image of scepticism: not only is there a reasonable possibility, it is a fact that here our normal senses are satisfied of reality while reality does not exist—even, alarmingly, *because* it does not exist, because viewing it is all it takes. (Cavell 1979, 188)

For him, the film's drama does not come from its illusionism but from its very anxiety because films block reality. Before a film, it is our contingency, which is expressed in the mythological, that defines our very absence from the filmic. "But movies also promise us happiness…because we can maintain a connection with reality despite our condemnation to viewing it in private" (Cavell 1979, 213). For Cavell, movies present us with the possibility of love and/or romance, which we cannot have in the rationality of literature. So, Cavell's view of film introduces a sense of contingency in which our wishes are addressed.

This contingency and scepticism of film and its satisfaction through the medium of cinema indeed found instantaneity and currency in the televisual in which "liveness" underlies a sense of reality. Thus when the filmic migrates into the televisual, it gains yet more Bazinian credibility in terms of its realism and/or its illusion of reality. It is this sense of the televisual which recurs in perspectival illusionism and photographic realism. The evidentiality of the recording which relies on photography's ability to record reality as such is transferred to the televisual as it relies on its capacity to serve as visual evidence of everyday reality. After noting how Walter Benjamin related that the shrinking of camera size would bring about the grasping of details with the use of captions, Fetveit notes that this relationship between the visual and the verbal, especially in reality TV, is about "an exploration of the visible surface of the here and now, avoiding abstract, symbolic montage and often pointing to its own status as visual evidence" (Fetveit 1999, 794). This sense of the televisual, beset with the promise of evidential liveness, creates a tension and sets the expectation of the viewers about the proximity of death (not only in the death of the characters, but also of the capturing of life) and of the obsession with reality on the part of the viewers.

Tying together the contingency of the filmic text promising happy endings through their own mythologies and the evidentiality of the televisual liveness, the Turkish television series *Valley of the Wolves* presents an unruly coexistence of fact and fiction, reality and illusion, by not only presenting itself as mythologically real, but also disrupting the border between reality and illusion, both in illusion and in reality. After its initial airing in 2003, the series—whose tagline is "This is a Mafia series" —blurred the lines between society and the underground by inviting and suggesting links between the state (including the Turkish intelligence service, the police, the army and also the bureaucracy) the Mafia, and international politics. In this respect, the male-audience-driven action-adventure series helped foster a paranoiac nationalistic ideology through both national and international conspiracies. These conspiracies revolved around the total control of Turkey by the "deep state" and at times by an international network of the Mafia, which is supposed to be in effect, in countries like the United States and Russia in controlling international relations and politics. I will first explain how the series is tied to Turkish society and politics with its crosscurrents that oscillate between fact and fiction and then, introduce the series' realism by tying it to the history of cinema in Turkey.

In the beginning of the television series, the lead character Polat Alemdar (Necati Şaşmaz), a successful intelligence agent, undergoes facial surgery and follows orders to penetrate into the heart of the Turkish Mafia, known as the Council of Wolves, in order to dismantle the organisation. However, Polat does not work for the intelligence service directly, but instead works for a cell of a fictional service known in the series under the name the Public Security Organisation (PSO). After the only two people who know Polat's real identity are murdered, Polat becomes an uncontrolled and unidentified person—a quality which allows him to climb the Mafia ladder before becoming the "baron" of the Wolves Council. In the process, Polat first befriends the Council's Istanbul leader Süleyman Çakır (Oktay Kaynarca), who is later killed by a rival mafia boss. This allows Polat to position himself as boss with a group of tight-knit helpers that all work for him. In the meantime, following the death of Polat's boss in the PSO, Polat plots with other agents of the intelligence service (PSO) and takes on new duties that bring him into the world of the international Mafia and politics. After the murder of the Council's baron by the international council, Polat not only becomes the baron, but also finds himself in the middle of different international duties, meeting some of the international council's members in the United States, including Hollywood actors Andy Garcia and Sharon Stone. Upon his return from the US, he and his helpers defend themselves in court, and he is released following the discovery of his true identity.

Following the season finale of the series in 2005, the producer Osman Sınav created a national box-office hit and an international controversy with a film based on the series, *Valley of the Wolves: Iraq* (Serdar Akar, 2006). Starting with an actual event that took place in Iraq in 2003 and known in Turkey as the "hood incident" in which the American army captured and humiliated a small team of the Turkish army's Special Forces in Iraq, the film revolves around fictional revenge. Polat Alemdar thus goes to Iraq on a special mission and kills the US colonel who is responsible for the event. The colonel is played by Billy Zane; another character, played by Gary Busey, is a Jewish-American doctor active in the illegal organ trade. The film became internationally infamous because of its openly anti-American and anti-Semitic overtones. The portrayal of the torture scene within the Abu Ghraib prison also helped to trigger its international renown. While the film was extremely successful in Turkey and watched by Turkish politicians, including the Turkish prime minister, it sparked a protest from the American army, Jewish groups and even led to pressure from German politicians who wanted the theatre chain Cinemaxx to stop exhibiting the film.

After the success of the film, the producers of the series launched a new, but a very short-lived instalment of the series called *Valley of the Wolves Terror* in 2007. This time, Polat Alemdar's mission was to stop the Kurdish separatists in Turkey. After the broadcasting of the first episode, the series was heavily criticised in Turkey (Anon 2007) not just because of its use of graphic violence, but because of the sensitivity of the Kurdish issue in Turkish politics, which has been plagued by the Kurdish Worker's Party's (PKK) violent attacks and the instability within the south-eastern part of Turkey, populated mostly by Kurds. After a two-month silence following the banning of the series by the Supreme Council of Radio and Television, The series relaunched under a new name and with a new storyline. The new series argued that intricate and clandestine international financial relationships were responsible for acts of terror in Turkey, which similarly led to attempts to halt the series. *Valley of the Wolves Ambush* which began in 2007 and still is on air begins with the story of the murder of a powerful Turkish businessman and how Polat is involved in helping his daughter. As Polat reveals the covert relations between four of the wealthiest Turkish business families, the state and the Mafia, he comes to sense that the "Global Gang" formed by the wealthiest business families in the world are indeed behind the entire plot to control the Middle East and Central Asia. As the series continues, Polat not only fights against a Turkish collaborator of the international forces who wants to control and lead Turkey, but also a separatist terrorist Muro (Mustafa Üstündağ) who later gives up his cause and starts to sympathise with Polat.

Since its conception in 2003, the series and the films based on the series continue to reference real events and/or dramatise them. To start with, Polat Alemdar is initially identified as a seasoned agent having connection with the "deep state," a presumably undisclosed security network in Turkey which guarantees the continuation of the establishment through various means, including violence, Mafioso relationships and other activities. Furthermore, parallels can be drawn between the fictional Polat character and a real-life undercover agent, Abdullah Çatlı, who was killed in an accident in 1996, despite various rumours and conspiracies claiming that he is still alive. A political scandal came to the fore when this accident occurred, and also led to a public campaign against the relationship between the state, politicians and the Mafia; the others present in the vehicle included a Kurdish MP, an upper ranking police chief and the alleged intelligence agent Çatlı. Not only did Çatlı's daughter claim that the character Polat was based on her father (Is Polat Alemdar

Abdullah Çatlı? *Haber7.com*, 3 November 2005) but the actor Necati Şaşmaz also sued some journalists who claimed that Polat was a cross between Abdullah Çatlı and Rambo. In response to a question on whether the real life person, actor Necati Şaşmaz and the fictional character he plays, Polat Alemdar are completely identical to each other, Şaşmaz responded that it is such a hodgepodge that even the court had difficulties in dealing with it (Şaşmaz 2008).

In the first instalment of the series, real events, such as the killing of a Mafia leader and Turkey's international political problems, are portrayed. Even more importantly, Rauf Denktaş, the founder and two-decades-long president of the Turkish Republic of Northern Cyprus (a state formed in 1983 which is only recognised by Turkey), appeared in the series. While in the series, Denktaş, appearing as himself, narrates the story of the Cyprus conflict from his perspective to Polat's intelligence agency boss, in reality, when receiving the series' crew at the Presidential Palace he said: "I was not an actor. As President Denktaş, I gave the interview which the press could not get to Anatolia in the *Valley of the Wolves*". Referring to Turkey as Anatolia, Denktaş thus allies himself with Polat Alemdar's cause against international plots, which are directed not only at Turkey, but at the entire Turkish diaspora.

This helps to explain why, when Polat Alemdar takes on the duty of avenging the humiliation of Turkish soldiers he also embarks on a journey towards international politics by helping the anti-American sentiment in Turkey to increase immensely after the Occupation of Iraq. As the third most seen Turkish film of the last two decades, *Valley of the Wolves: Iraq* not only triggered reaction from the Turkish public, but also made American politicians and generals feel the need to personally respond. For instance, the movie was discussed in the US Congress and by Condoleezza Rice, the US Secretary of the State at the time, who responded to questions by noting that the US had to work hard to regain good public opinion abroad (Rice Questioned about Valley of the Wolves, *Sabah*, 11 March 2006). Similarly, a general in the US Army, James Jones, according to a major Turkish daily's news story commented that while *West Wing* or *24* were just TV programmes, *Valley of the Wolves: Iraq* was different. After noting the necessity of distinguishing fact from fiction, Jones said: "It is clear that films shape opinions…but the important thing is the creation of public opinion according to facts and truths". The same news story notes that the US army warned US soldiers not to see the film, and that the Turkish Foreign Minister of the time, Abdullah Gül, stated that the film was nothing when compared to the films made in the US or in Europe

(Gül's Memorandum about Valley of the Wolves, *Milliyet*, 5 February 2006).

Valley of the Wolves: Ambush, on the other hand, starts with the re-enactment of the murder of Turkish businessman Özdemir Sabancı in 1996, and its later episodes introduce the murders of the Armenian journalist Hrant Dink and of German Christian missionaries, AKA Zirve Publishing House Massacre. However, in 2008, the series also integrated the Ergenekon trial into its storyline. The Ergenekon court case revealed an alleged military intervention plot which was planned by various ex-generals, bureaucrats and businessmen all of whom have alleged links to the "deep state." Moreover, according to the news media coverage of the trial the leader of the plot is unknown, while in the series he is revealed as an ex-general living abroad. In the series, events like the murder of a member of the Council of State, the bombing of a daily newspaper, Glock guns and hand grenades smuggled into Turkey and the murder of Hrant Dink are all connected to the a secret organisation called the "Elders," which is similar to the Ergenekon organisation (Polat Alemdar Versus the Ergenekon, *Taraf*, 4 February 2008). In a recently aired episode, two characters even made a bet on which team would become the champion of the Turkish football league (The Championship Bet in *Valley of the Wolves*, *Hürriyet*, 22 May 2009).

The series has created political reactions in its re-enactment of and references to real events, but what is even more striking is how the series became a part of everyday culture in Turkey, not just in terms of fan culture, but in how it defines people's lives and has led to violent incidents. To start with, after the killing of Çakır in the initial series, as a group of amateur football players observed a moment of silence for the character before a tournament game (Çakır's Funeral Prayer Is Held, *Yeni Şafak*, (17 April 2004), the actor who portrayed the murderer was beaten by a group of fans (Cerrahpaşalı Halit Who Killed Çakır in *Valley of the Wolves* Was Beaten Badly on the Street, *Habervitrini*, 15 April 2004). The murderer of a member of the Council of State, Alparslan Arslan, admitted in his statement that he used Polat Alemdar as his pseudonym (His Pseudonym Is Polat, *Hürriyet*, 25 May 2006). A survey done among high-school students found that Polat Alemdar topped the list of their idols, which generally continued in the following order: mother, father, teacher, aunt, uncle, older brother, Atatürk, etc. (The Scream of High School Students, *Hürriyet*, (22 September 2006). Such news can be added to various crime stories that often appear on the third pages of Turkish newspapers, hence the name "third page news". In the first few months of 2009, stories appeared about murderers who idolised Polat Alemdar, of small mobs referencing the series in their daily lives and in performing criminal activities, of a jobless Kurd nicknamed Muro shooting and killing one person in a small town's municipal building, and of a family starting court proceedings to change their children's names to the names of characters from the series.

All of these events introduced crosscurrents between real life and the fictional world of a television series and a film. They indeed come from part of the history of Turkey's popular cinema. As a country that was introduced to the Western invention of cinema in the late nineteenth century, Turkey not only kept oscillating between the West and the non-West in terms of its culture, but also produced a cinema which kept translating a Western form into a non-Western one. Turkish cinema has a background in the traditional performing and visual arts which relied on non-illusion and non-realism in many respects. This includes the inexistence of a proscenium dividing the stage from the auditorium in the theatre-in-the-round. Political satire was integrated into shadow plays, and the non-perspectival world of miniature paintings. Both cinematic and televisual fiction in Turkey carried elements of another sort of realism, perhaps fulfilling at its best capacity Cavell's rendering of scepticism in relation to film. Instead of displacing us from the world or blocking reality from the screen, the cinematic and televisual fiction in Turkey offered a contingency in which the mythological expression of fictional fulfilment is realised in both fact and fiction. If one looks at the history of popular cinema in Turkey, often very similar to what Gunning notes about early cinema, one may find frequent interruptions of diegesis through actors directly addressing the spectators, stars using their real names for characters and filmmakers openly deploying their life-stories in films. For example, the acclaimed Kurdish-Turkish director and actor Yılmaz Güney often had characters named after his real-life daughter Elif (from his first wife) in order to send her messages through his films because he was living apart from her. In this respect, such films are indeed more of a contingency that Cavell (1979) tries to introduce because they are not only about the fulfilment of the real-life wishes of the spectators, but also of the filmmakers as their texts bring their wishes to the surface.

When, therefore, one looks at the *Valley of the Wolves* television series and films from this angle, the non-Western realism of Turkey's cinematic and televisual culture appears as a specific instance of realism in which reality is transferrable from real life to the screen and vice versa. In other words, apart from offering a socially constructed fictional world in which social and political voices and ideologies are put together with a nationalist and anti-Western sentiment, *Valley of the Wolves* is also tied to the culture of Turkey, as it is left in-between the West and the non-West, the cinematic and televisual illusionism and the narrativised reality. In this respect, the reality of the narration and/or storytelling ties the filmic and televisual culture in Turkey to its historical cultural forms that bring together the presence of the storyteller or bard. It is this very presence of the storyteller not only in the fictional world but also in the real world of the storyteller's performance which denies the displacement of the viewer from the represented world. In this sense, modern forms of entertainment, be it cinema or television, may perhaps have taken the place of the traditional storyteller. The sense of realism on which I have tried to elaborate here however, is linked to this very function of the storyteller as a presence in the world, staged and viewed, and it is a residue of the contemporary television of Turkey. This is why it seems possible to argue that the liveness which allows for the convincing reality of television as the storyteller of our time, is coupled with the evidencing of reality in Turkey through both television news and the television series. Unlike reality TV, this evidentiality relies not on a play between fact and fiction, but on the direct transferability of fact into fiction and vice versa, by producing both filmic and/or televisual, as well as real, violence and aggression.

As it has led to various controversies, the series has been heavily criticised in Turkey. The entry for the series in the Turkish version of *Wikipedia* notes that it was criticised for its extreme nationalism and racism, for legitimising the culture of violence and the "deep state," for its expansionist and imperialist ideology, for encouraging armament and violence, for forcing a choice between "good" and "bad" Mafia, and for causing discrimination, creating a myth of male dominance and reinforcing patriarchal culture. That is why, unlike what television offers in terms of its creation of an expectation on the part of the viewers about an obsession with reality and the proximity of death, what is at times produced is the very fact of death and violence in a world in which the limit between fact and fiction, reality and imagined conspiracy is blurred.

Works Cited

Bazin, André. 2004. *What is Cinema? Vol. 1* Translated by Hugh Gray. Berkeley: University of California Press.
Cavell, Stanley. 1979. *The World Viewed*, Enlarged Edition. Cambridge, MA and London, UK: Harvard University Press.
Fetveit, Arild. 1999. "Reality TV in the digital era: a paradox in visual culture?." *Media, Culture & Society* 21 (6) (1999): 787-804.

Gunning, Tom. 2000. "The Cinema of Attraction: Early Film, Its Spectator, and the Avant-Garde". In *Film and Theory: An Anthology*, edited by R. Stam and T. Miller, 229-35. Malden, MA: Blackwell.
Stam, Robert. 2000. "The Question of Realism: Introduction". In *Film and Theory: An Anthology*, edited by R. Stam and T. Miller, 223-28. Malden, MA and Oxford, UK: Blackwell.

Websites consulted

Anonymous. 2004a. "Çakır'ın Cenaze Namazı Kılındı" (Çakır's Funeral Prayer Is Held). *Yeni Şafak* (New Dawn), 17 April. Available online at: http://yenisafak.com.tr/arsiv/2004/nisan/17/gkisa.html.
Anonymous. 2004b. "*Kurtlar Vadisi*'nde Çakır'ı Vuran Cerrahpaşalı Halit, Sokak Ortasında Sille Tokat Dövüldü" (Cerrahpaşalı Halit Who Killed Çakır in *Valley of the Wolves* Was Beaten Badly on the Street). *Habervitrini* (The Window of News), 15 April. Available online at: http://www.habervitrini.com/haber.asp?id=126497
Anonymous. 2005a. "Denktaş *Kurtlar Vadisi*'ne Girdi" (Denktaş Entered the *Valley of the Wolves*). *Sabah* (Morning), 18 February. Available online at: http://arsiv.sabah.com.tr/2005/02/18/siy107.
Anonymous, 2005b. "Polat Alemdar, Abdullah Çatlı Mı?" (Is Polat Alemdar, Abdullah Çatlı?). *haber7com*, 3 November. Available online at: http://www.haber7.com/haber/20051103/Polat-Alemdar-Abdullah-Catli-mi.php.
Anonymous. 2006a. "Gül'den *Kurtlar Vadisi* Notası" (Gül's Memorandum about Valley of the Wolves). *Milliyet* (Nationality), 5 February. Available online at: http://www.milliyet.com.tr/2006/02/05/siyaset/axsiy01.html
Anonymous. 2006b. "Kod Adı Polat" (His Pseudonym Is Polat). *Hürriyet* (Freedom), 25 May. Available online at: http://hurarsiv.hurriyet.com.tr/goster/haber.aspx?id=4469503&tarih=2006-05-25
Anonymous. 2006c. "*Kurtlar Vadisi*'ni Rice'a Sordular" (Rice Questioned about *Valley of the Wolves*). *Sabah* (Morning), 11 March. Available online at: http://arsiv.sabah.com.tr/2006/03/11/dun113.html
Anonymous. 2006d. "Liselilerin Çığlığı" (The Scream of High School Students). *Hürriyet* (Freedom), 22 September. Available online at: http://www.hurriyet.com.tr/gundem/5130419.asp?m=1&gid=112&srid=3428&oid=1.

Anonymous. 2007. "'Valley of the Wolves - Terror' on TV amid
    controversy" *Today's Zaman*. 10 February
    http://www.todayszaman.com/news-102446-valley-of-the-wolves---
    terror-on-tv-amid-controversy.html
Anonymous. 2009a. *"Kurtlar Vadisi'*nde Şampiyonluk İddiası" (The
    Championship Bet in *Valley of the Wolves*). *Hürriyet* (Freedom), 22
    May. Available online at:
    http://arama.hurriyet.com.tr/arsivnews.aspx?id=11705984
Anonymous. 2009b. "Anatomy of a Murderer"
    http://www.todayszaman.com/news-167746-turkey-press-scan.html
Cindemir, Kasim, Hakan Aytaş and Mesut Zeyrek. 2006. "Evet, Filmler
    Önemlidir" (Yes, Films are Important). *Hürriyet* (Freedom), 11
    February. Available online at:
    http://www.hurriyet.com.tr/dunya/3914052.asp?gid=51
Kuseyri, Alaz. 2008. "Polat Alemdar Ergenekon'a Karşı" (Polat Alemdar
    Versus the Ergenekon). *Taraf* (Side), 4 February. Available online at:
    http://www.haber50.com/30038_Polat-Alemdar-Ergenekon-a-
    karsi!.html
Şaşmaz, Necati. 2008. "Kadına Hak Ettiğinden Fazlasını Vermem" (I
    Don't Give Women More Than What They Deserve). Interview by
    Nuriye Akman, *Zaman* (Time) 24 February. Available online at:
    http://www.zaman.com.tr/roportaj_necati-sasmaz-kadina-hak-
    ettiginden-fazlasini-vermem_655997.html
(http://en.wikipedia.org/wiki/Valley_of_the_Wolves)

PART III:

CANONS REDEFINED

CHAPTER EIGHT

THE OLD AND NEW WAYS OF KURDISH FILMMAKING IN TURKEY: POTENTIALS AND RISKS

ÖZGÜR ÇIÇEK

I am staying in France with a special permit to shoot this film [The Wall]. I am allowed to remain in France to launch it. After that, I do not know. I do not want to talk about the future now—Yılmaz Güney, *The Middle East Magazine*, January 1983

From the 1900s until today, Turkey's political problems have mainly revolved around the status of minorities in the Turkish nation-state. After the end of the First World War and with the fall of the Germanic, Austro-Hungarian, Russian and Ottoman Empires, the Jacobin ideal of the nation-state came into prominence among the Turkish revolutionary intelligentsia, out of which the Turkish nation-state was founded. However, the status of minorities—the non-Turkish and non-Muslim ethnic communities—has not been clearly defined, and they have been forced to accept "Turkish identity" over their ethnicity. The largest non-Turkish ethnic minority group in Turkey is the Kurdish community. To this day, they are trying to preserve their ethnic identity and cultural heritage via their ongoing endeavours of taking an active part in state politics, resisting assimilation and resisting censorship; especially within their cinematic representations. Hence, in this essay, I will question the position of Kurdish filmmaking within the realm of cinematic production in Turkey. I will evaluate the existence of Kurdish filmmaking in Turkish cinema referring back to the theoretical framework of national cinema, and lastly by analysing *Yol/The Way* or *The Road* (Güney 1982). I will outline the controversial dynamics within Kurdish filmmaking in Turkey and what kinds of questions these raised, which I will explore in further studies.

The films about Kurdish people in Turkey and the struggles they face have a long traumatic past. For instance, Yılmaz Güney was the first director from Turkey to receive the Golden Palm at the Cannes Festival in 1982 with his film *Yol*. Being a director of Kurdish origin, Güney could only use the Kurdish language in a very restricted way due to politics of censorship of the time. However, films in the Kurdish language can now be screened in movie theatres, and their directors do not face the same obstacles Yılmaz Güney[1] once did. Nevertheless, films about the Kurdish question are not shown in as many theatres as mainstream Turkish films are. However, the change of attitude in governmental politics towards Kurdish art and cinema is somewhat promising. Thus, when we look at the history of Kurdish filmmaking from the 1980s up until today, and study Kurdish filmmakers like Miraz Bezar, Kazım Öz, Müjde Arslan, Özgür Doğan, Orhan Eskisoy and Hüseyin Karabey, we can find ourselves asking the following questions: How is the concept of national cinema defined in Turkey? How can the film industry in Turkey, with both Turkish and Kurdish directors, be analysed from the perspective of national cinema?

Before beginning to examine these questions in the Turkish/Kurdish context, I wish to articulate the theoretical framework of a "national cinema," in particular how this theoretical framework fails to acknowledge minority filmmaking.

Theoretical Framework on National Cinemas

In her article "Framing National Cinemas," Susan Hayward (2000, 91) elaborates on the concept of "national cinema", stating that when cinema is defined as national, it creates a frame for itself. This framing, she notes, tends to

> set the very territory of the nation *and* artifact, and nation *as* an artifact. In other words, they assume one-to-one relationship between "cultural artifact" – "cultural identity" – "nation/national identity" i.e.; the artifact "film" speaks of/for/as the nation.

In this definition, cinema turns into a "nationally bounded cultural artifact," and this creates a set of problems. Hayward (2000) suggests that when cinema becomes national and cultural, it is territorialised and thus, the national and cultural aspect of cinema turns the cinema into a "historical subject". It becomes a historical subject because

---

1. Editor's note: Güney was a prolific actor/director from 1963 onwards. His construction of himself as a legendary figure for the audience has also been studied elsewhere (see Akser 2009).

it stands for the nation—it is a means in which the nation can represent itself to itself (*qua* subject) and to its subjects. This produces a narcissistic, self-reflexive and self-fulfilling view of national cinema, one in which the historical subject/object becomes knowledge of itself and not the subject of knowledge. (Hayward 2000, 92)

Thus, framing a national cinema as a territorialised historical subject would mean an ongoing repetition of national history represented to/as historical subjects.

At this point, Hayward proposes an alternative way of conceptualising national cinemas. Referring to Tom O'Regan's (1996) work on Australian national cinema, Hayward suggests that,

[R]ather than talking about nationalism and national cinema as exclusive terms, we should seek to investigate the way in which society as a national whole is problematized and the kind of nation that has been projected *through* such problematization. In this regard, we can begin to see cinema as an effect of and as affecting that problematization. (2000, 93)

What Hayward rejects is a passive, self-reflexive and self-fulfilling cinematic form that speaks of/for/as the nation, which is a mere repetition of a nation's history. But she suggests a concept of national cinema that problematises the nation "through" an active cinema that affects the nation's problems. In this way, taking Hayward's perspective as a departure point, can representing the minority issues in cinema be a way of problematising the nation? How would this problematisation function in the Turkish and Kurdish cinema contexts?

Andrew Higson's approach to the concept of national cinema follows a different perspective. In his article "The Concept of National Cinema," he suggests that national cinemas are the product of the tension between "home" and "away," "between the identification of the homely and the assumption that it is quite distinct from what happens elsewhere" (Higson 1989, 67). From this perspective, he suggests two sets of national cinema conceptions:

On the one hand, a national cinema seems to look inward, reflecting on the nation itself, on its past, present and future, its cultural heritage, its indigenous traditions, its sense of common identity and continuity. On the other hand, a national cinema seems to look out across its borders, asserting its difference from other national cinemas, proclaiming its sense of otherness. (Higson 1989, 67)

In this respect, Higson's inward-looking notion of national cinema is what Hayward rejects and defines as problematic. His second notion of a national cinema that "looks out across its borders" asserting its difference and otherness to other nations is problematised later by Higson in his article "The Limiting Imagination of National Cinema," published in 1999. He suggests that this formula assumes a national identity or tradition that is already fully formed and fixed in place. Furthermore, it assumes borders to be effective in limiting political, economic and cultural practices. However, he argues that borders are "leaky" and that there is a degree of movement across them, and "it is in this migration, this border crossing that the transnational emerges" (Higson 1999, 67). So, for Higson, framing cinema as national limits the imagination of cinema, because, more than any other art form, cinema moves across and through boundaries. Further, he also underlines how a nation can be dispersed inside and outside of these boundaries.

In the same article "The Limiting Imagination of National Cinema" Higson also refers to Benedict Anderson's classic work *Imagined Communities* (Anderson 1991). Following Anderson's work, he underlines the importance of belonging to a community which is not dependent on a geopolitical space. So, diasporic communities can still share a common sense of belonging. Therefore, a nation can be:

[O]n the one hand community, on the other, diaspora. On the one hand, modern nations exist primarily as imagined communities. On the other, those communities actually consist of highly fragmented and widely dispersed groups of people with as many differences as similarities and with little in the sense of real physical contact with each other. (Higson 1999, 64)

An imagined community actually consists of people that are fragmented and dispersed with various similarities and differences and with little real physical contact with each other. This, as Higson articulates, brings about a "tension between unity and disunity, between home and homelessness" (Higson 1999, 65). Hence, belonging to an imagined community is what generates the sense of home and homelessness. Desire for and/or lack of belonging generates the tension between unity and disunity.

Further in his article Higson questions the effect of cinema in imagining a nation. He criticises the classical theory of imagined communities for being "not always sympathetic to what we might call the contingency or instability of the national. This is precisely because the nationalist project, in Anderson's terms, imagines the nation as limited, with finite and meaningful boundaries" (ibid., 66). Furthermore, he states that this limited conception of the nation is similar to the problem of defining national cinemas. When theorising a national cinema there appears to be a tendency to look at those films that narrate the nation as a finite, limited space which is inhabited by a tightly bound and unified community closed off to any other differing identities than that of the national one. Moreover, Higson notes:

> The "imagined community" argument sometimes seems unable to acknowledge the cultural difference and diversity that invariably mark both the inhabitants of a particular nation-state and the members of more geographically dispersed "national" communities. In this sense, as with more conservative versions of the nationalist project, the experience and acceptance of diversity are closed off. This seems particularly unfortunate as modern communication networks operate on an increasingly transnational basis, and cultural commodities are widely exchanged across national borders. (Higson 1999, 66)

What Higson wants to point out here is the cultural diversities within a geographically dispersed nation. His problems are related to thinking that, first, the nation is defined within borders and second, a national cinema is closed off to any other national identity. His main argument revolves around thinking about a transnational cinema, rather than a fixed and finite national cinema. However, from his perspective, while films cross borders, they still embody an original national identity that is built on cultural diversities. Furthermore, a national cinema should be open to embracing cultural diversities and other national identities. Because the integration of different national and cultural identities enrich the visual culture, the diversities in question then turn into cultural commodities in films.

Taking Andrew Higson's notions of national cinema into consideration, what is the distinction between the dispersed diasporic communities and the minorities of a nation? More importantly, how are we to theorise the cinema of an ethnic minority group that does not have a recognised nation-state and that does not want to merge within another national cinema realm/territory?

Up until now, I have discussed the necessary theoretical framework for analysing the first question I posed: "How can one think of the existence of Kurdish-themed and Kurdish-language films in Turkey as part of Turkish national cinema?" In order to offer more elaboration on this question, I have visited the concept of national cinema through some of Susan Hayward's and Andrew Higson's articles. Hayward argues that a national cinema should problematise the nation, rather than merely being a historical and national representation. However, she does not refer to the issue of minorities as a way of problematising the nation. In the same context, Higson argues that framing cinema as "national" limits cinema because cinema is transnational, in and of itself, rather than being national. Cinema is transnational because the borders of a nation are "leaky" and open to cultural and national diversity. Moreover, cinema, more than any other form of art can cross borders and travel in the circle of international film festivals. Although Higson argues for transnational cinema rather than a national cinema, he still presupposes a national origin for cinema that can become transnational. This argument also forms a valid theoretical approach for Kurdish films in Turkey. It is obvious, therefore, that the presence of Kurdish cinema within the realm of Turkish cinema complicates the definitions of national cinema.

In order to situate minority filmmaking, in particular the case of Kurdish filmmaking in Turkey, in the next part of this paper I will discuss Yılmaz Güney's cinema and how it created a landmark for new Kurdish cinema in Turkey. In this discussion Deleuze and Guattari's theories on minor literature (1986) and Hamid Naficy's work *An Accented Cinema: Exilic and Diasporic Filmmaking* (2001) will be immensely useful in supporting my argument that Kurdish cinema carries the marks of minor literature.

Yılmaz Güney and *Yol* (*The Way*)

Yılmaz Güney was born in 1937 in Adana, a southeastern city of Turkey. His parents were Kurdish; however, he defines himself as an "assimilated Kurd" who was cut off from his roots. He studied law and economics in the big cities of Istanbul and Ankara. However, at the age of twenty-one, he started his career in filmmaking, first as an actor, scriptwriter and assistant, and later as a director. In an interview given to Alfreda Benge just one month before his death in a secret location in Paris, Güney categorises his life story in three stages. Between 1958 and 1961, he took an active part in a minor movement within Turkish cinema, which tried to introduce social-realist subjects to mainstream filmmaking. This new trend was not very powerful and also short-lived. Although they worked hard to create a new mainstream or to intrude upon the mainstream as a form of resistance, they were not very effective. Between 1961 and 1963, he was imprisoned for publishing a communist novel, and when he was released from prison, he decided to combine two things: "first, this tradition of resistance and second, the popular approach to filmmaking" (Benge 1985, 35). He tried a synthesis of two forms: "On the one hand, I addressed myself to the consciousness and expectations of the audience;

on the other hand, I tried to communicate to the audience their own reality" (ibid.). However, he defines the outcome of this synthesis as decadent. Because after he became well-known and created strong bonds with his audience, he went further and introduced storylines which had previously been impossible to deal with. For instance, peasants-migrants that were flowing into cities in search of work, and (as he noted), people who had become *lumpenised* and desperate entered into the storylines of Turkish cinema.

> In other words, people who had become marginalized by our rapidly transforming society. People who had been pushed out became visible. People pushed outside the margins of society and the law. The peasants who became smugglers on the border, in mortal danger to earn a living…people who commit murder out of desperation…what these people actually felt, how they personally lived, entered our cinema. (Benge 1985, 35)

The point that Güney posits therein refers to Kevin Robins and Asu Aksoy's (2000) argument of the encounter between imaginary reality and the embodied reality of Turkish society. Güney's films become the site where the embodied reality of the society intrudes into an imaginary reality in the form of cinema. The result of this encounter, as described by Güney, is decadent. At this point, there emerges another encounter, which is the encounter of the cinematic work with censorship, that is to say, the intervention of state politics. Furthermore, in an interview, Güney notes that censorship limited his cinematic production:

> In all the films I made in Turkey, I have never been able to express a single one of my thoughts in the way I would like to have, let alone a serious matter like the Kurdish question, let alone an important question like that of the working class; even basic questions of justice and injustice which exist in our society, could only be dealt with partially and indirectly. (Benge 1985, 36)

Thus, in Yılmaz Güney's cinema, the nature of censorship motivated a new filmic language that is much more metaphoric, and that uses facial expressions rather than words. The restrictions motivated a narration that deals with social realities on the level of the image and sound rather than on words. Keeping these points in mind, I want to refer to Deleuze and Guattari's book *Kafka: Towards a Minor Literature* (1986) because I believe that the theories they introduce on minor literature are crucial in situating Yılmaz Güney's cinema in Turkey. In the same way that Kafka was a Jew and a writer writing in German in the Austro-Hungarian Empire and then Czechoslovakia, their theories on Kafka's literature can shed light on minority cinema—such as Kurdish cinema produced in Turkey.

Deleuze and Guattari state that the first characteristic of minor literature is that everything in a minor language is political. Minor literature directly refers itself to political interpretation, unlike major literature. Further, they define the characteristics of minor literature and state that:

> Minor literature doesn't come from a minor language; it is rather that which a minority constructs within a major language. But the first characteristic of minor literature in any case is that in its language it is affected with a high coefficient of deterritorialization. In this sense, Kafka marks the impasse that bars access to writing for the Jews of Prague and turns their literature into something impossible—the impossibility of not writing, the impossibility of writing in German, the impossibility of writing otherwise. (Deleuze and Guattari 1986, 16)

When Deleuze and Guattari's first definition of minor literature is taken into account from the perspective of Kurdish cinema produced in Turkey, similar processes of *deterritorialization* and impossibilities are at stake. For example, in the 1980s, Kurdish filmmaking in Turkey was marked by the same impasse that barred access to producing films in Kurdish, and that turned Kurdish cinema into something impossible. At this juncture, there were many impossibilities at stake: the impossibility of writing, speaking and representing Kurdish identity, the impossibility of Kurdish representation in Turkish, the impossibility of Kurdish language films, the impossibility of Kurdish representation otherwise. However, all these impossibilities did not bar Güney from producing films about Kurdish people. In recent Kurdish productions, some of these impossibilities have been lifted by the ongoing resistance of the Kurdish people; yet Kurdish cinema is still affected by *deterritorialization*.

Kurdish is a language of many dialects found in the Kurdish parts of Turkey. Following Deleuze and Guattari's minor literature definition, we need to evaluate Kurdish as a vernacular language from three perspectives: "the degrees of territoriality, *deterritorialization* and *reterritorialization*" (ibid., 25). On this trajectory, films in the Kurdish language are occupying a space within the territoriality of the Kurdish language. They have the agency and the desire of Kurdish *territorialization*. At this point, referring to Kafka's works, Deleuze and Guattari put forward a significant aspect of minor literature, which I argue would also be valid for minority cinema and Kurdish cinema in general. They point out that Kafka does not opt for

a *reterritorialization* through either the Czech language or High German
or with the spoken Yiddish.

> Instead…[h]e will feed himself on abstinence; he will tear out of Prague
> German all the qualities of underdevelopment that it has tried to hide; he
> will make it cry with an extremely rigorous cry…He will push it toward a
> *deterritorialization* that will no longer be saved by culture or by myth, that
> will be an absolute *deterritorialization*…To bring language slowly and
> progressively to a desert. To use syntax in order to cry, to give syntax to
> the cry. (Deleuze and Guattari 1986, 25-26)

In other words, "[w]riting like a dog digging a hole, a rat digging its
burrow. To do that, finding his own point of underdevelopment, his own
patois, his own third world, his own desert" (ibid., 18). What Deleuze and
Guattari argue along these lines is that the definition of minor literature
does not solely mean a literature that is a minor one in the realm of a major
literature. Aside from this, minor literature benefits from the exclusions it
has been put through. It does not cry over its exclusion, it gives syntax to
its cry. From this perspective, in minor literature there is not a desire for
power but rather, as Deleuze and Guattari perfectly express, "it is power
itself that is the desire. Not a desire lack, but a desire as a plenitude,
exercise and functioning" (ibid., 56). Minor literature does not mourn its
deterritorialization, but it will push it through to the end and bring it to an
absolute *deterritorialization*. Here, I want to illustrate these points by
looking at Yılmaz Güney's film *Yol* because I believe that this is the case
that would show what Deleuze and Guattari mean by minor literature that
just like a repressed people's language feeding itself with its lack.

Yol is about five prisoners on the way to their homes. They have been
released on a five-day-leave to visit their families. All of them live in the
eastern part of Turkey, indicating that they have Kurdish origins. The
period of their release takes places during the military coup d'état that took
place in 1980. The government has been overthrown, and Turkey is now
being ruled by the military.

Yılmaz Güney's *Yol* presents not only the lives of five male prisoners,
but also shows the reality of various cities and villages in the southeastern
part of Turkey. The cities are presented much like characters. Each of
them is introduced by an on-screen title when the character and the camera
enters each city. However, Güney does not merely depend on images for
characterising the cities; he also makes the audience hear the soundscape
of the cities in question. The sound of each city or village is crucial in the
characterisation of each place. In Gaziantep, for instance, the sound of the
city is composed of traffic, cars and horns. In Diyarbakır, our attention is

diverted to off-screen sounds of military planes and poor children begging for money. In Fırat-Birecik, the soundtrack is made up of bullets, crying children and the mourning of mothers and wives. In this respect, the audience does not just see the image and hear the dialogue; s/he feels the city and hears the city. The tension of the political climate lies within the soundscape, within the sounds of planes, bullets, cries and mourning. Although Güney does not reveal the Kurdish conflict directly on-screen, he uses alternative ways to indicate the presence of the Kurdish people in Turkey. The *deterritorialization* of the Kurdish people is coded with sound. Hence, he does not use narratives that include mourning; instead, the cinematic language feeds itself with its lack of dialogue and benefits from it by using sound in alternative ways.

In the scenes of Diyarbakır[2] when we focus on the soundtrack, we first hear a song performed by three children. This song is in Turkish; however, it is an arabesque song, arabesque here indicating a kind of music influenced by Arabic culture. Right after that we hear the Kurdish soundtrack music/dialogue. The arabesque music is different from the Turkish folk music that is heard on the screen, but we still see the source of the music, while the Kurdish soundtrack remains off-screen and is non-diegetic. With this music, the image we see is of Ömer[3] and his village with vast fields covered in yellow flowers. Ömer feels very happy; he kneels down and kisses the land. In a flashback, he remembers earlier days when he was riding horses with his brother on this fertile and untouched land.

At this point, I want to refer to Hamid Naficy's book *An Accented Cinema* (2001) and his notion of "Chronotopes of the Imagined Homeland". Naficy defines the cinema of displaced people as accented cinema. The accent comes from the displacement of the filmmakers and their alternative production modes. Within this perspective Naficy also refers to Yılmaz Güney's *Yol*, but before that he introduces Bakhtin's term "Chronotope," which literally means time-space (2001, 152). He notes that the space in accented films is attached special meaning and value. The space in question can be a country, a region, a town, a village or a particular street. No matter what it is or where, the space refers not only to a physical entity, but also to our relations to it and our relationships within it. He further notes that "since space is historically situated, displacement and emplacement have a temporal dimension—often linked to the dates of

---

2. On Diyarbakır, in the original version there is the title Kurdistan and because of this *Yol* was banned in Turkey until 2000, and when it was shown again in theatres the title Kurdistan was erased.

3. Ömer is the one with whom Yılmaz Güney identifies himself most, among the five in *Yol*.

a great homelessness or a grand homecoming" (Naficy 2001, 152). Further, Naficy states that one typical cinematic response to the rupture of displacement is to create a utopian chronotope of the homeland that is uncontaminated by contemporary facts. This is primarily expressed in the homeland's open chronotopes, its nature, landscape and ancient monuments. And this openness and uncontaminated nature of the space is suggested by long shots and long takes that situate the characters within their open spaces. Time in these open spaces is the present time which is experienced retroactively by means of nostalgia and loss. It is as though the experience of the present time in the open space would be incomplete if it is not mediated by memory, nostalgia and loss. The present time of the open space cannot fully be articulated without indicating what it has lost in the past. Thus, the wide shots that situate Ömer in his homeland are accompanied by the flashbacks of the past and with the Kurdish folk music heard in the background. The days he spent with his brother (who has never returned). Those times are gone, but what is left is the space, yet it too has changed.

When Ömer remembers the old days, he smiles and feels happy to be home again. However, his happiness disappears when he hears the sound of guns and bullets coming from his village. When he reaches his village, he finds out that Turkish soldiers are chasing some Kurdish rebels. They have guns, but when the guns are on the screen, the shooting cannot be heard. The sound of shooting is again off-screen. Apart from the sound of the shooting, we hear children crying and dogs barking. So the existence of the soldiers who are creating unrest is represented with sound. Later when the rebels surrender, the cries of the children and the mourning of his wife accompanies the soldiers who are taking the rebels away. Later Ömer learns that his brother is also a rebel and each day his parents fear finding his dead body. Ömer likes one of the girls in his village, but if his brother dies, or if he is already dead, Ömer will have to marry his brother's wife as tradition would not allow him to leave the wife a widow or the children orphans.

Apart from the cities each character visits, the public transportation system is another major element in *Yol*. Each character reaches his destination by a different mode of transportation, such as the train, the ferry, the bus, the minibus or on foot. With each vehicle, Güney presents the eastern people who are on their way to reach their destination. Thus, the crowd of people in each train compartment becomes a texture on which the character in question is not differentiated, but he is as he should be, a part of this texture. The exclusion from this texture takes place when Emine and Mehmet want to have sex in the bathroom, and the episode ends with an attempt by other passengers to lynch them. So, Güney presents a society that cannot tolerate any immoral behaviour and moreover, a society that becomes an agent of morality. This refers to the law of the tradition/patriarchy, which is stronger than the law of the state. The eastern people judge their issues on their own; the law of tradition comes before the law of the government. The state and the law cannot penetrate into this private space. Hence Güney not only employs a critical approach to the Turkish army and Turkish rule, but he also criticises the inner dynamics of Kurdish society, the rule of tradition and patriarchy. He is not just problematising the non-Kurdish realm, but there is also a critical eye on the Kurdish population, tradition and culture. However, the rule of tradition in the eastern part of Turkey underlines the fact that the eastern region has been left outside the system of law. Hence, as Naficy suggests, in *Yol* the characters are not only imprisoned in jail; their imprisonment is not particular to prison, they are also imprisoned in their homeland. They are imprisoned by the military forces, by the state apparatuses and by tradition.

Yılmaz Güney and his films mark the emergence of a cinema that is problematising the concept of nation. It is not mourning the *deterritorialization* of the Kurdish realm but adding the *deterritorialization* of the Kurdish language to its cinematic language and finding ways to use it in sound and in other cinematic tools. At this point, I must again refer to Deleuze and Guattari. At the end of the chapter "What is Minor Literature?" they argue that:

> [t]here is nothing that is major or revolutionary except the minor...How many styles or genres or literary movements, even very small ones, have only one single dream: to assume a major function in language, to offer themselves as a state language, an official language. Create the opposite dream: know how to create a becoming minor". (Deleuze and Guattari 1986, 27)

Here Deleuze and Guattari question the will to be major, but they suggest that this dream should be reversed to create "a becoming minor". The becoming minor stands for the nature of minor literature that is always in search of producing meaning and challenging its limited ways of representation. Considering these points, I argue that Kurdish cinema carries the marks of "minor literature" with its narrative dealing with different forms of censorship throughout the history of its production. Yet, the filmmakers never give up and, on the contrary, in fact, they benefit from that censorship as they continuously improve on the style and ways of narration which circumvent that censorship.

From this article, new questions arose about which I will continue to work on in further papers. I end this article on these following questions I would like to raise about the new Kurdish cinema produced in Turkey. Can there be another path for Kurdish cinema other than becoming a national cinema or a major cinema in the context of Deleuze and Guattari's formulations? Is there a risk that Kurdish cinema will end up in an ongoing process of *reterritorialization* if it tries to become major or national in a cinematic context? Following the route that leads to becoming major, is there a risk of losing authenticity? How do national cinema theories need to be re-theorised or re-articulated when the case of Kurdish cinema or minority cinema is considered?

Works Cited

Akser, Murat. 2009. "Yılmaz Güney's Beautiful Losers: Idiom and Performance in Turkish Political Film". In *Cinema and Politics: Turkish Cinema and the New Europe*, edited by Deniz Bayrakdar, 142-153. Newcastle-upon-Tyne: Cambridge Scholars Publishing.

Anderson, Benedict. 1991. *Imagined Communities: Reflections on the Origin and Spread of Nationalism*. London: Verso.

Benge, Alfreda. 1985. "Güney, Turkey and the West: An Interview". *Race and Class* 26 (3): 31–46.

Deleuze, Gilles and Felix Guattari. 1986. *Kafka: Toward a Minor Literature*. Minneapolis, MN: University of Minnesota Press.

Hayward, Susan. 2000. "Framing National Cinemas." In *Cinema and Nation*, edited by Mette Hjört and Scott Mackenzie, 88-102. London: Routledge.

Higson, Andrew. 1989. "The Concept of National Cinema". *Screen* 30(4): 36-47.

—. 2000. "The Limiting Imagination of National Cinema." In *Cinema and Nation*, edited by Mette Hjört and Scott Mackenzie, .63-74. London: Routledge.

Naficy, Hamid. 2001. *An Accented Cinema: Exilic and Diasporic Filmmaking*. Princeton, NJ: Princeton University Press.

Robins, Kevin and Asu Aksoy. 2000. "DEEP NATION: The national question and Turkish cinema culture" In *Cinema and Nation*, edited by Mette Hjört and Scott Mackenzie, 203-221. London: Routledge.

Yol (The Way). 1982. Dir. Yılmaz Güney. DVD. Imaj 2000.

CHAPTER NINE

NEW DOCUMENTARY, NEW CINEMA AND "NEW MEDIA"

TUNCAY YÜCE

My academic work began to evolve in the direction of documentary film towards the end of studying for my Bachelor degree in the early 1990s. Since then, documentary as a mode of cinematic practice has been the approach I have used in almost all my work. My work, either applied or theoretical, has involved critical evalution within the scope of film studies, or more generally, in media studies. One of the outcomes arising from these assessments regards the simulation theory of Jean Baudrillard, in particular, and consists of the fact that all the considerations in the aforementioned scope gradually evolved into two categories of assessing art: "truth" and "realism" (Yüce 2001). The discussion in Yüce (2001) on the specific examples of *The Truman Show* (Peter Weir, 1998) and *The Matrix* (Andy Wachowski, Lana Wachowski, 1999) was on trying to define the changing trends in film studies. Eventually, the depictions revealed through these films happened to be the first examples of use of digital cinema in the 2000s.

Video art of the 1960s and its extensions today have become what we consider the applications of "new media". It can be said that, over the years, film art has headed towards a definite direction, which had not been predicted by the "death of cinema" visions of Paul Schrader, Peter Greenaway, and others. In this regard, fiction films such as *The Matrix* (1999) and *The Truman Show* (1998) and non-fiction films such as the *Qatsi* trilogy (1983-2002), *Baraka* (1992) and *Samsara* (2011) are some good examples of the new direction. The subject of *The Matrix* and the way it was presented in the film, and the media concepts introduced by *The Truman Show* emphasise the level of narrative illusion cinema has reached. Furthermore, films in Turkish cinema such as *Mayıs Sıkıntısı/Clouds of May* (Nuri Bilge Ceylan, 1999), *Oyun/The Play* (Pelin Esmer, 2005), *İki Dil Bir Bavul/On The Way to School* (Orhan Eskiköy and Özgür Doğan, 2009) indicate the new direction of cinema to be docu-fiction: both fiction and non-fiction at the same time.

I do not want to argue that "the art of cinema is over". Rather, what I wish to say is that the art of cinema does not fit into its "shell" anymore with its production style and methods. I will address this issue in the following part of the article by considering Arthur C. Danto's "the end of art" discourse.

In the early periods of cinema, techniques that cinema borrowed from other branches of art were thoroughly studied. This was true at least until the 1920s. During the 1920s, cinema started to shape its own features with the contribution of sound. However, in the last decades, cinema has reached a more "specific" point in its "search" for its own style. The phenomena that I will point to here are those artistic or aesthetic pursuits constructed by adding prefixes such as "post-" or "neo-". Works that are produced in this context can in general be evaluated as efforts of finding a way of creating art. At this point in time, the assembly of "cultural objects" (Manovich 2001) through convergence, especially in computer and communication technologies, may reveal some innovative developments and/or complexities depending on the viewpoint taken.

Of course, each approach to film studies creates its own specific methodology in terms of its own content. This is, of course, very natural. However, what it is argued here is that fictional narratives in popular cinema are also approaching a limit. In other terms, it seems that films are now in a recycle mode; they are either in the realm of some kind of remake, or they are forcing the boundaries of the means of expression of cinematic form to tell a new story. Perhaps these assertions are not valid for non-fiction films, especially for documentaries. This is because the "documentary" filmmaking is a cinematic approach, as remarked by Bill Nichols, who claims that "a good documentary stimulates discussion of its subject, not itself" (Nichols 1991, x).

Even if they are constructed by using the "documentation" function of non-fiction cinema, production styles formed by "new media" within contemporary artistic production circles are carried through all types of media available today. Perhaps these are the "cultural objects" of our contemporary artistic productions that combine the documentary approach and the facilities of "new media". Time will question the validity of this argument. John Corner (2001) describes this tendency as a "post-documentary" phase and further states: "the term *documentary* is always safer when used as an adjective rather than a noun, although its noun usage is, of course, a form of abbreviation, championed by the cinema pioneers and established through sheer familiarity" (258). Corner (2001, 267) also states that:

> Neither postmodern skepticism nor the techniques of digital manipulation present documentary with its biggest future challenge. This will undoubtedly come from the requirement to reorient and refashion itself in an audiovisual culture where the dynamics of diversion and the aesthetics of performance dominate a greatly expanded range of popular images of the real.

Video art that began by artists' innovative use of a Sony Portapak camera during the 1970s\ without any doubt, as a new approach to the means of expression in cinema. However, in a short time, this new artistic production also developed its own language.[1] So much so that video has become one of the most sought-after media within contemporary art circles. Here, I need to make mention of "motion pictures" overflowing from movie theatres into art galleries:

> Now that there are no insurmountable technical limits, now that we can make our artistic medium do everything we want; we need to understand the moral limits much better than we have before. (Monaco 2001, 512)

Monaco (2001) continues his portrayal of a "digital revolution" as follows: "Interestingly, the traditional realists seem to gain more from the new technology than the fantasists" (513). These claims can be proven in a way by looking at Youtube's most "clicked" videos, generally the ones that are classified as documentaries.

> At one extreme lies "fully immersive" virtual reality, which attempts a full range of sensory impression, including three-dimensional video, full-range audio, and touch. At the other end of the scale we find basic, yet elegant, applications that simply allow us to control our point of view of standard images (ibid.)

"Hyper-real" images on the one hand and "standard images" on the other: most probably this comparison might be one of the most long-standing contributions in art analysis seen in recent years.

Bill Nichols states that realism in documentary cinema prepares this analysis by gathering "objective representations" of the "historical world"

---

1. In the 1950s artists like John Cage and later in the 1960s the Fluxus Movement were precursors to such developments (editor's note).

and "rhetorical overtness": "Documentary realism is not only a style but also a professional code, an ethic and a ritual" (Nichols 1991, 166-167). Documentary cinema uses the same means of expression as cinematic art. The technical modes of study used in films are relevant for both types of production, fiction and documentary. Both use elements of cinematic language, i.e. shots, editing, audio, and so on. However, in documentary cinema some elements such as script, decor, costume, acting, mise-en-scène, to name but a few, leave their place to real events and actual people in the world.

Cinema changes itself by using various technological means. These changes provide many opportunities in choosing a subject; realistic, fantastic, historical etc. Technological changes within contemporary art-making allow, depending on one's point of view, either some new possibilities for expression or some problematic concerns within documentary cinema. Looking at the possibilities of new expression, these technological developments in online editing, digital recording and exhibition give everyone a chance to tell their story. On the other hand, the increasing availability of the means of production can lead to confusion on the side of the filmmaker as to what to do. If we trust in the deep-rooted tradition of documentary film, I believe the outcome that arises is immaterial in respect to how it is limited by the artistic production. What really matters is the work itself. For instance, lately there have been discussions in Turkish cinema regarding the controversy surrounding the categorisation of certain feature films—are they fiction or non-fiction? These films include *Oyun/The Play* (Pelin Esmer, 2005) and *İki Dil Bir Bavul/On the Way to School* (Orhan Eskiköy and Özgür Doğan, 2009). What I would like to discuss via these examples is the difference between fiction and non-fiction films, as well as the situations in which these differences are significant or not. If we are to discuss art, cinema and documentary cinema, we should, first of all, consider interactions among them as well as the factors surrounding today's art. These considerations should, I believe, be made within conventional structures of the field. I believe, therefore, that qualifications through the prefixes such as "post-" and "neo-" will help us better understand the meanings of the prefixes. I also believe that the form that "new media" creates along with the content that the deep-rooted tradition of documentary cinema has supplied, gives us new hope for an abundance of creativity within contemporary art.

When we look at the phenomena of "new media" more closely, we immediately see that "new media" is composed of "cultural objects that are made and distributed by computer technology such as CD-ROMs, DVDs, virtual reality, computer multimedia, the internet, etc." (Manovich

2001, 37). The cultural objects described here by Manovich are, of course, not the ones that were described in James Luna's 1987 performance at San Diego Balboa Park Civilization Museum, where Luna presented himself "as a cultural object in a museum narrating the civilization adventure of humanity" (Antmen 2009, 294). According to Manovich (2001, 35), cultural objects that use computer technology during production but not in the distribution phase, such as magazines, books, television shows, and motion pictures, are not "new media". Following this short definition, I believe that when it comes to "motion pictures" in this huge arena, documentary cinema is the most exciting field of study. One reason for this is that contemporary image-making technology gives everyone the ability to create his or her own style, just like *cinema vérité* and *direct cinema* did during the 1950s and the 1960s by the easy-to-use and portable equipment available to filmmakers. One should not forget the works themselves produced within this cultural environment. Indeed, it is important how, why, and by whom these works were created.

In conversations about cinema, some films that were made with technical limitations are always later mentioned with regrets such as 'if I had made it today, I would have..'. It was the same with Stanley Kubrick's *Artificial Intelligence*" (Steven Spielberg 2001). According to Kubrick, he postponed making this film because of the technical limitations, and it was Spielberg who was lucky enough to remake it years later. In light of this, does new cinema lead to "remakes"? It also seems that in these "remakes" we are faced with an entirely different "new".

Artistic forms that are made using digital technology can be classified as follows: "image making, sculpture, installation and virtual reality, performance, music and art of sound, animation and video, software and video/computer game art, net art" (Wands 2006, 14). Here it is necessary to mention the artists and institutions that are important in the history of the "digital arts" which would eventually lead to "new media": Ben Laposky and Edward Varese in the 1950s; Billy Klüver, Andy Warhol, Robert Rauschenberg, Robert Whitman and John Cage during the 1960s; SIGGRAPH which was established in 1973; institutional support given to artists by Ars Electronica in 1979; artists focused on telecommunications and animation at the MIT Media Lab under the leadership of Nicholas Negroponte in the 1980s; the internet (speeding up in the middle of the 1990s) as well as interactive art taking advantage of digital technology today. Digital art received attention through museum exhibitions such as "010101: Art in the Technology Age" at San Francisco Modern Art Museum in 2001. This interaction between digital technology and museums is continually increasing (Wands 2006).

Art has chosen technology as a theme not as a tool in the digital culture
(Kimmelman 2001, 2). Compared to twenty years ago when the
technological tools of today's cinema were as yet unavailable, it is very
likely that one cannot totally understand the workflow of the contemporary
filmmaking production process. This is because of the changing styles of
production in film, such as "digital filmmaking"; this is the case in other
branches of art. In short, technology gives us an opportunity for artistic
production, and this causes new styles of expression to come about. What
other new developments these may bring to the field of art will be
understood in time. Kuspit (2004, 163) in this regard argues that

> art in fact seems to exist in the shadow of science and technology, which
> are worshipped more than it ever thought of being. Indeed, the ripest fruits
> of art seem like sour grapes compared to the ripest fruits of science and
> technology.

David Lynch created new possibilities of innovation in television with
his particular form of narration. Lynch did not want to return to television
after making the *Twin Peaks* series (1990-91). He also stated that he
expected an integration of the internet with television that would provide
an environment with more freedom. Time will prove whether such
predictions about cultural objects provided by digital culture will come to
be true as in Joseph Beuys' famous quote: "everyone is an artist". This
quote here is not a prediction but a statement as to how new media ensures
that everyone can become an artist, or the path to being seen or recognised
as one is now more open.

Art has been struggling with the debate of "stagnation and ending" for
a while (from the 1960s to the present day, according to Arthur C. Danto).
This point of view returns to almost the same data that was originally
presented and is made visible through various media. If we return to
Danto's ideas, the work of Vitaly Komar and Alexander Melamid
presented a series of paintings in New York's art world titled America's
Most Wanted and America's Least Wanted which were exhibited in New
York at the Alternative Museum under the title "People's Choice." In
1994. These were paintings that make reference to the history of art.
However, his comments continue as follows: "As a painting it has no place
in the art world. What does have a place in the art world is the
performance piece by Komar and Melamid which consists in the opinion
poll, the painting, the publicity, etc." (Danto 1997, 216).

If we combine Danto's thoughts together with those of John Corner,
we see that there is a point of intersection where different applications
within two different art branches (namely, painting and cinema) meet. Can

an artist who finds an opportunity to apply a different technique make new statements in art? We must wait and see.

Works Cited

Antmen, Ahu. 2008. *20.Yüzyılda Batı Sanatında Akımlar* (20th Century Art Movements). İstanbul: Sel Yayıncılık.
Corner, John. 2002. "Performing the Real: Documentary Diversions". *Television New Media* 3 (3): 255–269.
Danto, Arthur C. 1997. *After the End of Art*. Princeton, NJ: Princeton University Press.
Kimmelman, Michael. 2001. "Creativity, Digitally Remastered" *The New York Times*, March 23.
http://www.nytimes.com/2001/03/23/arts/art-review-creativity-digitally-remastered.html?pagewanted=all&src=pm
Kuspit, Donald. 2004. *The End of Art*. Cambridge: Cambridge University Press.
Manovich, Lev. 2001. *The Language of New Media*. Cambridge, MA: MIT Press.
Monaco, James. 2009. *How to Read a Film: Movies, Media, and Beyond: The World of Movies, Media, Multimedia: Language, History, Theory*. New York: Oxford University Press.
Nichols, Bill. 1991. *Representing Reality: Issues and Concepts in Documentary*. Bloomington: Indiana University Press.
Rush, Michael. 2005. *New Media in Art*. London: Thames and Hudson.
Spence, Louise and Vinicius Navarro. 2011. *Crafting Truth: Documentary Form and Meaning*. New Jersey: Rutgers University Press.
Wands, Bruce. 2007. *Art of the Digital Age*. London: Thames and Hudson.
Yüce, Ayşe and Tuncay Yüce. 2011. "Sanatsal Etkinlikler İçerisinde 'Yeni Medya' Olgusu" (New Media Phenomena within Arts Activities). *Sanat Yazıları Dergisi* 19: 81-93.
Yüce, Tuncay. 2001. Belgesel Sinemanın Gerçekçilik Anlayışı ve Türkiye'deki Örnekleri (The Idea of Reality in Documentary Cinema and Cases from Turkey), Yayınlanmamış Doktora Tezi, Dokuz Eylül Üniversitesi Sosyal Bilimler Enstitüsü/Institute of Social Sciences, İzmir.

PART IV:

NEW WAYS OF SEEING

CHAPTER TEN

WHY DO FILMS END BY THE SEA?
LAST SCENES IN CONTEMPORARY
GERMAN/TURKISH CINEMA

DENIZ BAYRAKDAR

"Before ending his film my father looked at the sea"
—D.B. (1929-2013)

Introduction

In my article titled "Remembering the Film with its Reality," I
discussed how Fatih Akın brought his character Nejad to a beach on the
Black Sea Coast and in doing so expanded Europe's borders to the Black
Sea via an imaginatively filmic link within his film *Auf der anderen Seite*
(*The Edge of Heaven/Yaşamın Kıyısında*, 2007) (Bayrakdar 2009, 125).
The German title of the film means "on the other side," while the English
title directly refers to heaven. The question I would like to pose is this:
Why does Fatih Akın end his film "auf der anderen Seite" or at "the edge
of heaven"? My observations are based on the final scenes of several films
in contemporary Turkish cinema as well as offFatih Akın's German-Turkish
film.

At the end of *The Edge of Heaven*, Nejad finalises his filmic journey at
the Black Sea Coast. The narrative line begins with Nejad's story in
Germany where he is a professor of German. He then changes his life by
becoming the owner of a German-language bookstore in Istanbul. At the
very end, he leaves all his identities behind and is depicted staring into the
sea just as the son of Ali, a first-generation immigrant worker
(*Gastarbeiter*). The film begins at a gas station, which comes a little bit
before this scene, and follows a filmic circle that is, in fact, a film-long
flashback. We have almost forgotten about the first scene that we are
brought back to at the end of the movie. It is in this way that the director
leaves the film on the other side of the sea/heaven. I would like to inquire

into the moment in which we look to the sea as a kind of contemplation that can be defined as an "oceanic feeling," a feeling embedded in several classic films' endings and specifically those in the auteur films of the 2000s in Turkey.

From the *Heimat* of National Cinema
to the *Rootlands of Transnational Cinemas*

The article which first attracted me to this subject was Alexandra Ludewig's "Heimat, City and Frontier in German National Cinema" (2001). In 2009, in the European Cinema course I taught at Kadir Has University, my students and I watched Andreas Dresen's film *Nachtgestalten* (1999), and I highlighted a statement by Ludewig about the transition from the *Heimat* genre to that of contemporary German cinema. Ludewig points out that *Nachtgestalten* comes to an end at the Baltic Sea (2001, 181), and she mentions previous German films which come to an end in the Alps and other well-known *Heimat* settings. She discusses the position of the Baltic Sea in contemporary Germany: it used to be a summer resort but now has become more industrialised and polluted, as a sea standing for "loss" and "disappearance of desire" and the new and old value system throughout the region. She also mentions the importance of the "oceanic feeling" in this "final" scene as a key point (ibid., 183).

The first time I read this article, I recalled the last scene of Fatih Akın's film *The Edge of Heaven*. The directors whom Alexandra Ludewig mentioned were late-period German directors and the end point they often reached was the Baltic Sea. One of the late-period directors, German-Turkish director Fatih Akın, also utilises a final scene in which Nejad journeys to the Black Sea Coast, and is ultimately left there by the director.

Black Sea: The Edge of Life/On the Other Side/
The Edge of Heaven

While *The Edge of Heaven* does not have a clear location, in the first scene from the film, we learn that the song played while Nejad was paying the bill in the gas station was written by Kazım Koyuncu,[1] a "Laz"[2]

---

1. Deniz Göktürk's article " World Cinema Goes Digital: Looking at Europe from the Other Shore" (2012) examines in detail Kazım Koyuncu and his importance in the film *The Edge of Heaven*.
2. "Laz" refers to a certain population living along the Black Sea Coast and their language.

musician from the Black Sea Coast. Kazım Koyuncu's style is a synthesis of the Black Sea Coast's Laz language and rock music. The sound of the song is meant to jog our memories, and it also functions as a meta-narrative reminding us of Kazım Koyuncu, who died from lung cancer at an early age. This meta-narrative contributes to Fatih Akın's auteurly oeuvre at the beginning of the film in creating Nejad's environment. In the second layer of the meta-narrative, we are reminded of the Chernobyl disaster which polluted the Black Sea Coast and the natural surroundings in 1986.

As we think of the fact that Nejad is there to wait for his father, we can feel that he has completed the circle and integrates the past he left behind by turning back to where the film begins. With this ending, the generations of both father and son unable to integrate social life between Germany and Turkey reach a level of contemplation; although we don't see the father anymore. The film begins in a relaxed way and ends with a sense of peace, but between these two coordinates Fatih Akın involves his characters in an endless and intermingled struggle between countries and generations. Reaching the end means becoming freed from feelings of degradation (Bayrakdar 2009, 13) and finding rest at the sea, a common mode of enlightenment for Fatih Akın, Nejad and the audience within the "oceanic feeling".

The research literature written on this emotion is comprehensive and ranges from theology and philosophy to psychoanalysis. In his article "Oceanic Feeling Revisited" (1998), William Parsons examines debates on the "oceanic feeling" through French author and reviewer Romain Rolland's correspondence with Freud (Rolland in Doré and Prévost 1990, 86-88). Parsons talks about psychoanalysis, religion, faith, and Eastern philosophy, and argues that the "oceanic feeling" includes all of us and conveys all the experiences that a person experiences: it has an essence indicating a whole that it is part of (Parsons 1998, 508).

Romain Rolland thinks that the true source of religion is a feeling that he refers to as an "oceanic feeling" and by sending a letter to Freud he suggests the latter take up research on the issue. Freud responds to Rolland's request, stating that he perceives the oceanic feeling as the moment of the primary narcissistic union between mother and infant (ibid., 501). Like Jung, Rolland was captivated by Eastern philosophy and its cultural sources.

According to Parsons, the "oceanic feeling" is eternity (ibid., 503). In his letter, Rolland limits it with respect to *The Future of An Illusion* by Freud. For him, the ocean is not the opposite of the intellect, but rather he argues that it could be treated as the equivalent to a desire for death (Freud

1927 in Strachey 1961, 23). It is completely independent of the dynamic, vital, creative, socially adaptable, and institutionalised aspects of religion's many accruements. In brief, the oceanic feeling exists in a meaningful manner different from ordinary religious experience; the "oceanic feeling" is the genesis of all the religions (Parsons 1998, 504).

Rolland comes to understand a certain point about the "oceanic feeling" through the concepts of the *natura naturans* and *natura naturant* he encountered while reading Spinoza (ibid., 508). Actually, this feeling brings about enlightenment for Rolland because it makes people think that everything is a reflection of God, and God is nature itself (ibid.).

If we think of Freud's claim that, in the primary narcissistic period, a child unifies himself/herself with the mother and sees her as bigger than he/she really is, we can see the relevance of the "oceanic feeling" as a gaze directed towards the sea, to which the gazer belongs and is destined to go. This is the point where life and death come together. Death is embedded in life: the "oceanic feeling" is a revelation beyond religion or the sum of religions and beliefs.

The "Oceanic Feeling" in the New Cinema of Turkey

Many films in Turkish cinema end with a character's gaze upon the sea. Ferzan Özpetek's *Hamam/Steam Bath* (1997); Nuri Bilge Ceylan's *Uzak/Distant* (2002), *İklimler/Climates* (2006), *Üç Maymun/Three Monkeys* (2008), Abdullah Oğuz's *Mutluluk/Bliss* (2007), Fatih Akın's *Im Juli* (2000) and *Auf der anderen Seite/The Edge of Heaven* (2007) are only a few examples of films ending at the seaside. This prompted me to ask: Why do so many films end at the seaside, especially films from the 2000s in Turkey? Is it something characteristic to our cinema or is it a wave that follows a geographical pattern? I began to note all the films that end at the sea with the aim of investigating these questions. From Europe to Hollywood and Far Eastern films, the sea has had an important symbolic role. Celluloid film with its translucent, opaque quality and the screen with its naked modus actually duplicate the feeling of looking at the sea for audiences. On the other hand, the sea represents a path for the director during the creation of a film; and it creates the oceanic feeling for viewers, bringing the two together at the same place and time on the horizon line and the seaside.

In François Truffaut's *Les Quatre Cents Coup* (1959), Antoine Doinel, played by Jean-Pierre Léaud as Truffaut's alter ego, finds himself at the sea at the end of the film. Antoine Doinel, the rebellious boy who escapes from reformatory school and experiences the beginning states of puberty after being rejected by his mother forever, runs away and reaches the sea. We are empathising with him at the moment of this liberation when he leaves his old life behind. His body cries out loud, although without a voice: "Let it be!" Antoine turns his back to the camera and looks at the audience for a moment, and Truffaut freezes this last moment, the very end and the death of the film. We see in his eyes the uncertainty of the very end. Antoine Doinel/Truffaut rejects at the very last moment the contemplation of the "oceanic feeling" and brings us to the juncture of death/life and then traps us there.

A half-century later in 2008, the German director Doris Dörrie made her film *Kirschblüten–Hanami*[3] (2008) using a genealogical structure interwoven with a German family melodrama in the 2000s and situates the film between Berlin and Tokyo. Trudi and Rudi are stereotypical parents with children living in Berlin; they have a lesbian daughter, a son who is a yuppie businessman and their youngest child lives in Tokyo. Trudi and her husband's lives are dedicated by work and daily tasks. This means that Rudi goes into the office the same way by train, eats the same kind of sandwich every day, and walks the same way home. The routine is shattered by the news that Rudi, the husband, will die soon. Trudi has to keep this secret to herself and continues her "self-freeing attempts" and tries to project them onto her husband. First, they visit their children in Berlin. The generation gap cannot be overcome; however, and they cannot live in the city and become confused. Their next attempt is the Baltic Sea, at a hotel at the seaside. Even in the interior scenes Doris Dörrie offers moments of redemption via tableaus of the sea.

Trudi, who is afraid of losing her husband, makes another attempt with a *Butoh* dance—"dancing with one's own shadow". To put the body in another soul, she undresses her skin and puts on a new ski. In the last dance, Trudi is able to succeed with her husband, and then she fades away unexpectedly. She cannot overcome the "Angst" at losing her beloved husband and dies. Rudi takes over his wife's "attempts" at freeing herself, and tries to fulfil the wishes of his wife, so he travels to their youngest son who lives in Tokyo. Soon, he discovers the cherry blossoms and Yu, the young girl who also transcends life through the *Butoh* dance, and tries to reach her mother's soul through a pink telephone. Rudi, neglected by his busy son, starts a strange relationship with Yu. As she tries to visualise their names, Rudi and Yu make a step towards the "oceanic feeling". It is a bond between father/husband, daughter/beloved, and "me and you" (*ich und du*). "*Ich und Du*" according to Buber's definition is about the duality

---

3. Thanks to Deniz Göktürk for introducing *Kirschblüten* to me.

of things and without this "I" we cannot exist.

> ...the man's world is double-layered according to his acts. The man's attitude is double-layered according to the double-layered basic words he speaks. The basic words are not single words but word couples. The one basic word couple is me-you. The other word couple is me. (Buber 1983, 3)[4]

Rudi and Yu—the old and the young—leave the city and make their way to Fujiyama. This was Trudi's imaginative *Heimat*, her motherland, whereas Germany was her *Vaterland*.

There they find Fujiyama veiling itself beyond the clouds, the guide says that the mountain is "shy". One morning Yu realises that Rudi is gone, but she knows where to find him. Rudi lays on the shores of the lake and Fujiyama is reflected in its foggy heights. A *nature mort* of a "picturesque" scene shifts the sad ending into a bright release for Yu and supposedly for Rudi as well wearing a kimono, and his beloved Trudi's blue knitted jacket and pearl necklace.

Doris Dörrie changes the sublime atmosphere in Fujiyama to a scene in a crematorium. The melancholy that Trudi and Rudi have transferred to the audience is covered up as their young son tries to put the rest of his father's bones into a bowl. He is not able to use the chopsticks to remove the bones, so Yu does it for him instead. From Germany to Japan, Dörrie draws a line in search of the "oceanic feeling".

Fatih Akın draws the imaginative line of genealogical evolution in time and space and brings Nejad, a third-generation German-Turk, to the Black Sea Coast. In a similar way, Doris Dörrie has Trudi and Rudi go to the Baltic Sea Coast, and then, after the death of Trudi, Dörrie brings Rudi to the hillsides of Fujiyama following the shadow of his wife.

America was the idealised "stepfather" for the directors of the New German Cinema, and Japan is one of the contemporary transnational countries[5] that has opened horizons along this genealogical chain; furthermore, Turkey can be seen as the root/rotational homeland for the generations that go back and forth, just as Dörrie's leading characters are the German couple Trudi and Rudi from the generation of World War II. For Trudi and Rudi, Tokyo is the *Sehnsucht* (*sehen und suchen* = to see

---

4. My translation: Buber uses the word *Zwiefalt* which does not exist in English. I translated the word as double-layered. It can also be thought of as double-fold.

5. Siberia is one of these destinations in Ralf Huettner's film *Ausgerechnet Sibirien* (2012). The film follows the pattern of the 1950s *Heimat* and *Fernfeh* (wanderlust; longing for distant lands) films. The man who is sick of civilisation will be cured in the wildness (Banaski (2012) in *Spiegel Online*).

and search) meaning both longing and nostalgia (Bayrakdar 2004, 18). She cures the void through the *Butoh* dance, and Rudi carries this void contemplating the lake near Fujiyama. Rudi's void is deeply related with the *Sehnsucht nach dem Sohn* (longing for the son) in Tokyo. She shifts her homeland from Germany to Japan.

According to Parsons, Rolland's concepts of the "Ocean of Being" and "infinite waves" can be traced back to Leibnitz by referring to Rolland's journal, and while at the Ecole Normale he noted:

> "Movement is attributed to the sea and, opposed to the immobile mountain..." (1956 in Parsons 1998, 510)

These words are almost audible in Dörrie's last scene. We see Rudi's body lying next to the lake covered by the shadow of Fujiyama in the background. The future and past melt together in this eternal present time and unite in the "oceanic feeling" (ibid. 1956 in Parsons 1998, 509).

Doris Dörrie converts the scenery of the Alps in the *Heimat* genre by former German directors by giving the "oceanic feeling" at the Baltic Sea. So, the final destination for Dörrie is the point where Fujiyama and the lake meet, instead of at the Baltic Sea.

In *Kirschblüten-Hanami* the scenic almanacs on the walls around the houses that convey the smell of death blend with the paintings from the walls of spiritless *Gasthofs*. When the complexity of Berlin and the Tokyo metropolis come together with the German town's silence, the shadow dance *Butoh*, which feels like an allusion, is truly understood. As "you and me," "woman and man," and "child and mother" are disrobed and meet in eternal ecstasy, the viewer obtains relief in the place he/she is, and we join the party, as well.

Dörrie gives Rudi the chance to experience a moment of "mystical ecstasy"[6] (Freud 1927), *nirvana*. And Fatih Akın brings Nejad from Hamburg to the Black Sea, his home country, in the same way he titled his early documentary film *Denk ich an Deutschland—Wir haben vergessen zurückzukehren* (*We forgot to return*, 2001) which is about him waiting for his father to come back.

The Baltic Sea as a victim of environmental disaster and industrialisation is translated by Fatih Akın into the Black Sea. The punk outsiders at the end of the *Nachtgestalten* by Andreas Dresen end up at the Baltic Sea and set the stolen car on fire. They escape from the city of Berlin and end up

---

6. Parsons points out that "Rolland characterized the moment of mystical ecstasy in terms of 'nirvana' and refers to the 'illusion' of individuality in terms of 'maya,' facts that clearly demonstrate an Eastern influence" (1998, 511).

there. In *Im Juli*, Fatih Akın brings a couple together, after a long journey from Germany, at the Bosphorus in Ortakoy, Istanbul. In *The Edge of Heaven* Fatih Akın's Nejad leaves Germany and Istanbul behind and ends up at the Black Sea Coast.

Nuri Bilge Ceylan's characters look at the sea where the grey border shades the sun, and the light's source is no longer seen. In *Uzak* (*Distant*, 2002), the character sits with his back turned to us at the seaside, and looks at the sea. The camera shows his face and then the silhouette of old Istanbul, and as we look at his face we continue to hear the sound of the sea. Especially, in the film *Üç Maymun* (Nuri Bilge Ceylan, *Three Monkeys*, 2008) Istanbul is transformed into a dystopian city, and the Marmara Sea is an uncanny (*unheimlich*, not belonging to a home), cold and depressing background against which the family tragedy reflects its death-drive. There is no more desire, no hope for "mystical ecstasy" at the Marmara Sea in Istanbul, a city of over seventeen million inhabitants and growing as more and more migrants from the eastern parts of Turkey move there; it is a place where people have to rapidly transform themselves and their values. The endings at the sea of Turkish films in the 2000s differ from other German and the German-Turkish films. In 2000s, Turkish cinema looking at the sea transcends "the oceanic feeling" and becomes a nihilistic moment in the "void".

Conclusion

As this article has discussed, the Black Sea has a similar significance to that of Alexandra Ludewig's Baltic Sea. Fatih Akın's *rootland* is a translated version or the evolving story of his new *Vaterland*, Germany. His conceptualisation of his *rootland*, Turkey, perpetuates the essence of Ludewig's statement that Germans have refreshed memories for a lost geography both politically and environmentally (2001, 176). Fatih Akın, from his perspective as a German-Turkish director, reflects the "oceanic feeling" which is destined by Andreas Dresen toward death in the Baltic Sea to a still uncertain future at the shores of the Black Sea. This experience is new for the audience. What shall we think of a man looking at the Black Sea with his back turned toward the screen/camera? Should we assume that he is hopeful? Dörrie has a definite answer to the desire felt for the "oceanic feeling". In her film, the "oceanic feeling" means death at the moment of contemplation. Truffaut prevented Antoine from acting at the point of his end and to the audience's relief. Fatih Akın's spectre of the "oceanic feeling" is embodied by Nejad, the son in a longer genealogical chain, looking at the sea stretch out to the horizon. It is not as restricted as Dörrie's hero Rudi—the father—whose horizon—the depth of the screen—is shadowed by Fujiyama.

Films ending by the sea in the cinema of Turkey in the 2000s direct our gaze toward the sea. We experience a "pause" in between: a move from the New Turkish Cinema (Suner 2010, 27) to the Cinema of Turkey or Cinema in Turkey (Arslan 2011) to continue our stories to remember our past, to forgive and end at the same "ocean".

There has been, not a *Heimat* genre per se in Turkey, but in the 1970s, Yılmaz Güney's films turned the camera to the east and southeast of Turkey. The 1980s films gave priority to the individual's and intellectuals' frustrations in Istanbul (such as Şerif Gören's 1986 film *Sen Türkülerini Söyle*). The 1990s films began in eastern Anatolia and ended on the roofs of Istanbul (*Eşkiya*/Bandit, Yavuz Turgul, 1996; *Hamam*, Ferzan Özpetek, 1997). Following the mobility line of migrants from the *Eastern Heimat* to Istanbul, cinema of the 2000s converted this so called "social realist" movement of the 1970s and the transition to the 1980s city life into the "void of the sea". A horizon exists, attached to the screen behind which "nothing" exists, but we still want to believe that there is "something".

Works Cited

Arslan, Savaş. 2011. *Cinema in Turkey: A New Critical History*, New York: Oxford University Press.
Banaski, Andreas. 2012. "Komödie *Ausgerechnet Sibirien*: Spiesser auf Sinnsuche" (Comedy "Ironically Siberia": philistine on the search for meaning). *Spiegel Online*. May 10. Available online at: http://www.spiegel.de/kultur/kino/film-kritik-komoedie-ausgerechnet-sibirien-mit-joachim-krol-a-832107.html
Bayrakdar, Deniz, ed. 2004. "Türk Sineması: Hayali Vatanımız?" (Turkish Cinema: Our Imaginary Homeland) In *Türk Film Araştırmalarında Yeni Yönelimler*, 13-23. Istanbul: Bağlam Yayınları.
—. ed. 2009. "Turkish Cinema and the New Europe: At the Edge of Heaven". In *Cinema and Politics: Turkish Cinema and the New Europe*, 118-132. Newcastle upon Tyne: Cambridge Scholars Publishing.
Buber, Martin. 1983. *Ich und Du*. Heidelberg: Lambert Schneider.
Göktürk, Deniz. 2012. "World Cinema Goes Digital: Looking at Europe from the Other Shore". In *Turkish German Cinema in the New Millennium: Sites, Sounds, and Screens*, edited by S. Hake and B. Mennel, New York: Berghahn Books. 200-211.
Rolland, Romain. 1990. Letter from Rolland to Freud, December 5, 1927. In *Selected Letters of Romain Rolland*, edited by F. Doré and M.

Prévost, 86-88. Delhi: Oxford University Press.

Ludewig, Alexandra. 2001. "Heimat, City and Frontier in German National Cinema". *Debatte: Journal of Contemporary Central and Eastern Europe* 9 (2): 173-187.

Parsons, William B. 1998. "The Oceanic Feeling Revisited". *The Journal of Religion* 78 (4): 501-523.

Strachey, James. 1961. *Sigmund Freud: The Future of an Illusion.* New York, London: The Hogarth Press.

Suner, Asuman. 2010. *New Turkish Cinema, Belonging, Identity and Memory*. New York: I. B. Tauris.

CHAPTER ELEVEN

"DO ONE'S DREAMS BECOME SMALLER AS ONE BECOMES BIGGER?": MEMORY, TRAUMA AND THE CHILD IN TURKISH CINEMA

EYLEM ATAKAV

The military intervention of September 12th 1980 repressed both the radical Left as well as the radical Right in Turkey whilst aiming towards a period of systematic depoliticisation in society. It crushed all political parties and particularly leftist organisations, while temporarily suspending democracy and thereby bringing normal political life to a complete halt. The considerable effort by filmmakers to come to terms with this national *trauma* has resulted in an outpouring of cinematic texts in Turkey since 2000. This growing body of films focuses on the consequences of the 1980 military coup on the lives of individuals (through the stories of children suffering) and call attention to notions of memory; remembering trauma, torture and most importantly, the child in film.

Babam ve Oğlum/My Father and My Son (Çağan Irmak, 2005) is one such text. It is a melodrama about a left-wing activist journalist after the loss of his wife during the birth of their son on the night of the coup. In the powerful opening sequence from the film, Aysu (Tuba Büyüküstün), who is ready to deliver the baby, is seen with her husband Sadık (Fikret Kuşkan) in the empty streets within the city, unaware of the curfew. Sadık's panic is highlighted by the fast tilts and shaky moves of the hand-held camera. His yell for help mingles with his wife's screams of pain as they realise they cannot go any further. The couple is shown in a long shot as Sadık helps his wife lie down on the grass at the park alongside the motorway. He removes his shirt to help with the birth; his nakedness highlighting his vulnerability. The soundtrack is funereal, tragic and like a requiem with forceful rhythmic, almost martial, underpinnings. It suggests death, symbolising not only the impending death of Sadık's wife, but also the death of the Republic and democracy as a result of the coup. The screen is darkened, followed by a scream and then opens onto the morning. The camera pans through the still empty and silent streets and finds the blurred image of Sadık sitting half naked on the grass with a baby in his arms and the bloody body of his wife behind him. As the camera closes in on him, we see the blood on his face and body. From his point of view, we see the misty image of an approaching military vehicle. In Irmak's cinema this gloominess is used to imply his state of shock. A soldier comes out of the vehicle and hesitatingly walks towards Sadık asking if there has been an accident. From the point of view of the soldier, we see Sadık, who is shown looking distraught and finding it hard to create sentences: "My wife is dead…the baby has been born…so much blood…No one was here…" He stops after each sentence and finally, with a cry in his voice, he asks: "Where is everyone?" The soldier replies in an alarming manner as his voice sounds slow and echoes as it mixes with the dramatic music used earlier: "There's been a coup!" The camera slowly pans around Sadık and closes in on the baby's face. The baby is alive; his eyes are open.

In view of the idea that cinema presents a medium of memory, this chapter looks at whether the process of depoliticisation is still effective in the representations of the coup in recent films. Indeed, what brings these films together is their use of children. In *Babam ve Oğlum*/*My Father and My Son* (Çağan Irmak, 2005), Deniz is born in the immediate aftermath of the coup, and the story is based on how he will survive when his father dies as a consequence of torture. *Beynelmilel*'s/The International (Sırrı Süreyya Önder and Muharrem Gülmez, 2006) young Gülendam loses her boyfriend when he is shot by the local military for his political activities in 1982. In *The Edge of Heaven* (Fatih Akın, 2007), Yeter has immigrated to Germany leaving her young daughter Ayten in Turkey after the death of her politically active husband and has been working as a prostitute. Ayten is imprisoned for following her father's path and becoming politically active as a student. *O…Çocukları* /Sons of a…(Murat Saraçoğlu, 2008) is based on children whose parents disappear after the coup and who are placed in an ex-brothel. The film focuses on one particular girl whose mother has to escape secretly from the police to Italy with a fake passport, and whose father is tortured to death. *Sonbahar*/*Autumn* (Özcan Alper, 2008) deals with the consequences of torture on a romantic relationship. In referring to these, I would like to signal the need to continue to examine the relationship between depoliticisation and cultural memory in the context of recent and contemporary films.

In this article, I argue that these films, on the one hand, use the child as an emotion-evoking imagery, thereby depoliticising the narrative; on the other hand, through their focus on the coup's consequences on individual lives and by focusing on the relationship between the child and the adult, they offer a route to critical consciousness that resonates in feeling and thinking ways across the individual and the collective—hence the personal and the political. In all these (adopting Kuhn's phrase) "memory texts" (Kuhn 1995, 5) personal and collective remembering emerge again and again. Yet they resurrect and recreate these memories while reminding us of a traumatic past that encompasses cultural memory. As Kuhn aptly describes, "although we take stories of childhood and family literally...our recourse to this past is a way of reaching for myth, for the story that is deep enough to express the profound feelings we have in the present" (2005, 1). Narratives of these films are shaped by the forgotten or the missing accounts of the coup. Hence, through telling stories about the past that were visually suppressed until now, they become the cultural products of national identity. They require cultural criticism. My concern here is with the way in which these stories about the past are told within filmic language, in the present; in other words, in the way in which the reminders of the past remain in the present. I am then interested in what Kuhn defines as "reconstructions out of fragments of evidence" (2005, 4).

Here, I explore the connections between public historical and political events and the personal. In fact, examination of this connection calls to mind the feminist slogan "the personal is political" as these films—through the stories of individuals—make the personal public, thereby politicising it. So, on closer scrutiny of these films, representations are essential to what is not shown and what is shown and how, and provide deeper meanings to the shadowy side of the past. These films, indeed, present new possibilities for understanding not only how films work as texts, but also how through images and representations, they (re)construct a nation's identity and history. These images figure largely as clues to the history and collective memory of a nation. As Richard J. McNally writes in *Remembering Trauma*, the subjective experience of relieving ourselves from our past is essential to our sense of personal (and in this case national) identity (McNally 2005, 28). My intention here is to consider the notion of identity by looking at cultural memory. To do so, I will analyse a scene from *Babam ve Oğlum* to identify how the relationship between child and adult is represented.

In an interview, the director of *Babam ve Oğlum*, Çağan Irmak, stated that his concern was to narrate a story, not to make a political statement despite the political nature of the subject (Dönmez-Colin 2008, 52). Hilmi

Maktav points out that the film illustrated the futility of risking the break-up of families for political ideals since real happiness could be found only within the confines of the family. He argues that "by placing family above ideologies; Irmak was depoliticising the audience...which was commensurate with the ambitions of the generals—a depoliticised Turkey" (ibid.). Dönmez-Colin also comments on films from that era and points out: "the most applauded film about the 1980 coup does not even name the coup or its leaders" (ibid.). These comments suggest that the film is not politically informed, yet they fail to expand on why this is the case. I argue here that the film, on the one hand, uses the child and his vulnerability as the centre of the narrative, thereby relying on the image of an innocent child and evoking emotion more than political consciousness; on the other hand, through the juxtaposition of images of torture applied to the adult and the child's imaginary world (which is shown as a fantasy inspired by the comic books he reads), it covertly turns the personal into the political.

First, I would like to focus on how the image of the child is used to evoke emotion in the audience. As Patricia Holland writes in *Picturing Childhood*, pictures of sorrowful children reinforce the defining characteristics of childhood-dependence and powerlessness (2004, 143). Deniz's mother dies on the night of the coup, and his father is dying after he is physically tortured for his political ideas. Both of the deaths are related to the political situation. Sadık decides to bring Deniz to his home village to live with his grandparents. Unaware of what will happen to him, yet at the same time constantly feeling discomfort due to his father's unloving behaviour towards him, Deniz becomes the central character in the narrative. Not only is his father a victim of the coup, but so too, indirectly, is the child. The child here figures in the imagery as "the most vulnerable, the most pathetic, and the most deserving of our sympathy". Throughout the storyline as his vulnerability is revealed more and more, the audience longs to protect him. And as Holland writes: "the boundaries between childhood and adulthood are reinforced as the image gives rise to pleasurable emotions of tenderness and compassion" (ibid.). Melodramatic codes of staging and lighting, deep focus, distorted close-ups and expressivity of sound, all coordinate to evoke appropriate emotional orientation to the text. To adopt Greg Smith's words on film structure and the system of emotions, the narrative is anchored by the emotional spectacle of a child in danger, thus providing a unifying emotion (Smith 2003). Hence the film's narration relies on sustaining its emotional appeal. The audience's concern, then, becomes the vulnerability of the child. Nevertheless, this strong sense of compassion and tenderness also invites the audience to think of the reasons that put the child in this condition.

Hence, the personal becomes political as the audience is invited to think of the consequences of the military coup not only on the child, but also on the mother and the father. The effect of torture for a political crime, a crime against humanity, is not known earlier in the film. In fact, none of these films reveals the reasons why the ones tortured are in prison or under police scrutiny. However, in the film, we are given the information that Sadık is a left-wing journalist whose article was banned, its meaning for the ones tortured and the public that is informed of it indirectly is brought to our attention.

Henry Jenkins' argument on the cultural positioning of children is worth noting here. He suggests that "the dominant conception of childhood innocence presumes that children exist within a space beyond, above, outside the political" (Jenkins cited in Wilson 2005, 331). Wilson points out—in relation to this—that keeping children outside the political, the conception or fantasy of childhood innocence works further to shore up a sense of the distinction and distance between adults and children (2005, 331). Yet, in the study of this film, this distance is blurred as much as possible through one particular scene that depicts torture.

Sadık is asleep. Next to him lies Deniz wide awake looking at his father. As he turns his head toward the direction of the camera, we find ourselves in his imaginary world in which he narrates the story. "Dark forces" come and kidnap him and throw him into a well where they have already thrown his father. The "nightmare-like" scene that he imagines represents the constant discomfort, unhappiness and vulnerability of the child. The consequences of the father's past are linked strongly to the present condition of the child. As in his imagination, he is shown being thrown into the darkness of the well, the following scene fades into the same darkness. This time we are in the nightmare of the father who will wake up instantly after seeing images of torture. He is suspended naked and blindfolded (this same image is seen in other films like *Sons of a...* as well). His face and body are bleeding while blood also comes out of his mouth. This scene brings the viewer up close to the image of torture, thereby disallowing distance. The juxtaposition of the two nightmare-like scenes creates a bond between the child and the adult and stresses how the two are interrelated. The adult lacks control as much as a child over its circumstances, its environment, and its own body. As Martha Nussbaum argues: "the adult, overwhelmed by experience, by emotions of intensity of negative affect, in the very experience of being overwhelmed involuntarily returns to the child's state of helplessness (motor, emotional or political)" (Nussbaum cited in Wilson 2005, 330).

I would like to finally return to the images of torture and how, indeed, they are politically charged. The film makes it clear what life is like in a culture that practices torture, both the individual and the collective effect of its introduction to social and political existence. As Kate Millet argues:

> For those who live for others and social ideas, the body defeats them with its pain and despair before the absolute solitude of human existence, essentially a solitude before death. A terrible knowledge is born of this pain. The scream of the victim is the body calling out to the soul, the self calling out to others. Both will go unheard, unanswered. The lesson of torture is silence. Just as the torturer boasts—no one will ever hear you, no one will ever know, no one will ever discover. (Millett 1994, 301)

This silence that is imposed on the tortured through the politics of cruelty turns into a voice through cinematic images. These images call for the consideration for the reasons behind torture particularly by linking the adult experience to the emotion-evoking image of the child. Indeed, the film ends the silence, breaking it and restoring the victim's voice. The systematic depoliticisation of the masses still has its effects on Turkish society; democracy is still fragile, and these may be reflected in the mode of production of films.

In an interview conducted with one of the leaders of İlerici Gençlik Derneği (The Association of Advanced Youth), Behzat Kocavardar shared his recollections of his political activities at the time, and his experience of the coup and the aftermath (including severe physical and mental torture).[1] One of his close friends was a student union leader at the time. After she had a child, she found that she could not move from the sofa for an entire year because she was so scared and in such shock. As her child grew up, she wet the bed at night until the age of fifteen, and could not talk because of the sense she had that all means of expression were closed to her. In talking about her experiences of depoliticisation, torture, and escape in the same interview, a member of İlerici Kadınlar Derneği (The Association of Advanced Women), Nuran Sayman told the story of giving birth to her second child in 1982.[2] When the time came for her to give birth, her friends and husband were unable to help take her to the hospital as they

---

1. İlerici Gençlik Derneği was established in 1976 and stil exists under the name of Tüm İlerici Gençlik Derneği. Its slogan, however, has remained the same: "Our way is the way of the working class". Mr Kocavardar was hesitant to give the names of his friends, which is why I do not disclose them here.
2. İlerici Kadınlar Derneği was established in 1975 and was shut down by the government in 1979 as it was the only women's organisation of Türk Komünist Partisi (Turkish Communist Party).

were still being pursued by the police for their political activities. A helpful mini-bus driver took her to the hospital and waited until after the birth.[3] When the nurse came to say that her husband was happy to hear that she gave birth, she could say nothing because she could not reveal that the driver was not her real husband. She named her child Savaş—war. Her first child was named Barış—peace. In such a way, names also reflect changing realities and the personal encapsulates the political. To a large extent, Turkey maintains the practice, both in first names and surnames, of naming people after virtues, objects or abstract concepts. Although this practice was once common in Western Europe, and can still be seen in many names, in Turkey names still have a deep and immediate political resonance. In 1986, Nuran Sayman procured an illegal passport to enable her to go to Germany. She had to lie to her son and say his father was in Saudi Arabia where he had found work. In their documents, her sons had false first names, but the same surname even though they had different fathers. At the time, Barış was nine and Savaş, four. As they travelled on the train, Nuran thought it wise to tell the older child what the names written on the passports were, and she waited for a moment when his brother was sleeping to tell him. As she was doing so, Savaş suddenly woke up and said "I want another name too". After the trauma of the flight to Germany, the children no longer wanted to know their parents' real names as they did not want to get confused about their names and identity.

More films are being made about this period and individuals' stories, as these films reveal, represent and help us remember the brutality, which ranges from casual torture to mutilation, disappearance and death. Through interviews with tortured left-wing activists, one listens to their stories, verbal accounts of how the 1980s military regime imposed its force and intimidated dissenters. The resulting effect was hidden in its many dark aspects and secrets from the past. While remembering trauma and thinking about memory, the need to turn oral culture into visual culture proves to be crucial. In the circulation of remembered stories and in the process of producing, selecting, exhibiting or representing the national, the cultural and the historical, the nation is, in fact, in the process of making itself. Overall, the child in the film discussed is not only used to evoke emotions (thereby seeming to depoliticise the narratives), but also through a complex nexus of emotions and in bonding a relationship between the child and the adult, they turn the personal stories into political ones.

---

3. A detailed account of narrative and industrial basis of film popularity can be found in Akser (2013).

Works Cited

Akser, Murat. 2013. "Blockbusters". In *Directory of World Cinema: Turkey*, edited by Eylem Atakav, 124-145. London: Intellect, 2013.

Dönmez-Colin, Gönül. 2008. *Turkish Cinema: Identity, Distance and Belonging*. London: Reaktion.

Holland, Patricia.2004. *Picturing Childhood: The Myth of the Child in Popular Imagery*. London and New York: I. B. Tauris.

Kuhn, Annette. 1995. *Family Secrets*. London and New York: Verso.

McNally, Richard J. 2005. *Remembering Trauma*. Cambridge and London: Harvard University Press.

Millett, Kate. 1994. *The Politics of Cruelty: An Essay on the Literature of Political Imprisonment*. London and New York: W. W. Norton and Co.

Smith, Greg M. 2003. *Film Structure and the Emotion System*. Cambridge and New York: Cambridge University Press.

Wilson, Emma. 2005. "Children, Emotion and Viewing in Contemporary European Film". *Screen* 46 (3): 329-40.

CHAPTER TWELVE

POST-APOCALYPTIC SCIENCE FICTION: A NEW GENRE IN TURKISH CINEMA?

ÖZÜM ÜNAL

Introduction

This paper intends to analyse the "post-apocalypse" theme in *Gelecekten Anılar/Memories from the Future* (Erverdi, 2010), a short science-fiction film from Turkey that treats post-apocalyptic themes in new guises. This paper will focus on the cinematic representation of dystopia and post-apocalyptic dread in this film; it will provide reasons why Turkish cinema has not produced films that are related to, or centre around the theme of post-apocalyptic science fiction. It will also ask questions related to post-apocalyptic narratives and their religious, historical and socio-cultural fear formation in relation to the methods of cultural and political theories.

André Bazin claims that witnessed images show audiences not only the features of the phenomena, but also the very existence of those phenomena, and that it offers audiences what has not been recognised before and represents its permanency (Büker 1989, 20). In other words, the cinema may be thought to be functioning as a mirror of society. He also highlights that "cinema presents spectator's information on objective actuality, which one cannot perceive with one's senses" (ibid.). Although this may seem a reductionist approach, cinema is a very popular instrument among all the various media of mass communication, so much so that it could also influence people's historical perspectives. Films and post-apocalyptic films, in particular, could be analysed in terms of the semiotic and structural workings of cinematic "post-apocalypse".

Before embarking upon a discussion of the semiotic and structural workings of cinematic "post-apocalypse," I define the origin of *dystopia* in the post-apocalyptic world. In the first part of the paper there will be a survey of dystopian narratives as religious, historical and socio-cultural forms of fear formation. Using these views in the section that follows, I will apply those characteristics to Turkish cultural history. The second part will focus on a thematic analysis of *Gelecekten Anılar/Memories from the Future*, a Turkish post-apocalyptic short film directed by H. Mert Erverdi (2010). Following these analyses, I will conclude by providing a speculation about the importance of engagement with the dystopias of recent decades, as they are the product of our dark times and the reasons why post-human futures are represented the way that they are within popular culture.

Cinematic Dystopia in a Post-Apocalyptic World

The classic dystopia is simply defined as a critical framework in the "utopian" future where the present state of society is magnified to the point of calamity. The idea of a post-apocalyptic world is quiet recent. In these stories what happens usually is that humanity is under threat of extinction. There is a new generation of survivors born from the ashes of the old order. In an interview with William Gibson by Timothy Leary in a 1989 issue of *Mondo 2000* Gibson described his approach to a dystopian world in *Neuromancer*, stating: "What's most important to me is that it's about the present. It's not really about an imagined future. It's a way of trying to come to terms with the awe and terror inspired in me by the world in which we live" (Gibson 1989, 58). Donna Haraway, in her seminal article, "A Manifesto for Cyborgs: Science, Technology and Socialist Feminism in the Late Twentieth Century," also asserts that: "the boundary between science fiction and social reality is an optical illusion" (Haraway 1994, 84). If both statements are true, then we currently live in an age that is akin to Baudrillard's dystopia idea that we no longer need to read science fiction literature because we are living it (Bukatman 1993, 323). It takes very little effort to notice that the contemporary moment is one dominated by an ideology of fear. Fear and anxiety have become the most effective way of both mobilising and demobilising populations. Representations of "the present or future [that] are sometimes shaped in the mould of supernatural terrors from the past" which bring "the millennial fear of Judgment Day into the high-tech present" were caused by the failure of imagination (King 2000, 53).

According to Elaine L. Graham, one element of a dystopian story is a "confusion of reality and illusion" (Graham 2002, 195). Considering the dystopian narrative's unalterable and inextricable link to the current point in time, I would claim here that the dystopian narrative's purpose is to "map, warn and hope" (Moylan 2000, 196). The anxieties about the future and the end of the world which are based upon various long-standing ecclesiastical prophecies about Judgment Day or Armageddon are drawn from holy books such as Islam's Koran (Thompson 2007, 24). Şerif Mardin indicates that, "for the society, Islam was not just a religion, but a lifestyle, the most important aspect forming their culture, also the most important concept that specified their judgment and basis of their actions" (Mardin 1976, 7). The term "apocalypse" and the concept "sin" are interrelated. In Muslim societies like Turkey, "apocalypse" in religious terms is the destruction of the world. Since it is human rage that causes the end of civilisation in the post-World-War-II science fiction stories, this particular genre was renamed "post-apocalyptic". As Rabkin indicates following: "World War II there has been a decline in positive, utopian visions about the future and an increase—particularly in science fiction— of visions of imminent decline and disaster" (Rabkin 1993, 121).

The overwhelming acceleration of technological developments and globalisation became the central cause in the creation of the post-apocalyptic genre in the second half of the twentieth century. Where did Turkey fit in to this power-related competition of technology? The modernisation process Turkey was striving for was entangled with domestic issues, as Zafer Toprak observes: "in the 1950s, Turkey tried to get to know itself, whereas in the 1960s, it was mainly interested in getting to know the world" (Toprak 1998, 260). Furthermore, Tanju Akerson claims:

> Turkish cinema, unlike in the West, was not a product of the industrial revolution. It was a product of a consumption economy established by the western type of production in underdeveloped countries. (Akerson quoted in Scognamillo 1990, 154)

Karl Marx claimed that human beings were social beings owing to the fact that they are themselves products of their very society. According to this assumption, we are all collective products of our society just like a commodity is a collective product from the factory where it was produced (Akçam 1993, 25). In fact, Turkey has constructed a fake expression of technology. The consciousness of the average Turkish citizen was not shaped around the advances of technology up until recently. The inaccessibility of technological advancements has been effective on the creative imagination within the society where film crews found simple solutions rather than the use of high tech. Turkish cinema imported Hollywood technical devices and recycled narratives to make films. The various cinematographic problems and weakened financial background of the Turkish cinema industry affected which genres would be produced in Turkey. According to film scholar Murat Akser (2013), even if technology was a direct part of the science fiction narratives in both Turkish and Hollywood films, Turkish film's "primary discourse is a positivist-technocratic one that valorises the uses of science and technology" (Akser 2010, 116). As a matter of fact, Turkish society neglects to focus on technological advances and "domestic development" unlike western societies, which have "aimed at reshaping or taming nature," so "the Turkish sci-fi superhero helps out those in need with good manners and virtue" (ibid.). As Akser asserts, there is an intertextual relationship to American cinema, which includes "imitation and an overt feeling of technical inferiority" (ibid., 133).

There have always been discussions about whether or not cinema could function as the memory reserve of society by reflecting the period in which they were produced. The cinema can never be thought of as distant from the value judgements, political and ideological tendencies. Hilmi Maktav (2000, 79) argues that the September 12, 1980 military coup gains importance in terms of two major perspectives. In the first place, it has changed people's historical perspective by influencing social perception; it also affected the cinema as a cultural product of the society. Secondly, films that were made in the second half of the 1980s present the chaotic atmosphere and turmoil of the pre-1980 period and the coercion years which happened after the September 12 military coup. That is to say, the grounding of the de-politicisation process began to be formed in the 1980s. Furthermore, as Nurdan Gürbilek defined, society could be said to have gone through a "social explosion" (Gürbilek 2010, 16-17). Amos Funkenstein earlier explained the significance and the position of "the present" within the complete insight into the theory as follows:

> The experience of memory is also a measure of time. The past is the remembered present, just as the future is the anticipated present: memory is always derived from the present and from the contents of the present. (Funkenstein 1989, 9)

As it was a significant tool of socialisation for the masses, Turkish cinema brought content of the past or present, repressing the tendency of exploring the infinite possibilities of an infinite number of possible futures.

Second quality of dystopian narrative is that one superior class or corporate power has domination over the other(s). Graham describes this superior group as "panoptic corporate powers" that "[have] access to all the fruits of technology" which they then manipulate to meet their own needs (Graham 2002, 194). Reorganising the underclass using technology which is controlled by the state or economic monopolies "on a capitalist basis," according to social theorist Oskar Negt, corporate powers (large panoptic organisations) attempt to withhold the underclass' "subjective means of expression" by reducing their communication for only leisure use, which creates a lack of "emancipatory usage," that is to say, lacking any sort of political voice (Negt 1980, 75). I would claim here that technology is essential in dystopian exercises of power. Dystopian narratives show "inhuman technologies and impersonal capitalism" that can use its own superiority to dominate humans that can be described as "an erosion and colonisation of human freedom" (Graham 2002, 195).

As with dystopian stories, however, there must be an exhaustion of ideologies and human inability to escape from calamities. Linguist George P. Lakoff asserts that when unable to interact with another natural life form, the human soul becomes deprived; nonetheless, memory remains too often trapped in an individual along with regressive nostalgia. By considering the dystopian world as a warning, the resistor in dystopian narratives has some element of anger resulting in hope for a better future. Raffaella Baccolini claims that awareness and responsibility are the conditions of the resistors in a dystopian world which shows that "a culture of memory—one that moves from the individual to the collective—is part of a social project of hope" (Baccolini 2004, 521).

Up until the Chernobyl nuclear disaster in Russia on April 26, 1986, Turkey had not been disturbed by a disaster caused by humans. Society was cowed into silence because of the disinformation policy on the media under pressure of the authorities. Furthermore, on 24 June 1986, the Turkish Minister of Industry and Trade Cahit Aral blamed the scientist who worked on the impact of Chernobyl saying: "Anyone claiming that the radiation (from Chernobyl) has affected Turkey is an atheist and a traitor". Political leaders from the president and prime minister down posed on newspaper pages drinking tea alongside headlines such as "A little radiation does you good". "I drink seven or eight cups of tea a day. Even 20 is harmless...We never dispatched any contaminated tea for sale...Even my wife drinks tea daily," said Cahit Aral. "Radioactive tea is more delicious, tastier," urged Turgut Özal. The newspapers went as far to suggest sexual potency due to radiation: "Does a certain level of radiation have an aphrodisiac effect?" (*Hürriyet Daily News*). Modern anxiety is the basis of the man-made-disaster theme whereas Turkey shows an attitude that one can assume to be the denial of an enormous shock. What happened was the justification of an on-going system that was in place to give the public the impression that there was no social unrest, everything was under control, and the nation was safe. Post-apocalypse stories depict the sharp reality of the survival of humanity after catastrophe. It could be argued that this tendency to deny catastrophes and not to recall the past estranges the Turkish people from the genre.

Turkish cinema was part of the creative process of collective memory that has a tendency to forget the past or a desire to escape from it. This tendency to bury the past or escape from one's own past creates a kind of a vicious cycle where the insistence on ignoring it increases its emphasis, influence and effect on the present day even more. This tendency to ignore the past had long been a strategy used in Turkish society. This kind of relationship between Turkish people and their past was deemed necessary to create and maintain its intrinsic characteristics for building a favourable identity for the nation-state by the Kemalist founders. Mesut Kara pointed out, "a society was constituted, which was getting individualised, isolated and fragmented. Briefly; a new human culture was created" (Kara in Makal 2007, 57). We may consider this in terms of politics exerting its pressure on cinema, and art cinema particularly—at once demanding an authentic Turkish cinema while making conditions for its production impossible.

To sum up, cinema is a medium that can be functionalised to create opportunities to come to terms with the future. The post-apocalyptic sci-fi genre can be a part of how we utilise the cinematic medium; thus, it deserves consideration.

Memories from the Future (Gelecekten Anılar)

"The pure present is an ungraspable advance of the past devouring the future. In truth, all sensation is already memory."
—Henri Bergson

Directed by H. Mert Erverdi, *Gelecekten Anılar/Memories from the Future* (2010) is the first post-apocalyptic short film made in Turkey. H. Mert Erverdi is an emerging director, who is currently working on a feature-length film project about a dystopia set in Istanbul.

Memories from the Future is a mood piece about a soldier in a post-apocalyptic world, whose personal memories are reconstructed and controlled by unknown authorities, and the only memory he has left is the image of the woman he loved, which enables him to endure whatever hardships he must face.

Figure 1 *Memories from the Future*

Memories from the Future criticises the meaning of memory. Maurice Halbwachs argued that repeated memories cannot be conveyed and recited intact; meaning they change in time, and "are conflated as they are continuously being revised" (Hutton 1994, 149). The mutant soldier reconstructs his memories each time they are repeated within the framework of his social context. One can deduce that the images from the past in one's memory cannot be the original images, but rather that those images are adapted to the current social framework and conceptions of today.

Memories from the Future is a non-narrative mood piece in which the dialogue is not in a known language. The narrative is accompanied by real-time sounds. There is an implicit understanding in this film that the images are mere vehicles for the voices to be heard. The visuals provide a strong aesthetic which allows an accessible reading. Deleuze says that movement-image binary destroys the very logic of representation. That is to say, its model would not be "a natural perception, but rather a state of things that is constantly changing, a stream of material, in which no anchoring point or centre of reference could be indicated" (Deleuze 1989, 86).

In *Memories from the Future*, "the altered-society structure" is exclusively prevalent throughout the film. The dark and gloomy atmosphere and the ambiguous ending to the movie reflect the altered-society structure with the clash between the soldier without memories and the constantly daydreaming main character.

The objects used for the film can be identified through their own particular iconography; for instance, gas masks are significant elements in the description of the post-apocalyptic setting of *Memories from the Future*. Rage is fixed on the gas mask itself. As Rabkin puts it "for the gas mask embodies many of the basic contradictions of contemporary capitalism" (Rabkin 1993, 121). Since capitalism's roots go deep down, to the survival-of-the-fittest, the pessimism, disbelief and rage against human nature are also aimed at capitalism and build on capitalist elements to portray the post-apocalyptic wastelands of *Memories from the Future*. The remains of the civilisation are important in the making of post-apocalyptic societies. *Memories from the Future* questions the position of the viewer.

In the world of film, nearly all post-apocalypse movies end with hope for survival of the human species and the suggestion of a communal rebirth to prevent total extinction (Broderick 1993,12-17). Although science and technology generally defeat any threat to human survival, what is rarer is an ending where human beings will not live on. Probably, a terminal ending is more acceptable in a novel than in the film where theatregoers expect, or even demand, a happy ending. *Memories from the Future* challenges the audience to question and also to have an opinion, although the film itself does not provide any suggested interpretations about its ending. There is little to none sense of hope at the end of the film; the ending is as uncertain as the memories we saw of the woman in the soldier's mind.

Works Cited

Gelecekten Anılar/Memories from the future. 2010. Dir. Hüseyin Mert Erverdi, Turkey.

Akçam, Taner. 1993. "Ulusal Meseleye bir kollektif kimlik sorunu olarak yaklasmak" (Approaching the issue of the national as a matter of collective identity). *Birikim* 45/46: 24-32.

Akser, Murat. 2010. *Green Pine Resurrected: Film Genre, Parody and Intertextuality in Turkish Cinema*. Saarbrucken: Lambert Academic Publishing.

—. 2013. "Blockbusters". In *Directory of World Cinema: Turkey*, edited by Eylem Atakav, 124-145. London: Intellect.

Anon. "Authorities lied on impact of Chernobyl in Turkey", http://blackraiser.com/cherno.htm_br (accessed February 10, 2011).

Baccollini, Raffaella. 2004. "The Persistence of Hope in Dystopian Science Fiction". *Science Fiction and Literary Studies: The Next Millennium* 119 (3): 518-21.

Bazin, André. 1967. "What is Cinema". Translated by Hugh Gray. In *Film Theory and Criticism*, edited by Edited by G. Mast and M. Cohen, 21-26. New York: Oxford University Press.

Broderick, Mick. 1993. "Surviving Armageddon: Beyond the Imagination of Disaster" *Science Fiction Studies* #61. Vol 20 (3): 1-19. Accessed Google online 2-14-2011.
http://www.depauw.edu/sfs/backissues/61/broderick61art.htm

Bukatman, Scott. 1993. *Terminal Identity: The Virtual Subject in Postmodern Science Fiction*. Durham, NC: Duke University Press.

Büker, Seçil. 1989. *Film ve Gerçek* (Film and Reality). Eskişehir: Anadolu University.

Funkenstein, Amos. 1989. "Collective Memory and Historical Consciousness". *History and Memory* 1 (1): 5-26.

Graham, Elaine L. 2002. *Monsters, Aliens and Other in Popular Culture*. New Brunswick, NJ: Rutgers University Press.

Gurbilek, Nurdan. 2010. *The New Cultural Climate in Turkey: Living in a Shop Window*. London: Zed.

Halbwachs, Maurice. 1980. *Individual Memory and Collective Memory*. New York: Harper and Raw.

—. 1992. *On Collective Memory*. Chicago: The University of Chicago Press.

Harraway, Donna. 1994. "A Manifesto for Cyborgs: Science, Technology and Socialist Feminism in the 1980s". In *The Postmodern Twin: New Perspectives on Social Theory*, edited by Steven Seidman, 82-115. UK: Cambridge University Press.

Hürriyet Daily News. 1997. "Tea was also contaminated," 24 February. Available online at: http://www.hurriyetdailynews.com/tea-was-also-contaminated.aspx?pageID=438&n=tea-was-also-contaminated-1997-02-24

Hutton, P. H. 1994. "Sigmund Freud and Maurice Halbwachs: The Problem of Memory in Historical Psychology". *The History Teacher* 27: 145-48.

Kracauer, Siegfried. 1985. "Theory of Film: Basic Concepts". In *Film Theory and Criticism: Introductory Readings*, edited by G. Mast and M. Cohen, 7-20. New York: Oxford University Press.

Makal Oğuz., Engin Ayça, Tamer Ay. and Mesut Kara. 2007. "Sinema ne kadar 12 Eylul" (To what extent is 12 September in cinema). *Cinemascope* 11: 55-62.

Maktav, Hilmi. 2000. "Türk Sinemasında 12 Eylül" (September 12 in Turkish cinema). *Birikim* 138:79-84 .

Mardin, Şerif. 1976. *İdeoloji* (Ideology). İstanbul: İletisim.

Moylan, Thomas. 2000. *Scraps on Untainted Sky: Science Fiction, Utopia, Dystopia*. Boulder, CO: Westview Press.

Negt, Oskar. 1980. "Mass Media: Tools of Domination or Instruments of Liberation? Aspects of the Frankfurt School's Communications Analysis". In *The Myths of Information: Technology and Postindustrial Culture*, edited by K.Woodward, 65-87. Madison, WI: Coda Press.

Rabkin, S. Eric. 1993. *Fights of Fancy: Armed Conflict in Science Fiction and Fantasy*. London: The University of Georgia Press.

Scognamillo, Giovanni. 1990 *Türk Sinema Tarihi 1896-1986 vol I-II*. Istanbul: Metis

Toprak, Zafer. 1998. "1968'i yargılamak ya da 68 kuşağına mersiye" (Trying 1968 or an Elegy for the Generation of '68). *Cogito* 14: 154-59.

Thompson, Kristen Moana. 2007. *Apocalyptic Dread: American Film at the Turn of the Millennium*. Albany: SUNY Press.

CHAPTER THIRTEEN

ARM-WRESTLING A SUPERPOWER:
REPRESENTATIONS OF THE UNITED STATES
AND AMERICANS IN TURKISH COMEDIES

ELIF KAHRAMAN

> *"They cannot represent themselves; they must be represented."*
> —Karl Marx

Introduction

In *Orientalism*, Edward Saïd uses the above quote by Karl Marx in order to explain the Orientalists' view of the Orient. Saïd mentions that the Occident views the Orient as incapable of representing itself. Due to this incapability, the Occident believes that it must be the one to depict the Orient. However, film has provided a way for the Orient to show that it can represent not only itself, but also the Occident. In recent Turkish cinema, comedy films have become the voice of the Orient. Representation is also important for creating an "I" that becomes an "us" with regard to nationality. In representing the "Other," the "us" is also represented. Here the concept of nation enters the battlefield of representations. In other words, while films try to represent the "Other," they also represent "us".

In Turkish comedies, Occidentalism is linked to the nation. The concept of nation is an inseparable part of communal identity, which creates a sense of belonging. Although Benedict Anderson states that the "nation is an imagined political community" (2000, 6), it is hard to deny the importance of "nation" in today's world. This sense of belonging creates boundaries for non-members and draws lines, which result in conflicts. Whether imagined or not, nationality has been a key factor in both the literal and metaphorical power wars in recent Turkish cinema. Due to its status as a world superpower, the United States is faced with many competitors, especially in the twenty-first century. This competition stems from the concept of "us" versus "them," which is a consequence of national identity. The "us" is a powerful side in the imagined world of binary oppositions. The dominant "us" is important for the representation of "them"; but, naturally, the portrayal of the represented one—the "Other"—is also affected by the one doing the representing.

Cinematic representation is a battlefield for the power relations between "us" and "them". In the cinema, impartiality is not required, and thus the battle between "us" and "them" can be played out. It is important to see who has the upper hand and will be able to win the game. Stuart Hall explains: "[t]here is always a relation of power between the poles of a binary opposition" (2003, 235). This is exemplified in the recent competition seen between Turkey and the United States in Turkish comedies where Turkey plays the powerful role.

In this study, "us" becomes the East and "them" is the West representing the conflict of the Orient versus the Occident. The nations are represented in cinema as Anderson states, "For these forms (the novel and the newspaper) [in this case, films] provided the technical means for 're-presenting' the *kind* of imagined community that is the nation" (2000, 25). In the representation of the nation in cinema, other nations are also represented. In recent Turkish comedies not only is the Turkish nation represented, American characters are represented as well. The quote from Karl Marx at the beginning elucidates the reason for the desire to represent Americans in Turkish comedies. However, in this case, it is the Occident that cannot represent itself and needs to be represented. This is significant as the Turkish victory in this arm-wrestling match reverses the power relations between the United States and Turkey.

American characters have increasingly been depicted in Turkish films, especially after the start of the Second Gulf War. As the United States was an invading force in the region, the relationship Turkey had with the United States was frequently reported on by the media. This raised the awareness of society and opened a new window in Turkish cinema. While this situation affected film plots in general, surprisingly, American characters were included in more comedies than dramas. As a result of the Iraq War, American characters were presented either as agents or soldiers. Non-agent or non-military characters were rare. This situation reversed the typical views of the powerful and the weak and the Occidental and the Oriental. Therefore, these representations should be examined in order to find out how the power relations have been reversed.

In addition, the style of film comedy provides a stage where power relations can be altered. Comedy discovers weaknesses in characteristics in a culture and naively attacks or makes fun of them. Using the features of the comedy genre, such as joking about real issues, these films provide a point of view for Turkish society in relation to the United States. As it is claimed in *AS Film Studies*, "films do not exist outside of a society and certain social relations" (Benyahia, Gaffney and White 2008, 15). In this study, I intend to show how American characters are portrayed in Turkish comedies as soldiers and agents while tacitly referring to the United States' involvement in recent wars.

In light of these ideas, this study's main question is: How are Americans represented in contemporary Turkish comedies? Representation represents an already existing subject. The act of re-presenting contributes a new dimension to the viewer's perspective. The construction of characters as types in cinema provides us with a framework of analysis for identity politics. In this case, Americans are represented as inferior in post-2000 Turkish film comedy. Accordingly, a cinematic battle takes place between the Turkish characters and the Americans. In this study, this cinematic battle is compared to an arm-wrestling match where two opponents use physical power—which is concrete and finite—to beat the "Other". Turkish comedies provide a new point of view about Americans. The American characters are represented physically, behaviourally and linguistically in different cinematic ways, which are also symbolic battlefields. In Turkish comedies, the American characters are constantly defeated, and the Turks are always victorious. With regard to the main research question and the battlefields, I intend to examine the different representation strategies, which include race, gender and the costuming of the American characters in order to determine the arm-wrestling strategy, which is then employed to defeat the Americans.

Turks and Americans: Occidentalism on Screen

The adage "never judge a book by its cover" implies that physical appearance influences the first impression that people have about another person. In a similar fashion, audiences form their first impression about another nation or country through film. To begin with, costumes are important because they represent the nationalities while also stereotyping the characters. Costume portrays race of a character. Here race is being used as a term here to separate "Occident" from "Orient". The Turkish comedies included in this study stereotype the Occident, i.e. the American characters, through their physical appearances. This is how the arm-wrestling match between the Turks and the Americans begins on the cinematic battlefield.

Clothing can give clues about the personality/occupation of those represented. Because soldiers and CIA agents represent Americans in these films, the characters generally wear formal clothing. This type of cold formal clothing, which allows the Turks to look superior, is used to defeat the Americans in the arm-wrestling match. Turkish comedies tend to characterise Americans as formal/inflexible and serious when they are not actually so. Secondly, race and gender are sensitive issues with underlying messages. In this point in time, it is important to draw attention to how race and gender are represented in order to ensure that racist and sexist points of view are not displayed. However, through stereotyping, Turkish comedies seem to attack the weakest part of American society, that is to say, its persisting problems with race and gender. This is done through the use of racist and sexist points of view as well as by making the American characters look and feel Oriental in their appearance. Hence the Americans, as representatives of the Occident, become what they fear: the Orient.

Overall, the American characters are for all intents and purposes represented as Oriental. Occidentalism in Turkish comedies takes its roots from Oriental ideas. It is like holding a mirror up to the sun and reflecting the sunlight back to the sun. This arm-wrestling match allows the Turks to beat the Americans, who are not superior despite being typically cast as Occidental. In this chapter, I analyse the physical representations of the American characters in three ways; clothing, race and gender and how each is used in these films as a way to beat the Americans in arm-wrestling.

Race, gender and clothing are important as they help create the first impression of the Americans. Concepts can then be used to show the relevant background issues. These concepts are divided into two: concepts of quality and concepts of process. Concepts of quality represent the supposed inherent appearance of the American characters, whereas concepts of process indicate the change in appearance of the American characters throughout the films.

Concepts of Quality

Silliness and Clumsiness: This concept is used both in the clothing of the American characters and in the representation of race and gender. Silliness and clumsiness are inferred from the style of the American characters' clothing. Here, clothing shows the characteristics of the American characters. The "Occidental" view of "America" for the Turks is that mainly white people are depicted in their television series aired on Turkish television. This concept enforces the stereotypical norms of race and gender by mainly depicting white Americans. Whereas in American films orientals are depicted as clumsy or ignorant. In recent Turkish film comedies, white Americans are put into the same mould as the other races in terms of silliness and clumsiness, and Turkish superiority gains the upper hand.

Whitening: This concept is used for the lack of characters of other races such as African, Asian, etc. in Turkish comedies. This exaggeration of representation is a reflection of how Turkish cinema views Hollywood. As previously mentioned, while white Americans are equated with non-white Americans in Turkish cinema, non-white Americans still have a lower status than their white American counterparts.

Man Fist: [1] This concept is used to describe the lack of female characters as well as to indicate the patriarchy that is featured prominently throughout the films in this study. Because the female characters are suppressed by men, their lack of representation is equivalent to male hegemony.

Concepts of Process

Orientalisation: This concept is used to Easternise—or Orientalise—the Americans' appearance and/or clothing. The American characters wear clothes typically worn by Turkish villagers. This makes the Americans Oriental in Turkey. This also indicates how Americans turn into Turks (lose their Americanness) after having spent some time in Turkey.

Worsening Characterisation: This concept indicates the change in the characteristics of the American characters when their clothes change. Although the characters are not represented positively, the change makes them worse than before.

Formality-in-reverse: This concept shows how American characters are mainly formal in appearance. They usually wear uniforms, but do not act as formal as their appearance suggests they would. Their clothing and behaviour are not consistent.

---

1. Here the concept of Man Fist means of a male fist.

Analysis

Clothing is the visual aspect of film that focuses on the physical representation of the characters. Physical appearance provides the first clue about a person. It is the first thing the audience understands about a character and helps form the audience's overall perception or first impression. Stuart Hall states that "[r]epresentation is an essential part of the process by which meaning is produced and exchanged between members of a culture" (2003, 15). So, representations of Americans have various meanings for the Turkish audience.

Clothing is an important part of the physical qualities of a character and gives clues to the personality of the American characters to Turkish society. The clothing of the characters has meaning for the audience (Benyahia, Gaffney and White 2008, 34). In addition, clothing becomes a part of the meaning that is inferred. As Hall puts it, "[t]he clothes themselves are the *signifiers*" (2003, 37). Hence, the clothes worn in the Turkish comedies included in this study symbolise the American characters and their personalities.

The Turkish films *Super Spy K9* (Bülent İşbilen, 2008), *Americans at the Black Sea 2* (Kartal Tibet, 2006)*,* and *European* (Ulaş Ak, 2007) all feature American CIA agents. Timothy Corrigan explains that "[c]ostumes …provide a writer with the key to a character's identity" (2010, 62). So, how does the clothing in Turkish comedies provide clues about Americans?

At first glance, silliness and clumsiness are evident solely based on the costumes of the American characters. The silliness and clumsiness of the American characters are hidden in the details, but stand out at second glance. In *Super Spy K9* and *European*, the agents wear formal clothing: men wear dark-coloured suits, ties, leather shoes, dark sunglasses and earpieces; women wear very short skirts, tight shirts, high-heeled shoes and earpieces. At first glance, the men's costumes stand out for their resemblance to agents in Hollywood movies that a Turkish audience would be used to seeing. However, at second glance, their accessories, such as their earpieces, are conspicuous. As agents, they must be camouflaged and should not stand out; however, the size of their earpieces indicates the agents are puppets controlled by outside forces. The costumes of the unnamed male agents in the film *European* reveal their identity. The size of their earpieces demonstrates their clumsiness and the failure of their mission. It also gives clues about their character and helps form the Turkish audience's overall impression of the Americans. They are formal, serious and dangerous; at the same time, they are conducting business which is not beneficial to Turkey. The strength of the American government is manifested by the CIA. However, as the CIA agents are portrayed as incapable and clumsy, this results in the weakening of the traditionally powerful CIA and is a loss for the American side of this equation.

In *Super Spy K9*, formal clothing was chosen for an American agent, but in a rather distorted way. The character, Ayse Kosovalı, who is half American through her father, is the only American agent in the film. Her costume is not casual, but not totally formal, either: a very short skirt with a slit down the side, a tight shirt with the top buttons unbuttoned and high heels. In its totality, her costume makes her anything but an agent. Her overt sexuality is not necessary for her job as an agent and influences the first impressions both the men in the film as well as the audience have of her. In addition, as an American character her being blonde is not surprising. She is dangerous since she is an agent, but is not a direct threat to the Turkish people because she is not fully American.

Worsening characterisation describes how the characteristics of the American characters change when they change clothes. But, it is not the same transformation as journalist Clark Kent turning into Superman. Rather, it is actually the reverse. Before the change in costume, Americans are not represented positively. After this change in costume, their situation worsens. In *Americans at the Black Sea 2*, there are five agents—three men and two women—who are undercover as tourists and thus seen wearing casual clothes. The men are wearing trousers, t-shirts and caps, and women are in short skirts and tight t-shirts. They are dressed like tourists encountered by Turkish people in real life on the streets. When in casual clothes, they are harmless, naïve and friendly, like tourists rather than agents. When they change into their black suits, which reveal their true identity, they become frightening and dangerous, pointing guns at the Turkish people who welcomed them thus far. To sum up, the agents who are fully American in *Americans at the Black Sea 2* and *Europeans* are depicted as dangerous and as a result, they do not have a relationship with the Turkish characters. Furthermore, their clothing reveals their true identity. In contrast, in *Super Spy K9*, Ayse Kosovalı is half American-half Turkish and as such, is characterised as a Turk with an American appearance. As a result, she is not as dangerous for the Turks as American agents usually are.

Soldier characters are found in the following four films: *Super Spy K9* (Bülent İşbilen, 2008), *Americans at the Black Sea 2* (Kartal Tibet, 2006), *Five Masqueraders – Iraq* (Murat Aslan, 2006), and *Ottoman Republic* (Gani Müjde, 2008). All these characters are in uniform. But what are the differences? *Formality-in-reverse* shows the difference between the clothing and the behaviour of the American characters. In *Super Spy K9*, the general wears a brown uniform, whereas a female soldier wears a skirt as part of her uniform. While the uniform worn by the male characters is formal and resembles a real uniform, the female characters have informal, sexy uniforms, designed to appeal to the male gaze, which is overtly erotic. In *Americans at the Black Sea 2*, the soldiers on the ship wear dark blue uniforms when they are with their admiral. When the admiral is not present, they do not wear their jackets. At the end of the film, when soldiers arrive at the shores of Turkey, they are in dark-blue camouflage, and their faces are painted. This indicates the instability of the characters, who transform easily from naïve soldiers to evil killing machines. In *Five Masqueraders – Iraq*, the soldiers wear light brown uniforms, which are worn in the desert for protection. While the Turkish characters wear green uniforms, which are unsuitable for desert conditions, they seize the well-prepared American army first literally, and then metaphorically, despite wearing the wrong uniforms. In *Ottoman Republic*, the American soldiers again wear dark-blue uniforms, but in some parts of the film, they wear different green-brown uniforms, which are similar to those worn by the Turkish soldiers, and thus by wearing the same colour uniform they admire the Turkish army. This gives way to the acceptance of the superiority of the Turks.

Race and Gender

The agents in *European*, *Super Spy K9* and *Americans at the Black Sea 2* are represented through racist and sexist point of views. *Whitening* is a key factor, which shows exclusion of other races present within western societes in Turkish comedies. Although Americans are not just white Anglo-Saxons, in *European* and *Super Spy K9*, they are portrayed as such. Racism does not only entail representing other races as inferior, it is also limits the visibility and speech of other races. Hall emphasises that:

> The meaning of the picture is produced, Foucault argues, through this complex inter-play between presence (what you see, the visible) and absence (what you can't see, what has displaced it within the frame). Representation works as much through what is not shown, as through what is. (2003, 59)

Disregarding African Americans, Asian Americans, and so on and only casting white Americans demonstrates the tendency toward racist views and/or white supremacy in America as depicted in Turkish sitcoms. While

Americans at the Black Sea 2 does include one African American (Melanie) and an Asian American (Li-Ting), who are agents in the film, the film still displays racist tendencies. When the group of agents in the film is considered, these two people are in the minority as there are also three white Americans. Whether in a small group such as this or a large one like a nation, the minority stays the same. Li-Ting and Melanie do not play an important role in the film; they merely support the white American characters. In addition, the involvement of these characters with the mission and their relationship with the Turkish villagers is relatively small when compared with the roles of the white American males. In addition to their rather small involvement with both the public and their colleagues, they also have fewer lines than the white males.

The sexist point of view in these three films is another issue. *Man Fist* is used to follow the representation of male dominance in Turkish comedies. There are no female American agents in *European*, which shows the patriarchal point of view. *Super Spy K9* has one female agent who is characterised in an overtly sexual way. In *Americans at the Black Sea 2*, the female agents Pamela and Melanie are not as active as their white male colleagues. Li-Ting's ethnic background is a more important defining characteristic than his gender and thus he is placed in the same position as the women. Furthermore, among the three, Pamela, as the only white person, is superior. In addition, the male gaze is dominant. The clothes of the female characters are chosen in order to provoke the attention of the male characters. While Melanie and Pamela dance in their underwear in a room, an old Turkish villager watches them from a tree. While this old man has a voyeuristic fetish in the film, the audience, watching the man watch the girls, partakes in the same voyeuristic pleasure. The focus of all the pleasure (in this film) is on these two women. Nitzan Ben-Shaul states that "Mulvey's major presumption was that films were a product of the 'patriarchal unconscious' and, therefore, served the patriarchal social order by replicating and reinforcing gender patterns that discriminated against women" (2007, 115). These three films support this idea by treating women solely as objects to look at for pleasure.

In contrast to the agents in these films, the soldiers are often of a different race and gender. In *Americans at the Black Sea 2*, there are African-American soldiers, but they are not as involved in the main storyline as the white Americans are. In *Five Masqueraders – Iraq*, there are African-American soldiers and one Asian American (the same actor plays Li-Ting in *Americans at the Black Sea 2)*. In *Super Spy K9*, there are African-American extras. In *Ottoman Republic*, the African-American characters are the servants of the white Americans. Interestingly, no Latin American characters are represented.

With regard to gender representation, three of the films have female characters. In *Super Spy K9*, the female soldiers appear to be more like models than soldiers. In *Five Masqueraders – Iraq*, there is only one female soldier character, and she is seen to be very emotional. This shows how the patriarchal order of society continues to portray women as hysterical. The fact that they are soldiers does not affect their personality. In *Americans at the Black Sea 2*, the role of the female soldiers on the ship is not as important as the male soldiers in the film. In short, the female characters, whether they are agents or soldiers, are primarily used to satisfy the male gaze. Like Ben-Shaul states, "Mulvey's conclusion was that the dominant type of filmmaking (mostly from Hollywood) mainly addressed the male spectator whose scopophilic gaze it pleasured" (2007, 118). Hence, American women are primarily represented in Turkish comedies in a way that appeals to the scopophilic gaze. Women are sole sex objects rather than individuals with personalities.

Orientalisation appears in only one way: turning American women into Turkish villagers who wear traditional clothing. In *Super Spy K9*, the unnamed female soldier, who is the American general's girlfriend, wears a red headscarf while helping the General eat *lahmacun*, a traditional Turkish food. In *Five Masqueraders – Iraq*, Tezcan dreams of a female American soldier in traditional village clothes—again with a red headscarf and *şalvar*, traditional Turkish trousers. The Orientalisation of American women allows Turkey to reign over them; therefore, Turkey gains one more point in the arm-wrestling match.

In comparison, Turkish characters differ in physical appearance. Rather than soldiers and agents, the Turkish characters in these films are civilians. This sends a powerful message as civilians get the upper hand without having to resort to military force.

On the other hand, superimposition is found in two scenes of *Five Masqueraders – Iraq*. In the first scene, the Turkish flag dissolves over American soldiers, and in the second scene the face of the American president dissolves into the Turkish flag. As Anderson points out, "*emblems* of nation-ness, like flags, costumes, folk-dances, and the rest" (Anderson 2000, 133), are symbols of nationality, which is a powerful symbol of Turkish dominance over Americans.

Conclusion

In conclusion, the American characters, or rather, Americans in general, have been overpowered by the Turks in the metaphoric arm-wrestling match on the cinematic battlefield. However, the defeat of the Americans in Turkish comedies does not stand out; rather, it is presented in an entertaining way using the features of the comedy genre. Clothing is used to characterise Americans while helping to defeat them by making them appear "Oriental" and presenting them in such a way that they are not taken seriously. Race and gender distribution has two functions: first, they are factors used to emphasise the Turkish superiority and secondly, they demonstrate the white and male hegemony in these films. In addition, the Americans lose strength as the problems in American society are emphasised. The American characters are naively represented and are in the background, and following the Turks' defeat of the Americans, victory cries can be heard. Hence, once again, "us" becomes superior to "them" in cinema.

Table 1: The Distribution of Race among American Characters

	White American	African American	Asian American	Latin American	Native American
Super Spy K9	√	X	X	X	X
Americans at the Black Sea 2	√	√	√	X	X
Ottoman Republic	√	√	X	X	X
European	√	X	X	X	X
Five Masqueraders Iraq	√	√	√	X	X

Table 2: The Distribution of Roles among American Characters

	Hero	Villain	Lover	Buddy
Super Spy K9	√	X	√	√
Americans at the Black Sea 2	X	√	√	X
Ottoman Republic	X	√	X	X
European	X	√	X	X
Five Masqueraders Iraq	X	√	√	√

Works Cited

Anderson, Benedict. 2000. *Imagined Communities*. London and New York: Verso.

Ben-Shaul, Nitzan. 2007. *Film: The Key Concepts*. Oxford and New York: Berg.

Benyahia, Sarah Casey, Freddie Gaffney, and John White. 2008. *As Film Studies: The Essential Introduction* (2nd edition). London and New York: Routledge.

Corrigan, Timothy. 2011. *A Short Guide to Writing About Film* (8th edition). New York: Longman.

Hall, Stuart, ed. 2003. *Representation: Cultural Representation and Signifying Practices*. London: Sage Publications.

Saïd, Edward W. 2003. *Orientalism,* London: Penguin.

Filmography[2]

Amerikalılar Karadeniz'de 2/Americans at the Black Sea 2 (2006). Directed by Kartal Tibet. Kenda Film. *Avrupalı/European* (2007). Directed by Ulaş Ak. Best Line Pictures.

Maskeli Beşler Irak/Five Masqueraders – Iraq (2006). Directed by Murat Aslan. Özen Film.

Osmanlı Cumhuriyeti/Ottoman Republic (2008). Directed by Gani Müjde. UIP Filmcilik.

Süper Ajan K9/Super Spy K9 (2008). Directed by Bulent İşbilen. Medyavizyon..

---

2. The translations of the titles are my own.

PART V:

NEW RECEPTION

CHAPTER FOURTEEN

A NEW LOOK AT FILM RECEPTION:
SUMMER THEATRES

HILAL ERKAN

Introduction

Open-air theatres were among the most important and widespread entertainment and socialising spaces in Turkey in the 1950s and 1960s, and as such they are a subject worthy of study because of their unique features and the roles they played within Turkish society during this period. The lack of research concerning open-air theatres and audience socialisation within these locations are important deficiencies in today's scholarship. In this study, "open-air theatres" will be analysed as the important entertainment and socialising places of the recent past.

Today, cinema is one of the branches of art that functions as a medium of communication addressing the masses. According to Metz, cinema is an advanced industry because of all the technical tools and equipment it uses, and it can represent all the institutions linked with filmmaking, including distribution, film exhibition and film reception (1977, 5-9). While cinema, in its simplest form, meets our need to communicate, one of our deepest and oldest needs, it also presents a complete and perfect spectacle of reality and enables the reconstruction of the world around us in the shape of illusion that consists of sound, colour and texture (Bazin 2004, 20).

With the invention of film production technology, cinema became an important entertainment apparatus and gained the adoration of the masses, which led cinema to innovate and become a large and important industry. As another result of this attention from the masses, "film screenings" (one of the elements of Metz's definition of the institutions of cinema) became a primary subject of consideration and theatres different in size and aesthetics started to be built. According to Evren, movie theatres created a communal activity, are dream castles of the masses where they live a kind of ritual in the modern age (1998). Theatres are not simply designed for films to be screened and watched collectively. They are also designed for improving the effectiveness of the film's plot and through removing elements that can distract the spectator.

Especially after World War I, an era when cinema evolved rapidly, the number of movie theatres also increased. Alongside indoor-movie theatres, open-air theatres used during the summer time were also established. Despite the worldwide popularity of indoor movie theatres as film screening locations, open-air theatres became an alternative location for spectators, especially in the summer.

As the number of films shot in the late nineteenth century increased, movie theatres also rapidly increased in number in the West. They also started to appear within the Ottoman Empire, which had numerous entertainment spaces such as coffeehouses, baths and promenades. In this era, alongside movie theatres, the number of Western-style entertainment spaces such as patisseries, playhouses and restaurants increased noticeably in the capital of Istanbul. According to Orçan who explains this expansion of people's socialisation "out of the neighbourhood," movie theatres brought a great brightness to daily life (2004, 104-5).

When we look at the historical chronology of the first movie theatres in the Ottoman Empire, we find that the cinematograph of the Lumière brothers was generally accepted as presenting the first film screening. According to official records, the first theatre was Pathé, established in Istanbul in 1908. It was followed by the Palas and the Majik theatres established in Beyoğlu (Onaran in Aydın 2008, 61). After these theatres opened one after another in Istanbul, theatres were then established in İzmir in 1909 and later in Ankara and Bursa (Çakır in Aydın 2008, 62). Between the years 1913 and 1916, when movie theatres in Istanbul were experiencing a huge explosion in numbers, open-air movie theatres started to be established. During this time, the Istanbul audience was discovered by foreign film companies in search of new markets. The first open-air movie theatre was opened in Şişli's Halaskargazi Street in 1913 (Evren 1993, 540). According to Yıldız, the reason behind the increase in the number of open-air theatres in later years was because of the establishment and success of the Yeşilçam film industry. Yeşilçam became an important presence, created an alternative to foreign films in the early 1950s, and reached a wide market which in turn quickly led to an increase in the amount of films that were produced (2007, 270).

Summer theatres have lost their prevalence and appeal today, but were important entertainment locations when domestic films were in high demand in the 1960s and the 1970s. When we think of the reasons for the summer theatres' increase in number, we can link this to a few observable facts. During that period, going to a movie theatre was an important leisure-time activity for possible spectators. As a result, both domestic and foreign film screenings increased in number. However, the indoor-movie theatres established during that period were not able to meet the increasing demands of spectators. Open-air theatres, which were less costly to establish than indoor ones, gained prominence as an alternative to indoor theatres and were an economically favourable way to increase film-watching locations in order to screen more films and to satisfy a larger audience. Hence, the insufficiency of indoor-movie theatre space is the reason behind the increase in the number of open-air theatres. That there were no indoor-movie theatres in rural areas certainly hints towards the impact open-air theatres had on film-watching experience

Despite both types of theatres being film screening locations, there are differences in the film-watching experience in indoor and open-air theatres. Since there are no walls surrounding the audience, open-air theatres offer more bodily and performative freedom to the spectators while watching the film. This freedom is based on physical comfort and the opportunity for greater participation as well as enabling emotional reaction to the film. These are places where the rules could be bent and allowed spectators to react with the film as they wished without restricting them. Richard Sennett calls this communication between the spectators within the open-air theatres "spontaneity" (Sennett 2006). The characteristic of "spontaneity" can be defined as something that enabled individuals to have the flexibility to express their inner dynamics or allowed them to experience something naturally and without the effect of an external force, which makes the open-air theatres "unique".

According to Vural and Yücel, while interpersonal and public relationships start losing their spontaneity as Sennett defines, the locations in which these relationships are experienced begin to turn into artificial places and relationships. This occurs because of the loss of the ability to express these inner dynamics, an aftermath of external pressure, which we can liken to products that lose their uniqueness because of serial production (Vural and Yücel 2006, 100).

The loss of spontaneity and freedom produced in public places, which enables social sharing, can be interpreted via Arendt's view regarding capitalist dynamics and their erosion of public opinion, meaning and importance. According to Hannah Arendt, capitalism creates intrapersonal individuals who see themselves in competition with others, and these individuals evaluate their place in society, not through and with each other, but with general production and consumption lines. They therefore lose empathy towards each other and prefer to live their subjectivity alone in contrast to discussion within a life of social interaction (Arendt 1969, 32-65). While the necessity of interacting with others in order to create a bond with audiences disappears when one retreats to the satisfaction provided by subjectivity, the urban fabric of today now consists of places such as plazas, malls and movie theatres "constructed" to isolate individuals pursuing leisure-time activity and entertainment instead of socialising them. Despite their multiplex offerings, these man-made, consumption-oriented places that are unable to move with the inner dynamics of the global age will flourish more and more. They are all uniform and according to Bilsel, with limited business, entertainment and leisure-time activities, these places only provide a simulation of public life. Further, Bilsel points out two of the facts revealed by such urban development to be, firstly, spatial fragmentation, which can be linked with these constructed places that are constantly monitored, and secondly, the social segregation necessitated by this spatial fragmentation. Spatial fragmentation of the city strengthens the social segregation, which can also be defined as a disintegration of society with socio-economic and cultural separations. This condition forces a separation between different groups in society with an emphasis on the increasing economic income disparity and a decline in the way in which these groups live. The city and the places/spaces within the city therefore move away from being shared social spaces and become pieces divided by social groups (Bilsel 2009, 2-4).

Looking at this from another vantage point, the spatial fragmentation and social segregation which contemporary civic centres and social living areas contain, are not reflecting a dialog and a dialogical statement based on polyphony referred to by the *carnival*, Bakhtin's connective and emancipating concept against pressure and monophony, but instead produce a monophonic statement which implies monotony and insistence. According to Vaneigem, the "ecstasy" that is the essence of Bakhtin's polyphonic and emancipating concept *carnival* is the exact opposite of the sickness of survival, which is the physical and the psychological result of the cold world of business and marketing at the root of capitalism. "The sickness of survival" which is placed against the ecstasy of the carnival by Vaneigem, is an unpleasant experience provided by the system (1994, 76-110).

While these critiques about "space" and the social relationships produced within these "spaces" explain the reasons behind open-air movie theatres and their unique and emancipating spatial features, these critiques also define the perspective this study will use to examine these particular spaces which have now lost their popularity. The open-air movie theatres united people from different age groups and socio-economic levels in an atmosphere of festivity like a *carnival* and open the doors to enthusiastic experience just as Vaneigem once dreamed.

This essay is based on interviews with two individuals who experienced the open-air theatres of the 1950s and 1960s. The main reason these individuals were chosen was because of their frequent visits to open-air theatres during that era and, most importantly, because their knowledge and experience encompass both rural and urban open-air theatres. However, this subject deserves a deeper examination through a series of interviews with more participants. For this reason, in future publications, this subject will be examined more deeply by recalling oral histories regarding open-air cinemas and the forms of socialising that occurred in these spaces.

Summer Theatres as Public Places

When we think of communication, we realise it is a process that enables thought, information and emotions to be shared and alongside all of this, for an individual to become socialised. An important question arises from this definition: "Where does communication take place?"

In the same way that the universe is linked to movement in time and space, communication cannot be separated from time and place. It is hard to talk about placeless communication. That is because a place has an important force behind the establishment or effect of communication. Place plays a "decisive" role when it affects the communication between people and the nature of communication. The decisiveness of a place is "a three-dimensional expression of the gap, the distance and the relationship between humans and objects" (Erdönmez and Akı 2005, 69), related to the configuration of the emptiness and/or fullness of the location. In other words, place is decisive because it either blocks our motions or sets them free. For example, when planning a city, designated spaces do not just define the places where people get together or are separated from each other, they also define the type of communication between placeas and individuals. Therefore, public places like streets, squares, boulevards, parks, theatres, cinemas, concert halls, cafés and coffee places have the power of determining the city's face and the communication between its people. Bilsel explains the efficiency of public places, which he defines as the "physical places" in which "people get together, see each other, are seen and [which] enable people to exist in public areas in their everyday life," in determining the communication and interaction among people with their quality of being accessible by everyone (2009, 4). According to

Arendt, who believes that public places form our concrete and institutionalised common world and help us to exist together, these places constitute our interpersonal relationships (1969, 45-60).

Even though each has a similar film-screening technique, open-air theatres are places where rules are more flexible compared to indoor theatres. Open-air summer theatres that allow people to consume food and beverages and provide them with freedom of movement and reaction are, in this way, quite like public backyards. Open-air theatres, which are not only used for watching films but also for moments of social sharing, are public places that help people to connect with each other and to socialise.

One oral history was given by Lale Çelik, who stated that the first things she associated with open-air theatres were summertime, wooden chairs and viewing the newest films. She adds:

> There were wooden chairs in open-air cinemas, tied together; the big screen would shake before the wind from time to time. The screen was so big that it was possible to watch the film from neighbouring houses. Open-air theatres were very valuable, especially for the people from small towns because they didn't have any other form of entertainment. Most of the villages, which had open-air theatres, didn't have any indoor/winter cinemas. People would wait until evening with excitement, and they would try to come early to the cinema to nab a seat. People would cook and eat early before they got to the cinema; young children and the elderly would be sent to their beds. In big cities, there was at least one open-air cinema in every neighbourhood. The film advertisements, especially in small establishments, were very interesting and entertaining. They would put a big poster of the film which was supposed to be screened at the theatre that night on a truck, and they would advertise it using a microphone; information such as the artists in the film, the starting hour, the theatre where the film would be presented to the public. This voice could be heard from our houses many times during the day, and the people would look forward with excitement to the evening.

There were certain ceremonial aspects revolving around this event, which included the advertisement of the films, the selection of the film to be screened and the finishing of housework after the theatre evening—all this because open-air cinema was one of the cheapest forms of entertainment. Indoor cinemas were too costly for the family of a low-level government clerk to be able to visit in the 1950s and 1960s. However, during that period, open-air theatres provided cheap entertainment to all members within the family with tickets costing only one lira and free entrance for children under twelve.[1]Open-air cinemas functioned as television does today, as a cheap and easily-accessible entertainment. Lale Çelik also emphasised the fact that open-air cinemas were very inexpensive forms of entertainment.

> Summer cinemas were places where people went to watch films and then afterwards, we went to sleep—just like watching TV in our homes. Furthermore, it was very cheap. The open-air cinemas in the towns and villages I visited were like neighbourhood cinemas. They were in all neighbourhoods; everyone could access them and because of their prices, everyone could afford them.

The oral history of Basri Çelik emphasised the notion that open-air cinemas were forgotten after television came into everyday use in life.

> Open-air cinemas were the source of all entertainment until we bought a television in the 1970s. After we bought a television, we stopped going to open-air cinemas, but they continued to serve the ones who didn't have televisions in their homes for a few more years.

Besides the function of screening films/providing entertainment as television does, another important quality of these places is in providing the comfort of a home environment. At the end of the interviews, both participants emphasised the freedom of consuming food and beverages in these places. Lale Çelik voices her thoughts about how spectators could eat and drink before and during the screening:

> Sodas, sunflower seeds, bagels, cucumbers, wooden chairs…you couldn't enjoy the film without those. The sound of sunflower seeds cracking would mix with the film's sound. Beneath the chairs would be full of shells, and we wouldn't stop eating fruit until the end of the film. Probably, the thing that annoyed the cinema workers most in the morning was those shells. Now it's forbidden to eat seeds in the cinema, but they were probably the biggest treat of the summer cinemas. Seeds, corn cobs, sodas in our hands…soda was very cheap back then. Inside there were people selling grapes, corn and seeds.

Regarding the food and beverages consumed in open-air cinemas in the past, Basri Çelik said:

---

1. By today's standards admission fees are ten times higher and tickets have to be purchased for children as well.

Most goods sold in open-air cinemas were sodas and fruit sodas. There were no packed ice creams available during that time; therefore, we would buy ice-cream cones and eat them while watching the film. Wooden chairs painted white, and the sound of the projector dominated the place. Tons of sunflower seeds overflowing from paper bags in your hands…Everyone would eat seeds in a hurry as if they believed that the more seeds they ate, the more they would enjoy the movie. Those who got carried away with the film wouldn't even notice the mountain of shells rising in front of them.

Open-Air Cinemas as Places Where Emotions are Expressed

At first glance, indoor and open-air cinema spaces do not appear to be that different from each other. In both, the spectator is carried away by the magical atmosphere and "faces the problems that he/she cannot confront in daily life with a relaxed attitude, catharsis as Aristotle defines, resulted from participating with what is seen through one's emotions" (Abisel 1999, 7), and thus, an emotional discharge is achieved. For Abisel, the most important difference between cinema and other forms of popular entertainment is the more concentrated emotional participation it presents. "A cinema audience's relationship with a popular film is based mostly on the emotional participation starting from the beginning. Anger, joy, sadness, and horror are some emotions, which can be felt and expressed when watching a film" (ibid.).

As the place where the viewer watches the film has a decisive impact on his or her emotional participation, indoor and open-air cinemas differentiate themselves from one another in the way of aiding or preventing the "expression" of different emotions. Indoor cinemas, which were established in the modern city/culture, have spatial characteristics that prevent the expression of emotions. Even though the spectator is left alone with him/herself after the lights go out and can participate emotionally and achieve a relaxed state, s/he cannot easily express verbally what s/he feels during the screening after the experience takes place. The walls and their predominance have a direct effect on the interaction the spectator has with him/herself, and especially with the others around him or her.

Contrary to indoor cinemas, summer cinemas have the spatial qualities that help them provide a high level of emotional participation and expression for the spectators. First, there is enough light for spectators to see each other's faces, since open-air cinemas are not just places for watching films, but also for chatting and having fun. As illuminated space, they help relatives, neighbours and friends see each other, which also enables them to observe each other's emotional responses during the film.

Sennett's statement that "how people react to each other, see and hear one another creates obvious differences on determining the emotional distance and the spatial relationship of their human bodies" (2006, 12) helps to explain both the force that enables interaction and the emotional expression between spectators in open-air cinemas. This feeling of connection and the loss of emotional expression is blocked by the spatial qualities of indoor cinemas.

Lale Çelik, who also believes that indoor cinemas prevent emotional expression, remembers the emotional intensity she experienced in open-air cinemas.

> Perhaps, summer cinemas were places where we experienced our strangest, most cheerful and saddest moments. Film characters seemed like ordinary people just like us. We were identifying ourselves with these characters, getting excited while they were struggling with the villain and sometimes supporting the protagonist boisterously and very loudly. I would cry while watching those films. Everything was allowed during the screening, to whistle, to cry, to yell, to laugh. You can't express yourself that easily in an indoor cinema. There are boundaries, and you'll be warned...

These shared emotions and the joy of watching a film in open-air cinemas can be explained by the revelation of emotions as a result of the sight of the other spectators' faces. According to Derry, films are communal, and they offer an experience to be shared by the masses. To provide this social experience, films are made to be screened in public places where spectators can observe each other (1987, 163). Even if Derry talks about film-viewing places in general here, it is hard to observe the reactions of other spectators within an indoor theatre. On the contrary, in indoor cinemas the spectator is focused solely on the film. The observation of others' reactions becomes possible only in the open-air cinemas.

Basri Çelik says that open-air cinemas helped people to socialise and share their feelings during the 1950s-1960s when these places were popular.

> Emotions would be shared always by crying and observing the other spectators who would also cry when watching dramatic Turkish films. In comedy films, the sound of the film couldn't be heard when we laughed out loud. Sometimes people who disagreed with the villain's actions would yell with discontent or even curse at him. Voices from spectators like "Shame on you, you've harmed him enough!" could be heard often. That would show people were immersed in the film and were expressing their

emotions freely. I would think that all the spectators in the cinema were relatives or the members of the same family. I cannot experience the same emotional intensity and joy in today's movie theatres or in front of the television.

Socialisation in Open-Air Cinemas

While public space creates a common ground connecting people to each other, the emergence of social life is linked with people's experiences of the "state" between place and space. One of the most important functions of public places is to create a place of social interaction. It is in the interactions of life created by the gathering of people at these places; the way people communicate with each other, the way that they socialise, that enables them to form a common identity. Another important feature of public places is to provide "encounters". While Anthony Giddens mentions Goffman's "typology regarding the boundaries of interaction," he defines "encounters" as a focused interaction materialised with face-to-face connections among routines (Giddens 1986, 103). Physically being together with other people, the connections between bodies, the gathering and/or forming of social synergy through these routine activities enable a social texture to be formed. However, gatherings are more "loose" and "temporary" structures compared to social synergy formed by two or more persons. On the other hand, social synergies as "gatherings that contain a plurality of individuals" form in more figural contexts (Giddens 1986, 120-21).

This is how being together at summer cinemas formed a social synergy in the "figural" contexts that Giddens describes. This social synergy is limited as "chronic" and "spatial" in terms of the place itself and the duration of synergy in the place. Summer cinemas limited to those figural contexts helped people to get together and to socialise in the 1950s and 1960s. In deciding on which film to go to and watch together after viewing the advertisements of the film, to get together at an agreed-upon time and even using these places to help people to make up with each other are some of the important details that show the socialisation effect of open-air cinemas. Basri Çelik, who connects friendship and the sincere relationships among the people at these places to the removal of class differences between people in open-air cinemas, commented,

> there could be people you don't know in front or behind you, but after the film finished you would talk of the film with those new friends. It would be very hard to get rid of the effect the film created. People also would make plans to watch other films in the upcoming days.

Lale Çelik explains the reasons she cannot enjoy contemporary summer cinemas:

> after years, one day here in Istanbul my friends said 'There is a summer cinema in Caddebostan Burak Cinema; shall we go?" I was surprised. In the end, we went to that cinema with a few friends. I couldn't find that communication, the sincerity, and the honest expression of emotion of the old summer cinemas in this one. People came, got seated, watched the film and then left, cold-blooded. In the old days in Ankara, people I saw in summer cinemas would greet each other with smiles, would chat about politics, business and their children's college education during the interval and after the film finished...

Melodramas and Love in Summer Cinema

Henri Lefebvre stated that place is not a background or scene of physical existence, considering it instead as a social product full of dynamic interactions, conflicts and contradictions. According to Lefebvre, place is both a product of and a mechanism constantly transforming society (Lefebvre 1995, 195). When Lefebvre's dialectic frame on place is examined, it can be said that while place determines social relationships, sometimes it becomes "determined" by society as a product of it. This shows that a place has a flexible structure. Thus, it becomes possible for people to change the meaning they attach to places and their functional features or add a new one onto existing functions.

Open-air cinemas are concrete examples of the meaning that people put on a place and how that can be transformed by people who share a unique physical location at the same time. The act of being together in an open-air cinema shows it as "a place or area where several social synergies occur, each containing more than one gathering" (Giddens 1999, 121). Open-air cinemas are ideal environments for some people to watch a movie, for others to chat while watching a film or for others to have contact among the members of the opposite sex. In this range of meanings that people put on a place, we see that the different gatherings and social synergies created by people who get together in a unique location transform the place into a "determined" entity.

Describing those different gatherings at open-air cinemas, Basri Çelik said:

> The young people who come from different houses in the neighbourhood would decide on the time they'd meet, and they would wait for each other in front of the cinema to go in and get seated in the same row. Young folks would wait for their fiancées, girlfriends/boyfriends or friends in front of

the cinema; engaged and married couples would enter the cinema hand in hand. In open-air cinemas, young people in love were interested in flirting or chatting with each other rather than watching the film.

Some people consider the age of *Yeşilçam* in the 1950s and 1960s the Golden Age of Turkish cinema. This was the time when summer cinemas were also popular, an era of Turkish cinema "where around three hundred films were produced yearly, and the number of production companies, movie theatres and people who work[ed] within the film sector increased daily" (Mutlu 2001, 111). In this period, open-air cinemas were widespread and the first important genre to attain success in Turkish cinema was melodrama (Arslan 2001, 194). Although melodramas faced criticism because they were often produced to make money, they also acquired the highest number of spectators during these years. According to Mutlu, melodramas, which are often criticised for their lack of rationality and logic, basically function to help spectators reach a catharsis rather than arrive at rational responses to everyday life. Melodramatic narration with the use of good and evil characters along with the obstacles that the protagonists faced is based on constant surprises, unexpected encounters and amazing, miraculous endings (Mutlu 2001: 111-8).

Lale Çelik believes that watching a film in an open-air cinema was a magnificent experience. She stated that she lived with the constant excitement of going and watching a film during the period when domestic melodramas were popular in the 1960s.

> We would go to the same film nearly every night until a new one came out, but every time we would experience new excitement as if we were watching it for the first time. We would be carried away with the film so much that we would read all the names projected onto the screen one by one out of curiosity. All the names from the artists to the extras, the electricians to the sound technicians and the director...we would take starring actors as role models for ourselves. After all, films during that period were like reflections of life. Maybe that's why we loved and embraced cinema...Cüneyt Arkın, Sadri Alışık, Filiz Akın, Erol Taş, Türkan Şoray...all of them were our heroes. Everybody wanted to become one of them...films were so emotional and exciting that sometimes we would get carried away with laughter and tears. Whenever the curtain fell, and lights were switched on, only then would we understand that the film was finished.

Yeşilçam cinema and especially Yeşilçam melodrama, which attracted large audiences to open-air cinemas and allowed for emotional release with its narrative structure are, in Bülent Oran's words "...an escapist cinema for the spectator. It is a cinema of stories where s/he can identify and find him/herself with it..." (Oran in Mutlu 2001, 120).

Conclusion

The increase in the number of films produced in the 1950s and 1960s when Turkish cinema started to reach the masses allowed the low-cost open-air theatres to be opened as alternatives to indoor theatres. There was an insufficient number of indoor theatres in the big cities, and they were almost non-existent in rural areas. During this time, summer theatres, which had spread in popularity not only to suburban neighbourhoods and larger provinces, but also to the villages of Anatolia, had allowed films to be screened by different sections of society. At that time, when entertainment venues were limited in number, open-air cinemas served not only as places to watch films but also as gathering places where people could engage in various forms of social interaction.

It is possible to form an analogy between open-air theatres that provided a location for different social experience beyond being places that allowed people to watch films together as described by Bakhtin's *carnival*, which has joy and festival in its roots. Bakhtin likens rituals in carnivals to a world of laughter full of passion, joy and festive atmosphere and provided resistance toward ideological boundaries (1984, 59). Rituals and the experience of summer cinemas are similar in how the social experience accompanying them is often direct, sincere and natural.

Summer cinemas satisfied the basic needs of people such as unity, joy and laughter, and these were found within the neighbourhood. These cinemas slowly began to lose their popularity in the 1970s when television put an end to the sovereignty of the silver screen. While the dominance that television exerted over cinemas was causing an important decrease in the number of open-air cinemas, individual interactions were confined to private areas; people stayed at home where they would be less likely to engage with other individuals and started to live through their own subjective and personal experience. In 1980s, with the rise of videos, the number of traditional cinema spectators declined even more as they stayed at home to watch films. Summer cinemas and also indoor cinemas started to close in large numbers and because of this, the makers of Turkish cinema started to experience serious financing problems.

Works Cited

Abisel, Nilgün. 1999. *Popüler Sinema ve Türler* (Popular Cinema and Genres). Istanbul: Alan Yayıncılık.

Arslan, Savaş. 2001. "Türk Tapon Filmlerini Oyun Olarak Okuma Denemesi"(An Attempt to Read Turkish Trash Films as a Game). In *Türk Film Araştırmalarında Yeni Yönelimler* (New Directions in Turkish Film Studies), edited by Deniz Derman, 185-201. Istanbul: Bağlam Yayınları.

Aydın, Hakan. 2008. "Sinemanın Taşrada Gelişim Süreci: Konya'da İlk Sinemalar ve Gösterilen Filmler (1910–1950) (The Development of Cinema in the Rural Areas: First Film Theaters in Konya and Films Shown)". *Selçuk Üniversitesi Sosyal Bilimler Enstitüsü Dergisi* (19): 61–74.

Arendt, Hannah. 1969. *The Human Condition*. Chicago: The University of Chicago Press.

Bazin, André. 2004. *What is Cinema? Vol. 1* Translated by Hugh Gray. Berkeley: University of California Press.

Bakhtin, Mikhail. 1984. *Rabelais and His World*. Indiana: Indiana University Press.

Bilsel, Cana. 2009. *Yeni Dünya Düzeninde Çözülen Kentler ve Kamusal Alan: İstanbul'da Merkezkaç Kentsel Dinamikler ve Kamusal Mekân Üzerine Gözlemler (*Dissolved cities in the New World Order and Public Space: Observations on Centrepetal Urban Dynamics and Public Space in Istanbul). Available online at: http:// old.mo.org.tr/mimarlikdergisi. (17/02/2009).

Derry, Charles. 1987. *More Dark Dreams: Some Notes on the Recent Horror Film, American Horrors, Essays on Modern American Horror Film*. Urbana: University of Illinois Press.

Erdönmez, M. Ebru and Altan Akı. 2005. "Açık Kamusal Kent Mekânlarının Toplum İlişkilerindeki Etkileri"(Effects of Public Urban Spaces on Social Relations) *Yıldız Teknik Üniversitesi Mimarlık Fakültesi Dergisi* 1 (1): 67–87.

Evren, Burçak. *Eski İstanbul Sinemaları: Düş Şatoları*, (Old Istanbul Theaters: Dream Palaces) Istanbul: Milliyet Yayınları, 1998.

—. 1993. "Bahçe Sinemaları" (Garden Theaters). In *Dünden Bugüne İstanbul Ansiklopedisi (İstanbul Encyclopedia From Past to Now)*, Vol. 6, 540-41. Istanbul: Kültür Bakanlığı ve TVY Yayınları.

Giddens, Anthony. 1986. *The Constitution of Society: Outline of the Theory of Structuration*. Berkeley: University of California Press.

Lefebvre, Henri. 1995. *The Production of Space*. Cambridge: Blackwell.

Metz, Christian. 1977. *The Imaginary Signifier*. Edited by Celia Britton, Annwyl Williams. Bloomington: Indiana University Press.

Mutlu, Dilek Kaya. 2001. "Yerli Melodramlar ve Ruhsal Boşalım" (Local Melodramas and Catharsis). In *Türk Film Araştırmalarında Yeni Yönelimler* (New Directions in Turkish Film Studies), edited by Deniz Derman, 111-20. Istanbul: Bağlam Yayınları.

Orçan, Mustafa. 2004. *Osmanlı'dan Günümüze Modern Türk Tüketim Kültürü (Modern Comsumption Culture from Ottoman Times to Now)*. Ankara: Kadim Yayınları.

Sennett, Richard. 2006. *Flesh and Stone: The Body and the City in Western Civilization*. New York: W.W. Norton.

Vaneigem, Raoul. 1994. *The Revolution of Everyday Life*. London: Rebel.

Vural, Tülin and Atilla Yücel. 2006. "Çağımızın Yeni Kamusal Mekânları Olan Alışveriş Merkezlerine Eleştirel Bir Bakış" (A Critical Look at Shopping Malls as New Public Spaces of Our Time). *İstanbul Teknik Üniversitesi Mimarlık Fakültesi Dergisi* 5 (2)97-106.

Yıldız, Pelin. 2007. "Film Sahnelerinde Sosyo-Kültürel Yansımalara İlişkin Türkiye'den Seçilen Örneklerle Analiz Çalışması" (On Socio-Cultural Reflections of Film Ssenes: The Sample from Turkey) *Gazi Üniversitesi Eğitim Fakültesi Dergisi* 27 (1): 261–75.

Interviews

Lale Çelik, Interview, İstanbul, 4 May 2009
Basri Çelik, Interview, İstanbul, 10 May 2009

CHAPTER FIFTEEN

INTERNATIONAL FILM FESTIVALS:
A CINEMA STRUGGLING TO EXIST BETWEEN
NEW RESOURCES AND NEW "DEPENDENCIES"

TÜLAY ÇELIK

Introduction

As a new film language emerged in post-1990 Turkish cinema, production relationships began to be determined by new dynamics. A large part of the components that shaped the production of post-1990 films found their source in the changes that took place in cinema between 1970 and 1980.[1] American distribution companies began entering the country, large theatres began to close; distributors dominated the new theatres and the implementation of "package programs" in the early 1990s reduced a films' chance of being screened which in turn also restricted opportunities for new productions. Subsidies from the Ministry of Culture began during this period, but fell short in light of films' production costs. The establishment of an economic relationship with the United States and the submissive policy the Turkish government adhered to in the field of

---

1. While Yeşilçam (the Turkish film industry of that period) was encountering its demise, directors attempted to make films independently with some of those directors even creating their own film companies. Thus, the first important steps of the post-1990 production period were taken. It is interesting to note on the other hand, that the conditions of art film production improved in the 1980s. Efforts to construct a unique cinematic language and examples of the concept of cinema which carried a personal imprint were encountered during that period: a few 'auteur' directors came to the fore and, with the visibility provided by international film festivals, expectations of orientalism became an issue. Also during that time, the films which could be regarded as art films competed with popular cinema especially Arabesk films which dominated the culture and began to increase in number with the post-1980 cultural transition.

communications led to compromises within the cultural arena. As the state was unable to play a constructive role within the field of film production during this period, a new understanding of production developed through individual efforts, which started in the 1980s and began to flourish in the second half of the 1990s. Production subsidies provided by Eurimages, which Turkey joined in 1990, became a significant factor in establishing this new understanding. While the field of "auteur cinema" began to take shape around the axis of individualism, popular cinema began to emerge as a significant presence during this period. Television, advertising and sponsorship became new components of film production.

On one side of the construct that emerged in the second half of the 1990s, there was the field of "auteur cinema," and on the other, popular cinema, which followed in the footsteps of Hollywood films and was dominated by, and fell under the influence of, distributors. The most important and threatening characteristic of a dominant cinema can be understood through the concept of the culture industry in that it communicates a particular ideology through cultural products. In order to find an audience and theatres in which to be viewed, "auteur cinema" in Turkey was forced to compete with popular Turkish cinema, and could not strongly hold its own against the dominant ideology. An interesting example occurs in 1996 when a large number of viewers went to the cinema to see *The Bandit/Eşkıya* (Turgul, 1996) for the first time. In contrast, *Somersault in a Coffin/Tabutta Rövaşata* (Zaim, 1996) was only able to attract a very small audience, but was the starting point for this new conception of cinema where the majority of film production was created through individual effort and produced universal, deep, lasting meanings, thereby putting forth a unique cinematic language, encompassing within it a quest for truth—and criticism of society from within.

In 2010, a full fifteen years after the emergence of this new concept of film production, directors who wanted to wriggle out of the tight confines of market conditions were forced to enter into new dependent relationships in order to make their own films. The fundamental reason for this dependency is the limiting circumstances of film production in Turkey. Ensuring the continuing production of films not tied to commercial concerns depends upon the coming together of many different components, most of them involving subsidies. Of these components, international film festivals occupy an important place. Before we can talk of the relationship of international film festivals and their likely effects on Turkish cinema through their fundamental characteristics and their functioning, it is necessary to mention, albeit briefly, the mechanisms of production outside the festivals in order to grasp the structure of film production today and to discuss the place of international film festivals in view of Turkish cinema.

In order to be more independent and to produce the films they want, the film directors who work in "auteur cinema" choose to become producers. Such a choice requires that the production be arranged by the director. Production becomes a creative process for the director, who has to find solutions to reduce the budget and to use it wisely. In this situation, we encounter a director who dominates the entire process of making a film. Inherent in the concept of director-producer, each director owns a production company (for more detailed information see Çelik 2009); however, the fact that a director has a production company does not mean that he can create his own budget. Especially in the field of "auteur cinema," box-office revenues usually do not provide the financial resources required to maintain the production process. The fact that directors establish production companies in order to become independent is actually a result of the imposition of other dependent relationships, because the three main resources that feed the film production process in Turkey—the Ministry of Culture, Eurimages and festivals[2]—require the director be linked to a production company.[3]

The other components of the process for film production, which can be viewed as the available financial resources, can be identified as sponsorship, television sales and DVD sales. However, this is not a means to provide for the production itself.[4] With this in mind, the main components of production in Turkish cinema would be the Ministry of Culture, Eurimages and festivals.

The support of the Ministry of Culture is important in the process of film production. Although it can be seen as a small sum when compared to other European countries, this support is necessary for the directors who have to work with low budgets to produce films since there are no other

---

2.In order to apply for the subsidies of both the Ministry of Culture and Eurimages, it is necessary to own a production company or to obtain the approval of one. Similarly, to facilitate the sales of the film through the festivals requires the existence of the production company. Funds abroad deal with the producers. Under these circumstances, every director has to establish—or to make a contract with—a production company before beginning the film-production process.

3. We encounter a new component added to the production process: the role of the executive producer. Due to the long production process, the necessity to provide the financing for the film from various sources and the necessity to carry out the international distribution work of the film, the collaboration with executive producers began.

4. The factors we mention are becoming a more important source of income for the popular cinema.

institutions or organisations in Turkey which provide such support. Furthermore, this support can often be seen as providing a major contribution which in turn is needed in order to create a budget which can then receive Eurimages' support. On the other hand, the fact that the Ministry of Culture can exempt the films from many obligations of repayment, on the condition that they are screened and receive awards in certain festivals, and leave the assessment of their quality to a group of national or international film festivals emerges as an ideological issue. We can talk about a particular network of relationships and a system of priorities in regard to the festivals within a national arena. International film festivals are institutions, which have commercial functions at their core (the commercial structure of the festivals will be discussed in detail in the next section). The state's decision regarding this cultural field signifies surrendering this cultural field to uncertain preferences, market conditions and the dependency relationships which shape the international network, and thereby impel the directors to follow the same course.

One of the important factors of the production process is the support of Eurimages. Although this support is not granted to many films, it creates activity in the field of film production and exists as an important option, especially for "auteur cinema". There has been an increase in the technical quality and improvement of relationships within international film production that is witnessed in the growing number of joint productions. However, in Turkey, some difficulties were experienced during the process of entering the co-production network which upheld European standards. This was due partly because Turkey had not yet fully broken away from the production mentality of the past. Today, important steps toward the elimination of shortcomings of the functioning of the co-production process can be observed. The start of joint productions with major (film-producing) countries has accelerated this process. Screening the film in the countries that have helped co-produce it for example, increases the number viewers as well as giving it an international audience all the while expanding the area of responsibility of the director. Another point that joint productions reveal is that pressure from the partners can be an issue and partner intervention is perceived as a variable dependent on the will of the director.[5]

International film festivals, which we discuss in this study with the thesis that they create a new dependency relationship, exist as an important factor which facilitates film circulation as well as one that determines the

---

5. For the study titled *Film Üretim Süreci* (*Film Production Process*), see *Post-1990s Film-Production Process in Turkey in the "Auteur Cinema" Field* (Çelik 2009).

production process. To see the relationship established with festivals in detail, it is necessary, first of all, to talk of the emergence of film festivals, the change in the structure of international film festivals and how these festivals function.

International Film Festivals

Film festivals, where films from different countries are viewed by an international audience, began to appear after World War II. Many different reasons can be mentioned regarding their emergence; however, what we do know is that cultural nationalism policies, and the aims and activities of the nation-state are at their origin (Stringer 2001, 136). Another reason is the desire to gain some field of existence via art films in relation to Hollywood (Elsaesser 2005a, 85-89). While, on one hand, the nationalistic aspect of film festivals comes to the fore, on the other, festivals have provided important opportunities for the field across the art film to demonstrate itself as an area where countries positioned themselves against Hollywood.[6] In the festivals, nationality becomes visible. However, festivals have also been very important within the context of finding opportunities for the international distribution of these art films, for their being accepted as an art, for their being rewarded and for balancing their artistic value with their commercial potential (Neale 1981, 35). Attention was drawn to the important "auteurs" of the 1950s and 1960s through festivals (Thompson and Bordwell 2003, 716). Furthermore, from the 1970s onwards, the place where new trends were introduced has also been in film festivals. Minorities and political pressure groups, women's cinema, gay and queer cinema, ecological movements (Elsaesser 2005a, 92-100), third-world political films (Thompson and Bordwell 2003, 716), all found an opportunity to express their views in festivals. In the context of bringing art cinema into existence, being a point of visibility for different areas and establishing and maintaining relationships in a multicultural perspective (Stringer 2001, 134), film festivals have been a locus in the world film culture (Thompson and Bordwell 2003, 716).

---

6. Here, it is necessary to remember Neale's views associated with the convergence of national cinema and art cinema: "Art cinema is always, then, a matter of balance between these two aspects [international and national]. The nature of this balance can perhaps best be exemplified by the fact that during the course of their international circulation, Art films tend nearly always to retain a mark which serves simultaneously as a sign of their cultural status and a sign of their national origin. This mark is that of the national language" (Neale 1981, 36).

The transformation witnessed in festivals since their emergence reveals that the festival structure should now be evaluated using different concepts. The growing internationalisation of cinema in connection with economic and political changes, the collapse of the Hollywood studio system, the proliferation of independent film production (Thompson and Bordwell 2003, 716) have also had a determining impact on the identity of festivals. The 1980s can be viewed as the decade in which these changes occurred. During this time, the classical festival centres begin to change. New festivals emerged in Asia, Australia and North America (Sundance, Toronto, and Montreal) and these festivals acquired an important status. These festivals, which follow global trends, greatly affect the international distribution and domestic screenings (Elsaesser 2005a, 91).

In the 1990s, as the number of festivals continued to grow rapidly, global distribution gained importance. While there were a hundred annual festivals in 1981, this number increased to seven hundred in 2001. The festivals became diversified in terms of duration, themes, genres, awards and categories. However, as the variety increased, a classification of festivals was initiated. The prestigious Class A festivals were the most effective ones in regards to the network that circulates films (Thompson and Bordwell 2003, 716-17). All of these changes reveal that festivals have an important role in marketing films made outside of Hollywood and in reaching the international audience.[7]

The fundamental characteristics of festivals, especially those associated with festivals' emergence and the changes to their structure are listed above: I would like to review and discuss the relationship to this film festival funding-distribution structure in regard to Turkish cinema and the crucial role of this relationship to production, by relating the experiences of directors who produced films in Turkey and participated in international festivals, while presenting example films. In the course of this review, studying many different components of film festivals, grouped in three main categories—Festival Funds, Criteria and Giant Distribution Network —will help to clarify the basic factors in determining the impact of international film festivals and allow us to see the functioning of the production process clearly.

---

7. Iranian "independent" cinema, which became popular through the festivals, achieved great international fame and reached audiences around the world thanks to the festivals (Kırel 2007, 401-403). Latin American cinema is considered as part of Europe also thanks to being invited to festivals (Elsaesser 2005, 465).

Festival Funds: Making a Festival Film

Applying for funds under the auspices of a film festival is not only beneficial in terms of receiving support, but also in facilitating a more comfortable entry into the later stages of the process of circulation by the prestige and recognition this support provides. Semih Kaplanoğlu says that he benefited from the Hubert Bals Script Development Fund under the scope of the Rotterdam Film Festival for the film *Angel's Fall/Meleğin Düşüşü* (Kaplanoğlu 2004). Kaplanoğlu wrote the script after the film received that support and began to look for a partner through Eurimages' applications. He says that the search for a partner was long because it was his second film, but indicates that, with the references he found through the fund, he was able to find a Greek producer. After he found this partner, the Hubert Bals Fund also supported the post-production. Kaplanoğlu states that this fund was important for his cinema:

> I had sent them a scenario. If this support had not been granted—because I had nothing, I mean; not even a company—if this support had not been granted, I may not have been able to venture onto this path. (Kaplanoğlu 2009)

Once the support from any fund is received, one reaches a certain level of recognition, and the process runs much more smoothly.

The contribution of the fund continues even after the film is completed. For example, after the completion of the movie *Angel's Fall*, the Rotterdam Film Festival, with which the Hubert Bals fund is associated, admitted the film into its competition section. When Kaplanoğlu was admitted to the Berlin Film Festival at the same time, he chose to go there. The process seen here proves that the support, which started with the script development fund, did not end there, because the references provided by receiving the support of a fund had a positive effect in the process of being selected for the Berlin Film Festival. The interest of the German and French media and the publicity surrounding the film after the screening in the Berlin Film Festival cleared the way for its director (Kaplanoğlu 2009).

Among the expectations, the sending of a film to a festival elicits reviews in the press. A director who attends a festival has a very high chance of securing his next film (Elsaesser 2005a, 97-98). Thanks to the visibility and recognition, a director has the opportunity to benefit from various funds for his next film (Thompson and Bordwell 2003, 716).

There are also various film development and funding platforms that are linked to the festivals. For example, the script of *Milk/Süt* (Kaplanoğlu,

2008) was selected into the Atelier program of the Cannes Film Festival. It was presented there to producers. Kaplanoğlu stated that these circles created opportunities to see who did what in world cinema (Kaplanoğlu 2009), and he also stated that after making acquaintances there, producers began to follow what the directors were doing. This increases the chances of support in the production process. There are also other organisations outside the scope of the festivals. However, these platforms still have some links—even if by way of personal relationships—to the festivals. One of these is the "Paris Project". As part of this platform, producers and directors meet every year in July. The projects submitted are viewed, and the directors meet with French producers, distributors and television executives. This is how Kaplanoğlu encountered and began working with Arizona Films, the French co-producer of his film *Milk*. Furthermore, this meeting resulted in his entry into the Cannes circuit: during the "Paris Project," Kaplanoğlu met the coordinator of the Atelier of the Cannes festival, who was following his film, and who then invited him to the Atelier.[8]

According to Zaim, festivals are important places where deals and acquaintances are made, and many of the established development platforms associated with these festivals facilitate ventures abroad. Zaim, who received post-production support for his film *Mud/Çamur* (2002), stated that being acquainted with the decision-making group made things easier (Zaim 2009).[9]

Another example of the relationship between funding and festivals is Yeşim Ustaoğlu's film *Waiting for the Clouds/Bulutları Beklerken* (2004).

---

8. Kaplanoğlu indicates that both the project-development platforms and festivals are important for meeting with many respected directors, discussing cinema and production conditions, meeting and establishing relationships with producers. On one hand, he adds that it has a motivating aspect but on the other he admits that it becomes an obligation since the films cannot be produced with the box-office revenues. "100,000 spectators on the average could allow me to make good films; then I may not feel the need to allocate so much time here [in the festivals] and I could focus on directing, but this is not possible" (Kaplanoğlu 2009).
9. According to Zaim, these funds are important contributions for the films about critical issues. "Projects tackling the Kurdish problem, Cyprus, military coups, sexual relationships and homosexuality—such as *Journey to the Sun* [*Güneşe Yolculuk*], *The Photograph* [*Fotoğraf*], *Goodbye Tomorrow* [*Hoşçakal Yarın*], *Lola and Bilidikid* [*Lola ve Bilidikid*], Mud [*Çamur*], *My Marlon and Brando* [*Gitmek*], *The Storm* [*Bahoz*]—have found the opportunity to benefit from these funds" (Zaim 2008a, 55). At this point, deducing that only the political films are supported by these funds would be a reductionist approach. These funds should be considered as opportunities for the critical attitude.

Having received support from the script development fund of the DAAD enabled the film to be screened at the Berlin festival (Zaim 2008a, 55). As these examples show, the funding which is one of the scopes of festivals, is an important component of the festival network and becomes a factor which renders obvious the role of festivals in the production process.

While the prestige of the festivals is a plus which affects the film's box-office revenues, the increasing chances of the directors to receive co-production offers[10] creates important opportunities (Elsaesser 2005a, 97). Furthermore, as mentioned in the introduction, the fact that, in some countries like Turkey, the reimbursing of funding received from the state is not required if an international award is won in a festival makes these awards all the more important for producers.

Criteria: Being Selected and Awarded

Another important contribution of the festivals is that they provide the films the opportunity to be shown to international audiences. Semih Kaplanoğlu, who became known through film festivals, stated that he did not take into account the international audience that he was able to reach through the festivals. He stated that it was normal for a film to go beyond its native territory and become recognised when it tells a human story. Then, he underlined how important it was to be recognised abroad as part of the "auteur cinema" of Turkey (Kaplanoğlu 2009).[11] And, Yeşim Ustaoğlu, who has participated and had many awards conferred at international festivals, chooses to highlight the nature of the film when it comes to the choice of the festival. She stressed that the film itself, no matter where in the world it is made, should be able to connect with its audience (Ustaoğlu 2009). The emphasis of both Yeşim Ustaoğlu and Semih Kaplanoğlu on the artistic quality of the film is an attitude that can be justified when considering the universality of a film in this arena; however, the conditions for entering into the distribution network should not be disregarded as they don't always depend upon the nature of the film. Here, many criteria play a decisive role.

---

10. In this area, the directors who identify themselves as political, avant-garde and independent received the state's support and made co-productions with televisions. Since they appeal to the general audience, they became international auteurs (Elsaesser 2005b, 468).

11. Directors are aware of the importance of being noticed. "This cinema was discovered and spread abroad by the foreigners through the festivals. Turkey noticed this later and began to acknowledge it. This acknowledgement happened five of six years later" (Kaplanoğlu 2009).

As producer Serkan Çakarer suggests, to be selected for a festival, the first criterion is the importance of the names of the director, the producer, the distributor and the references. The aforementioned funding has pre-eminent influence on providing these references. Çakarer stated that the project on which he is currently working had been awarded funding from the Sarajevo Film Festival, and thus it was directly qualified to participate in the competition. He also drew attention to the importance of personal relationships in regard to festival selections. For example, he said that if he were to apply with a new project to the San Sebastian Film Festival—which he previously attended and in which some of the projects that he produced received awards—he would be taken into consideration because of his past works (Çakarer 2009). To be featured in a festival increases the chances of finding joint production opportunities. Özcan Alper, who participated in the Locarno Film Festival, does not have any difficulties at the moment in finding partners and financing due to this type of recognition. Although he will be making his second film, he stated that he could easily find a partner from Hungary, Romania, Bulgaria or Germany.

While providing prestige and opportunities in the distribution network, the big festivals do not give monetary awards. The festivals organised in Turkey provide a certain amount of prestige within the country and can affect the number of spectators,[12] but they also give monetary awards.[13]

At the same time, the festivals have become the primary path for the circulation of parallel films (Elsaesser 2005b, 468).[14] There, the video distributors and cable television companies find new material to feed the

---

12. The film *Autumn/Sonbahar* (Alper, 2007) was bought by the distributors at the Adana Golden Boll Film Festival. In addition to this, the prestige brought by the festivals abroad is much more influential within the country. *Somersault in a Coffin* was not successfully distributed although it was released after receiving the Best Film Award in the Antalya Film Festival, but it was released again after receiving awards in the festivals abroad (Sivas 2007, 156).

13. On the other hand, it is necessary to emphasise that the money awards given by the festivals in Turkey constitute a very important support for the "auteur cinema" field. It should not be ignored that, with the ability of paying the debts, even if this is not regarded as a production variable—in this context, directors paying their debts should be taken as an important component of the production process—and the elimination of the obligation to pay back the support of the Ministry of Culture, the awards become a decisive factor in the film production process of the "auteur cinema" field in Turkey and this decisiveness is associated with the obstruction in the functioning of the production system.

14. Having signed contracts with the British Channel 4, Italian RAI, French Antenne 2 [now France 2] and German WDR, they upgraded the status of their television joint productions to the level of art cinema (Elsaesser 2005, 468).

communication line (Thompson and Bordwell 2003, 718). The festivals became a market where they buy films classified under the category of world cinema or New Wave, to meet their "auteur" quotas. This represents a new market for movies produced within a country like Turkey. In addition, the television companies also sell the films that they have been have been co-producers of in this market (Elsaesser 2005a, 92). Many films in the category of "auteur cinema" in Turkey receive support from the foreign television channels. Derviş Zaim's film *Mud* received contributions from the TV channels Rai Cinema and TSI (Sivas 2007, 157), and Kaplanoğlu's films *Milk* and *Honey* (Kaplanoğlu, 2010) received contributions from the TV channels Arte and ZDF.

According to Thompson and Bordwell, film festivals, as Hollywood's only competitor, now function as a global distribution system. Elsaesser talks about the coming closer of these two fields through film festivals and says that the distinction between them is becoming less apparent. The similarity between the functioning of the festivals and that of Hollywood becomes the manifestation of the evolution in the field which Elsaesser calls "world cinema" (Elsaesser 2005a, 103-104).

The first similarity seen between the two fields is related to the criteria for preparing festival programmes. After the 1970s, the process of selecting films shifted from nation and country to festival directors. This situation incidentally draws attention to small countries as it also established a structure where "auteurs" come to the fore. However, not only do small countries gain prominence but the "auteurs" of America also become the stars of the festivals (Elsaesser 2005a, 91). The festival awards have become the most effective way to draw attention. When we add to this the rumours (Thompson and Bordwell 2005, 718), scandals, talks, discussions and writings around the axis of the festival, we see that the agenda-setting clichés of popular culture and tabloid press are not any different from those of Hollywood (Elsaesser 2005a, 102).[15]

The festival directors and programmers have decisive roles. The festival programmers establish close relationships with the existing film

---

15. In this context, the media relations have a key importance since they possess the power to draw public attention towards the films. While establishing close relationships, predicting and debating the awards and bringing the hot topics to the forefront are regarded as a continuation of these clichés, a special attention is given to the field of criticism. The journalists and the press are presented with special opportunities. The FIPRESCI award is a significant honour for beginners. The critics take part in the jury and help determine the awards. The festival programmers and distributors pay attention to the critics in regard to the promising names (Thompson and Bordwell 2005, 718).

producers and find talented filmmakers to draw people in. The Class A
festivals send discovery teams all around the world to visit other festivals
and to watch works in progress (Thompson and Bordwell 2005, 718).
Again, the directors and programmers determine the different categories.
According to Elsaesser, through this process the world's annual film
production is, in fact, categorised and classified through these selections,
awards and accolades. The artistic level of discernment and appraisal is in
question. Elsaesser states that this undemocratic discernment is valid for
all categories. He speaks of a new power structure based on inclusion and
exclusion, namely, a hierarchy. This structure is known by the producers,
if not by the audience (Elsaesser 2005a, 96).[16] During the modernisation of
the Turkish Republic, the expectations of acceptance by the West may
prevail upon the consciousness of artists, and this can start the "self-
orientalism" process which progresses down through to the artists (Kırel
2007, 412).

The kind of influence relation we are talking about, in fact, becomes an
indication of the mechanism of establishing control through the auteur's
film and this control, while incompatible with the traditional qualities of
"auteur cinema," reveals another point which establishes a similarity
between the rules of Hollywood's distribution network in the world market
and the globalising festivals. In this sense, festivals give, in Elsaesser's
words, post-national cinema the tendency of European cinema and
reconstruct its identity (Elsaesser 2005a, 83-93). The most basic factor
pertaining to the rewriting of identity is the structure which affects the film
production process. According to Kırel, who uses Iranian cinema as an
example, being evaluated by the West takes into consideration the West's
ways of looking at the East. This, in turn, creates the danger of producing
under the influence of the images that affect the West and of orientalism.
There are common points about the content and the form of expression of
Iranian films in festivals, and this situation finds its source in the fact that
these films are produced for an international audience rather than their
own (Kırel 2007, 378-98). Furthermore, in this context, the uniformity of
festival audiences should also be emphasised (Elsaesser 2005a, 101).

The selection process to international film festivals seems to point to
an area where there are interventions on behalf of certain films. This issue

---

16. This is evidenced by what Kırel says in regard to the effect on directors of the
prestigious welcome the Iranian cinema receives—he sees it as a debt
relationship—in the festivals: "However, this debt, as any other, is the kind which
harbours some problematic and debatable areas within itself. Artists can transform
their subject at hand under the influence of this debt relationship" (Kırel 2007,
412).

is brought to the attention in relation to the joint producers and vendor firms when, the president of the Cannes Film Festival, Gilles Jacob, stating openly that there are interventions by the joint producers, their own view of what will sell with the films (Regnier and Sotinel 2006, 4), reveals that there is a direct routing mechanism in the festivals. The directors claim that the festival expectations do not affect their cinema. Semih Kaplanoğlu declared that compromising his film in order to be selected for a festival is out of the question.[17] While stating that staying true to the story told is more important, Kaplanoğlu stressed that he also has a responsibility to the people who believe in him, and if he were to do otherwise, there would be no reason left to try as hard as he does. Özcan Alper stated that festivals were not everything (Alper 2009):

> If one believes the work done by one's own conscience is right, even though there might be a little something lacking or in excess, one should be able to shrug off the rest. If one places these things—festivals and such—at the centre, one would slide off one's own centre.

Alper underlines the necessity for a director not to place too much importance on the festivals and to focus on the cinema they want to make (Alper 2009). Zaim has questioned the imposed expectations, which create the conditions of the intervention itself. First of all, he articulates his suspicions pertaining to the criteria employed in the selection of the projects.[18] "People who are making the selection have their own principles, but these principles are always vague" (Zaim 2009).[19]

---

17. "I cannot do this; if I do, then my current existence would be damaged. This is important: because the present moment, today's festivals, the world of the now and the film's adventure now do not concern me much. It may seem that I utter this too easily but it is something I say by thinking and knowing: what really matters is what the film will become in twenty years from now " (Kaplanoğlu 2009).
18. Zaim mentions the likelihood of the people who make the selections manipulating the selection criteria according to their own fancy, the grey areas in the selection process and the possibility of these grey areas making more room for people to manoeuvre (Zaim 2009).
19. In addition to the past festival and production career of the director which we mentioned in the previous sections, Zaim lists the selection criteria as follows: "The place of the film's context within the international balance of powers; where and how the film stands in this balance; the commercial potential of the film, the power of the seller, the power of the distribution company; the producer's influence capacity before the festival; the aesthetic and production value of the film...the film's capability of adding to the prestige of the festival; the attitude of the critics related to the festival towards the directors career; the attitude of the

According to Zaim, what receives a "yes" today may receive a "no" tomorrow or a similar project produced under similar conditions may encounter a completely different attitude (Zaim 2009).[20] Having to comply with certain criteria and being selected or awarded in this way only leads to serious limitations and manipulation. The directors are aware of this danger, and they are putting up a fight to protect themselves.

The Giant Distribution Network: Selling the Film

Festivals are the power grids of the management where social pressure is applied via the mediators, namely, festivals managers, curators and shoppers (Elsaesser 2005a, 83). This pressure becomes a force of intervention into the field of distribution. The coming together of a film production package exists even before a director is in question. What is now being determined in festivals is what will be showcased in art-house cinemas that year, which films will be screened in a few theatres allocated to festival films in the multiplexes. The films selected usually belong to independent distributors (Elsaesser 2005a, 91).[21]

The close relationship of Miramax, one of the biggest independent distributors, with the Sundance Film Festival is another important point. The structure established here is very different from the Hollywood monopoly but still there is a network of commercial relationships developed through the dependencies in question. The prestige which the distribution company gets from the festival is very important because a new "popular" field is emerging. This field consists of the films carried into the global market through festivals such as Cannes, Berlin, and Venice and film companies like Miramax. Elsaesser defines these films as "indie blockbusters" (Elsaesser 2005b, 92).

---

critics towards the film; the promotional and marketing budget of the film" (Zaim 2008b, 43).

20. Zaim states that Nuri Bilge Ceylan is the best example of this situation. The film *Distant/Uzak* (2002), which was not even selected to a parallel section of the Venice Film Festival, was selected to the Cannes Film Festival. Moritz de Hadeln was at the head of the selection committee in Venice. Previously, de Hadeln was in the management of the Berlin Film Festival at the period when *Small Town/Kasaba* (1997), and *Clouds of May/Mayıs Sıkıntısı* (1999) were selected for the festival.

21. Miramax (US), Sony Pictures Classics (US) and Castle communications (UK) are among these. The smaller ones among these companies are Sixpack (Austria) and Fortissimo (Netherlands) (Elsaesser 2005, 91).

Entering into contact with distributors takes festivals to the very important place of being launching pads (Thompson and Bordwell 2003, 717). As Kırel emphasised in the example of Iranian cinema, the films a nation produces in the field of independent and alternative cinema can earn money thanks to the distribution network they acquire through the festivals (Kırel 2005, 413).

Tevfik Başer stated that the distributors began to run after him after the acceptance of his film *Forty Square Meters of Germany/40 Metrekare Almanya* (1986) during the Critics' Week section of the Cannes Film Festival. Zaim adding that the chances of being distributed are lower in the parallel sections stressed that Turkey does not match the criteria for being selected in the main sections and explains the rationale behind this as follows:

When compared to the cinema of developed countries, Turkish cinema does not have the strength to create the momentum that will attract the attention of world media during festivals by bringing a "different" film and a star actor every year, continuously and consistently, which would benefit the big festivals. Turkish cinema—again, with some exceptions—is generally classified as the kind of cinema, which is showcased mostly in the parallel sections. (Zaim 2008b: 42)

Despite the fact that the film *Mud* received the UNESCO Award at the 2003 Venice Film Festival, it was not sold intensely outside of Italy and Switzerland (ibid.).

The competition sections render the films attractive for big sales and especially for the major sales companies.[22] For example, when *Milk* was selected for the competition section of the Venice Film Festival, The Match Factory wanted to buy the global rights to the film. There were no sales companies involved in Kaplanoğlu's film *Angel's Fall/Meleğin Düşüşü*. Many companies wanted to buy the film *Egg/Yumurta* (Kaplanoğlu, 2007) after it was selected for the Directors' Fortnight section of the Cannes Film Festival, but the director Kaplanoğlu, who wanted to decide which festivals he attends, chose to have a one-year trial partnership with a French-Spanish sales company. Eventually, he was not satisfied and thought that he could sell his films himself. However, when

22. Currently, there is no company capable of buying global sales rights in Turkey. Çakarer states that they are making an attempt to begin the preparations but since the well-known directors prefer to work with big companies, it would be difficult to realise at this stage. Yeşim Ustaoğlu thinks that it is necessary to support this infrastructure. (Ustaoğlu 2009, Çakarer 2009).

he experienced problems such as not receiving earnings following a sale to a country, not being able to make copies of the film in that country or to clear copies through customs, no longer wanting to be bothered by the exhausting process, he signed a contract with a big sales company. This company, The Match Factory, made a tempting offer to Kaplanoğlu after his film *Milk* was selected for the Venice Film Festival, bought both *Egg* and *Milk*, also showed interest in *Honey* and paid development money to Kaplanoğlu (Kaplanoğlu 2009).

The sales rights of Yeşim Ustaoğlu's earlier films were sold to a company called Celluloid Dreams. The sales rights of her film *Pandora's Box/Pandoranın Kutusu* (Ustaoğlu 2008) were bought by The Match Factory. Ustaoğlu said that these companies were more knowledgeable in sales, and that they followed and selected the festivals from which they buy; however, she stresses that she has the final word. Apart from the criteria of being selected by one of the festivals, the deciding factor in the selection of a film by these companies would be the screenplay—if the film is still in the script-writing stage—and the director's earlier projects. The Match Factory became connected with *Pandora's Box* during the script-writing stage and became one of Ustaoğlu's partners. Ustaoğlu stated that the company invested money that allowed for the completion of the movie and made a return on its investment from the sales revenues (Ustaoğlu 2009). As was the case with *Pandora's Box*, the company which holds the global sales rights of Ceylan's films *Climates/İklimler* (2006) and *Three Monkeys/Üç Maymun* (2008) was also the co-producer.[23]

Besides the large sales companies, the smaller ones also make choices involving the films appearing at festivals. However, these companies also pay attention to the films in the parallel sections (Çakarer 2009).[24]

The fact that large companies co-produce films brings the much-debated intervention issue to the table regarding the co-producers. As Semih Kaplanoğlu also indicated, the companies which possess a large sales and marketing network and know how to use it well create strategies in order to obtain selections at the festivals. Kaplanoğlu underlined the need to be on guard against the manipulation of sales companies, which are profit-driven, although they move through the field of art-house films, and he also emphasised his awareness that their world is different from the

---

23. *Climates* (2006) http://www.imdb.com/title/tt0498097/*Three Monkeys* (2008) http://www.imdb.com/title/tt1233381/
24. For example, the sales rights of the film *Summer Book/Tatil Kitabı* were sold to Wide Management after the film participated in the Forum section of the Berlin Film Festival.

director's world.[25] Although Derviş Zaim worked with a French distribution company for his film *Mud* and preferred to distribute *Waiting for Heaven/Cenneti Beklerken* (2005) and *Dot/Nokta* (2008) himself, he stated that he is in search of new opportunities. In regards to the film distribution companies, Zaim stated that the small companies may not reflect the intake of revenues exactly and that the big companies may be indifferent to the films; like Kaplanoğlu, he pointed out that the director's position is important when the sales companies want to intervene in the film (Zaim 2009).

Here, it must be underlined that the distribution revenues of a film are not very substantial. In these cases, it is obvious that the international distribution network, in fact, does not provide sufficient revenue to create a space for directors working in "auteur cinema," except if they are working with low budgets; however, we see that international sales have become almost a *sine qua non* condition for these cinemas to survive. Being able to get a film distributed harbours the danger of being exposed to the intervention of sales companies, in addition to that of other forces. As American "indie" cinema shows, the profits of low-budget films become attractive in the market in this sense.

Another important point about the festivals is that the directors are better known in the festivals than they are in their own countries (Thompson and Bordwell 2003, 716). The reason for this is the little space left by Hollywood; these directors can only find room for their work in festivals. However, market opportunities can be found through the festivals (Kırel 2007, 401-403). Turkish cinema has followed a similar path. While not well-known in his country, Nuri Bilge Ceylan is recognised on the stage of world cinema. One of the most significant reasons why Semih Kaplanoğlu's films are being watched abroad is through a similar mechanism.

---

25. Kaplanoğlu states that the functionality of the festivals is not very different from that of the commercial cinema and that there is a goal to make profit. He says it is necessary to wonder where the innocence of the films and production is and to be able to resist at certain points (Kaplanoğlu 2009). Kaplanoğlu states that the demands made—such as reading the script at the stage of filming, interfering with the editing, asking the film to be more understandable, cutting out certain parts, suggesting formats, meddling with the colours, etc.—although put politely by the companies, may aim at carrying the director to a certain point and underlines the importance of the director's stance and the addition of the rules related to his stance in the contract (Kaplanoğlu 2009).

Conclusion

Once the functioning of festivals and the outline of the Turkish cinema's relationship with them are demonstrated through the directors and films cited as examples, it can be seen that festivals are not only instrumental in facilitating the circulation of the films, but also exist as an important factor that determines the film-production process. The recognition brought by festivals guarantees a director of the film's production. The funding that is available as part of the scope of film festivals is an important resource for "auteur cinema"; the prestige of these funds increases the chances of the films being screened in the festivals, and this enables the sales of the films. On the other hand, granting global sales rights to a film to certain companies within the context of the festivals increases the number of components, which may interfere with the film-production process. When these companies become co-producers of the films, the only deciding factor regarding potential problems (or disputes) seems to be the will of the director(s).

The Ministry of Culture, Eurimages and the festivals, while being fundamental components of a film's production process, cannot finance film productions by themselves. In order to produce films, many components must be put together at the same time. Since it is difficult to find resources in Turkey and impossible for the films in the "auteur cinema" category to pay for themselves with box-office revenues, we encounter a structure which depends on an international platform in terms of support and distribution.

In regard to these dependency relationships, the conditions require both an economic and a cultural re-structuring. As we have seen, the concept of director-producer, the development of the executive-producer concept—that came about because of the complexity of the process and its structure, which also brings the producer to the fore—the establishment of the criteria to receive the Ministry of Culture's support related to the production process through festivals, and the economic and cultural conditions that of the co-production process create the important building blocks of this re-structuring. Assessing the components of the film-production process shows that the international dependency relationships are featured prominently. The dependency in question is both material and intellectual (Tomlinson 2004, 109), and equality is out of the question within this dependency construct. Under these circumstances, expecting the directors—who are evaluated unequally and are producing films in Turkey, which is defined as a developing country—to resist the co-production interventions with their personal influence would mean being unable to grasp the process as a whole and to ignore the ideological issues of the process.

When considering the production conditions that we have listed, the danger of the production-distribution relationship established in festivals, which influences the quality of the films in "auteur cinema" and thereby transforms them, can be clearly seen. The influx of festivals brings about not only intense activity but also consumption. The directors are aware that they can be forgotten, and this creates an element of pressure (Kırel 2007, 405). [26] This fluid market needs to be fed and supported with new products continuously. This necessity poses the danger of reducing the art film to a material for consumption because festivals try to gain a foothold as permanent structures striving to exist in a global market. [27]

Festivals have become an area where commercial cinema and art cinema are intermixed. As Elsaesser emphasised, the festivals, which form the centre of a globalised commercial entity, are aiming at building a new identity within the symbolic global economic system (Elsaesser 2005a, 83). There is a strong commercial mechanism that is advancing through the art-house cinema. The big festivals and the distributors linked to them have begun to control the distribution network of the entirety of world cinema. As this bustling market is always in need of new films, the films are reduced to a material of consumption.

While festivals have a commercial structure integrated into the global market and as Wallerstein stated, while the commercial mechanism is entwining itself around the particularistic and local culture (Wallerstein 1998, 137), the "director's cinema" that exists in Turkey at festivals, continues its production dependent on this structure and thereby endangers its quality as an art form. At the point where the selections and the awards take place, there can be a limitation, transformation and manipulation of culture. The explicit intervention of both the festival programmers and the sales companies as well as the director's creative limitations (due to his concerns over being selected) force the films produced as "auteur cinema"

---

26. Jafar Panahi's words reveal the pressure the directors feel: "We are conscious of the fact that the destiny of the Iranian cinema is in our hands, that it depends on us. While, on one hand, our country's cinema is becoming globally known, on the other hand, we are conscious that if we do not produce a film or two every year, it may be forgotten very easily" (Genç 2000, 83).

27. According to Stringer, conceptualisation is very important in order for the festivals to compete for global financing. The festivals "have to create their own sense of community, and hence their own marketable trademark or brand image" (Stringer 2001, 139).

in Turkey to try to survive in new dependency relationships at the level of content and form.

Works Cited

Çelik, Tülay. 2009. 1990 "Sonrası Türkiye' de 'Yönetmen Sineması' Alanında Film Üretim Süreci" (Film Production Process in Turkey After 1990 in the Field of 'Auteur Cinema'). unpublished PhD thesis, Marmara University, SBE/Institute of Social Sciences.

Elsaesser, Thomas. 2005a. "Film Festival Networks: The New Topographies of Cinema in Europe". In *European Cinema, Face to Face with Hollywood*, edited by Thomas Elsaesser, 82-109. Amsterdam: Amsterdam University Press.

—. 2005b. "Hyper-, Retro- or Counter- European Cinema as Third Cinema Between Hollywood and Art Cinema". In *European Cinema, Face to Face with Hollywood*, edited by Thomas Elsaesser, 464-84. Amsterdam: Amsterdam University Press.

Genç, Seray. 2004. 'Cafer Panahi ile Son Filmi ve İran Üzerine'. *Yeni Film* 4: 81-84.

Kırel, Serpil. 2007. "İran'da Sinema, İran Sineması ve Üretim Dinamikleri ve Anlatıya Etkileri Üzerine Bir Değerlendirme"(Cinema in Iran, Iranian Cinema and an Evaluation on the Effects of Production Dynamics and Narrative). In *Üçüncü Sinema ve Üçüncü Dünya Sineması* (Third Cinema and Third World Cinema), edited by Esra Biryıldız ve Zeynep Çetin Erus, 355-417. İstanbul: Es Yayınları.

Neale, Steve. 1981. "Art Cinema As Institution". *Screen* 22.(1): 11-39.

Regnier, İsabelle and Thomas Sotinel. 2006. "Il ne faut pas que ce soit le marché qui fasse la sélection" (Shouldn't it be the market which makes selection). *Le Monde*, 18 May.

Sivas, Âlâ. 2007. "Türk Sinemasında Bağımsızlık Anlayışı ve Temsilcileri" (The Idea of Independence in Turkish Cinema and Its Representatives). Yayınlanmamış Doktora Tezi/Unpublished PhD Dissertation, Marmara University SBE/Institute of Social Sciences.

Stringer, Julian. 2001. "Global Cities and the International Film Festival Economy".In *Cinema and The City: Film and Urban Societies in a Global Context*, edited by M. Shiel and T.Fitzmaurice, 134-44. Oxford: Blackwell Publishers.

Suner, Asuman. 2004. "Horror of a Different Kind: Dissonant Voices of the New Turkish Cinema". *Screen* 45 (4): 305-23.

Thompson, Kristin and David Bordwell. 2003. *Film History: An Introduction*, 2nd edition. New York: Mc Graw Hill.

Tomlinson, John. 2004. *Globalization and Culture*. Chicago: University of Chicago Press.

Wallerstein, Immanuel. 1998. "The National and the Universal: Can There Be Such a Thing as World Culture". In *Culture, Globalization and the World-System: Contemporary Conditions for the Representation of Identity*., edited by Anthony D. King, 91-106. Minneapolis: University of Minnesota Press.

Zaim, Derviş. 2008. "Your Focus is Your Truth: Turkish Cinema, "Alluvionic" Filmmakers and International Acceptance". *Shifting Landscapes: Film and Media in European Context*. Edited by Miyase Christensen and Nezih Erdoğan., 86-108. Newcastle upon Tyne: Cambridge Scholars Publishing.

Websites

İklimler / Climates (2006).
    http://www.imdb.com/title/tt0498097/ (accessed 02/07/2009).
Üç Maymun / Three Monkeys (2008).
    http://www.imdb.com/title/tt1233381/ (accessed 02/07/2009).

Interviews

Özcan Alper. Interview, Istanbul, 19 June 2009.
Serkan Çakarer. Interview, Istanbul, 25 May 2009.
Semih Kaplanoğlu. Interview, Istanbul, 9 June 2009.
Yeşim Ustaoğlu. Interview, Istanbul, 25 May 2009.
Derviş Zaim. Interview, Istanbul, 9 June 2009.

CHAPTER SIXTEEN

THINKING OUT LOUD:
ON THE ADAPTATIONS
OF *SEVEN HUSBANDS FOR HURMUZ*

PINAR ASAN

Introduction

Directed by Ezel Akay, *7 Kocalı Hürmüz/Seven Husbands for Hürmüz* did not follow the regular intervals of approximately ten years between the previous versions of the film—1963 (Suna Pekuysal), 1971 (Türkan Şoray) and 1980 (Ayten Gökçer) respectively—and was released twenty-eight years after the last instalment, in 2009. I do not intend to interpret the film in a manner that will shed light on the different social changes that Turkey underwent between the dates of the respective releases. However, although the film's story is set in the 1800s, it should be noted that each version is based on certain social paradigms pertaining to its production period's social, political and cultural setting. Their scripts, form and content were all closely associated with these components, and above all, within the framework of the same story each version presents quite different representations of femininity from the others in the series. From this point of view, by drawing correspondences in terms of form, content and representations of femininity, I will analyse the two versions that depict a woman's story within the framework of popular culture, namely, the film directed by Ezel Akay (2009) and the film directed by Atıf Yılmaz from 1971. I hope that, as I mentioned above, such a comparison will form a ground on which some facts concerning the time periods when the films were shot can be revealed. I want to discuss the parallel reading of the 2009 film in comparison to the 1971 film with a female protagonist, so I can illustrate the ways in which "women's films" were part of the social agenda, particularly during the 1980s in Turkey, and how this discussion is reflected in our day.

Vaudeville as a Genre

In Turkish popular culture, *7 Kocalı Hürmüz* was highly successful at the box office each time it was released. It has been imprinted in public memory and can almost be understood as having a cult following. Due to these possible reasons, many directors—all of whom are male—reinterpreted the story.

7 Kocalı Hürmüz is, in fact, part of vaudeville. It was written by Sadık Şendil as a theatre play by making use of traditional Turkish theatre and the *meddah* tradition. Born as theatre, using mostly comedy elements and satirising social problems, *vaudeville* means "the sound of the city" in French (Snyder 2000, 132). Starting from the eighteenth century, it was a genre frequently employed in the theatre.

The eighteenth century witnessed the Industrial Revolution and accordingly, developments of technology, urbanisation and new types of businesses. In Europe with the increase of unemployment and the gradual collapse of a land-based economy, access to job opportunities caused a great wave of migration to developing cities. With the urban settlement of the working class, the urban population increased. Therefore, working-class culture was articulated in the culture of the bourgeoisie and the aristocrats who had constituted the majority of the urban population up until that time. Thus, diversification in the products of urban culture was observed. With the rise of urbanisation, inter-class conflicts were beginning to be investigated. Theatre, as one of that period's popular arts, started to become a field where the life of the urban population was depicted, and society was critiqued. Migration to the cities from various parts of the country and the encounter with a cosmopolitan environment that resulted from such a migration led to diversification of genres, stereotypes and space depictions in plays. Comedy attracted great attention in the city as it was a genre that could continue the critical tradition that penetrated across social classes.

Developed around a simple story, a chain of incidents occurring along with constant misunderstandings, accidents and relationships becoming more complex, vaudeville combines the traditions of comedy and musicals. Characters are rather broad stereotypes and after continuous action, the story concludes with a happy ending.

Seven Husbands For Hürmüz as Vaudeville

Sadık Şendil's piece is set in the 1800s in Istanbul's Taşkasap district which is now within the borders of İstanbul's Fatih municipality. Hürmüz, the protagonist of the story, is illegally married to six men of different professions and hosts all of her husbands once a week. She provides them with a nice time according to their respective desires, receives gifts from them and makes her living in this way. This is the rough outline of both adaptations. However, in Atıf Yılmaz's version featuring Türkan Şoray, the story begins with Hürmüz noticing that her husband has six more wives and so creates marriages with more than one man in order to take her revenge. Brokenhearted Hürmüz (Şoray) follows her husband's lead in order to repair her hurt pride and to take revenge. In the Akay version, Hürmüz (Nurgül Yeşilçay) lives in a mansion inherited from her deceased husband who had been a pasha. The pasha, who we afterwards learn to be quite old, married the young and beautiful Hürmüz, but died after a short while. The difference in the two beginnings, namely, in the act of taking revenge, bears significant importance in terms of justification for Hürmüz's acts. The first story depicts an innocent woman who has relationships with more than one man because she was cheated on while in the second we see a woman who got married to an old pasha for monetary gain. Therefore, the former film adds comedy elements to the incident occurring after a dramatic event, but we do not see such a dramatic event in the second. Yılmaz's Hürmüz adopts melodrama and lets the story absorb it as pre-acceptance in a manner that does not disrupt the tradition of 1970s Turkish cinema. Attracting a female audience, who constituted a majority of the cinema audience during the 1970s, and adding elements of melodrama to the story, though the genre is within comedy, were efforts to consider the audience's desire to identify with the star. Increasing the sympathy towards the popularity of a famous star, comedy may be added to the star's assets. Türkan Şoray is one of the most important representatives within the tradition of melodrama in the 1970s and was the dubbed "the sultan" by the public, particularly by women audiences. Star persona, which is one of the attributes of becoming a real star and which was perfected by carefully working on that persona, was actualised in the star persona of Türkan Şoray. The most telling criterion that confirms this fact is a star's on-screen persona and star persona coming together in time and becoming undistinguishable for the audience. Although in her article titled "The Film Does Not End with an Ecstatic Kiss" (2002) Seçil Büker did not make a differentiation between a star's on-screen persona and star persona and used the concept of *image* (imaj), which she thought to express both concepts, the writer explains what Türkan Şoray means for Turkey as follows (Buker 2002):

> In the 1960s when the new city-dwellers started to rid themselves of their timidity, they were fortunate to find someone on the screen that did not

intimidate or ignore them. They were happy because they found someone
on the screen who was compassionate and warm and made them feel that
she was their peer. (Büker 2002, 170)

For the audience, this star was one of them. She was the one they cried
with, laughed with, got angry with—in short she was the thing with whom
they lived a part of their lives. She was both close to and far away from
them. Therefore, her promise to the audience was that she would
experience all these feelings with them at the same time. Şoray would have
been reminding the audience of her own persona, even though she was
acting in a comedy. In the Şoray version, Hürmüz is very loyal to her
husband Ömer. In the first few minutes into the film, we understand how
much she is devoted to her husband. She is the only one who sends money
to Ömer when he is in need. Ömer's messenger knocks on the doors of all
of Ömer's wives, and tells them that he needs money. All the women
complain, and they reject his request. Only Şoray's Hürmüz sends money
that she earned through her handicrafts. She tells Safinaz, who has
criticised Hürmüz/Şoray's behaviour, that Ömer is her husband, and it is
natural that she should send him money. However, Ömer wants this money
to make him appear important in front of the other men in the prison. He
says, "The horse neighs according to its owner. You will pat some people
with the back of your hand and some with your palm". This is how
Hürmüz's behaviour is justified from the perspective of the audience.
Besides, the story then turns to the revenge enacted by a woman who has
been cheated on. The audience now becomes the witness of the rightful
struggle of this woman, portrayed as a victim whose only desire is to love
and to be loved—although now she does also try to take revenge. This is
almost like her fate. Finally, the film concludes with a happy ending not
only to satisfy the loyal audience of melodrama, but also to reward "her
proper behaviour as a woman". Throughout the film Şoray's Hürmüz
intrigues those around her with a childish naughtiness that is far from that
of a femme fatale. This "naughty" woman is never represented as bad or
evil. On the contrary, everything Hürmüz does to get rid of her husbands
and to avoid sexual encounters with them becomes part of the parody
thanks to her "innocent" and "impish" nature. Her beauty and
attractiveness only serve as a superficial trap for men. However, she looks
for love just like an "ideal" woman might, and once she finds real love it is
implied she would be able to undertake the wife role assigned to her, the
part of wife to a man she has chosen out of love. So, traditional roles
assigned to women by a masculine culture such as altruism, loyalty and
loving are underlined throughout the story, and the narrative reproduces
these roles as if they are inherent in the gender roles of women.

It is an interesting fact that this version is directed by Atıf Yılmaz who did not reject the borders drawn by the audience and producers of melodrama, and would after a decade be called a successful director of women's films. In her 2005 article entitled "Vasfiye'nin Kız Kardeşleri" (Vasfiye's sisters) in her book *Hayalet Ev* (*Ghost House*) Asuman Suner examines the representation of women in Turkish cinema and mentions the rise of women's films after the 1980s as being pioneered by Atıf Yılmaz. However, with a firm determination, Suner argues that the only difference between the 1980s from the previous years was the inclusion of female sexuality in films. And she continues as follows:

> One of the most problematic aspects of women's films is that although they focused on female characters who struggled for an emancipation and took the risk of interference with society for that purpose, the movies always kept the outsider, voyeuristic, objectifying gaze (male gaze) in terms of the narrative positioning" (Suner 2005, 295

We witness this "outsider's gaze" in both films in different forms. The version dated 1971 explains the story to the audience through an unseen male narrator, whereas in Akay's version, the narrator is Safinaz, who did not go beyond being a stereotype in the former version. As a full-fledged character in the latter film, Safinaz appears on the screen at the very beginning. She tells us in advance that she will narrate a woman's story. We meanwhile see her sharing the same space with Hürmüz and other women. In this scene, which we later understand to be Hürmüz's henna night (a form of Bachalerotte party), Safinaz explains to us how a woman could be successful within the male-dominated culture and how this could set an example for other women, rather like a fairytale. Gülse Birsel plays Safinaz, a character previously depicted as Hürmüz's aunt in the 1980 version, whereas in Akay's version she is Hürmüz's best friend, confidante and assistant in her friend's intrigues. Safinaz says that our own day is different from the past; that men used to be with five women rather than contenting themselves with one and that now things are just the opposite. With the word "now" being used in a story set in the 1800s, Akay promises that he will offer a different perspective from the older versions of the film: that he will not depict the story as a woman's revenge plot and will turn it into a story observing feminine culture and life "more accurately". "Now, the times have changed," says Safinaz. "Now it is time for women to enjoy their lives". Before seeing whether Akay keeps his promise, it would be useful to mention the difference between the narrators of these two versions.

The former Atıf Yılmaz version has an ambiguous narrator. Mentioned as the "Voice of God" in documentary film literature, this voice explains to the audience what and how to think and receive information. The "Voice" offers an irrefutable reality which does not allow any other interpretations. It is added for the audience to get to know and understand Hürmüz and to increase audience's sympathy towards her. The "Voice" tells us the story as a fairytale at the very beginning of the film. This voice reveals that Hürmüz is not to be blamed for all these incidents and presents her sympathetically in every situation; therefore, this *voice* narration hoped to take a false "negative" impression to remove any negative impressions that the audience might already have of Hürmüz character from previous film versions. However, this voice belongs to a man. The story is clearly presented from a male perspective. Hürmüz thus takes part in this story not as a woman, but as a shadow, as someone who is inarticulate and as an object. As this view makes her inarticulate, it puts aside her positioning as "meaning creator," and imprisons her in the position of "bearer of meaning". In her classic article titled "Visual Pleasure and Narrative Cinema," (1975) Laura Mulvey simply defines this image as follows:

> Woman then stands in patriarchal culture as the signifier for the male other, bound by a symbolic order in which man can live out his fantasies and obsessions through linguistic command by imposing them on the silent image of a woman still tied to her place as bearer of meaning, not maker of meaning. (Mulvey 1975, 6)

In this regard, Ezel Akay at least manages to save Hürmüz, to a certain extent, from being the object of male fantasies and sets her free. Hürmüz's characteristics are consistent; they do not change either in the beginning or at the end of the film. Her purpose, pleasure and life are based on making use of weaknesses within patriarchal culture. In Akay's 2008 version, the narrator of the film is now a woman rather than a man. Because the film is the story of women who try to live in a man's world and under the male gaze. And these women are not only able to talk to men and to make fun of them, but they are also loud women. Seeming to make use of the silliness of her husbands and all men from the beginning of the film, Hürmüz wraps herself up in different personalities and plays the role that each of the men around her wants her to. She instantly shifts from one personality to another—such as the aggressive man's even more aggressive wife, the stammering man's naïve wife and the watchman's patriotic wife—and never thinks about changing the way she lives although she does get tired sometimes. In cases where things become too complicated, her best friend Safinaz helps Hürmüz to set the intrigues in order. Unlike the former version, comedy is used for critiquing masculinity. Women's talk is seen as foolish, and yet in matter of fact it is quite witty. Throughout the film, women use a rich female slang. We therefore encounter an unknown aspect of female culture, which was lost and ignored in the patriarchal culture. This language, which leads us to think about femininity almost as a subculture, is an indicator that women not only talked but also created a language which masculinity cannot access. In this context, slang is a point of resistance against the male-dominated language as mentioned by Mulvey. But is talking and expressing themselves with all the possibilities of language enough? More frankly, do Akay's women really talk?

Contemporary Hürmüz

Akay's Hürmüz is presented as a parody of the parody. And the director is quite self-conscious as he does so. Colourful costumes, songs, crowded choreographed scenes, mise-en-scène, camera angles, lighting are all quite refulgent and they border the grotesque. The grotesque aesthetic is spread all through the film as an element to subvert stereotypes. The audience is estranged, and situations get absurd with the use of such a film language. Attempts to reduce the screen into two dimensions occur as much as possible. Actresses and actors play to the camera and have exaggerated body language. Set in the 1800s, the story is told by emulating that period's aesthetic. Miniature and meddah traditions are absorbed and revealed throughout the story. The doctor reminds us of Abdülcanbaz; three old men, one of whom is Greek, are watching the whole story while smoking a hookah, and the German soldier emphasises the cosmopolitan environment of the Ottoman Empire. In all of these practices, Akay attempts to destroy classical narration techniques inherent in the 1970s Yeşilçam tradition and create binary oppositions within the story as good-bad and moral-immoral.

Despite it not being an adaptation, *Hacivat ve Karagöz Nasıl Öldürüldü?/Who Killed Shadows?* A previous film directed by Akay in 2005, was considered to occupy an important position within the popular culture, since it offered an alternative reality to Ottoman culture and the Hacivat-Karagöz story that was fictionalised in the official history. However, although based on the original text, adaptations can be successful to the extent that they contribute new perspectives and interpretations of the text. Just as covers of songs display differences from one musician to another depending upon the period in which they were produced, literary adaptations in film also display differences. These differences are mainly seen in form and content and offer a coherent reinterpretation and rethinking.

At first glance, experimentation with form in Akay's Hürmüz, seem to display a counter-position against many elements of traditional cinema's narration structure. Moreover, sexuality is not shown, rather, it is implied. The scene where the doctor examines Hürmüz can be called a representation of a lovemaking scene. Nudity is not shown, but catharsis is reached through implications of libidinal energies. On the other hand, Hürmüz, whose sexuality is intimated within the film, makes use of the weaknesses of masculine characters, and creates space to live for herself in her own way. Here, the story is interpreted in the exact opposite way from the 1971 version, yet even here Hürmüz cannot achieve complete freedom. This time, thanks to the men's weaknesses, Hürmüz manages ways of using masculine power to her favour, which became available due to the absence of masculine power. It is not a woman's story as seen entirely from the point of view of the woman; but it could indirectly be interpreted as showing that the female position is still "inferior" in society precisely by disallowing this viewpoint, that is to say, with a voyeuristic camera showing how women's predicament remains the same in some ways. This gaze is there to satisfy the male audience and through nature of its being shown in this way, allowing that type of gaze in future. Thus, the story is still not a woman's story, rather it includes criticism of masculinity. Unfortunately, the gaze is still male. In the bath scene, women entertain themselves and sing the song El-Hubb (Gökten Erkek Yağacak) *It's raining men* in the steam bath scene. In this atmosphere, they lose themselves in joy. This scene, which could well be grotesque with high-angle shots and sliding dollies, turns into a scene where beautiful women dance for the camera, an invisible eye. Here the setting does not allow the female audience to identify with the women on the screen or feel part of this carnival. The camera is always the outside observer, which connotes "voyeurism" of male gaze. In this scene, where women raise their hands up as if to beg God to give them charming males, the camera prefers to be above them, which has sexual implications. This is a reductionist view of the women's demand to God about what they could be asking for. It is not only sexual; but other types of domination more generally: they are also "inferior" in patriarchal, religious order. As if it adopts God's point of view, the camera does not choose a position among the women as if it were a member of its group. The presence of women within the space is felt merely through the ways in which the camera is viewing them. The camera slides behind the columns of the bath and makes the figures reappear from time to time. Hands of the women completely fill the screen as if begging to the gaze above. Who then, can be said to be the one above listening to the song, purportedly only for the women? Who is subject and who is object? How are the bearers and the receivers of the gaze positioned?

Conclusion

However, what Safinaz says "it is time for women to enjoy their lives" is true. The song addresses women experiencing their own desires. Unfortunately, the filmic form of Ezel Akay's *7 Kocalı Hürmüz* excludes the women of the film as the song speaks to the female audience. The function of the two dimensionality used in the bath scene is unequal to the more rounded dimensions used in the remaining parts of the film. There had been an expectation that it has a certain function throughout the film, but at this point in time in the film, it neither multiplies the textual meanings nor offers a new formal experiment to the audience. The steam bath, where women share intimately and which turns in upon itself spatially, could now have been opened to the audience, at least on the narrative level. The use of shot/reverse-angle shots that enables the reception of the space with its three dimensions and the figures therein might lead to such an opening. Kaja Silverman explains the effect created by shot/reverse-angle shots as follows:

> A particularly striking instance of this displacement would seem to be the articulation of shot/reverse shot relationships along the axis of a fictional look, which gives identificatory access to vision from within spectacle and the body. The theoreticians of suture argue that it is only through specular mediations that the viewer can sustain an identification with the camera. (Silverman 1996, 127)

Consequently, while the female audience's identification with Şoray's Hürmüz disturbs us in the Yılmaz version, why do we expect such identification with contemporary Hürmüz? Perhaps the answer is already there in the film. As Safinaz says, "Now, times have changed". Women perhaps want to identify themselves with characters that contribute to their struggle for liberation resisting the discourse of masculinity, which is still dominant in terms of the representation of women in Turkish cinema.

Works Cited

Büker, Seçil. 2002. "The Film Does Not End with an Ecstatic Kiss". In *Fragments of Culture: The Everyday of Modern Turkey*, edited by Deniz Kandiyoti and Ayşe Saktanber, 147-170. New Jersey: Rutgers University Press,.

Mulvey, Laura. 1975. "Visual Pleasure and Narrative Cinema". *Screen* 16 (3): 6-18.

Silverman, Kaja. 1995. *The Threshold of the Visible World*. London: Routledge.

Snyder, Robert W. 2000. *The Voice of the City: Vaudeville and Popular Culture in New York*. Chicago: Ivan R. Dee.

Suner, Asuman. 2005. "Vasfiye'nin Kızkardeşleri"(Vasfiye's Sisters). In *Hayalet Ev: Türk Sinemasında Aidiyet, Kimlik ve Bellek* (Ghost House: Belonging, Identity and Memory in Turkish Cinema). İstanbul: Metis Yayınları.

PART VI:

NEW METHODOLOGY

CHAPTER SEVENTEEN

CINEMA OF THRESHOLDS, WITHOUT GRAVITY, UNDER URGENT TIMES: DISTANT VOICES, STILL LIVES

TÜL AKBAL SÜALP

The real is far beyond the giant mountain in the land of the inferential past tense or the glorified alienated "outsider" and lumpen nothingness.

Turkey's cinema of the last two decades has gone through a series of specific, diverse shifts which distinguish it from the earlier cinema in some very significant ways; while these shifts can be studied from different angles they all share a very particular chronotope (time-space). I would therefore like to study the films of the late 1990s and the 2000s, which concern themselves with the tension between urban and rural space, within the context of the trauma of remembering and forgetting political history and the "global," social, political and economic effects of the 1980s. In order to understand and explore these complex and diverse appearances, we also need to analyse the particular way of looking at hybrid forms and aesthetic tendencies which lie over the tension between the cognitive search and survival strategies within the shifting space of global capitalist imperialism, which had been re-mapping and rearranging the world system.

Turkey's cinema in the last two decades has four main tracks. First track is male dominated lumpen urban melodramas. Second track is the way of stylistic new ways of narration. Third track belongs to women directors. The final fourth track is political filmmaking. It is a cinema of *thresholds* of a *chronotope* without *gravity* under the *urgent times*. Cinema of thresholds refers to the socio-temporal specificity. The major outcomes of the 1980s neo-liberal policies have been the deregulations of the international division of labour, the high rates of unemployment, the abolition of the organised oppositions and the oppression of the lower classes all over the world (Hardt and Negri 2001). The consequences of these transformations have been the vast zones of social leftovers, forced migrations, constant displacements, social confrontations, the seemingly minor but extensive number of never-ending wars, paramilitary groups and denials by society. Specifically, Turkey suffered three military coups: on 27 May 1960, 12 March 1971 and 12 September 1980. These events triggered long-lasting trauma in society with no time or space for mourning. Together with other conditions such as growing unemployment, Turkish society began to experience insecurity and desperation and individuals became indifferent as if lost in time and space. Cinema, cultural life and the daily practices within society all lost their once well-defined and accepted links to each other. The social participants (people within society) became out of touch with the various aspects of culture they had known well before the coups and could not understand how to navigate the new relationships. Society sank into a twilight zone. The position of political and/or social subjects became what appeared to be for all intents and purposes the social panorama which had in the last two decades, been questioned and was regarded as not a very noble thing to focus on. However, the state of not being a "subject" or the denial of being 'one' also created a shaky and clumsy positioning in the areas of art, culture and within day-to-day life. These precise experiences are objectified in the form of fractured urban practices, multicultural confrontations, distrust of strangers, economic hardship caused by the rearrangement of the division of labour and the trouble in configuring gender positions. These conditions produce and embrace a specific chronotope of daily culture after the 1980s, yet within the scope of this brief comparative study of post-1990s Turkish cinema, I will focus on the specific chronotope of social upheaval in Turkey.

In the aftermath of the 1980s, Turkey's cinema developed diverse characteristics. One of them is the alienated, "outsider" cinema; the "outsider" quality came from the directors' standpoint. They were able to detach themselves from the recent past—the memories of the political and social trauma—and become indifferent and numb. This historical specificity requires extensive discussion.

I suggest here that people who survived the 1980s, the ones who were lucky enough to be saved from the casualties of war and the neoliberal world system, hunger, famine and/or violence of any kind on the part of those in power became "hermetically-sealed" image/subjects. That they are not living in war zones, and deprivation does not keep them from being hunted and falling into other traps in which they become out of focus, *fuzzy* and visually *image made subjects*.

Fear and anxiety regenerate the forms of representation of a specific genre and aesthetic whenever a rearrangement and a redefinition of labour divisions are necessary. New cognitive maps of the crowded space of the industrialised and/or post-industrialised urban life are required. Having to deal with unemployment and confront this new shared space becomes a heavy burden for the male ego. Today the forms of this fear and anxiety are more layered, multicultural and widespread. The anxieties have been complicated by the breakdown of the socialisation of production and experience. Public life is fractured and fragmented, so are its spaces. In this transformed "film-noir" chronotope of our time, it seems that the city dwellers are forced to remap and reconfigure the conditions of coexistence, order, and division of labour, and reconceptualise the qualities of survival, along with remapping the definitions and experiences of the "self"/ "other" relationship on the levels of class, gender and ethnicity.

Filmmaking of this specific "film-noir" chronotope is characterised by a self-pitying, arabesque atmosphere, and it mainly employs expressionist poetics to allegorise social conditions and survival strategies. This "visualises" the experiences of the city by its confused inhabitants who are desperately seeking out an identity within it; this slant portrays a true urge to feel the gravity of the situation for the viewers, directors, inhabitants themselves. As a genre, we can see that it is not only specific to the post-war chronotope of certain geographies such as the Weimar Republic of the 1920s and 1930s or to the United States in the late 1940s and 1950s, but may also become visible in other hybrid genres with different expressionistic aesthetics, within different geographies and with the directors of our time.[1]

After the mid-1990s we also see films that have gradually distanced themselves from issues of class conflict and gender, instead reproducing the philosophical ideas idealising the lumpen attitudes and the feelings of futility. I believe that the refusal and disregard of social criticism along with the disgraceful attitude towards knowledge/production/socialisation of knowledge, the revaluation of apolitical, illiterate and prosaic daily experiences, and the sublimation of nationalism and racism seen in the 1980s fed this phenomenon. Herein lies the main question of directors' self-indulgence within this stylistic form. It is a sanctified male-lumpen lifestyle that urges them forward, with no self-criticism or analytical insight into society and the world system that makes them eager to glorify and polish this wounded underclass male ego, without being interested in

---

1. As I have studied earlier in *Zamanmekan: Kuram ve Sinema* (2004).

people's real problems and/or the meanings and experiences of unemployment, poverty and deprivations of life.

Arabesque Noir

The deep and consecutively developed economic crises resulted in high unemployment and growing poverty, creating feelings of hopelessness and helplessness among the silent, mainly male majorities. I believe this in turn brought with it great unease and even hatred toward the figure of "the other". In a majority of films of the 1990s, for example, women's roles gradually moved away from "involvement in dramatic action" to unimportant figures in the background. No meaningful dialogue was written for them. On the screen, new (stereo)types of femme-fatale characters started to emerge, but now from different backgrounds and classes. Most commonly these women were from the outskirts of town, from lower classes and shown to act as provocateurs and seducers who lead men to commit crime, violence and irrational actions while themselves later becoming the victims of this brutality and violence. Increasingly, verbal and physical violence was attributed to male characters, whose "shattered" life became full of drama and absent of women, the latter either not represented at all or merely as cartoonish, two-dimensional silhouettes. I therefore prefer to term this type of cinema *arabesque noir*. In *Gemide/On Board* and *Laleli'de Bir Azize/A Madonna in Laleli* (1998), two films that have complementing scripts and characters, the directors, Serdar Akar and Kudret Sabancı respectively, treat a bunch of male losers—"lost in nowhere" in the city and hungry for everything— as the heroes of the lumpen world. The style of both directors is built on glorifying this "lumpen world" in both films. One night in Istanbul this gang of male losers picks up a foreign woman, who is herself also a victim of the same global system, left her own country in search of economic stability and become involved in prostitution. She is depicted as a blonde female foreigner with no language and no expression. Members of the gang brutally victimise and rape her in their "blessed" lumpen attitudes. In this glorified underclass world, specifically used by Turkish directors, women play their part as the unknown, threatening "other," standing for all "others". These manufactured women symbolise both the fantasies and fears of the wounded male ego, and seemingly, of the directors, as well. In films of the 2000s it can be seen that women either appear as backdrops, mannequins or the newly-fashioned femme fatale characters in a private space such as the home and/or lower-class community surroundings, or simply do not exist in the stories at all. *İtiraf/The Confession, Yazgı/Fate*

(2002), *Bekleme Odası/The Waiting Room* (2004), *Kader/Fate* (2006) by
Zeki Demirkubuz, and *İklimler/Climates* (2006) but also in some ways *Üç
Maymun/Three Monkeys* (2008) by Nuri Bilge Ceylan, are examples for
this category of film.

On the other side of "arabesque noir," these are "melancholic films
characterised by rural escape. In this sub-category of unhappiness, a
somewhat nihilistic and existentialist boredom fills the films. These
feelings of futility are also related to the same social and historical
conditions mentioned above; as well as the same alienation with the social
realities of urban space, political issues, and memories. These "rural
escape" films either focus on the figure of the miserable, lonely, incurably
melancholic male who one day escapes from the city and goes back to his
hometown, yet still continues to be bored and does nothing, or on the hero
or anti-hero, who is unable to return home and wanders the city without
purpose, likewise feeling boredom and nothingness. Self-pity and the
deflection of blame onto others for their miserable life without
questioning history or society are the main feelings evoked in these films.

Desperately seeking an escape from difficult metropolitan conditions,
these films instead glorify rural life, the slowness of the towns and their
claustrophobic world and indirectly, the petty bourgeois life style as well.
It would also appear, however, that the desire for escape is more attached
to *time* than to space. In these films the slow crawl of time serves to
annihilate space. In this way, the little hometown seems less affected by
the assault of capitalist time, thus creating nostalgia for safe and well-
known "home" environments. These perceptions are highly significant yet
never clearly stated; it never becomes clear why the characters are
desperately running away. We can apply our analyses to all of Tayfun
Pirselimoğlu's films (*Rıza* 2007 and *Pus/Haze* 2009) and to the films of
Semih Kaplanoğlu, from the early, film noir-ish and outsider films,
Herkes Kendi Evinde/Away From Home (2001), *Meleğin Düşüşü/Angel's
Fall* (2005) all the way to his trilogy, *Yusuf Üçlemesi/Yusuf's Trilogy*,
named after the main character Yusuf: *Yumurta/Egg* (2007), *Süt/Milk*
(2008), *Bal/Honey* (2010). One should also mention Nuri Bilge Ceylan's
films, *Kasaba/Small Town* (1998), *Mayıs Sıkıntısı/Clouds of May* (2000),
Uzak/Distant (2002) and *İklimler/Climates* (2006) within this category
since Ceylan's films were a main source of inspiration for the
aforementioned directors. While Ceylan might seem to be the pioneering
figure within this category, his films about the escape to the nostalgia of a
small home town have dimensions that require further analysis. We can
see and understand the sources of boredom, conflicts and the contrasts

between the characters as well as the relation of background and foreground work.

Experiments in Narration

The second of the four tracks is a novel and innovative search for new ways of telling and showing. Within these new experiments in form there appears to be an amalgamation of the old and traditional forms of "showing and telling" with the newer emerging poetics. This emerging aesthetic searches for the new ways that filmmaking might envelope, and also bring to the fore, discussions of social and historical realities, as well as the dreams, fantasies and imagination surrounding the comprehension of these realities. If directors can indeed help us to face difficult moments in our collective past, then their films and the way in which they are made require close study. The search for new ways of telling and showing can serve to break down the domination of established ways of storytelling (whether modern or postmodern, conventional or avant-garde) and help us go beyond the simplistic dichotomies of fact and fiction, realism and non-realist forms, documenting and narrating, showing and telling.

In the 2000s directors Derviş Zaim and Ezel Akay both started searching for new forms of "looking" and "showing" and for different ways of storytelling. Zaim studied the archaeology of history, society, time and space in his specific film poetry as shown in his trilogy: paper marbling (*Elephants and Grass/Filler ve Çimen*, 2000), miniature, (*Waiting For Heaven/Cenneti Beklerken*, 2006) and calligraphy (*Nokta/Dot*, 2008). He was also dealing with the personal problems of being a filmmaker in terms of the responsibilities he felt toward portraying his personal and social history, the problems of looking and representing the source of the story, the reason for telling the story and its framing (*Fango/Mud/Çamur*, 2003). Ezel Akay started with a grotesque work for his first film (*Where's Firuze?/Neredesin Firuze?* 2004) and went on to direct the very innovative film, *Who Killed Shadows/Hacivat Karagöz Neden Öldürüldü?* (2006) a saga about the early folk version of the shadow-play duo, Karagöz and Hacivat. In 2009, he directed *7 Kocalı Hürmüz/Hürmüz with Seven Husbands* (2009), a folk tale about the life of a fictional woman during the late Ottoman Empire and how she (delicately and joyfully) manages to juggle seven husbands, one for each day of the week. Akay made these films the frontal-staging inspired by the traditional stage and show plays. In *Killing the Shadow* and *Hürmüz with 7 Husbands*, he questions all official storytelling and the dominant narration of cultural history. Moreover, he offers a different reading of the Ottoman Empire institutions and its multicultural carnivalesque surroundings. Another remarkable pioneering example of different approaches to storytelling is Ahmet Uluçay's film, *Boats Out Of Watermelon Rinds/Karpuz Kabuğundan Gemiler Yapmak* (2004) which depicts the down-to-earth relationships of two young boys who try to give birth to a film experience in a very small town. An outstanding example of independence for both Turkish and world cinema with a totally fresh and innovative look and a way of rendering the medium, he left behind a valuable legacy for filmmaking upon his death in 2009.

All the above films talk about minor histories, yet within a 'long shot' of 'History'. The directors' search for novel and genuine filmmaking is a *dream stalk* since they try to crystallise their analytical "look" in these dark and gloomy times of confusion and In presenting to us different way of seeing and comprehending. Their "dream stalk" offers highly innovative and freshening looks and asks for some residual way of spectatorship. Audience is not stitched up to the diegetic world of the films. Neither narration and narrative nor the story is for identification or suture. The real or, perhaps what we can term the truth, can be searched for in the ambiguity of the land of the inferential past, which might be called the logic of uncertainty and multiplicity. A particular culture of speech genre might have been creating some kind of sublime understanding of the reality on the one hand and might have been ridiculing the aura around the reality on the other, or both of them might have been working on parallel zones.

Because of the ambiguity that surrounds the way we talk and write, what happens sounds like a fairy-tale. Speech has been dominated by this logic for centuries. The cinema of Turkey needs multiplicities of tale like fictions to be able to grasp the idea of what is reality or about the truth that surrounds us more than verisimilitudes or imitation of life kind realisms. As opposed to the narration of fiction which pretends to be real, we might need a tale like fictions that never seem to claim reality while revealing the underneath of and ambiguity in realities. So the dichotomies around the fact and fiction can be reshuffled.

Bakhtin says: "Truth is not born nor is it to be found inside the head of an individual person; it is born between people collectively searching for truth, in the process of their dialogic interaction" (1998, 110). And Ballard reminds us that "everything is fictionalized, the role of the author is to invent the reality" (1984). Since what actually happened remains known only in the realm of the past, these directors search for the reality and truths embedded in ancient tales, shows and magic. Because the real might be too painful to face, and both remembering and forgetting are problematic, they prefer to raise the curtains up of the old shows and open up the boxes of fairy tales.

Interestingly, in-between the first two tracks of recent Turkish cinema one film stands out, Ümit Ünal's *Shadowless/Gölgesizler* (2008), the place of which among other films, regardless of its critique, suggests very crucial arguments. The film is based on Hasan Ali Toptaş's novel of the same title. Both the film and the novel question the subsistence of the absent existence of non-existent, presence of the absent which offers the problem of floating feelings about the self in the land of the traumatic history and/or the inferential past.

> Let us say, that moment, we were living in some other place, we were living in another time and from there we were dreaming here without knowing that were dreaming.
>   Maybe you have seen the ghost...that happens all the time when one looks at the glass so long, you always see a face. In fact, there is always a lost face for everyone, although they never could see it, but they always want to. (*Gölgesizler* 2008)

The dialogues in both the film and novel allegorise the problems I mention above, which, of course, are the carriers of the accumulated feelings.

The films *Who Killed Shadows/Hacivat Karagöz Neden Öldürüldü?* (2006), *Waiting for Heaven/Cenneti Beklerken* (2006) and *The Messenger/Ulak* (2008), *Dot* (2008), *Hürmüz with 7 Husbands* (2009), *Boats out Of Watermelon Rinds/Karpuz Kabuğundan Gemiler Yapmak* (2004) and *Gölgesizler/Shadowless* (2008) show us two facets of innovative search for meaning. On the one hand, these films question history, society, culture and the individual in a particular surrounding and seek answers to questions; on the other hand, they ask these questions using the different poetics of magical realism, fairytale storytelling and innovative visual shows which are the amalgamation of the visual entertainment habits throughout history.

Last but not least, it is worth mentioning two of Reha Erdem's films: *Hayat Var/My Only Sunshine* (2008) and *Kosmos* (2009). An outstanding filmmaker of this recent period, his films defy simple classification, yet they may be regarded as loosely associated with the second and third. In his last two films, he used the soundtrack to create another layer of meaning, creating another layer of meaning. He has also been developing an alternative and critical look to the themes he undertakes, and mostly these alternative looks have in some way been an answer to his earlier films. Furthermore, together with the innovative soundtracks, he has lately developed some very creative and alternative camera movements and angles that transform well-known spaces into.

Women Directors

Even though these directors belong to the same generation as the ones in the second track mentioned above, the third track separates itself in setting up a bridge between the second track and the fourth track that will be explained below. This third track came into existence through the work of leading women directors' brave and persistent stand in their approach to social and daily circumstances. The primary figures of this melodrama track, Yeşim Ustaoğlu and Handan İpekci, questioned social conflicts and bravely dealt with the question of the "other" and nationalism in *Pandora'nın Kutusu/Pandora's Box* (2009), *Bulutları Beklerken/Waiting for Clouds* (2004), *Guneşi Beklerken/Journey to the Sun* (1999), *İz/Traces* (1994) and in *Babam Askerde/Father is in the Army Now* (1994), *Büyük Adam Küçük Aşk/Hejar* (2001), *Saklı Yüzler/Hidden Faces* (2007) respectively. Tomris Giritlioğlu, whose earlier films dealt with the victims of the September 12th military junta has also persistently dealt with the plight of minority groups. Her films have shown forced migrations and displacement, and told stories that are related to traumatic moments of Turkish history. Yet her films have mostly been criticised as creating flat and popular stories out of social and historical traumas. *Suyun Öte Yanı/Other Side of the Water* (1991), *80. Adım/80th Step* (1996), *Salkım Hanımın Taneleri/Mrs. Salkım's Diamonds* (1999), *Güz Sancısı/Pains of Autumn* (2008) are among them.

The coup of 12 September 1980 and the military rule that followed has left a deep wound in Turkish society in recent past. A number of films were made on the subject; among them are: *Sen Türkülerini Söyle/Sing Your Songs* (Şerif Gören, 1986), *Ses/The Voice* (Zeki Ökten, 1986), *Kara Sevdalı Bulut/Cloud in Love* (Muammer Özer, 1987), *Av Zamanı/ Hunting Time* (Erden Kral, 1987), *Sis/Fog* (Zülfü Livaneli, 1988), *Bütün Kapılar Kapalıydı/All the Doors Were Closed* (Memduh Ün, 1989), *Uçurtmayı Vurmasınlar/Don't Let Them Shoot the Kite* (Tunç Başaran, 1989), *Bekle Dedim Gölgeye/I Asked the Shadow to Wait* and *Eylül Fırtınası/After the Fall* (Atıf Yılmaz, 1990 and 1999), *Babam Askerde/Father is in the Army Now* (Handan İpekçi, 1994) and *80. Adım/80th Step* (Tomris Giritlioğlu, 1995). Recently, directors from different generations have once again committed themselves to question the era of September 12th and started telling stories from the silently unremembered era that was left behind as if it was a faraway world from another time, another place. Although most of the films are tear-jerking melodramas, to some extent this enables emotional attachment with an audience who has lost the sense of that time, allowing the latter to remember and to remember and come to terms with the history of the recent past. Among them *Beynelmilel/International* (Önder and Gülmez, 2006) was able to earn some sympathy by telling a story with humour and being less exploitative. *After the Fall/Eylül Fırtınası* (Atıf Yilmaz, from the generation of the 1960s directors; 1999), *Vizontele Tuuba* (Yılmaz Erdoğan, 2003), *My Father And Son/Babam ve Oğlum* (Çağan Irmak, 2005), *Home Coming/Eve Dönüş* (Ömer Uğur, 2006) *International/Beynelmilel* (Sırrı Süreyya Önder and M. Gülmez, 2006), *Fikret Bey*, Selma Köksal, 2007), *Zincirbozan* (Atıl İnaç, 2007) and *O...Çocukları/Son of a B...* (Murat Saraçoğlu, 2008) are some of the other films that address the subject.

The whole-scale social unrest of the 1970s in Turkey was characterised by the students' and workers' movements' strikes and demonstrations that led to the detention, imprisonment, torture, disappearances and deaths particularly on the part of the left in the brutal coup of 1980 and the decade that followed. The coup can be read as a continuation of the violent attacks of the radical right-wing on the left. When compared to the same decades in the rest of the world, the 1960s and 1970s were different in Turkey in the sense that the whole of the political left and opposition movements were destroyed. Then we jumped into the era of the 1980s, "to the winds of desire of liberal economy" as it was the case all around the world. These films now try to recall the years of the late 1970s.

Directors such as Ustaoğlu, who do not fall into the trap of melodrama, are able to more delicately deal with all the above-mentioned problems in telling the stories of the minor and marginal people and brilliantly use the socially-produced space as a storyteller in their films. Both urban and rural settings bear marks of the recent history; urban as in *Traces* and *Journey to the Sun*, as the rural setting is in *Waiting for Clouds* and both urban and rural space in *Pandora's Box*. Layer by layer, these directors open up new paths for those who cannot speak for themselves, and render visible what so far remained unseen. While in her first film İpekci bravely touched on a taboo issue by exploring the story of the relationship between a retired judge and a little Kurdish girl whose parents were killed in a police operation, in her second, *Hidden Faces* (2007), she dealt with another controversial issue—the honour killing of women— and tried out a different editing technique so as to challenge the exploitative nature of the storyline of her film. Köksal, in *Fikret Bey* (2007), made a film about two old men one day in a disappearing factory through which the last thirty years of the turmoil Turkey has witnessed becomes readable.

The directors who worked in the gloomy era of the late 1990s and the 2000s continue to produce films about daily life experiences and try to show the conditions, histories and social practices behind the accepted, official line appearances. They have been changing the screen persona of the cities by including unfamiliar sounds and angles in their films. The well-known spectacle of the cities has been fading out and becoming far and distant. We now have different scenes from the alleyways. The looks and sounds seem to belong to the ones with different gravity when we see what is usually "not shown" and speak the "untold". These are the films that inhale and exhale the city of insignificant people and speak softly of the minor and/or oppressed and forbidden histories. We have the opportunity to comprehend the chronotopes of the 1990s and 2000s, and follow up with the differences and similarities. This cinema is based on the diverse forms of survival, struggle resistance and negotiation experiences of everyday life. The films emerge from the experiences of the other side and tell the stories of morphing encounters and habitations and of the passengers who do stand by for some time and/or coexist simultaneously. Today this complex chronotope can be seen as polycentric and most probably dialogical as well as in hybrid form. Because of all these mentioned specificities I would like to call this cinema *night navigations*.

Political Cinema

In the second half of the 2000s Turkey's cinema grew in box office numbers and in terms of popular and genre films of many different kinds. Directors from different generations made their first and/or second films in this period, and some popular comedians also made their debuts. Among them, the younger generation of filmmakers such as Özcan Alper, Kazım Öz, Hüseyin Karabey, Özgür Doğan, Orhan Eskiyerli, and İnan Temelkuran distinguished themselves with their sharp, political films. The significant appearance and apparently significant commitment of these young directors in taking political stands opened up the fourth tract of political cinema. Their films are mostly easy to watch for the general audience, but they are sharp and brave in what they talk about and create an emphasis on the importance of documentary film as part of cinema in Turkey in making use of this form. We can point out films such as *Sonbahar/Autumn* (Özcan Alper, 2008), *Bahoz/The Storm* (Kazım Öz, 2007), *Gitmek/My Marlon and Brando* (Hüseyin Karabey, 2008), *İki*

Dil Bir Bavul/*On the Way to School* (Özgür Doğan and Orhan Eskiyerli, 2008), *Bornova Bornova* (İnan Temelkuran, 2009), *Çoğunluk*/*The Majority* (Seren Yüce, 2010) which bring new perspectives to the documentary filmmaking style.

Lately, we have seen a diverse cinema that is greatly concerned with the uneven, unequal development and distribution of metropolitan life. *Kara Köpekler Havlarken*/*Black Dogs Barking* (Mehmet Bahadır Er and M. Gorbach, 2009), *Başka Semtin Çocukları*/*Children of the Other Side* (Aydın Bulut, 2008) and *Köprüdekiler*/*Men on the Bridge* (Aslı Özge, 2009) can be cited as examples of such films. They swing in-between positioning themselves outside in, inside out. When they touch on *cinema vérité* in their approach, they might be involved in and/or interfere with their objects. In this sense what they do is a representation, and this representation involves object and subject positions within a hierarchic nature that also creates the gaze of *terra incognita* and *voyeurism* over what is represented. I believe that these out-of-focus and chaotic positionings result from the long run of depoliticisation policies in recent history.

The polycentric, dialogical and multicultural chronotope allegorises for us the fractured urban experience, multicultural confrontation, distrust of unknown others, strong discomfort in material life caused by the rearrangement of the division of labour, and the trouble within the configuration of gender positions. I therefore suggest that when we look at the dark and the gloomy streets of different geographies it is important to try to make sense of whose territory is defined, who is excluded and how. Darkness encapsulates the invisible and behind the veiled we might see the off-screen spaces of different geographies holding the possibility for dialogic encounter.

Works Cited

Bakhtin, M. M. 1998. *The Dialogic Imagination: Four Essays by Mikhail Bakhtin*. Edited by Michael Holquist. Translated by Caryl Emerson and Michael Holquist. Austin: University of Texas Press.

Ballard, J. G. 1984. "Introduction to Crash". *RE/Search* 8/9: 96-98.

Hardt, Michael, and Antonio Negri. 2001. *Empire*. Cambridge, MA: Harvard University Press.

Süalp, Z. Tül Akbal, and Aslı Güneş. 2010. *Taşrada var bir zaman* (There is a Time in the Countryside). İstanbul: Çitlembik Yayınları.

Süalp, Z. Tül Akbal. 2004. *Zamanmekan: Kuram ve Sinema* (Timespace: Theory and Cinema). Istanbul: Bağlam Yayıncılık.

Filmography

1986
Sen Türkülerini Söyle/Sing Your Songs. Directed by Şerif Gören.
Ses/The Voice. Directed by Zeki Ökten.
1987
Kara Sevdalı Bulut/Cloud in Love. Directed by Muammer Özer.
Av Zamanı/Hunting Time. Directed by Erden Kral.
1988
A ay/Oh Moon. Directed by Reha Erdem.
Sis/Fog. Directed by Zülfü Livaneli.
1989
Bütün Kapılar Kapalıydı/All the Doors Were Closed. d. Memduh Ün.
Uçurtmayı Vurmasınlar/Don't Let Them Shoot the Kite. d. Tunç Başaran.
1990
Bekle Dedim Gölgeye/I Asked the Shadow to Wait. d. Atıf Yılmaz.
1991
Suyun Öte Yanı/Other Side of the Water. d. Tomris Giritlioğlu.
1994
Babam Askerde/Father is in the Army Now. d. Handan İpekçi.
İz/Traces. d. Yeşim Ustaoğlu.
1996
80. Adım/80th Step. d. Tomris Giritlioğlu.
1998
Gemide/On Board. d. Serdar Akar.
Kasaba/Small Town. d. Nuri Bilge Ceylan.
*Laleli'de Bir Azize/A Madonna in Laleli..*d. Kudret Sabancı.
1999
Eylül Fırtınası/After the Fall. d. Atıf Yılmaz.
Güneşe Yolculuk/Journey to the Sun. d. Yeşim Ustaoğlu.
Kaç Para Kaç/A Run For Money. d. Reha Erdem.
Salkım Hanımın Taneleri/Mrs. Salkım's Diamonds. d. Tomris Giritlioğlu.
2000
Filler ve Cimen/Elephants and Grass., d. Derviş Zaim.
Mayıs Sıkıntısı/Clouds of May. d. Nuri Bilge Ceylan.
2001
Büyük Adam Küçük Aşk/Hejar. d. Handan İpekçi.
Herkes Kendi Evinde/Away From Home. d. Semih Kaplanoglu.
İtiraf/The Confession. d. Zeki Demirkubuz.
2002
Uzak/Distant. d. Nuri Bilge Ceylan.
Yazgı/Fate. d. Zeki Demirkubuz.

2003
Çamur/Mud. d. Derviş Zaim.
Vizontele Tuuba d. Yılmaz Erdoğan.
2004
Bekleme Odası/The Waiting Room. d. Zeki Demirkubuz.
Bulutları Beklerken/Waiting for Clouds. d. Yeşim Ustaoğlu.
Karpuz Kabuğundan Gemiler Yapmak/Boats Out Of Watermelon Rinds. d.
Ahmet Uluçay.
Korkuyorum Anne/I'm Scared Mommy. d. Reha Erdam.
Neredesin Firuze?/Where's Firuze?. d. Ezey Akay.
2005
Babam Ve Oğlum/My Father And Son. d. Çağan Irmak.
Meleğin Düşüşü/Angel's Fall. d. Semih Kaplanoglu.
2006
Beş Vakit/Times and Winds. d. Reha Erdem.
Beynelmilel/International. d. Sırrı Süreyya Önder & M. Gülmez.
Cenneti Beklerken/Waiting For Heaven. d. Yeşim Ustaoğlu.
Eve Dönüş/Coming Home. d. Ömer Uğur.
Hacivat Karagoz Neden Öldürüldü?/Killing the Shadow. d. Ezey Akay.
İklimler/Climates. d. Nuri Bilge Ceylan.
Kader/Fate. d. Zeki Demirkubuz.
2007
Bahoz/The Storm. d. Kazım Öz.
Fikret Bey d. Selma Köksal.
Rıza d. Tayfun Pirselimoğlu.
Saklı Yüzler/Hidden Faces. d. Handan İpekçi.
Yumurta/Egg. d. Semih Kaplanoğlu.
Zincirbozan d. Atıl İnanç.
2008
İki Dil Bir Bavul/On the Way to School. d. Özgür Doğan and Orhan
Eskiyerli.
Nokta/Dot. d. Derviş Zaim.
Bornova Bornova d. İnan Temelkuran.
Gitmek/My Marlon and Brando. d. Hüseyin Karabey.
Gölgesizler/Shadowless. d. Ümit Ünal.
Güz Sancısı/Pains of Autumn. d. Tomris Giritlioğlu.
Hayat Var/My Only Sunshine. d. Reha Erdem.
O... Çocukları/Son of a B.... d. Murat Saraçoğlu.
Sonbahar/Autumn. d. Özcan Alper.
Süt/Milk. d. Semih Kaplanoğlu.
Üç Maymun/Three Monkeys. d. Nuri Bilge Ceylan.

2009

Kara Köpekler Havlarken/Black Dogs Barking. d. Mehmet Bahadır Er.
Kosmos d. Reha Erdem.
Köprüdekiler/Men on the Bridge. d. Aslı Özge.
Pandora'nın Kutusu/Pandora's Box. d. Yeşim Ustaoğlu.
Pus/Haze. d. Tayfun Pirselimoğlu.

2010

Bal/Honey. d. Semih Kaplanoğlu.
7 Kocalı Hürmüz / Hürmüz with 7 Husbands d. Ezey Akay.
Çoğunluk/The Majority., d. Seren Yüce.

CHAPTER EIGHTEEN

INBETWEENNESS AS A MODE OF RESISTANCE IN REHA ERDEM'S CINEMA

GÜLENGÜL ALTINTAŞ[1]

Dead ends...corridors... Isn't a human being an eternal creature that thrives within labyrinths of unknown ends; that feels vitality in the darkness in which we are lost, and while chasing the unrevealed, rises up from his/her wounds each time he/she tumbles over?[2]
—Reha Erdem

Reha Erdem's films are like the pieces of an investigation, the elemental *problematique* of which is set on the conflicts of human beings in their quest for freedom and happiness. Here, following Raymond Williams' understanding of social practice of everyday life, I consider culture in its broadest possible meaning; I intend therefore to refer both to the clash within social practices that regulate the conditions of living in a group, and to the conflicts that arise from the process of culturalisation— which is also a process that conducts people towards creativity and exploration.

I have written on this subject in a previous article, "The Realm of Dried Dreams" which was published in *The Cinema of Reha Erdem: Love and Rebellion* (2009). Here I will repeat certain parts of my earlier argument, while opening up long parentheses in between the lines, in order to further discuss the circumstances of *inbetweenness* in Reha Erdem's cinema. The state of *inbetweenness* in Reha Erdem's films is an ongoing theme, which is experienced through the films' main characters in various

---

1. This article is a shorter and modified version of the article "Kuru Rüyalar Alemi" ("The Realm of Dried Dreams") first published in *Reha Erdem Sineması: Aşk ve İsyan* (The Cinema of Reha Erdem: Love and Rebellion, 2009), and it is republished here with the permission of Çitlembik Publishing.
2. My translation. From Reha Erdem's article "Love and Rebellion" (2009)

ways, and also expressed through the representation of the filmic space as constructed within *in-between* places. In the following pages, I will discuss different instances of *inbetweenness* in Reha Erdem's films, especially the representations of adolescence as the *time* of *inbetweenness*, and the *in-between spaces* of this experience, with a special emphasis on the possibilities of resistance which these *in-between time-spaces* may reserve.

I believe Reha Erdem's filmography is part of a long-running project, a philosophical pursuit dwelling on various questions such as, what is truth, what is morality, what is love, what is time, what is it to be human; the films pursue a constant, on-going conversation with each other while collecting these questions, as well as their answers. In his latest film *Kosmos* (2009), Erdem repeats all of these questions once again through the quest of his hero, Battal/Kosmos—a mysterious, saintly character, who has stepped out of the social (the order of humanity) and transcended himself through the seven mystical floors of cosmos. With *Kosmos*, Erdem's pursuit comes to a point of closure, and I believe with his next film he might surprise his audience by beginning a new period within his filmography.

But let us put aside wishes and predictions about the future of Erdem's cinema, and concentrate on his existent films. The first thing I would like to draw attention to is how Reha Erdem's films approach the experience of adolescence as an opportunity. How adolescence, the state of being in between childhood and adulthood, is considered in Erdem's films as a mode of resistance and how different forms of *inbetweenness* generate similar meanings.

The state of adolescence in Reha Erdem's films is not determined according to the character's age or according to what stage of life they are in but by their relationship with authority and the stand they take against it. In these films, adolescence is not only considered as a stage of initiation, but also to be an experience which proclaims the cultural constraints on the character's empowerment and individuation. This is why Erdem tells the stories of different characters going through the state of adolescence over and over again at different ages and under different circumstances. Yekta in *A Ay/Oh, Moon!* (1988), the children of *Beş Vakit/Times and Winds* (2006), and Hayat in *Hayat Var/My Only Sunshine* (2008) are in adolescence as a consequence of their age; on the other hand, Ali and Keten in *Korkuyorum Anne/What is a Human Anyway?* (2004) are captives of a constant state of adolescence, as a result of the oppression in the world of adults they can neither escape nor internalise successfully. Adolescence is sometimes experienced as regression resulting from an outer threat, a setback to adulthood—as is the case with Selim in *Kaç Para*

Kaç/A Run for Money (1999); or sometimes it is a stage that is never fully experienced, that is passed over during the transition to adulthood—as is the case with Ömer's little brother in *Times and Winds*, who reads poems and prayers by heart like a ventriloquist dummy sitting on his father's lap.

Adulthood in Erdem's cinema is not related to physical maturity, rather, it is a kind of identity, acquired by the internalisation of oppression that is enacted in the world of adults. The "bedridden fathers" in the films (Yekta's and Hayat's grandfather, Ömer's father), "men who cough all the time" (the tailor in *Kosmos*) or the constantly sneezing mother, Neriman, in *What is a Human Anyway?* all seem to be crippled by the societal oppression they have internalised. Their constant sneezing and coughing are like a futile attempt to dislodge this oppression. The "coughing man" becomes a consistent and often-used symbol in Erdem's iconography. This theme—which is fixed not only in the visual world of the film but also in the soundtrack symbolises the price that is paid for adulthood. It paradoxically also indicates a loss of power that is conceded in order to be able to exercise power, to take one's share of the power which is held by adults.

The *Time* of *Inbetweenness*

Bilgin Saydam defines the transformation of the "compliant child" to the "adult agent" as a *mother-fugal*[3]/*father-driven* quest. In a nuclear family, a child withdraws from the mother and becomes attracted to the father figure, while, on a more social scale, this quest is directed towards the "collective consciousness". According to Saydam, "in order to allay the distress caused by being conscious," this quest from time to time should change its direction back to the womb, following the umbilical cord and "reach back to the source of life" (Saydam 1997, 54-5).

Reha Erdem's adolescent characters do not want to be torn apart from the "source of life" and hold on to their childhood tenaciously, wielding their adolescence (their *inbetweenness*) as a mode of resistance against the repression of *father-driven* action which is summoning them to the "collective consciousness". The *mother-driven/father-fugal* activity of these adolescent characters, which reverses the *mother-fugal/father-driven* type of action, is represented in the films in two ways. Sometimes it is as an escape from the patriarchal culture to nature (nature being the source of life—*Times and Winds*, *My Only Sunshine*, *Kosmos*); and sometimes, the

---

3. *Mother-fugal* refers to the term *centrifugal* here; centre being the mother as the source of life.

mother-fugal action is represented directly as a type of action towards the mother's womb, as in the case of the adolescent/adult characters of *What is a Human Anyway?* (Ali and Keten).

This *mother-fugal* action is both ludicrous and tragic at the same time. Whenever the adolescent characters of the film *What is a Human Anyway?* —who are decidedly over-age to be adolescent—pluck up their courage with the intent to leave their "mother's womb," they get scared to death by the outside world. Immediately, they return to take shelter in the womb, because the world outside where the *father-driven* action summons them is truly a dreadful one. It is a world where adults run wildly after flocks of little boys in the streets to circumcise them. When they succeed in catching them, it becomes a world that then sets up festivals of merry-making with a flush of victory. It is a world where soldiers forcibly drag off young men to mandatory military service to kill and perhaps die in a far-off land; it is a world where the police threaten people with torture to make them confess to crimes they did not commit. In such a world, not everyone has the guts to let go of the umbilical cord and take on the *mother-fugal/father-driven* quest.

All the male characters in the films who do take on this quest are either physically disabled by combat or become hypochondriacs like Mr. Rasih as a result of living with constant anxiety. At the end of *What is a Human Anyway?*, Keten—who is trying to adjust himself to the world of adults to be competent in love—makes a dash out of his mother's womb, but before he can drift apart, he finds himself stuck on a gigantic phallic rock screaming at the top of his lungs, "Mom, I'm afraid" (which is also the original title of the film in Turkish).

The way in which Yekta in *Oh, Moon!*, Hayat in *My Only Sunshine* and the children of *Times and Winds* constantly escape to nature—as if they are searching for something while they idly wander about the hills— is also an example of *mother-fugal* action. In *Times and Winds*, whenever Ömer, Yakup and Yıldız are reminded by their parents that it is time for them to start to take on responsibilities and pay the price for growing up, whenever they are scolded by their father or beaten by their mother, they take shelter in nature. Nature swaddles them in her compassionate arms. According to Bilgin Saydam *mother-fugal* action is "an escape/drifting apart from the swallowing, squeezing, imprisoning, slashing, melting mother (who is stuffing the child back into the womb, thus triggering regression), an escape/drifting apart from the instincts, intense emotions and exhilaration that deflates the consciousness" (1997, 57). Every time the children in *Times and Winds* take refuge in nature, it is as if they experience a little death of their own. While their bodies are covered with leaves, blending themselves with earth and stone, instead of a deep sleep, it is as if they dissolve in death that *deflates consciousness*.

A Universal Condition of Discontent

Within this context, Reha Erdem's approach to culturisation as a process resembles the way that Freud approaches civilisation as a *universal condition of discontent*. According to Freud, it is not possible to resolve the conflict of interest between the individual who is in search of happiness, and the society that is seeking to provide order. Therefore, the condition of discontent is the price we have to pay for the security and comfort of living together as a community and it cannot be eliminated on a social level.

> There is no sovereign recipe in this matter which suits all; each one must find out for himself by which particular means he may achieve felicity. All kinds of different factors will operate to influence his choice. It depends on how much real gratification he is likely to obtain in the external world, and how far he will find it necessary to make himself independent of it; finally, too, on the belief he has in himself of his power to alter it in accordance with his wishes. (Freud 1989, 67-8)

Reha Erdem's characters cling to their childhood, where the search for happiness and self-satisfaction is not considered selfish; in so doing, they defend their right to happiness with a timid but pertinacious manner against the adults who remind them that it is time to pay the price for growing up. Yekta in *Oh Moon!* (when she confronts her grandfather), Ali in *What Is a Human Anyway?* (when he deliberately withholds his father's medicine while his father is having a heart attack), Ömer in *Times and Winds* (with his constant attempts to kill his father) and Hayat in *My Only Sunshine* (when she abandons her grandfather to death), each act with this same determination. The acts of violence and the vengeance directed toward the father figure is the reflection of their enmity directed at the patriarchal order.

But adolescence is transitory and growing up is unavoidable. Each one of them strives to find out for himself/herself by which particular means (s)he may achieve felicity. In *Oh Moon!*, Yekta transforms into her aunt Neyyir in submission, after she embarks on the same journey as her mother/aunt by sailing away in a boat. Ali (in *What is a Human Anyway?*) denies his identity with obstinate and hopeless resistance in order to acquire the right to remain a child. In *Times and Winds*, Ömer, who is obsessed with the idea of killing his father, is appealed to satisfy his desires through a symbolic act. Hayat (*My Only Sunshine!*)—the strongest amongst all of these characters—takes shelter in love, the only expedient way for selfishly pursuing happiness in the world of adults.[4]

Hayat's itinerary is a quest for her womanhood. She searches for it in a masculine world—she gropes around to find herself as a woman among the ruins of war we hear from a distance (in the soundtrack of the film) even if we cannot see it. Hayat has nothing to learn from her mother who greets her daughter's first menstrual blood with a slap to her face. All she might have learnt is getting ashamed of her womanhood and to hide it as a wound. She learns about womanhood from abusive men and women. She learns quickly, but she does not obey. She waits mutely, quietly, forcing the borders she is trapped in. There is also this young man who does not violate the borders Hayat puts between him and herself—a young man who gives voice to his love with songs. Of course, a feeling as intense as love, can only find its expression with *arabesque* music which creates a kind of extrinsic contrast and excessiveness within the pale, masculine world of the film. Hayat approaches this man one step at a time and finally she takes his hand, she escapes with him, sails away with him in a boat.

The sea Hayat sails away on symbolises the opportunity for another kind of femininity different from the passive role imposed upon Hayat by the rapist male and abusive female characters in the film. Hayat finds the particular means by which she may achieve felicity on her own; she chooses her own path to a liberated adult womanhood. She invites the man of her choosing by putting on the lipstick given to her by a prostitute. Lips—like the labria—are a door opening to the inside of the body. Then she puts the lipstick on all around her face. She paints her face with the lipstick. She also marks the invisible doors of her body, of her soul; she opens herself to love, she invites love to her*self*.

Hayat's case is a special one among Reha Erdem's characters as she is the only character who acquires an adult identity other to the feminine/masculine identity imposed by the oppressive patriarchal order. All the other characters complete their adolescence with defeat or like Ali or Keten, they are condemned to experience their adulthood as a state of constant stuttering.

From such a perspective, the films do not suggest adolescence as a permanent utopia. Adolescence is not an end in itself, but a passage where different opportunities can be embraced; *inbetweenness* is not a happy, but a *discontented* experience. It contains prospects of freedom, but at the same time the dangers of entrapment and oppression. Reha Erdem's films

---

4. It is worth noting here that the name "Hayat" means "life" in Turkish.

do not affirm adolescence as a shelter to be escaped, but perhaps suggest adolescence as a kind of sensibility, which we should maintain throughout our lives.

The *Space* of *Inbetweenness*

If adolescence is the *time* of *inbetweenness* in Reha Erdem's films, Istanbul is the *place* of its experience. The representation of Istanbul in Erdem's films is not a usual one. With each film we witness another Istanbul, fictionalised by Reha Erdem specifically for his character's quest.

In an article on *Oh Moon!*, *A Run for Money* and *What is a Human Anyway?*, Feride Çiçekoğlu remarks that in these three films characters sail away on a boat as if they are trying to "row out to an *other* time-space, in order to escape from the feeling of constraint which results from living in a city that broke its ties with tradition but could not pass onto the modern" (2006). When Çiçekoğlu's article was published, *My Only Sunshine* had still not been filmed. I believe it would also be appropriate to add this film to the list. According to Çiçekoğlu, that boat is *Foucault's boat*—a space of *heterotopia*. Çiçekoğlu refers to Foucault's article "Of Other Spaces" (written in 1967, but published in 1986 just after his death) and defines *heterotopia* as the "*other* time-space". Çiçekoğlu reminds us that, in this article, Foucault designates the boat as the *heterotopia par excellence* and warns us about how "[i]n civilizations without boats dreams dry up; espionage takes the place of adventure, and the police take the place of pirates" (quoted in Çiçekoğlu 2006).[5]

---

5. Foucault explicates heterotopia in its relation to utopia by using mirror as a metaphor. According to Foucault, a mirror is a utopia because it enables us to see ourselves in a non-existent place. But a mirror, at the same time, is a heterotopia because it also occupies a physical space as an object. Relying on this simple reasoning, it is possible to think of heterotopia as a space where we dream of utopia. With its perfect design, utopia is a place, which is closed in on itself, immutable, fully accomplished and closed to change. However, heterotopia—the place where utopia is designed—is the space of dreams, which is incomplete and left open to variations. It is the journey we take to utopia—to the good land—installed in our imagination by Thomas Moore in the shape of an island. This is why Foucault defines the boat, the *techne*, which shares the same etymological root with the word craft in Ancient Greek, as the perfect heterotopia. Heterotopia is the site where all spaces become intertwined in the mesh of eternal time, where "the entire history of humanity [reaches] back to its origin" (Foucault 1984); a site, which is not like the site of utopia that belongs to ideal human societies, but to utopic thinking which is in search of the ideal.

Kevin Hetherington in *Badlands of Modernity: Heterotopia and Social Orderings*, refers to the *badlands* of modernity as heterotopias—defines *heterotopia* as a *space of otherness* and reminds us that it is also important not to transform *heterotopia* into a perfected and idealised site (1997). The spaces of *heterotopia*—which comprise both the possibilities of resistance and oppression—are transformed into utopias when they are idealised and thus lose their emancipatory qualities. When *heterotopia* transforms into utopia, the space of resistance disappears, for utopia is a space of domination and not of freedom; its system is closed to change and variation. *Heterotopia* can remain as the space of dreams (and not of an order), only as long as it can preserve its state of *inbetweenness*. This is why we should keep in mind that every *heterotopia* has two exits from both ends: one opening onto the *good* land of dominance (to utopia) and the other to the *badland* of terror and chaos (to dystopia).

Returning to our subject, we will now look at several different heterotopias in the world of Reha Erdem's films. In the film *Oh Moon!*, the house in Hisar where Yekta grew up and refuses to leave is a *heterotopia* in its truest sense. The unfinished structure is a place that embraces many different places from different periods of time, each flowing simultaneously in the stories told in its different rooms by Yekta's aunt, Nükhet Seza. This is a magical place where Yekta dreams of her mother passing by the window in a boat every night, and, when she falls asleep on its cold stone stairs, a place where the secrets of the past are revealed to her in dreams. In *My Only Sunshine*, the house Hayat lives in is built on the shore where a creek flows into the Bosphorus—making it hard to distinguish where the house starts and the sea ends. All these heterotopias in Reha Erdem's films have two doors opening out to different ends; one opening to the sea and the dream space of the boat and the other opening to the city (or to the town), which is the space of domination. Hence, neither of these houses is represented as idealised spaces; they remain open to the threats from the outer world and also preserve inner threats, of molestation by fathers and grandfathers.

In *A Run for Money* and *What is a Human Anyway?* however, we see different heterotopias within the different images of Istanbul: heterotopias closed in on themselves through constraint, and heterotopias with dead ends. What has changed is not the space itself but the characters' experience with the space and their perception of themselves. In *A Run for Money*, Istanbul transforms into a dark labyrinth; its streets do not run to the sea but into each other; even its *boat* is like a floating prison without egress. The whole site is an entanglement that echoes Selim's self-inflicted moral dilemma. We share Selim's point of view; that is why—like

Selim—we are also blinded to the opportunities that lie behind closed doors, thinking they cannot be opened. Nevertheless, we also know that the space would untangle itself if Selim could make a choice between morality and wickedness, if he could only break the social codes that besiege him. When he first finds the bag of money, he sees the possibility of another Selim for a moment in the thief's look. So he takes the bag, but he cannot understand what he has done; he cannot complete his transformation and continues to vacillate. At the end of the film, he is so shattered by complex emotions that he tumbles from the balcony and gets lost in the cloisters of the labyrinth. In the ferry scene—where Selim chases the thief, and at the same time, is being chased *as* the thief—the ship becomes the perfect metaphor of the *heterotopia* that is closed off in which Selim is held captive by his moral dilemma.

The representation of the city of Istanbul in *What is a Human Anyway?* seems quite different from the one in *A Run for Money* with its soft and colourful texture and high-key atmosphere, but when we look beyond the surface, they are quite alike in terms of the way the space is tangled with dead ends. The world in the film *What is a Human Anyway?* is not as dark and gloomy as the world of *A Run for Money*. Woven with soft and warm colours, it is as if the whole world has turned into a little apartment building where an extended family lives together, committed to each other with love and affection. All roads lead to this apartment, and the stories of different generations are repeated over and over again through the flux of time. In this big family, everyone cares for one another on their own terms and wishes each other only the best. They want the boys to be circumcised, young men to be soldiers and men to be manly; they each want the other to conform—not necessarily to be happy, but for everyone to be the same, not necessarily to be themselves. The world of the characters, who do not want to conform, is transformed into a hell by this extended family's "goodwill" and the heat in the weather creates a stifling atmosphere. Ali wants to stay a child, but he cannot; Keten wants to be a man, but he cannot; Aytekin is a fugitive who escaped mandatory military service; Çetin is a fugitive who escaped a circumcision, but none of them can escape far enough. The representation of the city resembles a labyrinth, like the one seen in *A Run for the Money*, which is closed on all sides, woven with fear and shaped by the power of social constraint. We repeatedly see Ali and Aytekin pushing their broken car on the streets of this labyrinth until they reach the apartment building.

However, momentary *heterotopias* can be nestled in this closed utopia. As the camera travels back slowly, we realise that the lush, green hill where Ümit and Ali meet is a small island surrounded by the city and traffic. The love Ali feels for Ümit creates a territory of liberation within the space of fear and constraint, which gradually disappears as Ümit (which means *hope* in Turkish) walks away. However, the ship is, again, not a space of adventure and exploration, but rather a floating prison where the police chase fugitives; the scene of Selim chasing thief in *A Run for Money* is repeated in *What is a Human Anyway?* with Aytekin and Ali. Of course, there are also boats in this *heterotopia*. Like the other characters mentioned previously, Aytekin and Ali also sail away on a boat, but they are anchored to the shore so tightly by their fears that before they can sail very far away, they get lost in a thick cloud of mist and can hardly find their way back to the shore. The boat, which carries Yekta to her mother and Hayat to love, carries Aytekin and Ali back to the order they wish to escape, for Aytekin and Ali do not experience their adolescence as a rebellion but as a regression.

These fragmented images of Istanbul with closed and open sites of *heterotopia* gather in our imagination into one single image of Istanbul, image of "a city's plurality: Istanbul with its sea and its islands, its Bosphorus, ships, small neighbourhoods and apartment buildings; a city which comprises both spaces of resistance and oppression; a city which can be the setting of any story, which can derive its colours from any period of time; a city which is as profound and as scary as a dark cloister and at the same time, as wide and expectant as the sea itself; a city which takes shape according to the journey of the protagonist; an incomplete, fragmented and unfinished space: a *heterotopia*.

Earlier on in this chapter I have claimed that if adolescence is the *time* of *inbetweenness* in Reha Erdem's cinema, then Istanbul is the *space* of this experience. Reha Erdem is interested in the city of Istanbul in the same context as he is interested in the experience: as a passage, as an opportunity, as a state of *inbetweenness*, as a means of rebellion where the constraints of society and the oppression of culture on individual being appear to be as overt as possible. In not one of these films however, is adolescence proposed as a resolution, or either they idealise the *heterotopias* they have constructed into utopias because a passage by its definition is somewhere one should pass through. But in what way? To which side? This is the hero(ine)'s own choice. Erdem's characters shall *find out for themselves by which particular means they may achieve felicity*, depending on how resistant and uncompromising, how resilient and daring they are, or they will be lost like Selim.

Province as *Time*

Within this context, *Times and Winds* and *Kosmos* should be discussed separately as films shot outside Istanbul. The village in *Times and Winds* and the small town in *Kosmos* are both representations of the province in explicit contrast with the representation of the city Istanbul as the heterotopic site of *inbetweenness*. Reha Erdem states that the province for him is the expression of the "present tense": a poetic time differing from the *trade-off speech* of the city where there is "no place for vagabondage or redundancy" (Erdem2009). In line with this, it is possible to claim that, in *Times and Winds*—which is a film that contemplates time—Reha Erdem approaches the province as a *tense* rather than a space.

In the village of *Times and Winds*, time flows quite differently from the passing of time in a modern city. At the beginning of the film, the old grandmother of the village tells the story of Yakup: "his father's father's father was also like him". The time of the story does not flow according to calendrical time, but flows naturally as the generations follow each other. The inhabitants of the city are moulded from the circular time of nature. They live within a traditional order, a traditional culture. They have patriarchal values, which they have bequeathed to modern men, and also they have institutions, which are adopted from them. For instance, they have schools where poems of patriotism are memorised by heart, where oaths are to be read every morning with shrieking enthusiasm in front of the bust of Atatürk. They are both shaped by nature and shape and cultivate nature in between the walls they have built. The conflict Ömer, Yakup and Yıldız face is not any different from Yekta's or Hayat's. When they escape confrontation with the adults who only remind them of their obligations, and take shelter in nature, they put themselves in a timeless sleep blended with stone and grass. Not only do they escape from their obligations, they also step outside culture and time. Their timeless sleep which "deflates" their "consciousness," the little death they experience with each escape, proves that the condition of being human is shaped by culture, and every culture has its own flux of time, whether it flows in cycles of twenty-four hours per day or through the cycles of the religious service.[6] Outside culture there is no time; outside time there is no human being.

Reha Erdem states that time in the province (as being the province itself) is as poetic as nature is for him, and yet, the representation of the

---

6. The original name of the film *Times and Winds* is *Beş Vakit* in Turkish which refers to the five different time periods in a day that is reserved for the religious practice *salaat*.

province in his films does not affirm this approach. The province in Reha
Erdem films is not represented as variable, fluid and expectant to different
possibilities as the *heterotopic* images of the city Istanbul. However these
heteropic images of Istanbul are also presented as closed and therefore
utopic Instead, both in *Times and Winds* and in *Kosmos* the site is rather
immutable and tightly woven within the laws of society and constraint.
This isolated image of the province, which is almost *islandised* on a
mountaintop surrounded by wild and desolate nature, bears the qualities of
a *utopia* rather than *heterotopia*.

The Unsurpassable Order

Plato—described by Neil Postman as "our first systematic fascist"
(1993)—said that for a site to be ideal, it should not be bigger than a place
where the leader of those living there would be able to call out to them.
The little town in *Kosmos* is introduced to the audience as an ideal site
where trustworthy, hospitable and generous people live in peace. If utopia
by definition is the ideal human society, then the town in *Kosmos* is a
utopia, and like any utopia it is an island, surrounded by desolate nature,
where the *topos* is closed in on itself without any prospect of change. The
film is shot in the eastern Turkish city of Kars, whose borders to Armenia
are kept closed as a result of the political and historical conflict between
the two countries. The fact that the filmic location is a *city with closed
borders* enriches the readings that can be made in reference to the fictional
town of the film as a utopia.

The name of the character who threw the town into chaos is Battal: a
stranger who comes from nowhere and is headed nowhere; a hero who
ascended himself through the seven mystical floors of cosmos and
descended back with the secret of life. Neither natural laws (for instance,
gravity or the continuity of time) nor the laws of the society (like morality
or chastity) can constrain Battal. He is a hero whose energy bestows
miracles and also receives life as a miracle. If humans can only be defined
within a culture, then Battal is not human. He does not speak our language,
but speaks with the screams of wild animals. He speaks a transcendental
language, the language of love. Only those who have the love in their
hearts can speak his language. "Language is the house of being, in its
home man dwells," said Heidegger. Stepping out of the order of man—the
home in which man dwells—Battal has also stepped out of language. He
speaks unceasingly, but no one can understand what he says. His words
are like a dysfunctional medium, resembling the camera that cannot
capture the image of Yekta's mother. It is an invention of man that can

only behold the images of this world; that can give voice only to the things that belong to this world.[7] Within the confines of language, Battal is devoid of responsibility. This is why his name is Battal, which means both "extraordinarily big and sublime" and for that reason, something which is "no longer fit to be used, oversized and unwieldy".' Battal cannot create any true miracle inside the *home in which man dwells* and is reduced to a healer who finds remedies to what modern medicine cannot, therefore, he can only gain acceptance as a functional part of the system. With all his transcendence, Battal cannot adjust himself to this world. Each time he moves he crashes or breaks something or brings something down, and afterwards, like a wild animal he gets scared of the destruction he has caused.

According to Freud, the fundamental contradiction of any society is the fact that the world cannot be changed without serious consequences on behalf of both the individual and the society. *Kosmos* is a film proclaiming this conflict with its premise.

In the film, a satellite falls close to the town and is considered by Battal as a message from beyond, from the transcendent order of the chaos, from the cosmos. When the inhabitants of the town want to see this miracle, the invisible borders of the town suddenly become visible: the soldiers cut their way through the crowd and tell them that there is no passing beyond the bridge. The bridge is more like a gate to the town than a bridge, because it sets an exit in-between the town and desolate nature which surrounds it. Only Battal can go beyond that border, but the transgression of the border evokes a very serious forfeit both for Battal and for society, in the form of a child's life symbolising the future, survival and the continuation of the society.

Conclusion

At the beginning of this article, I stated my opinion that Reha Erdem's films are complementary pieces of a long-running project investigating the conflict between human beings and culture through their quest for happiness. If Reha Erdem had not shot *Kosmos*, then this investigation would have been left incomplete. Reha Erdem builds the world of the film *Kosmos* with the stones he carried over from his earlier films, such as the tailors who give form to the body through social codes, soldiers,

---

7. Within this context the delirium and raving of Battal resembles the hero of Kim-Ki Duk's film *Bin-Jip* (3-Iron, 2004) who silenced himself in order to leave the *home we dwell*.

policemen, families; crippled bodies, crippled souls, coughing men and a war we cannot see, but hear its dreaded sounds... All of these come together and find their place in the pale and cruel male-dominated world of *Kosmos*. *Kosmos* is the film where this investigation comes to an end, and the iconography of Erdem's films and characters are gathered together along with the questions which had been asked in his earlier films. Battal's journey in the film clearly shows that the members of the community shall not violate the borders which are drawn around it: if they are meant to live together, if both the men and women would like to remain human beings, they shall not step outside of culture. Outside of culture there is no human being; outside of culture there is only a kind of death that annihilates consciousness—resembling the deep sleep Ömer, Yakup and Yıldız endlessly fall into in *Times and Winds* and alternatively, the sublimity of Battal, which transcends this world.

Since humans placed their own laws over the laws of the cosmos, then his or her "mind, the incredible ridges and grooves on his or her brain will be truncated by a trade-off economy" (Erdem 2009); and each one of them will find out for himself/herself through which particular means (s)he may use to escape this carnage. Battal dashed into this truth and went back to where he came. Along with him, the moon—the key image of Reha Erdem's iconography—that stands for a transcendental order beyond the order of humanity—the cosmos—abruptly disappears from the sky.

Works Cited

Çiçekoğlu, Feride. 2006. "İnsanlar İkiye Ayrılır..."(There are Two Types of People), *Radikal İki*, April 9th.
Erdem, Reha. 2009. "Aşk ve İsyan" (Love and Rebellion).In *Reha Erdem Sineması: Aşk ve İsyan* (Cinema of Reha Erdem: Love and Rebellion). Edited by Fırat Yücel. İstanbul: Çitlembik Publishing.
Hetherington, Kevin. 1997. *Badlands of Modernity: Heterotopia and Social Orderings*. London and New York: Routledge.
Foucault, Michel. 1986. Tr. Jay Miskowiec. "Of other spaces." *diacritics* 16 (1): 22-27.
Postman, Neil. 1993. *Technopoly: The Surrender of Culture to Technology*. New York: Vintage Books.
Saydam, Bilgin M. 1997. *Deli Dumrul'un Bilinci* (Mad Dumrul's Consciousness). Istanbul: Metis Publishing.
Sigmund, Freud. 1989. *Civilization and Its Discontents*. New York: W.W. Norton.

CHAPTER NINETEEN

SPATIAL REALISM: FROM URBAN TO RURAL

HÜLYA ALKAN[1]

The city is not just a visual background in recent Turkish films, but also a dramaturgical element giving direction to the story. Istanbul naturally has the leading role in representations of the city as a living space. Most of the stories happen—and almost all Turkish films are made—in Istanbul, which had a particularly privileged place in the cinema of the 1950s and 1960s; indeed it was a reference point as a city to such an extent that "Yeşilçam" was a more widely used designation than "Turkish cinema" as all production companies were located on this street in Istanbul. The Istanbul of this black and white period was teeming with sights: its streets, its tailfin-style cars, taxis, the unique beauty of the Golden Horn, people holding their luggage at the Haydarpaşa train station, the awe of seeing the city for the first time written all over their faces, the Bebek seaside, the waterside houses, mansions, and old Beyoğlu patisseries—these are all recorded in the filmic memories of those times. A transition occurs in the history of the Republic of Turkey at the end of 1950s. This is the era when migration from rural to urban environments increases its pace.

> The representatives of the closed rural community structure, a mass the Republican ideology could not yet transform or reach, come to power. It encompasses both the official ideology and the opposition. It is culturally conservative, traditionalist and closed from within. Yeşilçam cinema comes into existence, is brought into existence for these audiences, it is the cinema of the audiences. (Engin 2003, 23)

---

1. Translated by Neşe Ceren Tosun.

In my MA thesis "The Representation of Istanbul in post-90s Turkish Cinema," I base my argument on how urbanisation and Istanbul in particular are used as a romantic background in the films of the Yeşilçam period and are positioned as *indoor space*. Asuman Suner acknowledges this point as follows:

> In Yeşilçam's classic melodrama, Istanbul fulfils the function of a very familiar, domesticated and almost transformed background into an indoor one. (Suner 2005, 215)

Istanbul takes its place in Yeşilçam melodrama with its widely-known and commonly-used locations. Yeşilçam cinema, which started in the 1950s and 1960s, produced mostly melodramas and romantic comedies, which were mainly filmed in these spaces. In these films, Istanbul appears as an image. The waterside houses or mansions inhabited by the rich bourgeoisie are depicted with the Bosphorus or the Princes' Islands as their background location. Narrow streets with rough, cobblestone pavements and single-story slum houses with violets or magnolias hanging from the windows where poor youngsters or young girls live, also regularly appear in the background as a location. Similarly, the piers, the ferries, the ports become the sites of the regular boat tours in the frames of these films. The tea gardens overlooking the Bosphorus where lovers arrange to meet in the woods where cars stop to view the landscape from a hill can also be said to be among the main sites of Yeşilçam cinema.

Istanbul is usually depicted as an urban place longing for the West in the films during this period.

> [These films] presented sections of the lives of the rich strata longing for the West and made the audiences long for the Western Istanbul lifestyle, and the audiences were consoled by these dreams in the 1960s and the 1970s when Turkish cinema was very popular. As such, those who lived in the Eastern part and rural areas watched stories that were Western and urban. (Öztürk 2005, 418)

One of the distinctive features of this era, the class struggle, is defined along the binary of rich/poor as parallel to good/bad, while the distinction of living space is made between luxurious waterside houses or mansions and the slums with narrow streets where the middle class or lower-middle class resided. This situation is represented through an emphasis on the poor family trying to cope with the urban environments, and on the rich families, who are the real owners of the urban class.

The poor families usually live in a warm, cosy atmosphere. The members of the family support and sustain each other. We can qualify this as an approach that makes sure that the poor, constituting also the majority of the national viewership, feels content with their state, despite the class contradictions, seeing how degenerate the morals and family values became in richer circles, so as to envy the poor. (Abisel 1994, 74)

Atıf Yılmaz's *Ah Güzel İstanbul/Oh Beautiful Istanbul* (Atıf Yılmaz, 1966) is one of the most memorable and most famous Istanbul films of the Yeşilçam era. Istanbul is vital in this film not only to the extent of lending its name. The theme of migration toward urbanisation is valid for this film, as well. The fact that it is a woman who dares to come to the urban space by herself is what distinguished this film from others. The script was written by Safa Önal and features Sadri Alışık and Ayla Algan. The film, revolving around the story of an Istanbullite gentleman and a woman who has just come to the city to be an actress, also depicts the Istanbul of the 1960s through the protagonists' stories.

Atıf Yılmaz's *Ah Güzel İstanbul* distinguishes itself among the Yeşilçam films in its depiction of the city from the eyes of a sophisticated man rather than from the eyes of the man from the countryside just arriving in the city or the slum dweller. (Çiçekoğlu 2007, 96)

Post-1980s, some filmmakers preferred to tell the stories of modern life and urban people; Atıf Yılmaz's films about women are great examples of this trend. Most of these post-80s films are a direct reflection of the arabesque musical genre[2] that depicts the reality of people living in slums on the silver screen. During this period of 1980s arabesque films, Istanbul is seen through the eyes of the migrant, the man from rural areas.

---

2. Nurdan Gürbilek in her book *The New Cultural Climate in Turkey: Living in a Shop Window* (2011) defines arabesque as follows: "Arabesque is a musical genre that is anachronic, that is open to the impact of different times and of different cultures as it is not the product of a single tradition or a synthesis. To a certain extent, it owes its inclusivity to the fact that it has no inside, it renders music and lyrics a surface woven out of symbols. In that sense, it is nobody's music. The listener of arabesque does not listen to a music that belongs to him/her, s/he listens to a music that is foreign to him/herself but also does not belong to someone else either; a music that is not Turkish, folk, or popular music. The call of arabesque, its call to the foreigners of the city lies here: Music, such as popular music, Arabic music, Tavern music, folk music or hymns that come from different spaces and times, but belong to nobody can be freely incorporated in this genre. It is possible to move from one genre to another without stopping too much in any single one of them" (2011, 30).

Generally, these films start with the arrival to the city from the country. Haydarpaşa, as a symbol of entrance to the city, appears in the initial frame. The foreignness of the newly-arrived man from the country to the city is emphasised through his first glimpse of the city. Istanbul is depicted through the eyes of someone who comes from outside; the migrant holds the central position from the placement of a point of view and the ratio of storylines related to their lives during this era.

In the 1990s or the beginning of 2000s, as evidenced by the films of directors such as Zeki Demirkubuz, Fatih Akın, Nuri Bilge Ceylan, Derviş Zaim, Ümit Ünal and Yılmaz Erdoğan, the urban space of Istanbul becomes "an actor" in the script. In the post-1990 period the migrant and the native are entirely mixed in Istanbul. It might even be said that the migrant populations dominate the structure and culture of Istanbul. Practical and psychological problems arising from unemployment, housing problems, cultural and moral degradation, the disappointment of the migrants, fading hopes, isolation, attempts at some kind of individualisation and alienation appear in this post-1990s Istanbul. Cosmopolitan Istanbul takes centre stage with its slums, huge buildings, business centres and the new Beyoğlu—even İstiklal Street has a new structure—along with the new meanings each has acquired.

> Turkish cinema is not solely focused on Eminönü, Haydarpaşa, Galata Bridge or Beyoğlu, Salacak and Bosphorus landscapes anymore. The slums, outskirts, small enclosures, along with films such as *Büyük Adam Küçük Aşk* (Big Man, Little Love), *Güneşe Yolculuk* (Journey to the Sun, 1999) and *Eşkıya* (The Bandit, 1997), on the one hand, document the fact that the problems of the East have now moved to Istanbul and on the other hand describe an urban environment that is globalising and getting wilder. (Öztürk 2004, 131)

We view Istanbul with its alienated communities and individuals, its psychological and social problems, its backstreets, dark forces and dangers. The glorious profile of the city, its natural beauty or historic buildings, are rarely featured. From this moment forwards, filmic Istanbul consists of the streets the crowds fill or the narrow streets squeezed in between the big buildings, boring civil offices and business centres where the individual is emphasised, and where urban psychological realities are reflected.

> The naturalist pictures with Dostoyevskian and Beckettian inclinations from the new Turkish cinema, as exemplified in Zeki Demirkubuz's desperate little people, take Istanbul as their stage. Similarly Nuri Bilge Ceylan's *Uzak* (*Distant*) depicts the psychologies of the characters that

come to Istanbul from the countryside. These films enact an Istanbul and characters that are not anymore Sait Faik's Istanbul—with space for humanitarian solidarity and mercy. (Öztürk 2002, 47)[3]

Istanbul is represented in post-1990s films in a more realistic fashion. The films rip off its romantic pedestal, with more emphasis on alienation, focused on its modern urban image, full of dangerous and illegal lifestyles, and even as a city that is getting dirty. This gritty side of the representations of Istanbul in Turkish cinema eventually contaminates other representations of the urban as well as well as of small towns. Anatolian cities and rural towns that are chosen as the sites of films appear with their own culture and the names of the spaces in the films, and their names become not only the titles of the films, but also the place where the films are located. This transition can be attributed to the fact that these directors were born and raised in the country. They want to tell their own stories, a quest for belonging that is shaped by place become the basis of their films.

From Istanbul to Anatolian Towns

Local dynamics are represented in a realist manner through human relationships and culture in this cinematographic inclination from a cosmopolitan metropolis to Anatolian towns. In the journey that starts with Nuri Bilge Ceylan's trilogy *Koza*/*Cocoon* (1995)*, Kasaba*/*Small Town* (1997)*, Mayıs Sıkıntısı*/*Clouds of May* (1999), the story told belongs to the director, to his reality, to his own family.

One of the very important features that realist cinema has in common with the documentary is that it establishes a link between the characters and the surrounding life and objects. (Daldal 2003, 255)

In addition, as Siegfried Kracauer's understanding of realist cinema outlines, it is in these films that the location chosen corresponds to where the director spent his childhood, Çanakkale-Yenice. Similarly, in *Karpuz Kabuğundan Gemiler Yapmak*/*Boats Out of Watermelon Rinds* (Ahmet Uluçay, 2004), the director films his own story about where he is from,

---

3. Sait Faik Abasıyanık (1906-1954) was one of the greatest Turkish writers of short stories and poetry. He created a brand new language and brought new life to Turkish short story writing with his harsh but humanistic portrayals of labourers, fishermen, children, the unemployed, the poor. A major theme was always the sea and he spent most of his time in Burgazada (one of the Princes' Islands in the Marmara Sea).

Kütahya-Tavşanlı (Mid-Anatolia). *Dondurmam Gaymak/Ice Cream, I Scream* (Yüksel Aksu, 2005) emphasises local and cultural elements by focusing on the local culture and dialect in Muğla (Aegean). The emphasis on localisation gains intensity in more recent films. *Sonbahar/Autumn* (2008) takes place in Hopa (Black Sea), and its mountains appear in the first frame. *İki Dil Bir Bavul/On the Way to School* (Orhan Eskiköy and Özgür Doğan, 2009) has the particularity of being a re-enacted documentary. It tells the story of a teacher from Denizli who is assigned to a primary school in the village of Demirci, in city of Şanlıurfa's town of Siverek (South East Anatolia). It tells the story of the teacher and what happens with the Kurdish students who do not speak Turkish. *Tatil Kitabı/Summer Book* (Seyfi Teoman, 2008) is the story of a family from Silifke (Mediterranean) during one summer told from the point of view of the family's youngest son, Ali. In İnal Temelkuran's film, *Bornova Bornova* (2009), neighbourhood is so important it gives its name to the film. The screenwriter Engin Günaydın bases the story of *Vavien* (Durul Taylan and Yağmur Taylan, 2009) set in Tokat, Erbaa Mid-Anatolia) on his own story. The first two films of Semih Kaplanoğlu's trilogy *Yumurta/Egg* (2007) and *Süt/Milk* (2008) are set in Izmir-Tire (Aegean) where the director spent his childhood, and the last part, *Bal/Honey* (2010) takes place in Çamlıhemşin (Black Sea).

To tell the stories of the rural areas is, of course, not a new choice for Turkish cinema. However, as opposed to the films about villages made in the 1960s in line with the official state ideology of the time, the films about the countryside in the 2000s do not have a condescending narrative that looked down upon villagers but are told from within, from the very centre of the country. The desire to present the town as it is has caused recent directors to develop a language of their own for telling the stories that take place within the countryside or rural areas through cinematic technique and content.

In the following pages, I will look at examples of what I define as autobiographic localism. Among the films that tell the stories of local areas based on elements from directors' own life experiences, I will look at Nuri Bilge Ceylan's trilogy. Ceylan's films utilise the process of autobiographic localism, in juxtaposition to the style of the films of Semih Kaplanoğlu. Furthermore, the film *Vavien* will illustrate where the process is at the moment in terms of its different styles of content and technique— here emphasising the elements of plot and story.

In the journey of Ceylan's trilogy *Koza*, *Kasaba*, and *Mayıs Sıkıntısı*, the narrative has an autobiographic slant that includes elements of the director's own story, reality, and even family. Ceylan looks with an outsider's eye at his hometown in this autobiographic narrative that is the result of stories that involve him, his childhood and his family, depicting the outside world and the interior world with great authenticity. The fact that he knows the town very well and also the characters and surrounding countryside greatly contributes to the meaning of the film. Ceylan was born and grew up in Yenice, a town in the district of Çanakkale (Marmara). He tells the story of his town by first photographing then filming the initial images that made an impact on him there. It is not coincidental that the rest of the story is set in Istanbul. In *Uzak*, we continue to follow the biography of the director.

> The dreamy *Kasaba*, clearly based upon the childhood memories of Ceylan and his elder sister, evolves into a conscious comparison of adult livelihood in rural and urban settings in *Mayıs Sıkıntısı*. Ceylan reflects on his "alter ego" on the screen with an elegant humour. (Taşcıyan 2009)

The trilogy conveys a lot of information about the director-script writer. It allows us to participate in the lives of the townspeople, to lose ourselves in the slow pace of time as it runs in the town. Ceylan is a director who constructs his language of expression with long sequences, with much importance to detail. Nature, the flora, and many other things that are valuable to the townspeople are conveyed in long sequences.

> Ceylan likes long sequences, stable frames and slowness as they leave time to think to the audience, because even though nature changes incessantly, it looks stable to the eye. The world turns, the clouds pass, flowers flourish, the day turns into night and the night turns into day, the sun shines, it rains, the climate changes, kids grow up, people grow old. (Taşcıyan 2009)

In *Mayıs Sıkıntısı*, various scenes depict an introspective look at Ceylan's family and the life in the town: the child character, who is dreaming of a musical watch, is supposed to carry an egg without breaking it in order to win the watch in a race, and is saved with a ruse when the egg is broken. The father's long-time resistance and struggle to save his trees from being cut down, or the authenticity of Ceylan's own mother's voice calling her son to watch TV are other examples of this introspective regard.

Returning home, to the past

The main protagonist of *Mayıs Sıkıntısı* is Muzaffer, a young director attempting to shoot a film. He goes back to his hometown Yenice in

Çanakkale in order to fulfil this goal using his family as the cast. The relationship between the director Ceylan and the character of Muzaffer is explicit throughout the film. In other words, it is through Muzaffer that one approaches the events, people and the town. The previous films of the trilogy, *Koza* and *Kasaba*, are referred to when Muzaffer shares scenes he shot with his family. Thus, the lives of the actual director and the protagonist are enmeshed throughout the trilogy. As one of the outcomes of the autobiographical characteristic of the film, this state shows that the eye of the director shifts from the interior world to the exterior world. when Muzaffer, or in other words, the urban character exposes false attitudes towards life.

The first two films of Semih Kaplanoğlu's trilogy *Yumurta*, *Süt*, and *Bal* are set in Izmir-Tire where the director spent his childhood; the last is set in Çamlıhemşin in the Black Sea region. This trilogy similarly includes narratives from the director's own stories, life and hometown, Tire; however, Kaplanoğlu distinguishes himself from Ceylan in his breach of the spatial unity within his third film, shifting the story from the Aegean town of Tire to the Black Sea town of Çamlıhemşin. The chronology of the trilogy is reversed: while *Bal* as the last film of the trilogy depicts the childhood of the character Yusuf, *Yumurta*, as the first film of the trilogy, is about middle-aged Yusuf. In *Yumurta*, Tire as a place, its way of life and its culture are reflected throughout the film and the fact that local people also appear as actors with their local dialects sustains that reality.

> It is possible to create a link between Nuri Bilge Ceylan and Semih Kaplanoğlu. Ceylan tries to understand the rural in *Kasaba* and *Mayıs Sıkıntısı*, yet with a rural that is in the urban and in himself. Yusuf in *Yumurta* goes through a similar process. As we stated, it is not nostalgic, we can repeat that this experience is a re-awareness. (Büker and Akbulut 2009, 57)

Tire, like Ceylan's Yenice, is a place one wants to leave. We can conclude this from Yusuf's chats with his ex-girlfriend where he constantly states he wants to leave Tire. This need for escape from the town is equally emphasised in the film *Vavien*, which will be discussed in the following section for its distinction from the films of Ceylan and Kaplanoğlu in terms of its style. The main protagonist of that film, Celal, also loses hope in his hometown: all his expectations are placed in and depend on a nightclub singer from outside the town. While he dreams of a new life, the townspeople, and his wife, ignore his dreams.

Like Muzaffer, who goes back to his hometown to shoot a film in *Mayıs Sıkıntısı*, Yusuf in *Yumurta*, upon receiving the news that his mother has died returns to Tire, in other words, to his childhood, to his home, to his town, and to his past. The elements that make up the story are real, and belong to Tire and the way of life there the director knows very well. The home has a major role in the trilogy as it also appears as the remembered space, as the space that makes the connection with the past of the narrator. As Kaplanoğlu states in some of his interviews, one is constantly looking for the home where s/he was born. As in these films and also as the actual reality of the director shooting the film, the home is a space that is either left behind, returned to or remembered. In Yusuf's mother's house, her picture and Yusuf's circumcision pictures are placed side by side. The spatial reality is not limited to the indoor shots in the films. It is in the light of the director's past knowledge of the area that Birge is chosen as the location where some religious/cultural rites (such as animal sacrifice) will be carried out in the Aegean region. Similarly, the rituals that are shown as the people who visit the house after the mother's death talk among themselves, as they bring food to the house of the deceased, when the child carries the water to the tomb and the prayers afterwards with their hands facing the sky, are all specific to the town.

In *Süt*, the identity of the strong, hardworking woman who is also able to ride a motorcycle is reinforced through the increased visibility of the woman in the coastal Aegean towns. Other characters are also based on the director's past impressions. Kaplanoğlu shares the following about his process of character formation:

Sometimes I ran into people with whom I lived together in Izmir, from the times we wrote poems, from when we dreamt of being poets; they all have various occupations now. Some sell cheese, some work at their father's shop, some do metal work, and when I meet them and talk to them again, I ask myself if I had continued under these conditions, if I stayed there and did another job, whether I would continue writing poems, doing other things. That's how the character of Yusuf's friend came into being. (Çiftçi 2009, 51)

The opening scene of Sut deals with taking out the serpent that one character has swallowed while sleeping: the person hangs upside down from a tree with his head towards the source of fire and the serpent that is still alive in his body comes out of the mouth. This initial scene demands specific knowledge of town life; it depicts the fact that serpents are regular visitors to households and that people have developed methods of dealing with everyday problems in ways specific to the town. The writing of prayers in small pockets of tissue or paper as an alternative method of dealing with life's daily problems is another important piece of insider information about the town. In *Yumurta*, the guests who come to visit Yusuf after his mother's death tell him: "You are not going to worry. There is nothing one can do," and in doing so expose their calm attitude that is enmeshed with spirituality.

Bal has an ambient feeling that is clearly set somewhere in the eastern Black Sea region, yet without a specific spatial description of the location. The profession of hawser making that is highlighted in *Yumurta* is also shown in great detail in *Bal*. The making of thin hawser is a monotonous task, which requires moving between the spinning wheel and the rope. Beekeeping is also depicted in all its details in the film as a profession demanding patience, supported by spatial realities.

The Town Is Quiet and Time Flows Slowly

In the above-mentioned films, it is emphasised that life in the town is slow, and the relationships are very close. The elders of the town are the strongest signifiers of the slowness of time. Ceylan and Kaplanoğlu attribute to the elderly and to being elderly a central position in town life. In *Bal*, calm and silence reigns in the narrative of the town. The scene where the corner-shop owner makes a small gesture to Yusuf, who has been wandering the streets of Çamlıhemşin, to send his greetings to Yusuf's father is an example of how slow time flows: prior to his small gesture, the corner-shop owner has been sitting still in exactly the same way for hours.

> If the city is the space of sounds and noises, then the rural is the space of silence or natural sounds. The meeting of the spoon and the glass becomes a language, and one that is peculiar to rural life. (Büker and Akbulut 2009, 41)

These two trilogies are similar in terms of their language of expression. Among their common features are long sequences including scenes where the camera does not even move at all (which at times have been criticised with the label of art-house cinema), expressive moments without dialogue that can be defined as silent communication (the main character has the least possible communication with the others), the choice not to use music, including amateur actors alongside professional ones in the cast, the absence of a plot, prioritising visual representations and so on.

The town and the rural space appear as independent places of existence rather than those of a nostalgic space. Ceylan's and Kaplanoğlu's films share as part of their common style, the absence of identification by the audience with the protagonist and the lack of a defined, clear ending. The film is built on actions rather than on events. While life goes on with this slow pace, the film ends with a deep silence and the credits roll.

What about *Vavien*?

The last film I would like to analyse in this work is *Vavien*, directed by Durul Taylan and Yağmur Taylan. Written by Engin Günaydın, it is based on his own life story in which he also has the leading role. The film was shot in Günaydın's hometown, Tokat-Erbaa. Even though it is the story of a town similar to those in Ceylan's and Kaplanoğlu's films, *Vavien* distinguishes itself with its plot, with the characters of the protagonists, with its clear story line and with the protagonists' dialogue which strengthens its local-cultural features. When seen as a way to reflect the town's reality, it is very different in terms of its form from the films of Ceylan and Kaplanoğlu. The protagonists are played by professional actors in this story that is told from within - from the centre meticulously. However, it is still the scriptwriter Engin Günaydın's proximity to the characters in this script, and his knowledge of the spaces and of the town that gives the film a strong sense of realism. To give an example, the film is set, and was shot in Günaydın's electrician brother's own shop.

Celal, the protagonist of *Vavien*—defined as a black comedy by many—has an unhappy family life despite the fact that Celal's wife also unconditionally loves her spoiled son. Even though the electrician's shop is not doing very well, they take the time and the money to go to a nightclub in Samsun with Cemal, Celal's elder brother and co-owner of the shop. In the story, each of the protagonists' specific characteristics is emphasised and they each have something to hide from the rest of the family. The secrecy that hangs in the air is also consistent in the way the film starts; something secret is being planned and that sets the story in motion.

The town of Erbaa appears along with its way of life, its people and a view of nature that surrounds the town. In the film much occurs to give a sense of the place and the people who move within it. Male and female roles in the scene where the whole family goes to have a picnic attest to that fact. The two brothers' adventures in the nightclub, Celal's wife Sevilay's phone conversations with her father in Germany, her father's insistence on keeping the money he sends a secret, Celal's son's secret meetings with the neighbour's daughter, etc. are examples. The story is strengthened with humour and makes great use of language, dialect, and dialogues to express the local cultural elements, unlike the previously mentioned films.

Conclusion

The post-1994 Turkish cinema tends to accommodate more local, authentic and "living" town stories, including autobiographical references —most clearly observed in the first films of many of the directors and scriptwriters. It is possible to say that, despite the differences of style, the fact that the directors and scriptwriters are all familiar with the space/place of filming, that they have an insider's eye to the story, is an important step in reflecting the reality of each of the towns. The town is a living space for most of these directors rather than a nostalgic space. In *Vavien* and the two other trilogies I have comparatively analysed (*Yumurta-Süt-Bal* and *Koza-Kasaba-Mayıs Sıkıntısı*), it is possible to discern that the town and its people have a clearly defined way of life. The people's professions, their relationships, what happens to them, the places, and dialogue all provide a slice of reality. It allows the audience to witness life, culture and the day-to-day world of the townspeople during the films' time frame.

What soothes us at the end of *Vavien*, clearly the product of good observation, is the content smile of the main protagonist, telling us it will all be fine. The fact that the classic storyline is breached (the guilty are not punished, the wife continues to love her husband as unconditionally as before) is a direct reflection of the town, of the local culture and what happens there. The wrongdoings, lies, crimes are veiled. Maybe it is at this end point that this film resembles the others: it ends with a happy family portrait at a certain point in time, but life is seen to continue, the image is not frozen. It ends exactly as *Yumurta* ends. Both films end with an ordinary scene of having breakfast.

Works Cited

Abisel, Nilgün. 1994. *Türk Sineması Üzerine Yazılar* (Essays On Turkish Cinema). Ankara: İmge Publications.

Büker, Seçil and Hasan Akbulut. 2009. *Yumurta: Ruha Yolculuk* (The Egg: A Spiritual Journey). Ankara: Dipnot Publications.

Çiçekoğlu, Feride. 2007. *Vesikalı Şehir* (Documented City). Istanbul: Metis Publications.

Çiftçi, Ayça. 2009. "Anın İçine bir An Daha Açmak..." (Opening Up a Moment within a Moment) *Altyazı*: 51.

Daldal, Aslı. 2003. "Kracauer, Basit Anlatı ve Nuri Bilge Ceylan Sineması" (Kracauer, Simple Narrative and Cinema of Nuri Bilge Ceylan). *Doğu-Batı* 25: 255.

Engin, Ayça. 2003. "Yeşilçam Sonrası"(After Yesilcam). *Antrakt* 75: 23.

Gürbilek, Nurdan. 2011. *The New Cultural Climate in Turkey: Living in a Shop Window*. London: Zed Books.

Öztürk, Mehmet. 2003. "İstanbul'un Modernleşmesi ve Sinema" (The Modernisation of Istanbul and Cinema). *Varlık*: 47.

—. 2004. "Kentte Sinema Modern Binbir Gece Masalları" (Cinema in the City: Modern Arabian Nights), *İstanbul* 50: 131.

—. 2005. *Sine-masal Kentler: Modernitenin İki Kahramanı Kent ve Sinema Üzerine Bir İnceleme* (Cinematic Cities: On the Two Heroes of Modernity). Istanbul: Donkişot.

Suner, Asuman. 2005. *Hayalet Ev, Yeni Türk Sinemasında Aidiyet Kimlik ve Bellek* (Ghost House: Belonging, Identity and Memory in New Turkish Cinema). Istanbul: Metis Publications.

Taşcıyan, Alin. 2009. *Nuri Bilge Ceylan'a Göre Kainat* (The Universe According to Nuri Bilge Ceylan). Available online at: http://www.nbcfilm.com/3maymun/press-alinkainat.php

CONTRIBUTORS

Murat Akser is a lecturer in cinematic arts, in the School of Creative Arts, University of Ulster, UK. Between 2006-2013, he has been an associate professor of cinema and media studies, chair of new media department and the founding director of the Cinema and Television MA program at Kadir Has University Istanbul, Turkey. He has his MA in Film and PhD in communication and culture from York University, Canada. He works extensively on political economy of film festivals, film genres and has recently published a book-length study of Turkish cinema from Lambert: *Green Pine Resurrected: Film Genre, Parody, and Intertextuality in Turkish Cinema.*

Hülya Alkan Akyüz got her BA in Media and Communication Systems at İstanbul Bilgi University where she continued her academic career as a TA. She has an MA in Cinema and Television from Dokuz Eylül University İzmir. She started her on-line professional life at Medyanova as food and beverage content editor. She later joined Doğan Online as an editor for news, art & culture channels. Currently, she is working as an internet editor at Microsoft. She is also a columnist at art and culture pages on Milliyet.com.tr

Gülengül Altıntaş graduated from Istanbul University, Radio, TV and Film department and continued her studies at UCLA Content Creation for Entertainment Media program. Her short films and video projects were shown at festivals and received awards. After receiving her MA degree in Film TV from Istanbul Bilgi University, she is now studying through her PhD degree at Bahçeşehir University Department of Media and Film Studies and working as a full-time lecturer in Film and TV department.

Savaş Arslan is Full Professor of Film and Television at Bahçeşehir University in Istanbul, Turkey. He hold his PhD in Art History from Ohio State University. In addition to contributing various articles on cinema, arts, and culture to different journals, magazines, and edited volumes, he has three books: *Cinema in Turkey: A New Critical History* (Oxford University Press, 2010), *Media, Culture and Identity in Europe* (co-editor, Bahçeşehir University Press), and *Melodram* (in Turkish, L&M, 2005).

Pınar Asan is a faculty member at Bahçeşehir University, Department of Photography and Video. She is a graduate of Radio, television and Cinema Department from Faculty of Communication, Marmara University.

Eylem Atakav is a Reader in Film and Television Studies at the University of East Anglia, where she teaches courses on world cinemas; women and film; women, Islam and the media. She is the author of *Women and Turkish Cinema: Gender Politics, Cultural Identity and Representation* (2012) and the editor of *Directory of World Cinema: Turkey* (2013). She is currently working on two edited collections: *Women and Contemporary World Cinema* (with Karen Randell) and *From Smut to Softcore: Sex and the 1970s World Cinema* (with Andy Willis).

Zahit Atam is a film historian, has written widely on the history of Turkish Cinema and the cinemas of Third World. Has has been studying as a sociologist, the intellectual, political and philosophical roots of New Turkish Cinema, and deciphering of the political and cinematic heritage of Yılmaz Güney. Atam had his BA in Philosophy from Bogazici University and MA in Film from Marmara University. He is currently pursuing his PhD in sociology at Mimar Sinan University. Atam has been writing on cinema and policits for the last 25 years to numerous books and journals. He is the author of *Yakın Plan Yeni Türkiye Sineması* (Close Up New Turkish Cinema).

Deniz Bayrakdar is professor at the department of Radio, Film, and Television at Kadir Has University. Since 1998 she has been organizing "Turkish Film Studies Conference" and published ten edited volumes in this series. Her publications include *Cinema and Politics* (2009, Cambridge Scholars); *Mapping the Margins: Identity Politics and the Media*, Hampton Press, New Jersey, ABD (2006, coedited with Karen Ross). *Gender and Media* (1996, coedited with Ross & Dakovic), *Communications Revolution* (1996, coedited with Lotherington) among others.

Tülay Çelik is an assistant professor at the Fine Arts Faculty, Visual Communication Design Department, Sakarya University, Turkey. Her PhD thesis was on "Film Production Process in Turkey After 1990 The Field of 'Director Cinema'". Her research and publications are mainly on ideological representation of dreams, minimal tendencies and narration, low budget films, international film festivals and new dependencies in cinema. She makes short films and teaches Turkish cinema, film theory, film history, and world cinema.

Özgür Çiçek is a recent PhD at State University of New York Binghamton Philosophy, Interpretation and Culture Program. She has graduated from MA program in Film and Television Istanbul Bilgi University. She has been teaching as a lecturer in film studies at Işık University, Istanbul Technical University and Bogazici University since 2009. Her areas of research and publications range from Deleuze to Kurdish cinema and Bollywood.

Aslı Daldal is an Assistant Professor in the Department of Political Science at Yıldız Technical University and an affiliated film instructor at Boğaziçi University. She received her Ph.D. from Boğaziçi University, Department of Political Science and has done research at Duke and Columbia Universities. She is the author of *Art, Politics and Society: Social Realism in Italian and Turkish Cinemas* (Istanbul: ISIS, 2003 and New-Jersey: Gorgias Press, 2010) and *1960 Darbesi ve Türk Sineması'nda Toplumsal Gerçekçilik* (Istanbul: Homer, 2005). Her research interests are mainly on sociology of cinema, film theory and cultural studies.

Hilal Erkan is a PhD candidate in Media Studies at Yeditepe University. She had her MA From Gazi and BA from Eastern Mediterranean University. She is the author of *Orientalism in Hollywood Cinema* (in Turkish from Kırmızı Kedi, 2009).

Selim Eyüboğlu studied film at the University of Milwaukee, Wisconsin (B.A.) and at the University of Kent at Canterbury (Ph.D.) He has taught film studies at the University of Kent at Canterbury, The Polytechnic of Central London, University of Warsaw, Boğazici University and Istanbul Bilgi University. Currently a full professor at Department of Cinema and Television at Bahçeşehir University, Istanbul, Turkey. He is also a film critic and a photographer, producing 'cinematic photographs'.

Seth Feldman is a full professor of Film Studies at York University in Toronto. A founder and past president of the Film Studies Association of Canada, Professor Feldman has served as dean of the Faculty of Fine Arts at York University, and as director of York's Robarts Centre for Canadian Studies. Seth Feldman has published widely on national and international cinemas. He has edited three anthologies on the subject of Canadian cinema, among them the seminal *Canadian Film Reader*-- the first textbook to be published on Canadian film and two books on Dziga Vertov. He is also the author of 26 documentaries for the CBC radio program, *Ideas*. Currently, he is the principal investigator on a four year research project into the Canadian films at Expo '67. He is currently finishing a book on documentary.

Elif Kahraman is a PhD candidate in Public Realtions at Istanbul University. She has an interdisciplinary background and holds two Master of Arts degrees in Cinema and Television and American Culture and Literature. Her research and articles are mainly on discourse, narrative and style in cinema, discourse analysis of media, American culture and its reflection to cinema, and Turkish Cinema.

Murray Pomerance is Professor in the Department of Sociology at Ryerson University. He is the author of *The Last Laugh: Strange Humors of Cinema, The Eyes Have It: Cinema and the Reality Effect* (2013), *Alfred Hitchcock's America (2013), Michelangelo Red Antonioni Blue: Eight Reflections on Cinema* (2011), *Edith Valmaine* (2010), *The Horse Who Drank the Sky: Film Experience Beyond Narrative and Theory* (2008), *Johnny Depp Starts Here* (2005), *Savage Time* (2005), *An Eye for Hitchcock* (2004), and *Magia d'Amore* (1999), and editor or co-editor of more than sixteen volumes including *Shining in Shadows: Movie Stars of the 2000s* (2011), *A Little Solitaire: John Frankenheimer and American Film* (2011), *A Family Affair: Cinema Calls Home* (2008), *City That Never Sleeps: New York and the Filmic Imagination* (2007), and *Cinema and Modernity* (2006). He edits various series: "Techniques of the Moving Image" (Rutgers), "Horizons of Cinema" (State University of New York Press), "Screen Decades" with Lester D. Friedman (Rutgers), and "Star Decades" with Adrienne L. McLean (Rutgers).

Zeynep Tül Akbal Süalp has been teaching cinema, media and cultural studies in various Universities for the last twenty years. He has been a visiting professor at Humboldt University in Berlin in 2011. She recently has become the chair of Cinema and TV Department at Bahçeşehir University. She has her BA degree in Psychology and studied Political Science, Cinema Studies and Sociology (Cultural Studies) in New York and İstanbul in MA and PhD levels. She has been writing articles on cultural studies, cinema and critical theory in some journals and the editor of four books and author of the *ZamanMekan: Kuram ve Sinema/ TimeSpace: Theory and Cinema* (Bağlam 2004) and co-author of the short fiction: *Wanting Book Odd Notebook*. (MudamCamp de Base &

:mentalKLİNİK, 2004) and also co-author of the book titled From *Liberties To Losses and Afterwards* (De-Ki 2008) She has been also the coordinator of The Communication On The Road VYZ Project since 2010.

Özüm Ünal is a recent Ph.D. in American Studies from Kadir Has University, Istanbul. Her fields of specialization include the 20th Century American literature, women studies and film studies. Given her personal background and her studies in American Literature, she is also interested in issues related to science fiction cinema with a special focus on the clusters of body, technology and identity. She is currently working as a research assistant at Bahçeşehir University, Faculty of Arts and Sciences, Department of American Culture and Literature.

Tuncay Yüce completed got his BA in Cinema-Television Department from Dokuz Eylül University. He earned his MA from Fort Hays State University. He completed his Ph.D. in Cinema-Television at Dokuz Eylül University. He became assistant professor in Cinema-Television Department at Mersin University since 2002. He has opened two individual exhibitions both nationally and internationally. His works are composed of opportunities of the conventional forms of photography, cinema and video along with the new possibilities of new expression styles of 'new media' art.

INDEX